The Hospital

ALSO BY BRIAN ALEXANDER

Glass House

The Hospital

Life,
Death, and
Dollars
in a
Small
American
Town

BRIAN ALEXANDER

St. Martin's Press ☙ New York

First published in the United States by St. Martin's Press, an imprint of St. Martin's Publishing Group

www.stmartins.com

Design by Meryl Sussman Levavi

Library of Congress Cataloging-in-Publication Data

Names: Alexander, Brian, author.
Title: The hospital : life, death, and dollars in a small American town / Brian Alexander.
Description: First edition. | New York : St. Martin's Press, 2021. | Includes bibliographical references and index.
Identifiers: LCCN 2020040125 | ISBN 9781250237354 (hardcover) | ISBN 9781250237361 (ebook)
Subjects: LCSH: Public health—United States. | Public health—United States—Finance. | Public health administration—United States.
Classification: LCC RA445 .A4418 2021 | DDC 362.10973—dc23
LC record available at https://lccn.loc.gov/2020040125

Our books may be purchased in bulk for promotional, educational, or business use. Please contact your local bookseller or the Macmillan Corporate and Premium Sales Department at 1-800-221-7945, extension 5442, or by email at MacmillanSpecialMarkets@macmillan.com.

First Edition: 2021

1   3   5   7   9   10   8   6   4   2

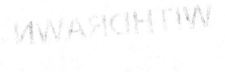

To the memory of Bruce Alexander,
writer,
who kept waiting to see a doctor
until his Medicare kicked in

Contents

A Note to Readers

In some cases, the names of people have been changed in order to comply with applicable medical care privacy law, or to protect anonymity. Those names marked by an asterisk are fictitious. In several cases, minor details of scenes have also been altered to avoid disclosing identities.

We have assembled the most enormous medical establishment ever conceived, and people are sicker than ever!

—Paddy Chayefsky, *The Hospital*, 1971

They're all sick when they come in here. They're horribly unhealthy. If they were healthier I'd see a lot fewer.

—Lori Bolton-Sell, chief probation officer,
Williams County, Ohio, 2019

The Hospital

Prologue

There was nothing special about that morning. It was just a winter Monday—cold, but of course it would be cold, being almost mid-February 2019. Nothing like twelve days before, when Jim Watkins, the chief of the Williams County Health Department, had taken a photo of his car's instrument panel to immortalize the reading of −15. A couple of sub-zero days in midwinter weren't unusual for this far northwest corner of Ohio, but even the crusty old farmers agreed that fifteen below was a little extreme.

At the Seasons coffee shop, talk about the "polar vortex" had faded, and High Street and Main Street had been plowed. Some side streets were still coated, but passable, and piles of crunchy snow, turning grimy, took up a few parking spaces in the CVS lot. The lawn of the county courthouse in the Bryan town square was covered in white, offsetting its extravagant Baroque/Romanesque mishmash of red brick and sandstone. Long strands of Christmas lights still swooped down from its peak. The main county roads and the state routes were clear, too, so most people were getting to work okay. Everybody kept an eye out for deer leaping out of frozen cornfields—the roadsides were dotted with the carcasses of struck deer this winter. Drivers sometimes ended their commutes in the ER because of them, or because they slid on the black ice that lay camouflaged like land mines.

Phil Ennen slipped into his long, brown overcoat, wrapped a scarf around his neck, and placed a rakishly wide-brimmed fedora on his head to prepare for his own commute—a walk of about 150 yards across Garver Park to the hospital, where he was chief executive officer. He could see the building out his front door. At night, watching TV or lying in bed, he could hear emergency medical helicopters arrive and take off from the hospital's landing pad. Only 8,500 people lived in Bryan, and Ennen knew all of them, or so it seemed, so he'd wonder who was strapped onto the gurney and what had happened and how bad it must have been to require flying the patient to Toledo or Fort Wayne.

He was fifty-five years old. He'd worked at the hospital for thirty-two years. He called it "my shop," as if he were a cobbler making shoes. Ennen was protective to the point of defensiveness about his shop.

The aesthetic critique was one example. The hospital stood out in a town of late nineteenth- and early twentieth-century architecture, especially since the 2009 rebuild. The rectangular orange and green exterior cladding panels and the intersections of the building's wings created a modernist, alien dissonance. A few residents had taken to calling it "the Lego blocks place," as in, "You goin' over to the Lego blocks place to get yerself checked out?"

What really got to him, though, was the "Band-Aid station" crack. "That place is just a Band-Aid station," people would say, and Ennen would smile to cover his seething.

He grew up in Bryan. Most knew him as one of the Ennen brothers, Mary Helen and Jack's kids. His father owned a small manufacturing company up in the village of Pioneer that made parts for Detroit's cars. His mother worked at the hospital he now ran. He met Mary, his wife, in the first grade at St. Patrick Catholic School. She was the daughter of Jim Ebersole, the barber who owned Mel and Jim's Barber Shop on the square.

So Ennen understood the small-town way of simultaneously demanding community respect from outsiders while internally scoffing at any homegrown institution as second-rate. He steamed just the same.

Sometimes it felt like the town—even the whole county—didn't give a damn about the work he did on its behalf. Running a small independent community hospital was never easy, but it was especially brutal now. Many hospitals in many towns like Bryan had winked out over the past decade. They'd gone bankrupt, or been absorbed (and sometimes gutted) by bigger regional health systems, or the towns themselves had slowly become more memory than living reality until there was no point in having a hospital there at all. Hundreds more such hospitals, over six hundred by some estimates, were in danger of collapse.

Ennen's "shop," Community Hospitals and Wellness Centers, or CHWC, lost money every month of 2018. It was being dogged by big hospital chains in Toledo to the east and Fort Wayne to the west. Both had been gobbling up small independents like CHWC for over a decade in a crazed rush to consolidate before they could be targeted themselves by even bigger predators.

Twenty-first-century America had become a healthcare country. At almost 18 percent of the entire economy, health was the nation's largest industry by far—a $3.6 trillion enterprise. CHWC was a tiny mote in that universe, but as was true in many towns across the country, the hospital was now the largest employer in Bryan, still standing as an independent, nonprofit, homegrown community asset. Ennen and his board of directors wanted to keep it that way.

That was the business. But there was also supposed to be a mission. Ennen said he believed in the mission of the hospital, but the mission and the business were so intertwined they'd become inseparable: Most days an outsider couldn't tell the difference.

###

"Dr. Stalter, we need you!"

Marv Stalter may not have heard, or may not have registered, the urgency of the shout. He was across the ER in Exam Room 3 with a seventy-seven-year-old woman. She had bladder cancer. There were tubes sticking out of her back. The tubes diverted urine from her kidneys and drained it into a bag.

She'd been in Room 3 for a while now, since a Williams County Emergency Medical Service ambulance dropped her off. A ride in the ambulance was often the only practical way to get somebody from the Genesis HealthCare nursing facility, the one off Center Street past the YMCA, to the hospital. Genesis HealthCare was a huge outfit that traded on the New York Stock Exchange and had about four hundred nursing-care facilities in thirty states and $1.16 billion in revenue. But ambulances for emergencies weren't part of its service, so the Bryan outpost called on Williams County employees to pick up the slack.

This wasn't the first ambulance ride for the woman in Room 3. She'd been in and out of the ER several times, then had been admitted to the hospital, stabilized, and released. This time Genesis called the ambulance when she began moaning in an "altered state of consciousness." That's why Stalter was looking her over: The cancer and the drugs and the malfunctioning kidneys and being seventy-seven and dying and not wanting to be dying had affected her mind.

She should have been placed in hospice care a long time ago. Stalter knew it the last time he'd seen her in the ER and he knew it now. The cancer wasn't going anywhere. It was going to kill her, but the family and the patient either didn't want to talk about hospice or could not get into hospice.

A young guy, a skinny twenty-year-old, sat, then stood, then sat, then paced, his hands shimmying like the frayed ends of electrified wires, in Room 5, the room designated for psychiatric cases. Stalter, who'd given the kid a quick look, knew within seconds how it would go—the meth mouth gave it away. Just about every tooth the young man still possessed was pocked with an open cavity. He was miserable all right, but he was miserable mainly because he was tweaking and his mouth hurt like hell and he was probably jonesing for an Oxy or a Perc to make the pain go away.

Stalter would let him jones for a while. He'd offer unsolicited and unwelcome advice about meth and rehab, knowing the young man would deny being an addict or using meth (as if Stalter were born yesterday). The two of them would play their roles—Stalter because he was a doctor and was supposed to say the words, and the kid because he wasn't going to do anything to piss off the guy who could make him feel better.

Stalter had also taken a preliminary look at the patient in Room 7, Marc Tingle, a fifty-four-year-old contractor from out in Edgerton, near the Indiana state line. He didn't like what he saw. Tingle had walked into the ER saying he had chest pains, a numb left hand, nausea, and sweats, even though it was 27 degrees outside. Stalter noted Tingle wore dentures. He thought to himself that fifty-four was pretty young to be wearing a complete set of dentures.

Tingle appeared fit and healthy, but he'd probably hosted a fair amount of gum disease. Over the years, a payload of bacteria could have drifted from his mouth into his arteries, aggravating cardiovascular plaque and leading to clogged blood vessels. So Stalter told Heather Gaylord, the nurse in charge of Room 7, that Tingle merited close monitoring while she collected data. But now she wasn't collecting data. She was shouting.

"Dr. Stalter, we need you! *Now!*" she yelled, as Tingle emitted an "Arrrggghh!" that boomed through the ER.

Without waiting for an answer, a nurse shoved back the curtain at the entrance of Room 7 and ran through the central staff station. Stalter, hustling in the opposite direction, nearly bumped into her.

"V-fib!" somebody shouted. Nurses converged on Room 7. Stalter pictured Marc Tingle's heart quivering like a Jell-O mold at a hot summer picnic—just quivering, not pumping, and therefore dying. The steel-band pain in Tingle's chest tightened again. "Accckkkk!" Tingle exclaimed from under an oxygen mask, sounding like gears being stripped on an old Mack truck.

Gaylord stood to one side of Tingle, her eyes—her face—blank with concentration as she began handling equipment. Shayla Carlisle, short and usually petite but now about seven months pregnant, climbed almost on top of Tingle's body. She pressed her hands up and down, up and down, against his chest as hard as she could. Her breath came in loud bursts, as if she were trying to breathe for him.

"Respiratory to ER immediately!"

Barb Rash, the director of the emergency department, was upstairs in the staff exercise room when she heard the hospital-wide PA announcement. She'd just changed into her pink and purple workout clothes—the yoga pants, the colorful T-shirt, the sneakers.

"Clear!" Stalter barked. "Shock him with 300!" Tingle's body arched off the bed. He released a tremendous grunt of pain and surprise, but his heart continued to quiver. Carlisle resumed: up and down, pressing hard, perspiration beginning to bead on her forehead.

Tingle's daughter, Summer, wanted to be in the room, but she was terrified of being in the room. She stepped in and witnessed the building chaos around her father, then stepped out into the hallway, then back in. And then out. She just couldn't think. Her hands shook. She sobbed. She held a cellphone to her ear, but why? What would she tell her mother, who was on the other end of the line? And so the phone came away from her ear and she stood still like a deer on County Road 10 when headlights shone into its eyes. She was standing there as the respiratory team rushed past her pushing a big cart equipped with twenty-first-century machinery and supplies.

More people crowded into Room 7. Stalter ordered injections. Gaylord and the other nurses ripped open slender plastic envelopes to release syringes. Pieces of plastic and paper and sections of tube floated to the floor: a snow of medical garbage.

Stalter relieved Carlisle, who was sweating now. She wanted to keep going—she recognized Tingle, because they attended the same church over in Edgerton—but she knew she couldn't: she'd used up her strength. She stepped around the curtain, breathing hard and looking grim.

Carlisle saw Summer, frozen except for her tears. "We're doing everything we can," she told her. She put her arm around Summer's shoulder and guided her into an empty exam room across the hall. "Call the cath lab!" Stalter ordered, and a nurse called up to the third floor.

The seventy-seven-year-old woman in Room 3 moaned.

A young nurse, handsome, dark-haired, buff from workouts, stood just outside Room 7—there was no more space inside—and pulled a syringe out of its packet. He held a small drug bottle up to the needle, but his hands shook. He was a good nurse, but still new. A man was dying. Everything had to happen fast: right now, and all at once, but with precision. Nobody could make a mistake. He moved the needle away from the bottle and took a deep breath to steady his hands. He pierced the bottle with the needle and drew out the correct dosage.

Barb Rash swept into the room in a smear of pink and purple. She'd left her ID badge and her scrubs upstairs. Rash was a veteran ER nurse with a veteran's cool. She sat down on a vacated stool at Marc Tingle's feet and helped coordinate the teamwork.

Every syringe, every tube, every unsealed drug bottle—every single item—carried a small sticker with a barcode printed on it. Before letting the envelope or wrapper or box fall to the floor, the nurses and Rash peeled off the stickers. Whether Tingle lived or died, all those barcodes would be scanned so the price of every item could be recorded for billing. Within seconds of arriving, Rash's T-shirt was decorated with small stickers.

"Give him another!" Stalter barked, unleashing another frenzy and another blizzard of litter. "Ready," somebody said. "Clear!" Marc Tingle's body arched. He groaned, yet his heart did not stop quivering. About two minutes had ticked away on the clock: It was a little after four in the afternoon.

▮▮▮

Half a mile away, Keith Swihart, thirty-nine, stared straight ahead into the tremendous flat-screen TV in the front room of the old, decaying two-story box of a house he rented in Bryan. He was watching cars whine and growl their way around Daytona International Speedway. In what was meant to be a dining room, small radio-controlled cars and trucks, along with the parts and tools for working on them, rested together on a workbench. He was happy—as happy as he could be. He had his RC cars, his black recliner, his TV, and a race. Everything else was chaos. The rooms were in chaos: papers, bits of old cereal, used bowls, a giant tub of puffed cheese balls, bags, pieces of toys, a half-eaten granola bar, unopened business-size envelopes, a child's sock, uncased pillows, a thin mattress all lay scattered or piled into mounds. Keith's body was in chaos: blood vessels were weakening and breaking, and he was losing sight in one eye. And his spirit, too, was chaotic as it wrestled with grief, confusion, anxiety.

But the recliner in which he sat with his legs up was an island in that sea, the last bit of real estate—psychic and physical—Keith could claim as his own, under his own control. So he focused on the cars and let himself mold into the lounger. His buzz-haircut head lay back against the cushion, and he said, "I'm doing good, buddy, doin' good." Through his thick-lensed glasses he watched very fast cars go round and round a track, his face impassive.

Keith had been working since he was thirteen, when, like a lot of rural midwestern teenagers, he took a job detasseling corn, walking the rows of growing stalks and snapping the pollen-bearing tassels from their tops to prevent pollination. It was hot work and hard, but it paid okay and lasted just a few weeks during the summer season, so it was nothing to complain about. From then on, he just about always had some sort of job—and he didn't complain much about any of them. "Complaining don't do no good," he'd say. If anybody asked how he was doing, Keith would answer, "Doin' good, buddy, doin' good."

Keith loved anything with an engine. By the time he was seventeen years old, he was spending his extra cash in junkyards. He'd sift through the used springs and carburetors and universal joints that were no longer true, and when he was done, he'd have everything he needed to rebuild "a junkyard car" with his own hands. Practically, anyway. He'd race his cars on public roads outside of Burr Oak, Michigan—population 850. Sometimes he'd race his buddy Josh Bell. Drag racing on the roads was illegal, of course, but out in the country, there weren't many deputies or highway patrol cars to stop you.

After high school, Keith went to work. There was a tool-and-die shop and then a Japan-based company called Hi-Lex Controls. It operated a plant in Litchfield, Michigan, a wide spot of about 1,350 people right off Michigan Highway 99, which runs along the St. Joseph River. Roughly forty miles north, give or take, of the Ohio border, Litchfield was about a forty-five-minute drive east from Burr Oak. The factory was a white metal barn of a place that sat on what was once a prairie cornfield. Keith made window regulators, the guides and cables that let auto passengers push a button and watch a window slide down into the door—or back up again. He liked it. He was working in the auto industry. The job paid okay and came with benefits like a health plan. Keith got married and had a son.

One day, as he was working on the line at Hi-Lex, he passed out—fainted dead away. Unbeknownst to Keith, he'd developed type 2 diabetes. He was only in his early twenties, but he wasn't shocked. His mother, Pat, a nursing assistant, was obese, and his father, Terry, a truck driver who hauled cars and dirt, was a fat man, too. Pat died in the summer of 2001 at age forty-nine of ovarian cancer. Terry died in November 2008 at fifty-nine of a diabetic heart attack.

By the time he fainted at Hi-Lex, Keith had packed over 300 pounds on his five-foot-eleven-inch frame. But he figured that if he could lose some weight, get more exercise, and stop eating so much pizza, his system would right itself and the diabetes would disappear. He was prescribed insulin to help control his blood sugar, but it was expensive, even with his Hi-Lex-supplied health insurance. He couldn't see spending so much money on a drug if he didn't absolutely have to. So, though he used the insulin, he took less than the doctor prescribed. Sometimes he went without. He did lose weight—nearly 150 pounds. He tried to eat healthier foods. He took walks. By doing all that, he brought his blood sugar down to around 200 milligrams per deciliter of blood—far better than it was the day he collapsed: To his way of thinking, this was a victory. (Normal blood sugar is roughly 100 milligrams per deciliter, so 200 sustained for long periods can still cause damage.)

The auto industry was crushed under the financial dominoes that fell during the Great Recession of 2008–2009. Chrysler declared bankruptcy on April 30, 2009. General Motors followed on June 1. Thousands of autoworkers lost their jobs. And as the car giants suffered, so did the companies that supplied them—the toolmakers, the glassmakers, the metal-stampers, the plastics-molders. Some of these manufacturers employed a few hundred people; some employed a few dozen. Many were located in small towns and rural villages in southern Michigan and in northern Ohio and Indiana, towns like Litchfield.

The U.S. economy had lost 1.2 million jobs by November 2008—the month Terry Swihart died. Keith's would be one of them, and his work-supplied insurance would go with it. By June 2009, the nation's unemployment rate was 9.5 percent. Michigan's stood at over 15 percent, while Hillsdale County, Michigan, where Hi-Lex was located, hit 20 percent. (In

1933, at the deepest point of the Great Depression, the unemployment rate climbed to 25 percent.)

There were no jobs in the world Keith knew best, southern Michigan. He finally managed to land one at a Pepsi bottler and distributor near Lansing, but that didn't last long. He skipped insulin more often. He skipped eye doctor appointments. He stopped seeing a dentist. His marriage dissolved under the torrent of instability, and now he had to pay child support. By the time he was thirty, Keith, who hadn't done much of anything wrong aside from a little drag racing of junkyard cars, found himself being lashed by the American Way of Life. But if anybody asked how he was holding up, he'd say, "I'm doin' good, buddy, doin' good."

■■■

A lot had changed in Bryan, though you couldn't tell at first glance. From his office high up on the hospital's fourth floor, Ennen could see across High Street to the white water tower with the big blue BRYAN on it, the letters leaning forward as if to announce that the "Fountain City" had momentum. He could see the Spangler Candy Company plant—the Dum Dums lollipop people—sprawled below the water tower. The company had been there for over a hundred years. He could see the railroad tracks beyond and the freight cars headed east and west, day and night, and the trees in their winter nakedness and the flat farm fields to the north, raked by the wind that never seemed to stop. If, as a boy, he had walked up to the top of the county courthouse and looked out of the tower, the picture would have been the same.

Bryan didn't look different, but it was. Up High Street toward Main, and on the other side of Main, there was the trouble. There were about 36,800 preternaturally homogenous people spread over Williams County's 421 square miles of tiny villages, fields, and lakes, but there could be as much as eight years' difference in average life expectancy from one part of the county to the next, and even from one part of tiny Bryan to the next.

Such disparities played out in Ennen's hospital every day. It was playing out three floors below him right then. He'd attended Bryan High with Marc Tingle. Their paths were already diverging as teenagers, and would diverge even more over the coming decades, until the village contractor with the dentures and the bad heart found himself dying in the CEO's hospital.

As it happened, what was true in Williams County was true all over

America, including places with huge healthcare systems and giant universities with medical schools. America had spent a century arguing about medical care but had not settled a thing. After all that time, all that arguing, and all that money, America was sick, and getting sicker and dying earlier with every passing year. Ennen and his shop were supposed to do something about that, but what—especially when the hospital was struggling to stay afloat? And what had created those differences in the first place? Could a hospital, even a financially secure one, intervene in any meaningful way? In many cases, CHWC *was* a Band-Aid station, though not the kind its local detractors implied. It was a battlefield clinic in an amorphous and mutating social and economic war that was killing people.

The weapons used against the people CHWC cared for were as deadly as any disease: Both the Ohio and the federal minimum wages were less than they were forty years before, after adjusting for inflation. Pensions had disappeared. Unions had been driven out of workplaces. As they were, wages fell and more of the nation's wealth flowed to its richest people. Consolidated industries and financial engineers ruled the lives of employees. And as inequality spiked, health insurance evolved into an unaffordable, often useless racket. The hospital took in the casualties, patched them up, and released them back into what had become a one-sided conflict.

The business of the hospital, as difficult as it was, was much simpler than its mission. Income, expenses, return on investment—these were quantifiable. Ennen ran a business. His shop spoke the language of business. His own title, CEO, was borrowed from business; hospitals once had had "administrators." The gray area intersection of the business and the mission was the tough part. Performing like a business while simultaneously taking on a mission nobody fully understood meant that one goal would always be in tension with the other.

To make matters worse, the board, a huddle of local pooh-bahs, was showing signs of impatience. Whether it was with Ennen's leadership, with his manner, with the finances, or with all of it was hard to say. Ennen sensed this and resented it. He'd spent years massaging rules, making deals, and weaving through a national healthcare landscape everybody thought was crazy—all in the name of protecting CHWC. He had succeeded in doing so and been praised by the board. If the board was going to become meddlesome now, he sometimes thought, he just might walk out without saying a word to his ostensible masters. Let *them* run it.

That was just the fantasy of a somewhat frustrated middle-aged man. Ennen was far too much the responsible bourgeois, too much the old-school Catholic boy, too much the Bryan native son to ever stage such a drama. So instead he started for home carrying his brown leather satchel—a tallish, lean figure bent against the cold and the stress.

Part I

Autumn, 2018

1

A Ready Haven of Refuge

The Battle to
Control Health

Them old Dutchmen, them old Germans—they'd work all day in a factory in Bryan, then head home to work on the farm. It was like they couldn't be sure the factory would last, and they wanted to hang on to the farm, just in case—because a farm is forever, you know. So them old fellas worked twelve, fifteen, eighteen hours a day, and you never heard 'em complain. People in Bryan, Ohio, have been telling that story for generations. It's true, mostly.

Williams County was a place of hard work. Always had been. Pancake-flat land, out of the way—tucked under Michigan, spooning against Indiana—at first it was such hard work just traveling across it that white settlers didn't bother. The Great Black Swamp covered much of northwest Ohio, including Williams County, making it so boggy that trails simply disappeared. So, while the southern parts of Ohio were growing cities and towns, the northwest was still a wilderness. Fort Defiance was there, in what is now Defiance County. General "Mad" Anthony Wayne had the fort built in 1794. He used this sole white outpost as a base from which to annihilate Native American villages for fifty miles around.

By 1830, twenty-seven years after Ohio became a state, there were still only 387 people in Williams County. Twenty years later, just 265 people lived in the new city of Bryan, the county seat. The Germans, the Dutch, and a few English, Scots, and Irish eventually did come for the water, the trees, and the land under the trees. They could dig down five feet and have all the water they wanted. In some spots, like the site of the courthouse in Bryan's town square, the pressure underground was so great that natural fountains spurted from the earth. And so Bryan became known as the Fountain City, while outside of town early farmers cut and sold wood, drained the resulting fields, and planted crops.

Williams County's geography could seem bleak and featureless, especially in winter, but railroads loved it because they could lay track across the land as fast as they could hammer the spikes. In 1855, the Michigan Southern and Northern Indiana Railroad connected Bryan to Toledo and Chicago. With the rails came new markets for Williams County farmers and incipient manufacturers. Thanks to the railroads, Bryan's population grew nearly tenfold between 1850 and 1870, to 2,284 people.

Resource-based businesses like tanneries, wood mills, and the wood asheries that made lye and potash gave way to the Bryan Plow Company, the Bryan Manufacturing Company (makers of wheelbarrows), and corn and wheat mills. Then came the Bryan Specialty Company (makers of school bus and truck bodies), machine-tool makers, Spangler Candy, Bard Manufacturing (a maker of furnaces), Ohio Art (a metal novelties manufacturing company), and other, smaller enterprises. By the time of the stock market crash in 1929, Bryan was growing, prosperous, and looking to become a modern, progressive city.

One thing it did not have, however, was a hospital. Other parts of the Midwest, flush with money from burgeoning industries, were busy building community hospitals and clinics, vaccinating people, and improving sanitation. But health in Williams County, just as in some of the other rural counties in the United States, lagged behind. Dr. M. V. Replogle, the county's first health commissioner, reported in 1922 that "conditions over the county are very bad in many places. People are negligent as to health conditions. Sewage and sanitation are faulty in several of the towns." That year, the county reported thirty-nine cases of diphtheria, eighty-three of scarlet fever, twenty-seven of typhoid, two of spinal meningitis, seven of syphilis, and twelve of tuberculosis.

Though a smallpox vaccination had long been available—Massachusetts passed a mandatory smallpox inoculation law in 1809—outbreaks were common in Williams County. In 1924, a local epidemic of 149 cases forced its schools to close. Alarmed, the county finally mounted a vaccine drive. The inoculations worked: the following year, there was one case of smallpox.

People sometimes killed themselves. In 1918, George Hutchinson picked up a .32 Colt revolver and put it to his head. Floyd Detiviller hung himself with some baling wire. David Kaiser slit his throat with a straight razor in 1927. John Rang stepped in front of a Wabash train.

Those who were sickened by disease or damaged by injury had few options for medical care. A handful of doctors practiced in the county, but most were concentrated in Bryan, with a few more in Montpelier, a village about ten miles north that was becoming a railroad nexus.

If a flour mill exploded, or a grain farmer drove his truck through a rail crossing into an oncoming New York Central locomotive, or a gas station owner was shot in a holdup, or a manure spreader entangled a boy—the kinds of traumas that happened with uncanny regularity—the wounded had to be driven west into Indiana, or south or east into other counties. They sometimes died on the way.

Bryan was fifty miles west of Toledo, and fifty miles east of Fort Wayne (named for Mad Anthony). Yet, despite its rail connections to the outside world, it was self-contained. Social innovations like the hospital movement took a long time to penetrate.

By 1900, science and technology had expanded medicine to where hospitals were ceasing to be asylums for poor people to wait out disease or die in the process, while the rich were treated in their own homes. Wilhelm Roentgen invented the X-ray machine in 1895. Joseph Lister pioneered sterile surgery with antiseptic carbolic acid mist in 1865, and by 1900, steam sterilizers were common. The Mayo brothers were operating on hundreds of patients every year in Rochester, Minnesota. In 1906, the Ohio Medical Society urged every county to build a hospital, while all over the United States a great burst of construction put hospitals even in small cities.

But the doctors of Williams County were ambivalent about a hospital. The unquestioned medical authorities in the community, they enjoyed their status and their monopoly on the market. On one hand, a hospital equipped with the latest gear and tools could improve the medicine they practiced. On the other, it could threaten their dominance by attracting competing doctors.

Bryan's promoters, however, realized that the city had fallen behind. To be considered a modern community, a town needed a hospital not just to treat the sick, but also to attract new manufacturers. So in 1915, the Bryan Businessmen's Association started a campaign to bring a hospital to Bryan. "Few towns in our class are without a hospital and many smaller ones have this most needed [of] conveniences," the *Bryan Press* reported of the effort.

Theirs was the vision of a hospital as public good and community asset. There was little mention of money, except that the lack of it would be no barrier to treatment. "A city hospital will save lives and add comfort to the sick," the *Press* added. "It will always be a ready haven of refuge for those in distress. It will give absolutely free service to the sick in need and without money. . . . It will lessen the number of persons dependent upon the city and county for charity."

But money, like Satan, proved to be an inescapable companion to the angels of mercy. Bryan wanted its refuge, but it didn't want to pay for it. The hospital idea died.

Three years later, as the worldwide Spanish influenza pandemic killed tens of millions, local leaders resurrected it. The fire chief suggested saving money by transforming an old school on Bryan's Cherry Street. The chief's enthusiasm failed to sway tightfisted taxpayers.

Meanwhile, the rest of the country, including some rural areas, kept building. In 1918, the same year the chief tried to turn the city's voters, there were 5,323 hospitals in the United States (including such types as mental hospitals and tuberculosis facilities). By 1926, there were 6,946 nationwide. In Ohio, there were 85 hospitals in 1921; five years later, there were 146.

With the rise of the American hospital, and with hospitals taking on the same role as libraries, country clubs, schools, and parks as keystones of a successful community, many towns and counties, and sometimes associations of rural counties, voted for taxes or bond issues to support the creation and operation of hospitals as a public service. Other areas were bestowed hospitals by religious organizations, mainly Catholic. In the early years of the century, entrepreneurial doctors opened small proprietary hospitals. And in some towns benefactors donated money for hospitals just as Andrew Carnegie built libraries. (Bryan took Carnegie's money to build its library in 1903.)

Dr. Henry Winzeler volunteered himself as Bryan's hospital benefactor. A former dentist, Winzeler had founded the Ohio Art Company in a nearby town in 1908 to make metal novelties, including picture frames. Four years later, Bryan boosters like the Spangler Manufacturing Company (later renamed the Spangler Candy Company), the *Bryan Democrat*, and a couple of banks raised $4,000 to finance Winzeler's moving the business into a Bryan factory. Over the next fourteen years, Ohio Art's business was good. Winzeler grew wealthy and grateful. So in 1926, he offered to give $25,000 (about $351,000 in 2019 dollars) to Bryan so the city could finally build its hospital. All he asked was that the city come up with a matching $25,000.

During a public meeting in September to discuss Winzeler's offer, most agreed a hospital was needed and welcome. By general consensus, Bryan turned over the exploration of the enterprise's feasibility—and leading of a fund drive—to the local chapter of the Woman's Christian Temperance Union, guardian of probity and health. The WCTU had helped turn the famously hard-drinking United States into a dry country (officially, anyway) with the passage of the Volstead Act in 1919. If any group could ram a hospital through, it was the WCTU.

At first the organization's persuasive powers proved irresistible. On September 15, townspeople gathered again to hear the news that the WCTU had recruited a list of prominent people to join an investigative committee to find out how other towns in the region financed hospitals. Most agreed that by passing a levy of, say, 2 percent of a year's income, it should be possible to raise the town's matching $25,000 and supply an endowment to run a new hospital.

One of Bryan's leading ladies rose to suggest that Bryan's stores join the effort by setting aside a day during which sales proceeds would be donated to the hospital. Another proposed that churches each "adopt" a room. The mayor stood to say the kinds of things mayors say, about the glories of Bryan and the can-do determination of its people. Then a reverend recited a prayer, and the school band played a coda. Bryan's future hospital appeared as sure as the coming day. The only note of wariness was sounded by a doctor representing most of the county's physicians. A hospital, he said, was not an institution for profit-making; Bryan should expect it to operate with a deficit.

Williams County was feeling the tide of modernity. Prosperity had arrived. The merchants could indeed afford to give a day's proceeds. The banks were flush. Industries were hiring. Health had become a national passion with the discovery of vitamins, which were formulated into the tonics advertised in the Bryan papers. The new "science" of eugenics that promised to perfect the white race received a firm embrace from communities across the country.

The very day the WCTU announced the list of committee members, the county fair in Montpelier, the biggest event in the county by far during the 1920s, opened its gates. There, for the first time in its history—and like many other county and state fairs at the time—the fair held a eugenics-inspired healthy children contest. Just as cows, pigs, and sheep were judged, kids in two classes, ages two to six and six to fourteen, were weighed and measured. Judges examined their teeth, hair, skin, posture, hearts, lungs, noses, and throats. The winning children in each age group received $5.

But once the new hospital committee set to work, they found that the world of medical care outside of Williams County was complicated and contentious. Innovations in medical science had birthed a new era not only in health but also in business and economics—and the nation was already roiled by what was becoming known as a crisis in medical care. That crisis wouldn't stop. It rolled on and on, affecting every human being in the country and every town that built, or hoped to build, a hospital.

At the time Winzeler made his offer to Bryan, the United States was realizing that it was one thing to build hospitals but quite another to pay for them. The poor—at least, those considered the "deserving poor," a designation often made at the discretion of a doctor—sometimes received charity care from both physicians and hospitals. The rich could pay. But the working class found itself caught in the pincers of having an income, but not enough of one to buy care and medicine. By 1926, medical costs had become a pressing national issue. "When pneumonia or typhoid strikes down a breadwinner or when a major surgical operation becomes necessary, poverty may soon knock on the door," the *New York Times* opined.

The debate about cost, about who should receive care, and about how it should be paid for was peaking in 1926, but it harkened back to a campaign from a decade before. By 1915, at the time Bryan first debated building a hospital, half the states had adopted workers' compensation laws to benefit those injured on the job. More would soon follow. But there was no national system of health insurance. If a working person contracted pneumonia, he or she might lose weeks, or even months, of paychecks, and then be dunned for the bills for treatment. Families were ruined.

J. P. Chamberlain, a Columbia University academic and a member of the American Association of Labor Legislation, described the challenge and its solution in a union magazine: "In European practice, workmen's compensation schemes are but one factor in a rounded scheme against the hazards of life. Is workmen's compensation to remain the only social insurance plan finding root in American soil? If not, what is to be the next step, at least in practical discussion and legislative proposal? Logically, the next step would seem to be to institute sickness insurance."

Business owners, especially manufacturers who employed large workforces, wanted no part of any such plan. At a 1916 conference in Washington, D.C., called by the International Association of Industrial Accident Boards and Commissions, Frank Dresser, representing the National Association of Manufacturers and the National Association of Machine Tool Builders, floated strains of an argument in opposition to national health insurance that would become etched in the American psyche for a hundred years.

First, he argued, the poor are the responsibility of government. Perhaps, Dresser conceded on behalf of his clients, a string of "diagnostic consulting stations" could be established in communities and in the neighborhoods of big cities. These centers would become a hub through which local physicians could work and local health conditions could be monitored. Establishing such a chain of centers would be expensive, Dresser said, but the cost would be tiny in comparison with insurance for all. Medical care would not be free at these consulting stations, "save [for] the poverty stricken, who now and always must receive it. There is no greater reason for giving free medical service than free food."

As for doctors, many believed in treating the indigent without charge, but they liked the idea that the government would take the poor off their hands. After all, carpenters weren't expected to build houses for the poor, they reasoned, so why should doctors be expected to give their services away?

Second, Dresser argued, the poor weren't poor just because they got sick. They were poor because they were indolent and lacked self-discipline. "There is an equally great wage loss through voluntary absences or absences caused by intemperance, by ball games, by the many personal reasons," Dresser said. "These voluntary absences upon our inquiries more than equal the combined absence and wage loss due to both sickness and industrial accident."

Health insurance, he said, would only enable the worst habits of the lower classes. "Insurance," he claimed, was not "'health assurance' but 'poverty insurance.'" If the working class wanted health insurance, it should band together and insure itself with its own money. This would encourage personal responsibility.

Personal responsibility and individual effort were qualities that had built the country so far, Dresser implied. In America, you were on your own. Europe, a continent of decadent nations, had few lessons to offer: "We are not yet ready therefore to assent to the advantage of a system so startling to our American theories and ideals."

The idea of social welfare as an alien virus and an extravagant and morally damaging handout to the undeserving and inferior was supported by the "science" of the insurance industry—most prominently by the work of a statistician named Frederick Ludwig Hoffman. At the time of the push for state compulsory health insurance, Hoffman, an immigrant from Germany, was a vice president at the Prudential Insurance Company.

Like the other large insurance firms, Prudential stood to lose part of its life insurance business if proposed health insurance schemes became law. At the time, life insurance included small funeral benefits, which were a big reason members of the working class bought life insurance in the first place: They didn't want to be buried in paupers' graves. A government plan for sickness insurance could include a small funeral benefit, too, cutting into the big five insurance companies' business. But Hoffman didn't just promote a professional conflict of interest. He was a racist whose racial and political biases drove him to oppose any government involvement in the medical care of the nation.

Hoffman first became nationally known by way of an 1896 book he wrote called *Race Traits and Tendencies of the American Negro*. It soon became a landmark in the literature of scientific racism. Though he had married the daughter of a prominent Georgia family—a woman who became an official with the United Daughters of the Confederacy—Hoffman claimed his German upbringing rendered him free of any racial animus based on American sectionalism. He also insisted that, though he never earned a college degree, his was a life of objective science.

And when he studied data, he was forced to conclude that "previous to emancipation, the negro enjoyed health equal if not superior to that of the white race." Under slavery, Negroes were "healthy in body and cheerful in mind." Since emancipation, however, African American health and life expectancy declined precipitously, the result of dissipation brought on by personal failings like laziness, sexual immorality, failure to save money, and criminality. The intrinsic nature of African American lust and lawbreaking was obvious, Hoffman argued. The many lynchings of black men accused of rape proved it.

These traits, he wrote, were exacerbated by the eagerness of whites to provide charity and support to emancipated slaves—not by poor living conditions, poverty wages, or lack of education. At a time when social Darwinism was part of mainstream thought, Hoffman had come to believe the Anglo-Saxon race's personal responsibility and self-reliance made it far better equipped to thrive in the battle for survival. Providing aid, education, and political rights would only make the state complicit in a perversion of nature—to the detriment of the objects of the aid, and to the state itself.

By the 1915 campaign for sickness insurance, Hoffman was considered an eminent authority. He'd been president of the National Statistical Association, and vice president of the National Tuberculosis Association (now the American Lung Association). He helped to found the American Society for the Control of Cancer (now the American Cancer Society). He was widely consulted on all matters relating to health, statistics, and insurance, which placed him in the center of the debates over a national health plan.

Hoffman was especially valued by anti-national-insurance forces like Dresser, the manufacturers' representative, because he'd been raised in Germany, where Chancellor Otto von Bismarck had pushed a national health insurance law through the Reichstag in 1883. Advocates like J. P. Chamberlain favored a plan based on the German system. Hoffman, eager to portray himself as a completely loyal American during the days of World War I—and viscerally opposed to any hint of socialism—provided dubious statistics to show that the German system was not just a failure, but anathema to the American Way of Life. Here, then, was a recognized expert—a German to boot—who could tell the American people and their political leaders the truth about the failed German system.

An alliance of industrialists, insurance companies, and physicians used these talking points in campaigns to defeat proposed state health insurance laws. Labor split. American Federation of Labor chief Samuel Gompers opposed the initiatives, believing that if unions won higher wages, workers could afford their own benefits without relying on employers or the government; by contrast, some in his own organization and other labor leaders favored state health insurance.

During World War I, it was easy to oppose anything approved by the German kaiser. Afterward, hoisting Germany as a bugbear carried less resonance. But Germany was quickly replaced as the metaphor for disaster when a new fear gripped the United States after the 1917 Russian revolution: Bolshevism. Soon any national plan for health insurance was painted as collectivist—not just un-American, but anti-American.

In 1919, a proposed health insurance law in New York faced opposition from a new organization called the New York League for Americanism. In reality, the league was a front for insurance companies, industrialists, doctors, and their allies in the state legislature. The New York State League of Women Voters commissioned an investigation into the activities of the League for Americanism and released the results in early 1920.

The investigation found that the group exerted "powerful and perilous influence" with its money and "pseudo-patriotic propaganda." It identified the leaders, including Frederick Hoffman of Prudential. The League for Americanism, charged the women, had convinced physicians to join with it in opposition to social welfare bills like health insurance by branding such legislation as "Bolshevistic."

Unfortunately, the League of Women Voters report was released shortly after nationwide "red" raids on alleged leftists, radicals, and anarchists, instigated by U.S. attorney general A. Mitchell Palmer. The mass arrests of over three thousand people on January 2, 1920, proved to be the zenith of the first Red Scare. Many arrestees were soon released, and Palmer, subsequently investigated by Congress for abuse of power, faded from American political life. But the linking of national health insurance to communism and revolution proved potent. The New York bill died, and from then on, the American Medical Association seized the Red Scare banner as its own.

▮▮▮

In 1924, two years before the Bryan WCTU formed its committee, Dr. Morris Fishbein assumed the editorship of the *Journal of the American Medical Association* (*JAMA*). Fishbein became the AMA's face and its most powerful—as well as most famous—member. He wrote newspaper columns, magazine articles, and books. He opined on quackery, diets, politics, and American life. He spoke on the radio and gave speech after speech. Under Fishbein's leadership, the AMA transformed itself into part trade union, part political lobbying force, and part market-controlling cartel. He used his power to protest any perceived intrusion of government into medical practice. Medical care was the domain of doctors, and hospitals, Fishbein believed, were to be run by and for them.

The lessons from 1919 were clear. The American people, and the politicians who depended upon their votes, were terrified of any policy that smacked of socialism, communism, or Bolshevism, no matter how benign its intent.

Fishbein's opposition to the National Maternity and Infancy Protection Act (also known as the Sheppard-Towner Bill) proved to be such a case. The bill was originally sponsored in 1918 by Congresswoman Jeannette Rankin of Montana, a Republican. It was reintroduced in 1919 by a Democrat, Texas senator Morris Sheppard, and a Republican congressman from Iowa, Horace Mann Towner. The bill provided money to states for use in programs such as establishing prenatal-care clinics and nurse visits to the homes of pregnant women and newborns. Rural areas were intended to be a special target for the very reasons M. V. Replogle of Williams County pointed out: poor education, sanitation, and public health practices. The measure passed both houses of Congress by wide margins in 1921.

Fishbein believed that if government money supported maternity-care clinics and home nurse visits, patients had fewer reasons to pay private physicians. "Sheppard-Townerism is inevitably an inroad of the State into medical practice," he told a meeting at Yale University in 1927. "The legislation is economically unsound. It did not accomplish what its proponents claimed for it." In fact, the infant mortality rate declined significantly, from 76 per 1,000 live births when the law was passed to 65 in 1927. Even so, under pressure from the AMA, Congress dismantled the law, and its funding ceased in 1929.

It was true that doctors in rural places like Williams County were sometimes desperate for income; they were no richer than many of their patients. Shelby County, Indiana, for example, was a county much like Williams, with one main small town, Shelbyville. In 1930, doctors in Shelbyville charged between $1 (about $15 when adjusted for inflation) and $2 for an office visit. Outside Shelbyville, an office visit could be had for as little as 50¢. House calls cost about two bucks, though some doctors charged for mileage. Those fees usually included medicine. A doctor delivering a baby in the local hospital billed about $25. A tonsillectomy cost $35. The median net income of a Shelbyville County doctor in 1930 was $3,066 (about $45,000 in 2019 dollars).

Though most doctors—especially in rural communities—weren't getting rich, many of their patients still couldn't afford care. "The medical care of indigent persons was paid for by the township," a report on a survey of Shelby County stated, "but a considerable amount of free work was done by the physicians." Receiving a free office visit, though, did not mean a patient could pay for the actual treatment. Dentists in Shelby County earned even less than the physicians, but half the Shelbyville workers diagnosed with cavities didn't return to have them filled because they couldn't pay the charges.

The same situation applied to working-class people in big cities. "Health is, for the most part, a commodity which can be purchased," Matthew Sloan, president of the New York Edison Company—a utility company and one of the nation's major employers—said in 1929. "The difficulty now is that its cost is beyond the reach of a great majority of people."

In 1926, when Winzeler made his hospital offer to Bryan, an Ohio machinist could expect to earn about 67¢ an hour in a fifty-two-hour workweek, for a yearly wage of $1,800. A $2 office visit to a Bryan doctor represented about three hours of that machinist's wages. A simple hospital tonsillectomy would cost a week's pay.

Starting in 1927, a group of academics, social workers, physicians, and others tried again to take on the affordability crisis. With foundation support—department store magnate E. A. Filene's Twentieth Century Fund was an early donor—they hoped to research the nation's health and the system (or lack thereof) for delivering it, and then propose solutions to its problems.

Though not an official government inquiry, the Committee on the Costs of Medical Care was a heavyweight group headed by Dr. Ray Lyman Wilbur, a physician and past president of the AMA, as well as the former president of Stanford University and the sitting U.S. secretary of the interior. Over the next five years, the committee created an enormous number of damning reports, many of them newsworthy.

Even as the science of medicine improved, the committee showed, healthcare was still based on a nineteenth-century model of the kindly sole practitioner collecting a fee each time he (almost always a he) performed an exam or administered a treatment. In the three representative southern counties studied, people were too poor even for that level of care. After basic costs of living, a family's amount of spendable cash could add up to as little as $99 per year. Doctors were poor, too: in Chester County, Tennessee, the average net annual income of a physician was $991.

African Americans could be shut out completely, denied medical care at any price or restricted to segregated and inferior hospital wards. This was true not only throughout the South, but also in some northern cities.

Nationwide, the rich reaped the benefits of modern medicine at far higher rates than the poor and working class. An American manufacturing worker in 1929 earned an average of $27.36 per week, or $1,422.72 per year. (By 1932, that would drop by over 33 percent.) About 2.3 percent of households had annual incomes of over $10,000 per year. But those rich households accounted for 9.8 percent of hospital cases. People earning an Ohio machinist's income accounted for about 5.2 percent. Households earning $10,000 or more per year accounted for about 7.5 percent of all X-rays; those with a machinist's income, 2.5 percent. Lab tests, surgeries, and special nursing care all showed such disparities. The rich were not an especially sickly group. The imbalance mostly derived from the working class's inability to afford the level of care the rich received. So it often did without.

"As one ascends the economic scale, medical care becomes more adequate," the report observed. "This results in a postponement of death in a certain number of instances."

In all, the committee found, the United States spent $3.6 billion on medical care. Almost 30 percent of that amount went to physicians, 23 percent to hospitals, 18 percent to drugs and other medicines, 12 percent to dentists, and 5 percent to nurses. Only 3 percent went to public health.

While individual doctors may or may not have been earning a lot of money—that depended on where they practiced, who they treated, and where they'd gone to medical school—there was no doubt the cash pie was growing bigger by the day, and everybody wanted a slice of it. Doctors, drug companies, hospitals, and equipment makers were all aggressive in protecting and growing their pieces. Doctors even fought with each other over who could do certain operations. They formed specialties in an attempt to exclude general practitioners.

The AMA and local medical societies acted like cartels to block experiments in medical payment that sought to make care affordable. In Los Angeles, Dr. Donald Ross and Dr. H. Clifford Loos formed the Ross-Loos Medical Group, the country's first group care plan (patients paid a set monthly subscription fee of $1.50), in 1929. The Los Angeles Medical Association expelled them. They carried on anyway. Other physicians who deviated from AMA orthodoxy regarding payments were denied hospital privileges or were harassed.

In its final majority report, the committee sought to explain why medicine was no longer what the country had once known. It had changed, and the way it was organized and paid for had to change, too. The release of the report would seem to have come at an auspicious time: in late 1932, three weeks after the election of Franklin Roosevelt and a few days after Thanksgiving. The country, shocked by the crumbling of its economy, was in a mood to experiment with new solutions to economic problems and social welfare.

The majority report envisioned centers—hospitals, in most places— where medical professionals of all kinds could be based. Public health should be expanded to all people, the report argued. The writers of the majority report envisioned something like the water and sewer districts that had brought clean water to cities and towns. A combination of community-based group plans, like the Ross-Loos model or the one pioneered by steel and ship-building magnate Henry Kaiser, would make care affordable for most. In areas where group fees had to remain very low due to poverty, the local group would receive federal money via the states to augment the fees.

Some physicians, especially in rural areas, would make more money because they'd receive salaries. A panel of local citizens would govern each group. The committee's majority made a point of insisting that it didn't favor a general, nationwide plan of free medical care to all to be paid out of federal taxes—and that private practice would still be available to those who preferred it.

"Partial socialization of medicine was advocated today by the Committee on the Costs of Medical Care," began the United Press story on the report's release. Those words were accurate, but "socialization," when linked to medicine, had become a red-flag word. The branding begun more than a decade before, and beaten out continuously since by the drums of the AMA, proved powerful.

The plans were immediately attacked as communistic, first by the minority report of the committee itself—made up chiefly of doctors—and then by the AMA, through Morris Fishbein. In the December 3, 1932, issue of *JAMA*, Fishbein scoffed: "One must view the expenditure of almost a million dollars by the committee and its final report with mingled amusement and regret. A colored boy spent a dollar taking twenty rides on the merry-go-round. When he got off, his old mammy said: 'Boy, you spent yo' money but where you been?'" He then attacked Filene, implying the retailer ran a little pink. He called the proposed group practice idea "medical soviets" and warned of the "destruction of private practice."

Three days later, Fishbein spoke to the Michigan State Medical Society. He again attacked Filene. But he also pointed out that hospitals—and the whole advance of modern medicine, with its technology and tests and drugs and new army of employees—were the root cause of the fuss over cost. This was exactly the point raised by campaigns for national insurance in 1919 and 1920. It was also the rationale behind the formation of the Committee on the Costs of Medical Care a decade later. But Fishbein still demanded that doctors rule the new world of medical care, just as they had the old one.

The AMA could live with the government removing the dead financial weight of the poor from its back (though even that was a regrettable intrusion of the state into medicine), but everything else was an anti-American conspiracy on the part of "the great foundations, public health officialdom, social theory, if not socialism and communism"—all of whom were pushing "utopian fantasies." Fishbein argued that the public should trust doctors and the AMA, not politicians, squishy-headed academics, social reformers, or labor unions.

"It is absurd for the editor of a leading American medical journal to express the view: '. . . the right to say how medicine shall be practiced must remain with the medical profession,'" countered Isidore Falk, a microbiologist and professor of public health at Yale who became influential within the Roosevelt administration.

Sure, Falk argued, government has no business telling doctors how to treat an individual patient. But having a medical degree gave doctors no right to dictate the overall organization of care for the population. "The interest of lay people is centered not on what the physician shall practice, but upon how he shall be paid for his services. . . . Neither denials nor hard names will create a current or stem a tide," Falk wrote. "The times call for action and the problems for wise and judicious solutions."

The hard names and the calls for action continued. Despite attempts among some physicians to rebel from within, Fishbein and the AMA, often relying on Cold War anti-communist jingoism, would win far more battles than they would lose during the next thirty years. When Harry Truman proposed a national health insurance plan after World War II, the AMA countered with one of its own—to be run, managed, and controlled by the AMA. A *JAMA* editorial written by Fishbein accused Truman of trying to take "the first step toward a regimentation of utilities, of industries, of finance, and eventually of labor itself. This is the kind of regimentation that led to totalitarianism in Germany and the downfall of that nation."

When John F. Kennedy proposed the precursor of Medicare for the elderly, the AMA mounted a full public relations blitz, including a 1962 recording by Ronald Reagan that was shipped to AMA women's auxiliaries so it could be played at local meetings of housewives. Should Kennedy's plan become law, Reagan told his listeners, "you and I are going to spend our sunset years telling our children and our children's children what it was like when men were free."

Blue Cross and the rise of the health insurance industry, Medicaid, Medicare, Obamacare, health privacy laws, patients' bills of rights—they'd all come, each involving a legislative and public relations war. But a true reorganization of medical care that provided for all Americans would die and be resurrected over and over again, killed each time by some variation of the "socialism" charge invoked for a century by corporations, by Fishbein, and by their allies.

The talk would go on and on, costs would continue to rise as inexorably as the sun, the working and middle classes would be crushed over and over again, the poor would still be poor. The real problem of American health didn't have much to do with medicine. But Americans would continue to talk about the crisis in medical care as they had done for a hundred years— and most of that talk would be about the leaves and twigs and branches and miss the roots altogether.

■■■

Bryan's own 1926 committee traveled to hospitals in the region to examine how those communities funded the ongoing operations of their facilities.

Almost all of them ran deficits, just as the doctor had warned of at the meeting. Only two broke even or achieved a surplus—a Catholic hospital in Garrett, Indiana, that used unpaid nuns for much of its labor force, and one in Morenci, Michigan, that was owned and run by a physician who opened it as a for-profit business.

Some towns passed levies to support their hospitals and cover deficits—a socialization of medicine—but Bryan's residents now considered such measures out of the question. Modern twentieth-century medical care in a hospital was just too expensive. A *Bryan Press* headline in January 1927 announced the bad news: "Hospital Must Wait Until Town Can Afford It."

Three years later, the Depression kneecapped Williams County's progress. Many of its residents were pushed into poverty. By the end of 1933, there were 930 fewer cars and trucks in the county than there'd been in 1929. Just about every public worker took a pay cut. Teachers were reduced to $50 per month. Factory layoffs and a price collapse on harvested crops led to desperation. In Williams County two people committed suicide in 1929. Five people killed themselves in 1931 (including M. V. Replogle, the first county health commissioner), and eight did so in 1933.

The federal government helped keep the county afloat. FDR's Agricultural Adjustment Act, which provided price supports and direct payments to growers, cushioned Williams County planters. By 1936, when the act was declared unconstitutional by the Supreme Court, hundreds of thousands of dollars in federal money had flooded into the pockets of more than 1,100 of the county's farmers. Most farmers approved of such socialism.

Meanwhile, the Works Progress Administration put unemployed laborers to work. The WPA built the concrete bleachers for Bryan's high school athletic field by Garver Park and constructed a shelter house at the county fairgrounds in Montpelier. It built the city swimming pool and extended the water mains to the city limits. In 1935, the federal government erected a new post office on Main Street, just off the town square. The Civilian Conservation Corps recruited young men to go into CCC work camps around Ohio with the offer of food, clothing, and a place to sleep. They were paid $30 a month and were encouraged to send twenty-five of that back home to help support their families. In 1935 alone, twenty-six thousand Ohio men enrolled.

All that federal money streaming across the United States indirectly bolstered Bryan's larger manufacturers. Even during the Depression, most people could afford a penny for a piece of Spangler candy. Just before the 1929 crash, an inventor and entrepreneur named John C. Markey sold more than two thousand shares of ARO Equipment Corporation, a company he wanted to start to manufacture grease guns for use in service stations. People who had cars needed to keep them running, so business was good for auto garages.

ARO expanded, adding pneumatic tools to its line. It found nationwide markets and then began exporting. By 1940, ARO was listed on the New York Curb Exchange (the predecessor of the American Stock Exchange). It entered the aircraft accessories business and had net sales of just over $1 million in 1939. ARO became Bryan's largest employer, and its workers enjoyed the protection of the machinists union.

But meanwhile, medical care suffered. The state slashed subsidies to the county health department. In 1929, it provided $1,820. In 1934, the department received no money until September, when it was given $412. The health department board didn't even meet during the fall of 1933. "CANCLD. No Funds," noted the secretary.

Much of the burden for the health of residents fell on the heroic county nurse, Miss Greene. During the last four months of 1932, she drove her car 4,855 miles on official business. She lost about $35 a month from her take-home wages by paying for the cost of those trips from her own money. When physicians prescribed hospital care, Greene often provided transportation. In 1932, she drove fourteen patients to the hospital in Wauseon, Ohio, which was more than thirty-five miles away, and ten patients all the way to Toledo.

People who lived in the western half of the county sometimes drove across the state line into Angola, Indiana, to a small proprietary hospital owned and run by a Johns Hopkins–trained surgeon named Donald Cameron. Cameron, who practiced in Fort Wayne, married the daughter of the U.S. congressman who represented Angola. He soon realized that Angola, like Bryan, had no hospital, and that if he opened one, he'd be the only board-certified surgeon for hundreds of square miles. So he bought a former private home along Angola's main street and opened a little hospital there in 1926, the same year as Winzeler's offer to Bryan.

Since some Williams County residents were already coming to his Angola outpost, and others in the eastern half of the county were going to hospitals in Hicksville, Wauseon, and Toledo, Cameron concluded that with another hospital in Bryan he could plug the leaky Williams market and capture most or all of that county's business as well. He purchased two lots along the front of Garver Park, next to the school and the athletic field, and in the spring of 1934 announced his intention to turn the land into a 40-by-80-foot two-story hospital building. He figured on fifteen beds and promised the most up-to-date equipment. It would be the kind of place Morris Fishbein and the AMA advocated: a doctors' workshop, owned and run by a doctor. The profits would flow to Cameron.

Hundreds of people toured the new building when it was completed in early April 1936. A few days later, Art Radabaugh, a man from Edgerton with a bad case of appendicitis, became patient number one. Bryan finally had a hospital.

2

Everybody Is Coming
After This Hospital

Surviving
the Business

Phil Ennen walked into the fourth-floor boardroom, just down the hall
from his office. The auditors from Plante Moran were already seated.

"How's it going, Phil?" asked one.

"We're open!" Ennen replied.

Ennen wielded sarcasm the way some people said good morning—an
effect of growing up with mostly brothers in a big Irish Catholic family
that used mordant bons mots as love taps. In Ennen's case, the dark jokes
overlay a sometimes exquisite sensitivity.

Thirty days before, on October 1, 2018, Community Hospitals and
Wellness Centers had entered a new fiscal year. Every month of the past
year had ended in the red, and there wasn't yet any sign money had stopped
leaking—the first month of this year would end in the red, too. The hospital's operating loss for the past year would turn out to be nearly $1.5 million
on patient revenue of $79.6 million, for a −2 percent operating margin.

CHWC was a nonprofit hospital, like nearly 60 percent of all U.S. hospitals. (About 20 percent of hospitals, usually city-based, were owned by
states or other government entities, and another 20 percent were for-profit,
like those belonging to big outfits such as Hospital Corporation of America.) As a nonprofit, CHWC was organized as a 501(c)(3) private charity,
freed from most tax liabilities. But it was very much a business, too, and it

could go bankrupt. So Ennen always sought to make a small margin—an "operating surplus" in the official lingo—to invest in new equipment, people, and the physical plant. Big nonprofit chain hospitals in suburbs often made a 6 percent margin, and sometimes much higher than that. Unlike a state-owned hospital supported by taxes, CHWC couldn't afford to lose money for long. Thus the meeting with the three auditors from Plante Moran, an international accounting firm based in Cleveland, who had come to find out if they should prepare a damning "going concern" statement for the annual report. Such a statement would alarm debt holders, not to mention the community.

Ennen saw more at stake than just a black eye for the hospital. Well into the second decade of the twenty-first century, CHWC had become a keystone of the Bryan economy. It may have been tiny—the flagship fifty-bed hospital in Bryan, the twenty-five-bed hospital in Montpelier, and a clinic in Archbold, just over the Fulton County line to the east—but it was the biggest employer and most sophisticated outfit going in Bryan, and it was Ennen's responsibility. Local people, Ennen, and the board of directors were all adamant that CHWC remain an independent community hospital—a Bryan and Williams County asset—even as such hospitals elsewhere folded or were taken over by bigger chains, one after another. CHWC was part of a dying species, and everybody knew it.

Sometimes in secret, some of Ennen's own leadership team—the vice presidents who sat in offices along a carpeted corridor on the fourth floor—whispered that a takeover was inevitable. His chief financial officer, Chad Tinkel, figured it could happen within three years, maybe five at the most. The geology of American healthcare had shifted since the days when Donald Cameron opened his little shop. The CHWC of today stood athwart tectonic plates whose movements were lubricated by a massive flow of dollars. The hospital had little chance of avoiding being swallowed. But Ennen believed he could juke and jive his way through American healthcare to keep CHWC as it was—and even to grow it.

Phil Ennen was not only a Bryanite but the George Bailey of Bryan—the man tantalized by thoughts of what his life would have been like had he lived and worked in the bigger world. His two daughters and son had gone off to college and were now making lives in faraway cities. He remained a big wheel on a small bike. He served on local boards. He acted in community theater. He established a charity drive for a big civic project. He was the man who saw all the flaws in his hometown, sometimes losing patience with it. He once even tried to leave Bryan for a job elsewhere, yet he loved and defended the place. Ennen didn't think it was healthy for the hospital to have the outsize economic and social roles it did, but that was how it was, and it had become his life's work to keep the place alive.

The Plante auditors sat on one side of a square formed by four tables. A sink on the back wall seemed intended to have been a wet bar, but it had never been used as one. A silver shovel hung on the wall above it. A framed photo with a group of smiling people looking uncomfortable in suits and ties commemorated the day the shovel had been used to break ground on $62 million in renovations and new wings that turned CHWC into "that Lego blocks place." The bonds were floated, the money borrowed, the ground broken—and then the worldwide economy imploded in the Great Recession. Ennen took over as CEO in January 2008, just in time to catch the fallout.

The five vice presidents—Tinkel; Wade Patrick, chief information officer; Angelia Foster, vice president for human resources; Mike Culler, chief operations officer; and Jan David, vice president for patient care—entered and took their seats across the table from the auditors. Chitchat subsided, and an uncomfortable pause settled over the room.

"Well," one of the accountants began, "where do you stand today?"

Ennen waited a beat. "I have no response," he said.

Ennen could be tetchy inside the hospital. He could sometimes be impatient, defensive, brusque. He hated meetings, often sitting silent and grim-faced in the back of a room and projecting impatience, as if he couldn't stand to wait while others arrived at an answer he already knew. He also hated process, and he hated meetings about process most of all.

Plante Moran had been the outside auditor for the hospital for more than twenty years. It had a large hospital practice, with clients around Ohio and up in Michigan—some of whom had been forced to shut down, or been taken over, or been bought out. Each one had a tale of its own, but they all shared the same basic outline. The auditors weren't going to be surprised by anything Ennen might say: this meeting was about soothing them out of a damaging "going concern" judgment, and everybody in the room knew that by the time it was over, Plante Moran would be soothed.

Back in March, and again in September, CHWC had broken loan covenants with Fifth Third Bank that required it to maintain a cash-to-debt ratio of 1.25 (meaning that for every dollar of debt, CHWC had to have 1.25 dollars of money). Even one breach would allow Fifth Third to take the hospital from the board. Nobody believed any such thing would happen—not yet, at least—but a covenant break was a serious matter, and Plante wouldn't be doing its job if it didn't at least consider the notion that the break signaled a risk that CHWC might not be viable in the long term.

The bank didn't want to own a hospital, so, of course, if it ever took over CHWC, it would sell it off. But when Bucyrus Community Hospital, south of Toledo, went bankrupt and was then bought out of bankruptcy and folded into a health system chain, the lenders, Plante calculated, didn't recoup all the value. That was a perverse bit of good news for CHWC: Fifth Third had to know that the bank was much better off letting CHWC slide on the covenants.

CHWC paid $4.5 million per year in principal and interest on debt of $55 million. As a sign of Fifth Third's wariness, CHWC was being forced to maintain $19 million in the bank, so Fifth Third already had a protective cushion.

Ennen argued that, covenants aside, CHWC was financially healthy. True, the losses over the 2017–2018 fiscal year whittled away at the hospital's "days of cash on hand," a figure representing how many days it could remain open in a hypothetical scenario in which it received zero operating income. Days of cash, a common metric in the hospital industry, indicated how close to bankruptcy a hospital might be. In March, CHWC had 324 days of cash on hand. Now there were 295, but some hospitals had 30 or less.

Plante Moran understood all of this but was concerned about the trend. Fifth Third, one auditor said, "is going to want to know if the breaches are a blip this year, or if this is the way it's going to be the next two, three, four years. What will you do going forward?"

That was the question on everybody's mind—on Ennen's, on the board's, on the hospital staff's, on the mayor's, and on the county commissioners'. Tinkel, CHWC's chief financial officer, worried more about the covenant breaches than Ennen did, and some of his fretting had rubbed off on the board. Though it had a long history of keeping its hands off the management, the board had grown nervous about the breaches over the summer and fall. Ennen could feel it pulling against the reins. For the first time, it asked him and his leadership team to hire an outside consulting firm to help draft a strategic plan for the future.

Ennen thought the prospect of consultants was a useful bit of information to drop to Plante as a way of saying "we're on it"—that the hospital was
engaged in change to create better fiscal outcomes—but he didn't appreciate
the board's instruction to hire outsiders. He had a near-overweening confidence in his ability to manage out of trouble. He knew what to do, and he
didn't need to spend tens of thousands of dollars on consultants to tell him.
"Initiatives," he told Plante, were already under way.

Ennen had started the initiatives in the spring, when it was becoming
clear that CHWC was in the middle of a tough year. In June he told the
board that CHWC wasn't in "panic mode" but that everyone should prepare for an honest reckoning: necessary changes were coming. He needed
twelve, maybe eighteen months to execute those changes. Meanwhile, the
hospital would operate on a cliff edge. The board, he thought, gave him the
autonomy to "find a glide path that gets the job done."

The challenges to CHWC weren't mysterious; they were systemic and
long-term. As a Plante auditor said, "The pressures on a rural community
hospital are great." People in Williams County, as in a lot of rural counties, were growing older, poorer, sicker, and more reliant on Medicaid and
Medicare. More than two-thirds of CHWC's income was paid by the government, but the hospital collected a lower reimbursement from Medicaid
and Medicare than it did from insurance companies. Private, employer-
based health plans helped less than they might have because CHWC was
so small it had little leverage with which to negotiate contracts with those
insurance companies.

The Montpelier facility of CHWC was classified as a critical access
hospital—a designation most often bestowed on hospitals of twenty-five
beds or less that were distant from another hospital—so Medicare paid it
101 percent of "reasonable costs." That guaranteed 1 percent margin from
Medicare in Montpelier helped, but not enough.

CHWC benefited from the expansion of Medicaid under the Affordable
Care Act—Obamacare. Before then-governor John Kasich bucked his own
Republican Party to expand it, about 15 percent of Williams County residents had no health insurance. After the expansion, that figure dropped
by half, helping more people afford hospital care and improving Ennen's
customer base. But the Republicans in the legislature remained steadfast in
their desire to dismantle expansion, and Donald Trump ran for president
on the threat to do so. Ennen knew he had to be prepared for the possible

disappearance of Obamacare, and for the loss of coverage for about a thousand Williams County residents.

Hospitals could try to milk a few extra drops of revenue out of the system by playing with the codes that designated medical diagnoses and procedures. An industry had arisen over decades to help do just that. In 1994, for example, the hospital received a pitch from a firm called Quest Health Enterprises. "I'm sure you'll agree that President Clinton will quickly push for legislation to <u>CONTROL</u> the 'high cost' of healthcare," it began. "If Congress enacts these proposals into law, then healthcare providers will certainly experience the following:

1. Reimbursement deterioration without recourse.
2. Cash flow insufficient to meet current liabilities.
3. Bottom line 'red ink.'"

And "even if Congress puts the 'squeeze' to your hospital in the name of 'managed competition,'" the company promised a "pricing solution": a software that could massage billings "**TO PUT MONEY IN YOUR CHECK-ING ACCOUNT**"—sort of like upcharging in a restaurant.

By 2007, Quest was charging hospitals $1 million a year to license the software. But such manipulations had reached their limits: there was no more cash to be gained. And just cutting expenses wouldn't work, either. Choosing layoffs and deleting services would lead to a cascade of other decisions, none of them pleasant. Which services to the community do you eliminate? How many employees? How much do you reduce wages and benefits? Besides, cutting could eventually prove self-defeating: as services declined and equipment aged, people might stop coming.

Ennen wanted to try a combination of cost reductions and new investment. Some job openings would go unfilled to lower the employee count. CHWC's nurse-to-patient ratio on the medical/surgical floor was one registered nurse for every three patients, while other hospitals in the region used a one-to-five ratio. Ennen had told his nursing leaders that if the hospital were taken over, "corporate" would set the ratio at one to five, so CHWC had better do it on its own, and now. About eighty employees were sixty-two or older, and some were continuing to work only because CHWC's health insurance plan was cheaper than Medicare. Ennen thought he might be able to nudge such employees onto Medicare so they could step away from the hospital. If any of their positions had to be refilled, he could hire a younger employee at a lower wage.

Such trimming around the edges, though, wasn't ever going to counter the long-term trends that were killing independent community hospitals. The big health systems were getting bigger partly to give themselves more leverage with insurance companies and suppliers so they could drive down their costs and drive up their own pricing power—and partly to fend off rivals who were doing the same thing. Ennen believed the federal government was encouraging such consolidation, or was at least unsympathetic to protests against it, because it was simpler for CMS, the Centers for Medicare and Medicaid Services, to deal with fewer giant outfits than with many small ones.

CHWC sat in the crosshairs of Parkview Health in Fort Wayne, to the west, and of ProMedica in Toledo, to the east, both of which eyed CHWC as a possible acquisition. In 2010, faced with uncertainty about the future of the hospital, the Bryan Medical Group, the county's physicians partnership located across from the hospital on High Street, had voted to sell itself to Parkview.

Ennen had tried to counteroffer by suggesting the creation of a foundation—something like what the Cleveland Clinic had done—that would join the for-profit medical group with the nonprofit hospital, but the doctors weren't convinced. "We were symbiotic with the hospital in the past," explained Diane Conrad, the group's lead physician. "But we looked for a safety net. There was no security at the hospital." Now, thanks to the big Parkview sign at the physicians group, a lot of people in Bryan thought the hospital already belonged to Parkview.

CHWC was forced to talk to both Parkview and ProMedica about entering into joint ventures like an ambulatory surgical center and a cancer center. The board didn't like the talk about deals with the big systems, but it recognized that CHWC had little choice. There was, after all, nothing stopping Parkview from building a surgery center of its own and starting a war for customers. But as one board member told Ennen, a joint venture was Parkview's chance to "leverage in on us."

During the summer, as the talks proceeded, Ennen compared them to "dancing with a fella, and the fella grabs your hip, tighter and tighter. We will try to keep creating space, but keep the Parkview dance card open as we go across the floor. And then ProMedica will sidle up and say, 'Hey, let's talk.'" Ennen hoped to play one big boy against the other to get what he wanted without climbing completely into bed with either. "The problem is there's not a lot of comfort or even trust between the organizations."

Now, in the Plante Moran meeting, he skipped all the backstory details but cautioned that the situation with the board was delicate. "Parkview will put co-management on the table," he told the auditors of the possible joint ventures. "That's a bridge too far for our board." He expected that, should a joint venture come to pass, Parkview would want its signage on the Bryan hospital's property. "That," he said, "would be emotionally very difficult for the Bryan board." He described ideas for investments CHWC might make on its own.

CHWC had survived so far because it had financed more—not fewer—services, giving the people of Bryan and Williams County reasons to stay local for medical care. Unusually for a small town, CHWC ran its own radiation oncology center to treat cancer patients. Ennen had placed a young woman named Kim Owen, a Williams County native, in charge of it, acting as a management mentor for her. The center was one of the few "service lines" to make a profit.

The hospital also ran its own cath lab for performing cardiac catheterizations, during which stents were inserted to prop open arteries. The cath lab was the most profitable part of CHWC. It was run by a doctor named Damoder Kesireddy, a native of India who had come to Bryan decades before.

Building on the examples of the cath lab and the radiation oncology center, Ennen created more clinics within the hospital. Just a month before the Plante Moran meeting, CHWC had opened a gastrointestinal center headed by a new hire, a young doctor named Matt Cooley.

The year before that, he established a women's clinic by recruiting a Michigan ob-gyn named Hanan Bazzi. Ennen pursued Bazzi with a special determination. The other ob-gyns in town were Parkview doctors, which meant Parkview reaped their service billings even if those doctors used the hospital's facilities. Also, one of those doctors was older and would retire soon, which would leave the community shorthanded. And in the modern American world of hospitals, many procedures were now being performed on an outpatient basis because payers believed it was cheaper. Birthing babies remained an inpatient staple, and Ennen wanted to be sure CHWC could harvest as much revenue as possible by having his own ob-gyn on staff.

Bazzi was a hijab-wearing Muslim. Ennen had worried she'd be reluctant to come to an overwhelmingly white, Christian, and conservative county where many residents could—and did—quote the Bible in casual conversation, where 69 percent had voted for Donald Trump, and where a local politician could blame problems associated with a Bryan business on the fact the owner was "not of American extraction" and know he wouldn't hear any disapproval.

Bazzi grew up being the different one. Born in Texas, she spent most of her childhood in North Carolina. She was a sophomore in high school and wearing the hijab on September 11, 2001. Kids taunted her. They tried to tear off her hijab and slammed her locker door shut when she opened it. "They'd say, like, 'Go back to Afghanistan,'" she recalled, "and I was, like, 'I was born in Texas, thank you very much.' We would go to a mall or restaurant, and we would hear comments."

The idea of coming to a town like Bryan, in a county like Williams, gave her pause because she had young children and didn't want them to experience the same prejudices. Ennen, however, impressed her by admitting that while he couldn't guarantee community reaction, he'd stand with her, come what may. When she visited Bryan, he and his wife, Mary, hosted a dinner party at their home and didn't serve alcohol. Bazzi noticed. She also noticed that the people she met at the hospital seemed nice and welcoming. And Ennen's deal was a better offer than she'd get almost anywhere else in the country. Though she was fresh out of her residency, she'd head up her own clinic and could design it however she wanted, modeling it after the one at the University of Michigan—where she'd trained—if she chose to. Since then, Bazzi had been joined by Samar Hassouneh, another Michigan transplant and another Muslim.

Sometimes when she was out in Bryan, Bazzi would notice suspicious looks. When she ran on the YMCA's indoor track wearing long pants and her hijab, she could sense eyes following her. At school, her children faced questions—some good-natured, and some not—about the clothes they wore, and about why they didn't eat in the daytime during Ramadan. But she faced little outward disapproval and received no hate mail. Ennen did. "Are you hiring Isis?" it read. "The only good Muslim is a dead Muslim." He didn't tell Bazzi.

She and Hassouneh seemed to have little trouble attracting patients. "The vast majority of my patients—I love them, and they love me," she said. But the clinic was still losing money, as had been expected during its start-up phase. Bazzi and Hassouneh ordered in-house lab work and radiology images, both of which made a profit. But, for the time being, the clinic itself was a drain.

Before establishing the ob-gyn center, Ennen opened a pain clinic—a joint venture with a pain management medical group—and a wound clinic, headed by George Magill, a former ER doctor. Magill's office lost money, too—but, again, the ancillary services derived from the clinic made up the difference. In time, Ennen believed, all the clinics would show a profit. He just needed the board to give him the twelve to eighteen months he asked for: his glide path.

Turbulence in the glide path was already appearing, however. Neither Bazzi nor Hassouneh was sure if they'd stay in Bryan beyond the three years of their contracts. Bazzi and her family left almost every weekend to visit relatives in Dearborn, Michigan, so she wasn't as invested in Bryan as her home as Ennen had hoped. When Trump ratcheted up his anti-Muslim rhetoric, her doubts grew. Both she and Hassouneh found themselves formulating plan Bs.

Bazzi also ran into conflict with the Parkview ob-gyns. Traditionally, the local doctor on call at night or over a weekend delivered the babies, no matter which doctor had cared for the mother during her pregnancy. But when Bazzi started in Bryan and took her first on-call assignment while her family went to Dearborn, her phone didn't ring. So she checked in. "Oh, yes," a labor-and-delivery nurse replied. "We have a patient in labor now." When Bazzi asked why she wasn't called, the nurse explained that a Parkview doctor was delivering the baby. Bazzi believed the Parkview doctors were freezing her out—delivering not only their own patients but hers, too, when she wasn't at the hospital—as a way to keep the revenue within the Parkview practice. "Okay, they wanna play that game?" Bazzi thought. "They wanna shut me out? I will deliver my babies, whenever it is. It doesn't matter if I'm on call or not: I will deliver my own patients."

If Bazzi or Hassouneh decided to leave, it wouldn't be easy to recruit replacements. But the Women's Clinic was the least of Ennen's personnel worries: Kesireddy's retirement carried more potential danger. Kesireddy was in his seventies. His stamina for work had become legendary; his family had to force him to go on vacation. Hospital staff joked that someday he'd just die in his scrubs and fall into a patient's bed. But not even Kesireddy could stop time. At some point he was going to retire—the betting was in two years at the most—and since he was the only interventional cardiologist in the county, the cath lab would have to close if Ennen was unable to find a replacement.

The hitch, however, was that Kesireddy was a Parkview doctor, so recruiting such a replacement was Parkview's responsibility. The big health system could decide to cut off CHWC from the cath lab revenue by refusing to hire a new interventional cardiologist, instead referring patients to the Parkview "mother ship" in Fort Wayne. Then CHWC would have to hire its own doc, assuming it could even attract such a physician to a rural town, or concede the cath lab income.

Another personnel issue had started as an annoyance but was now growing into a problem. Kim Owen, the radiation oncology center director, was beginning to rethink her own career with CHWC—though it wasn't Plante Moran's business, and it wasn't generally known around the hospital because Ennen and those concerned were doing their best to keep it quiet. Over the previous summer, she'd complained of being harassed by a contract physician. He allegedly sent non-work-related texts after hours, invited her to dinner, brought small gifts to the clinic, and left an apple with a corny message: "An apple a day won't keep this doctor away."

As his approaches continued, Owen spoke to Ennen, saying she wanted to try to manage the situation herself. Ennen agreed, giving her some advice about how to shut the doctor down without causing a lot of drama. The doctor backed off, but not for good. When Owen reported that to Ennen, he called the doctor. You've been in the wrong, he said. The behavior had to stop immediately. If it didn't, Ennen would take it to the medical staff—and that was the last thing the doctor, or Ennen, wanted. "That uncorks a variety of bad things, like a more public airing, perhaps questioning," Ennen said. At the time of the Plante Moran meeting, the harassment had eased—at least as far as Ennen knew. Owen, though, had begun to think it might be worth taking some of the phone calls she received from headhunters looking for radiation oncology managers.

Ennen also faced necessary, but expensive, cash outlays, including for new technology. The hospital's phone system was collapsing. Wade Patrick, the CIO, figured a replacement would take about half a million dollars. The hospital used an electronic medical records (EMR) system that had been cobbled together in the rush to comply with a 2009 law called the Health Information Technology for Economic Clinical Health (HITECH) Act. The law created a land grab by both established corporations and startups to supply the EMRs, and big hospital operators adapted whichever system they chose to their own needs. Community hospitals struggled to pay for the systems, and setting them up proved devilish. Because Parkview owned the medical group across the street, and because those doctors used Parkview's system, CHWC was under pressure to adopt that system for itself. Doing so would save money and time, but it would also be one more dance with Parkview with its arm wrapped around CHWC's hip.

Ennen didn't hide any of this information from the Plante auditors, but he didn't volunteer any of it, either. As far as he was concerned, the less discussion, the better. The meeting was a chore to be gotten through.

Outside the modern walls of CHWC, the people of Bryan wrestled with their own financial crises. A decade after the Great Recession, Bryan residents still spoke of it the way an older generation remembered December 7, 1941. It was a disaster—not just because of the immediate events that triggered the recession, but also because of the way it landed atop thirty-five years of setbacks, compressing the discrete elements of Bryan's long decline into a focused lens of desperation.

There was a time when, on spring and summer Friday afternoons, people in Bryan could stand outside, look toward the county airport, and watch the private planes streak overhead. The planes carried ARO Equipment executives and customers, or Bard people, or Ohio Art people going to New York or Chicago. ARO had about two thousand employees, dressed in either blue work shirts or short-sleeved white shirts with ties and a couple of pens in their pocket: the engineer's uniform. The ARO executives drove Buicks and Chryslers and served on boards and civic organizations.

During World War II, ARO made pneumatic tools for Rosie the Riveter and breathing masks for high-altitude pilots. Then it supplied NASA. Every piece of equipment was stamped with BRYAN, OHIO USA. Ohio Art shifted from making metal picture frames and little tin toys (the company's main building was on Toy Street) to putting an Etch-A-Sketch in the hands of seemingly every kid in America. BMWs and Mercedes dotted the headquarters parking lot. Up in Montpelier, about three hundred people worked at Mohawk Tools, making specialized industrial drill bits and other cutting devices for use by carmakers and aircraft manufacturers. The salesmen, executives, and customers at all these companies packed the Orchard Hills Country Club, just outside Bryan, and stayed at the Colonial Manor, a nice little motel near Ohio Art.

But then came the Reagan era and the explosion of mergers, acquisitions, and leveraged buyouts. In 1985, Todd Shipyards, in deep financial trouble, raided ARO to add its solvent pension fund to Todd's assets. Todd failed anyway, and ARO was handed off to industrial giant Ingersoll Rand. Ingersoll shut down the huge Bryan plant by the water tower and sent the jobs to North Carolina, a right-to-work state where there were no machinists unions, and to plants in India and China.

Ohio Art sold off the Etch-A-Sketch to a Canadian toy outfit and became a tiny fraction of its former self as it returned to its roots in metal lithography, making items like decorative boxes for Jack Daniel's bottles. Mohawk, caught up in a wave of consolidation of auto suppliers, shut down about the same time as ARO. There still was a Mohawk Special Cutting Tools company, but it was now based in Shannon, Ireland. Montpelier's school sports teams were still called the Locomotives, but the railroad jobs were mostly long gone, too.

The details may have been different, but hundreds of communities throughout Ohio, Michigan, Wisconsin, Indiana, Illinois, Pennsylvania, and upstate New York could tell similar stories. The planes stopped flying, the country clubs' fairways grew over with weeds, and empty windows faced the town squares.

When the recession hit, unemployment in the United States rose to 10 percent, but in Williams County it was 17.2 percent. About 60 percent of the county's land was devoted to growing corn, soybeans, and a little wheat—but farms had consolidated into big operations, so only a few hundred people still farmed full-time. Many worked for small manufacturers, and many of those were tied to the car industry. The recession made clear what had been denied for decades: nothing would ever be the same again.

By late 2018, unemployment had receded, and just about anybody who wanted a job had one. The jobs seemed fragile, though. As the CHWC leadership confronted the hospital's budget woes with the auditors, Valerie Moreno, a forty-six-year-old wife, mother, and Williams County native, confronted hers. She'd recently left Multimatic, a company in Butler, Indiana, across the state line. Multimatic made dashboards for Ford F-150s and Silverados, as well as a bumper for the Tesla Model S. Valerie inspected welds, mainly, and applied clips and screws. The job wasn't bad, but she wanted to move on: she was classified as a temporary employee, despite working seven days a week, which was why she made only $12 an hour. Her husband worked at a metal fastener manufacturer, but still, money was always tight. So Valerie kept looking. She found a spot at Sauder, a maker of institutional furniture. She worked in Stryker, a village in eastern Williams County, but because she'd just started, she had no health insurance and no paycheck yet.

Marc Tingle, the village contractor who would find himself dying of a heart attack in the CHWC emergency room, felt the recession coming before many others did. He worked in assembly plants—first near Bryan, and then in Indiana—putting together manufactured homes: the single-wides and double-wides that housed a lot of people in the rural parts of both states. For a while in the early 2000s, the companies, owned by big, out-of-state corporations like Warren Buffett's Berkshire Hathaway, couldn't keep up with demand. They offered sketchy loans to buyers with poor credit scores, who then snapped up the homes. But many buyers couldn't make the payments, so their homes were repossessed, and manufacturing slowed until finally, as the recession hit, it stopped altogether. By then, Tingle, realizing the $35 hourly wages were stopping, too, had started his one-man contracting business and left his health insurance behind. While the vice presidents and Ennen talked to Plante Moran, Tingle was on a job, swinging a hammer.

Meanwhile, on Cherry Street, Keith Swihart was also trying to figure out how he could survive. Back in March—when CHWC was first breaking the loan covenant—his wife, Stephanie, sat crumpled over in the little dilapidated house she shared with Keith and their son, Caleb. Her abdomen ached. She was having a menstrual period, but there was so much cramping and bleeding she worried something was wrong.

Though she worked off and on as a home health aide, Stephanie feared doctors. Not just doctors, really. Stephanie feared the medical system, whatever that meant: all the machines and clinics and hospitals and bills and people who always said they knew more than you. And while they did know more than you—that was true—they had a way of making you feel small about it. And everything cost so much money. Stephanie was afraid of a lot of things, not just medical stuff, but at that moment in March something medical was happening, so Keith begged her to see a doctor. "I have insurance," he argued. He did have insurance, along with a job, a 401(k), a wife, a child. A lot had changed since he left Michigan. He figured the bad times were long behind him.

After being laid off at Hi-Lex, after working for the soda bottler, after his divorce, Keith realized he was going nowhere in Michigan. He knew a few people down around Angola, Indiana, and in Bryan—and though in 2010 the economy was disastrous in those places, too, he decided to drive south to see what life there might bring. Keith first bunked with a friend named Chad Underwood. Chad was a good dude. He helped Keith get a used automobile and other things Keith needed to start a new life, and he introduced him to his friends.

Then Keith found a job in Ashley, Indiana. Ashley Industrial Molding manufactured thermoformed reinforced plastic parts—for example, a piece for the Oshkosh mine-resistant military vehicle. It made parts for tractors. Between the military orders and the reviving farm economy, Ashley's business was improving.

Keith always was a good worker. In his early twenties, he'd worked for a computer numerical control (CNC) machining company, and they liked him so much they sent him out to Las Vegas for a few days of training. Vegas was crazy. The New York–New York Hotel had manhole covers with steam coming out of them, like the real New York streets he saw on TV. Keith had never forgotten that, but he didn't have much desire to go back: Keith wasn't a Las Vegas guy.

Keith met Stephanie through Chad. "She saw me, and looked at me, and we started talking, and it was really comfortable," he recalled. "And one time she asked me, 'Why don't you come see me?'" Christmas Eve was coming up. Keith tried to plan a good first date. He thought of a movie, but the theaters closed early on Christmas Eve, so they went to the Applebee's down in Defiance. Keith fell in love right away. "She had a smile. It was one of them things—you see the smile. Her green eyes, red hair—I mean, she had a smile like no other. And she had the personality."

Stephanie, Keith, and Chad became a trio of best friends. Sometimes they all hung out with Chad's fiancée, the mother of his three children. Keith always said he wouldn't have the life he found if it weren't for Chad.

Keith made good money at Ashley. He figured that with overtime and with the money Stephanie made, some years they brought in $60,000 before taxes, maybe more. The drive to Ashley from Bryan could take him an hour, even ninety minutes in the snow or ice, which made for a long day, but the hassle was worth it. Keith reckoned the health insurance was decent, too. It included some pretty big deductibles for him and his family—and a big number for any medical costs he'd have to pay if the shit really hit the fan—so he tried to economize, including on his insulin. But he knew a lot of people who didn't get health insurance at all, so he figured he had a pretty fair deal.

He and Stephanie married in 2011. They were happy, but it wasn't all bliss. He felt the pressure of his new responsibilities. Not only did he pay support for his own child, but Stephanie, who at forty was almost a decade older than Keith, had had other relationships with other men. She'd given birth to five children of her own. They cost money, too. Then, in 2013, Stephanie gave birth to Caleb, who, as it turned out, was autistic and non-verbal. And some of Stephanie's relatives weren't working much. Cash just had a way of drifting out of the house. In his darker moods, he figured he was supporting eight people: an exaggeration, he knew, but *still*.

Despite such friction, Keith always called Stephanie his soul mate. He appreciated the way she held the household together and looked after Caleb while he was at work, the way she kept an eye on him and made sure he took his insulin. She called Keith, whose childhood nickname was Teddy, "Teddy Bear." They were the best thing that had ever happened to each other, they said. "We had a good marriage," Keith said. "We did stuff together," like going to NASCAR races so Stephanie could watch her favorite driver, Kyle Busch, and to RC car events. "I am now married to the most wonderful man in the world," Stephanie said.

After a long time of feeling controlled by events and powers he didn't understand, "I was in control," Keith said. "Things was goin' good." When he looked back, he wondered if the spiral down started with what happened to his friend Chad. Chad suffered from what Keith called "mental issues." He wasn't sure just what those were: maybe Chad was bipolar, or just had basic depression or something. Anyway, in late 2016, Chad seemed to get worse. There was some family trouble, too. So Keith invited Chad to come live with Caleb and Stephanie and him in the green-shingled house they rented for $600 a month on Cherry Street. He wanted to return the favor

Chad had done him. Chad wouldn't even have to pay anything—he could get himself straightened out, maybe get some counseling somewhere. Chad was open to the idea, but he wanted to think about it for a while.

On January 9, 2017, close to dinnertime, Chad called Stephanie. They were talking on the phone when Chad stuck the barrel of a rifle into his mouth and pulled the trigger. He was thirty-six years old when he became one of the 920 people in Ohio who would kill themselves with guns that year. "That messed her up pretty bad," Keith said of Stephanie.

Ever since Caleb's birth, Stephanie had been fighting some anxiety and depression of her own. They both adored their son. "My child—when he smiles and looks at me and laughs . . . ," Keith said, not finishing the sentence. "It's one of them things. If I had a bad day, he's the one who gets me through my day." And for the world, for their relatives, for themselves, they focused on that smile: not on the squirmy havoc and their son's sometimes impenetrable remoteness and their worry about his future. Inside, though, Stephanie couldn't escape the anxiety. Over time, it enveloped her. Then Chad's suicide left her as brittle as a dried autumn leaf.

Later that year, in October 2017, Stephanie noticed she cramped and bled more severely than usual during her menstrual period. At Keith's urging, she made an appointment to see a doctor over at the Parkview group on High Street, across from the hospital. Stephanie was, as Keith liked to say, "a big lady." At about five foot seven, she weighed 295 pounds. Maybe her weight influenced her bleeding condition, or maybe not, but after examining her vagina and cervix, the doctor found nothing worth noting. Stephanie would not let the doctor perform a Pap smear to test for cervical cancer—she was too afraid. Besides, the last time she'd had the test, the results were okay.

That she was bleeding abnormally was obvious, so the doctor cited the medical name for it—menometrorrhagia—and prescribed Mirena, an intrauterine device (IUD) containing the hormone levonorgestrel. Usually women have an IUD placed to prevent pregnancy, but sometimes it's used to prevent heavy periods, and that's what the doctor had in mind.

Though Stephanie told the doctor she'd have the IUD inserted, gave her consent for its insertion, and was then tested to be sure she wasn't pregnant, she didn't follow through. Her fears were stronger than her desire to stop the cramping and bleeding. She needed a psychiatrist as much as she needed a gynecologist, but Williams County didn't have a psychiatrist.

Stephanie tried to control her ache and bleeding with birth control pills, but they didn't help. She became anemic. She started taking iron supplements; they made her constipated. Then she was injected with Depo-Provera, a hormonal birth control that lasts about three months and can stop periods.

The bleeding subsided until the gush of blood and the abdominal pain in early March 2018. Again Keith urged Stephanie to see a doctor. But the bleeding soon stopped so Stephanie decided not to go. Six days later, though, she was worse, plagued with a fever and nausea. Keith drove her over to the ER at the CHWC Bryan hospital. A computed tomography (CT) scan of her abdomen appeared to show inflammation around her colon: perhaps Stephanie had appendicitis.

That day, CHWC transferred Stephanie to Mercy Health St. Vincent Medical Center in Toledo—part of a chain of twenty-three Mercy hospitals across Ohio and Kentucky. Keith drove Stephanie there. The doctor in the St. Vincent's ER decided Stephanie was suffering from sepsis and admitted her. Over the next five days, she was treated with IV fluids and antibiotics, and though the sepsis subsided, another CT scan revealed a mass on her cervix. The way Keith remembered it, "When she was in St. Vincent's, they said they thought they seen something on one of her CT scans, but it didn't go any further."

The bills added up: the office visit in October 2017, the pregnancy test, the CHWC ER charge, the CT scan, red blood cells to treat her anemia, five days at St. Vincent's in Toledo, and separate bills from providers to the hospitals—the radiology company that worked inside the Bryan hospital, the ER staffing company that covered CHWC's ER, a pathology corporation in Toledo. Keith had never heard of any of them before the bills came.

Keith's insurance covered a lot of it, but he was still on the hook for thousands—he never did know the exact amount. The mailman dropped the white envelopes through the door slot on Cherry Street, but between trying to care for Stephanie, looking after Caleb with help from Stephanie's niece, and working, Keith was already swamped.

By June, Stephanie's abdominal pain wrapped itself around her back, worse than ever. Though still reluctant, she made an appointment with the CHWC women's clinic. Samar Hassouneh knew within minutes of beginning her examination that cancer had invaded Stephanie's cervix and that it was well advanced. Bits of Stephanie's cervical tissue crumbled away the moment the doctor touched it. Hassouneh sent this tissue to the hospital's pathology lab, where pathologist Shannon Keil confirmed invasive squamous cell carcinoma. Hassouneh knew the diagnosis had come far too late—Stephanie was about to die.

During the month after her visit to Hassouneh, there would be ER visits to CHWC via Williams County ambulance, a urinary tract infection, a kidney-related emergency (fallout from the cancer), drives to Parkview Hospital in Fort Wayne for oncology treatment, testing, then admittance to Parkview on July 22, where, finally, at 7:44 in the morning of July 23, Stephanie died. She was forty-six. The last twenty-four hours of her life produced bills for drugs, supplies, labs, the ER, respiratory care, pulmonary function tests, vascular diagnostics, echocardiology, a CT scan, blood, doctor's fees, and observation adding up to over $41,000, but she was still dead.

Keith didn't like to admit it because he thought it sounded bad, being a diabetic and all, but he drank some after Stephanie died. He'd get Caleb down to sleep, sit in the recliner, and drink. He knew he shouldn't. He knew he should take care of himself, but he didn't do that, either. He missed insulin shots. When Stephanie was alive, the house had been bedlam even on good days, thanks to Caleb. Now anarchy ruled. A relative of Stephanie's came by a lot to look after Caleb and to do some cooking; for a little while she practically moved in. But she couldn't replace Stephanie.

Keith was low. Designing, ordering, and paying for a headstone for Stephanie's grave consumed his energy. And when he looked at Caleb and thought about driving to work in Ashley—where he'd be an hour away if Caleb needed him—he decided he had to quit his job, figuring he could go to work at the big distribution center for Menards, the home improvement retailer, where lumber and other supplies were shipped in and then shipped back out to stores around the region. The center was up by Holiday City, a tiny collection of motels and gas stations near the Ohio Turnpike about twenty minutes from Keith's home. Menards always seemed to be hiring. Keith couldn't see any other way.

███

For decades after it opened in 1936, Donald Cameron's Bryan hospital cruised along as an unremarkable part of the local fabric. A year after opening, Cameron united his Angola and Bryan operations into a single tax-exempt charitable corporation: Cameron Hospitals, Inc. He imagined himself in the mold of beneficent medical pioneers like the Mayo brothers, the Menningers of the Menninger Clinic in Kansas, and Cleveland Clinic founder George Crile. He would bring medical excellence to rural America.

Cameron was Morris Fishbein's apex exemplar of the doctor as Caesar, master of his own empire. Like Fishbein, he despised even a hint of government involvement in medical care. He despised taxes, welfare, and regulation, too. He believed "there should be available to taxpayers a list of the recipients of welfare in each county" because "a little more available publicity would keep the names of a fair number off the dependency roll." Taxpayers, he argued, "could at least dream about . . . a requirement that the name of every citizen put on the welfare recipient list be automatically removed from the voter list. Candidates for public office would not have to cater to this class of citizens." In the United States, Cameron believed, there was almost never a good excuse for anybody to be receiving aid from the government. Poverty was evidence of moral failure. While medicine's newfound abilities to save lives proved a boon to mankind, "among indigents, a medical triumph often adds to the taxpayer's burden."

Cameron was particularly galled after 1946, when the federal government entered the hospital-building business. The passage of the Hospital Survey and Construction Act, called the Hill-Burton Act after its sponsoring senators, Republican Harold Burton of Ohio and Democrat Lister Hill of Alabama, provided in-kind grants and loans to communities wanting to establish nonprofit hospitals. Cameron saw the law as "an example of waste and extravagance with taxpayers' money." "Almost any geographic taxing unit," he argued, "which will take the usual pauper's oath that it is too poor to build its own hospital may apply to the federal government for a grant in aid, and if approved by the State Board of Health may receive a gift from our rich uncle."

Hill-Burton hospitals built in nearby counties competed with Cameron's own in markets he hoped to dominate. (They "surround us," he complained.) Cameron tried to enlist the help of state and federal legislators to shut down Hill-Burton, but building hospitals proved too popular with both Republicans and Democrats.

Cameron did take charity cases: few were turned away for lack of funds, and he boasted that his hospitals admitted "many colored people." (Hill-Burton, reflecting its origins as a compromise between two senators from opposite sides of the Mason-Dixon Line, permitted states to discriminate against African Americans in admittance policies.) But whether or not to provide such charity care should, Cameron believed, be his decision to make. He'd used his own money to build two small hospitals where there'd been none, and now he felt entitled to be left alone to manage his business on his own terms.

His hospitals were lucrative. The nonprofit corporation leased the hospitals from him, and he headed and controlled the board. The hospitals provided him with an arena in which to practice surgery and, of course, to collect his fees. He recruited and set up doctors in small, one-man practices in villages by purchasing houses they could use as both residences and offices. The new doctors understood that, in return, they were to refer patients only to the Cameron hospitals, where Cameron was the head surgeon. Fee-splitting—similar to a kickback and now largely outlawed, in which one doctor pays another for a referral—was standard procedure. The hospitals also offered on-site offices to doctors who, in turn, paid 25 to 30 percent of their fees to the hospital via a pooled fund. They also paid a monthly fee to Cameron personally. By 1962, Cameron was receiving $500 a month (about $4,200 in 2019 dollars) from the funds in Angola and Bryan.

In 1959, in the middle of an IRS investigation of the Cameron hospitals' business arrangements with doctors, Cameron sold the buildings, real estate, and equipment to Cameron Hospitals, Inc., which then deeded them to the people of Angola and Bryan, respectively. The municipal court set up a new board of directors, and the hospital became a private, nonprofit community asset. In an effort to resolve the appearance of participating in a for-profit outfit operating under the guise of a nonprofit, the doctors formally signed an agreement to create the Bryan Medical Group and to move out of the hospital and into a building across the street. Cameron retired from the board and severed his business relationship with the corporation in 1964.

Thanks to Bryan's prosperity, the hospital continued to prosper, too—at first. It expanded and renovated. But Cameron was right about the Hill-Burton hospitals. They did siphon off some of Bryan's business. Thanks to improved highways and the growth of specialty medicine, more Williams County residents chose to drive to Fort Wayne or Toledo to see specialists. In 1952, the county's townships built Williams County General in Montpelier, offering patients a public option within the county itself.

By 1973, the hospital found itself in deep trouble. Parts of its physical plant were old, and so was the equipment. When Phil Ennen's mother, Mary

Helen, began working there as a nurse, she was so appalled by the unsafe conditions that she quit. Small-town people weren't stupid, she said; they knew lousy care and facilities when they saw them, so they'd stop coming. And they did. A short time later, though, she was offered a job as chief of nursing. Come back, hospital officials told her, and do something about it. So she returned—only to be fired after confronting doctors about their poor treatment of "her" nurses.

Grant Brown, a board member who owned Brownie's Drive-In—a Bryan institution—had a son who lived in Columbus. His son had become friendly with a man named Oreste "Rusty" Brunicardi, who happened to be director of patient care at Ohio State University's hospital. Brown called Brunicardi, telling him that the Bryan hospital was about to go broke. As a favor, could Brunicardi come up to Bryan to troubleshoot? It'd be temporary, maybe three years—just long enough to plug the money drain. Brunicardi told his wife they were taking an unexpected detour to a small town in northwest Ohio but that they'd soon be back in Columbus. The detour lasted thirty-five years.

Once in Bryan, Brunicardi responded to the crisis by mounting an immediate fund drive for $150,000 and by launching a campaign to reinforce the idea that the hospital was a community asset. Then he spent. If Bryan didn't have a service patients needed, he tried to supply it. After the nurses kept mentioning Mary Helen Ennen, he hired her, and both she and her husband, Jack, befriended Brunicardi. He recruited staff doctors. He spent on new technology and specialized care, even establishing the radiation oncology center. "Just because we choose to live here in a small town doesn't make us second-class citizens," Brunicardi would say. He built the clinic in Archbold in hopes of fending off westward expansion by Toledo giant ProMedica. He figured Fulton County doctors could refer patients to the Archbold clinic, then on to Bryan if necessary, and not to ProMedica's facilities.

Brunicardi ran his strategy partly by ducking and dodging through an increasingly complex and chaotic healthcare maze—bending a rule here, avoiding a rule there. He managed with little oversight by the board. He also recognized that healthcare was a political enterprise as much as a scientific or financial one, so he made sure state and federal politicians heard his voice. "I'd go to the doctors and say, 'Look, this person is going to get elected. Would you please make a $100 donation [to the campaign]? We're going to need his support.' And then I'd send it in on the letterhead of the hospital."

He slowly convinced reluctant county and Montpelier officials that two hospitals in the same county duplicated services, and that the competition for patients damaged both. He assumed administration of Williams County General in 1978. In 1986, they formally merged. Williams County General's status changed from public (meaning it was supported by taxes) to private nonprofit (meaning that it was controlled by a private board but qualified as a nonprofit organization under the federal tax code and supported itself on the fees it charged).

Mary Helen and Jack retired to Florida immediately after Phil graduated from Bryan High. So he attended Florida State, then entered the school's master's program in public administration while working for the Florida legislature. On a visit back to Bryan to see his longtime girlfriend, Mary Ebersole, he took her to dinner at Sam's, a diner in a one-stoplight village called Blakeslee. There, Ennen—a man given to quoting Looney Tunes cartoons, old movies, and the sorts of books English majors read in class—looked across the wooden table at Mary and proposed by asking, "So, we gonna do this?" Knowing what she did about the Ennen clan's preferred forms of communication and Phil's sense of humor, Mary considered the proposal romantic.

After a spring wedding in Bryan, Mary moved to Tallahassee, and the couple settled in. As Ennen was finishing his master's degree, he received a permanent job offer from the legislature. Then, on another visit back to Bryan, he walked into Brunicardi's office just to say hello. "I've been trying to find you," Brunicardi said. "You have a few minutes to talk?" Brunicardi offered the twenty-three-year-old Ennen a job as chief operating officer of the hospital at a starting salary of $26,000 and with the understanding that one day he'd fill Brunicardi's shoes as CEO. Ennen didn't know a thing about running a hospital, but to Brunicardi, that was the point. He wanted an apprentice he could shape in his own mold.

"His mom and dad were special people," Brunicardi told me. "I just felt he would be a good person because he knew what it would take, and because he was very intelligent. I always had it in my mind he would take over, from the very beginning."

The Ennens liked Tallahassee. But they were both Bryanites. And here was a job that promised to one day put Phil at the top of one of the town's most important institutions, and at a good starting salary. By saying yes, he could be set for life while many of his peers were still trying to find their way.

Brunicardi retired in December 2007 as the undisputed leader of what was now Community Hospitals and Wellness Centers. When he drove out of town, he passed through the intersection of Main Street and Brunicardi Way. Though Ennen took over as CEO in January 2008, for over a decade after, staff members would still ask, "What would Rusty do?"

Just as Brunicardi hoped, Ennen had absorbed many of his lessons. For example, Ennen's personal politics were what used to be considered pragmatic middle-of-the-roadism before the age of Trump but since then could be called moderately left. Trump disgusted him. Even so, he held a fundraiser at his home for Bob Latta, the Republican congressman who represented the district and whose main accomplishment was carrying water for Trump. But Latta held the office, and Ennen wanted his ear.

Ennen managed CHWC with nearly the same amount of independence from the board as Brunicardi did—and Brunicardi had taught him that the CEO could, and should, run the place in any way that got the job done. American healthcare was an absurdist game of Jenga. You had to juke and shuffle your way around it and through it, and you couldn't wait for permission to hustle. But almost from the moment he took over, Ennen faced turmoil unlike anything Brunicardi had. There was no playbook for guiding a community hospital through the deepest economic downturn since the Great Depression.

People stopped coming to the hospital because they couldn't afford it. "It has become clear the national and international economic problems will not be resolved quickly," Ennen wrote to the employees in October 2008, nine months after becoming CEO. "Effective immediately, I am placing the hospital on a fiscal watch." He limited overtime, incentive pay, travel, and hiring.

Those measures weren't enough. A month later, he cut $1 million in employee benefits. The first layoffs came two weeks after that; more followed. Ennen felt each one. He recognized, in a way few others in Bryan did, that the hospital wasn't just a place where sick people went for care, or an amenity that could attract business, like in the old days. In this new economic realm, it *was* the business: an economic lifeline to the town. "In many cases, I know we have employees who are the only family member with a job due to cuts all over the area," he wrote in December 2009. "The economic recovery that Washington keeps talking about has not arrived in Northwest Ohio."

The hospital eventually did begin to recover, and Ennen, who'd proven he was more than Rusty Brunicardi's protégé, would be chosen by peers to a term as president of the Ohio Hospital Association. But by then the Bryan Medical Group, seeking safety, had sold itself to Parkview. That meant more and more patients were being referred to Fort Wayne. And CHWC's customers emerged from the recession changed. Forces from outside their community had triggered fear, not only about work, but about the foundations of life in America.

■■■

A few days after the meeting with the auditors from Plante Moran, a group of about twenty new hospital hires sat in chairs behind institutional-style tables facing a white screen. The new-employee packets at their fingertips lent a first-day-of-school air. Some had long experience working in hospitals; others had none. It didn't matter. They were gathered for an indoctrination into the CHWC tribe.

Kim Jerger was already an honorary member—he'd been born into it. He sat smiling in his scrubs, thinking about his mother, who had worked at the hospital when he was young. If he were to walk out of the room and go to a window facing Garver Park, he could look down on the old family home, a small white clapboard-sided house where, on icy or snowy nights that turned driving into a life-or-death adventure, half the hospital staff, so it seemed, would camp out on the living room floor. He graduated from high school with Phil Ennen's brother. Brunicardi's son was a best friend. The two teenagers earned a little extra spending money by helping Brunicardi compile a database of rural hospitals.

Now he was back, after making a career of nursing. He'd climbed the rungs of the healthcare ladder, moving from one hospital to the next in Ohio and Indiana: Cincinnati Children's; the Mercy hospitals in Urbana and Springfield, Ohio; a hospital in Fort Wayne, where he worked in infection control. But he'd had enough of the larger systems. The other hospitals were too commercial, too bottom-line, too paternalistic, too alienating, and not at all what he remembered from his old Bryan days. The Fort Wayne hospital trapped itself in a financial morass and in poisonous staff politics.

So when CHWC looked for a director of perioperative services on the surgery floor, he leapt.

Nurses from other hospitals formed part of the incoming class, too. There were also a couple of clerical workers, a former law enforcement officer, and a maintenance man.

One by one, the vice presidents entered the room to introduce themselves, make a short speech, and cover a few points pertaining to their areas of responsibility. The introductions, though, weren't the most important message: Over and over, they talked "family," "friends," "community." CHWC was different, they said. CHWC put the patient first because the patient was the old woman you saw in Walmart, or the kid on your twelve-year-old's soccer team, or your junior high English teacher.

Jan David, the vice president for patient care, started. A nurse at the Bryan hospital for decades, David was a slight, soft-spoken woman with dark, bobbed hair who never seemed to remove her white hospital coat. The patients, she said, are our people: they are us, and we are them.

Chad Tinkel, the chief financial officer, followed. The picture of the buttoned-up accountant with his brown shoes, sweater vests, closely clipped hair, and nondescript glasses, Tinkel embodied the notion of CHWC as local family. He'd grown up in Bryan, attended Ohio State, and graduated with an accounting degree. Like Ennen, he'd married a Bryan girl, Jodi, whose mother was in labor at the hospital at the same time as Tinkel's. Jodi had gone to medical school and now worked as CHWC's staff medical cardiologist.

Wade Patrick, the chief information officer, was a newcomer to Bryan. A brick wall of a man, with a shaved head, Patrick had worked as a bar bouncer back in college at Purdue and still regularly heaved weights at the gym. Though he'd been hired on only about a year before, Patrick embraced the family ethos, too: his romantic partner, Janice Bearer, worked as a nurse in the ER, and his daughter was about to start work as a medical scribe in the ER. His time at other hospitals was still fresh in his memory, he said, teaching him that "we've got something special going on here."

Mike Culler, another native Bryanite, was a part-time farmer. Tall, balding, bespectacled, with an excitable manner and a still-strong Ohio country accent, Culler held Ennen's old job: chief operating officer. He was married to Dina Culler, Ennen's executive assistant.

Ennen entered. "Welcome," he said, "to this crazy family we have." He told the incoming employees how he'd been there thirty-two years—the only hospital he'd ever worked at. He meant it to be a statement of continuity, but then he warned that the continuity—the "family"—was under threat. "None of our customers want to be here," he explained, but the customers paid the bills, and the hospital and their jobs depended on that money. So customer service and safety remained, now and always, the priorities. "There's a lotta stress in our world right now," he said. "There's a lotta stress in the town. But we're still this independent organization. We are bucking the trend right here. It's just us. Nobody owns us, and we'd like to stay that way. In order to stay that way, the patients have to like us."

Angelia Foster, vice president for human resources, whose show this was, spoke last. Like Patrick, she was a newcomer, and more than any other member of the C-suite team on the fourth floor, she projected a corporate veneer. She'd trained as a consultant at Arthur Andersen, once one of the biggest accounting firms in the world. She was steeped in the business and process of modern American management to a greater degree than anyone else in the organization.

Foster arrived at CHWC after having worked for another community hospital, Passavant Area, in Jacksonville, Illinois. Passavant was also once independent before a chain, Memorial Health System, took it over. Foster worked there at the time. Just before starting at CHWC, she had been diagnosed with breast cancer. She told Ennen she'd give up the job she'd just been hired for, explaining that she didn't want to burden CHWC's own health plan and that there'd be a delay before she could occupy her position. Ennen promised to wait and insisted she accept.

A nurse new to the staff had a question regarding guns. She wanted to carry hers. "What is our policy on concealed carry?" she called out. Foster explained that guns were not allowed in the hospital. "Can we at least have a gun in our cars?" the nurse asked.

Foster broke the room into small huddles and assigned each group's members to introduce themselves to one another and explain what had brought them to CHWC. "I've worked for ProMedica," a newly hired nurse explained of her time with the Toledo-based chain, "and it's nothing like it is here." CHWC, she said, was much more laid-back. And then she invoked the words "family" and "community."

"I've been through the different systems," another nurse added. "Three name changes, bought twice, and the fourth time, I was back in the

ER"—a position she had tried to escape. That's what awaited CHWC should it fall to outsiders. Her testimony was all that the retired law enforcement officer, a longtime Bryan fixture just starting his new job as a hospital security officer, needed to hear.

"Everbuddy is comin' after this hospital," he said, his voice growing louder with each sentence. "Those people can't *stand* to have a facility like this. I've lived in this town fifty years, and most of 'em involved in the community, for fifty years, and it makes a difference" that the town has its own local community hospital, he explained. But, he warned, "investors, 'n this 'n 'at, they know what's happenin' here. They're chompin' at the bit to take this over."

All these fears—all the machinations and plans and glide paths and financial intrigues—overlooked a paradox hinted at by Ennen: CWHC didn't make any money by keeping people out of the hospital. It depended upon the sick and the accident-prone. It *needed* people to have heart attacks and blocked arteries so they would fill Kesireddy's cath lab. It *needed* the diabetics, the smokers, the obese, the cancer-stricken. Its life depended on them because CHWC was a business in search of customers. Luckily for the hospital, there was no shortage. On a micro scale, CHWC was a family home where the ill and injured could come for solace. The family was dysfunctional sometimes—and not everybody loved everybody else—but it was Ennen's family. On the macro scale, CHWC was a piece on a political and economic chessboard, and if Ennen wanted to help realize the ambitions of that family, he had to play like a master.

3

Chasing the Symptoms

Searching for the
Roots of American
Sickness

Chris Spielman stood tall and square-jawed on the stage of the fancy, techno-sleek auditorium at New Hope Community Church, preaching the gospel of medical faith. "I am a cancer warrior!" he exclaimed to the packed house. With the conviction of an old-time evangelist trash-talking Satan, he assured his audience that technology and belief and perseverance and money would someday defeat the scourge. "Cancer has zero chance!"

The capacity crowd had paid $15 each, driving a couple of miles north-east of Bryan to the church's campus on a colder-than-usual October day to eat some lunch and see Spielman in person. When Phil Ennen was help-ing plan the first Michelle Bard Geary Community Cancer Symposium, he knew how important a big-name headliner would be for luring people into seats to listen to a day of talk about cancer.

Spielman, the former Ohio State linebacker, NFL player, and Fox net-work football analyst, was as big an Ohio hero as you could find outside of a reincarnated Woody Hayes. His wife had died of breast cancer. In the years since, Spielman had become a professional speaker, charging between $10,000 and $20,000 a talk to tell the inspirational story of his wife's life and death and how it changed the course of his own career.

The symposium was the kind of event Ennen loved: an ideal mix of business and mission, part big-time show biz, part health, part good public relations—a few more eraser strokes rubbed against the "just a Band-Aid station" label. In the morning, the CHWC dietician and diabetes educator gave a cooking presentation. There were continuing medical education sessions for local physicians, a blood draw for disease testing, and health screenings. Spielman's job was to fire up the crowd, to convert them into cancer warriors, too.

Cancer didn't care about pep rallies or attitude. It couldn't be defeated by "warriors." It wasn't even one disease. But no matter: Spielman preached hope by transmuting cancer into black-and-white simplicity, and his audience gobbled it up.

Earlier, though, Jim Watkins, the county health commissioner, had delivered a more sober and more complicated message to a smaller crowd. Like it does everywhere, the U.S. Census Bureau divided Williams County into defined tracts. As it happened, the bureau split Bryan into two census tracts: the east side and the west side, with Main Street running down the middle. Watkins and a young health department employee named Megan Riley realized they could use the tracts to explore health data, including cancer. So they collected five years' worth of numbers, from 2010 through 2014.

Watkins told his audience that people in all Williams County census tracts got cancer. People on both sides of Main Street died of cancer. But when he showed a bar chart of who died and when they died, his audience gasped out loud. On the east side of Main Street, the side where Keith and Stephanie and Caleb lived on Cherry, the age of death from cancer averaged sixty-nine. On the west side, it averaged seventy-six. In a town of only 8,500 people—perhaps 10,000, if you included those who lived just outside the city limits—Main Street turned out to be a stark dividing line.

CHWC's director of compliance, a nurse named Cathy Day, still recovering from breast cancer treatment herself, would later compile numbers just for 2017. Bryan was a little town, so there weren't that many total cancers diagnosed in one year, just twenty-three—what statistics experts call a small sample size. Even so, Day concluded, "nearly double [the number of] patients from the east side of Bryan were diagnosed with cancer in 2017." And just as Stephanie had experienced, "the stage at the time of diagnosis was advanced in the east side of Bryan."

And it wasn't just cancer. Watkins and Riley's numbers showed that throughout Williams County, there was more than a nine-year difference in average ages of death from all causes between the tract with the earliest age of death and the tract with the latest. The same sorts of gaps—only wider ones—existed in the state and the nation. In Franklinton, a neighborhood in Columbus, the average life expectancy was sixty. In Stow, a suburb of Akron, the average life expectancy was a little over eighty-nine. Throughout the United States, there was as much as a twenty-year life expectancy gap among counties, and vast disparities between states. In the early 2000s, death rates for white people in Louisiana, a state with a median income of $37,472, were 30 percent higher than rates for whites in Minnesota, with a median household income of $56,000. The difference for blacks in the two states was 37 percent. As of 2016, a seven-year chasm had opened between states with the highest life expectancy and those with the lowest.

As a whole, Williams County was not a particularly unhealthy part of Ohio; by several measures, it was about average. When the Robert Wood Johnson Foundation issued rankings for counties all over the nation, it showed that Williams ranked in the top third in Ohio. That finding, though, caused some local health and welfare professionals to roll their eyes. "I think they got the wrong county," one said, laughing.

Comparing Williams County with the rest of Ohio was setting a low bar. Ohio ranked forty-sixth out of the fifty states for "health value"—the health of the population combined with healthcare spending. The state ranked dead last in drug overdose deaths, forty-fourth for infant mortality and adult smoking, forty-third for premature death, and forty-second for life expectancy and oral health. Ohio's health was declining. The state found that "negative trends in premature death, life expectancy and overall health status indicate that the health of Ohioans has worsened in recent years." In 2010, as the Great Recession eased, 815.7 people out of 100,000 (age-adjusted) died of all causes every year. By 2017, 849.7 died, placing Ohio among the deadliest states in the nation. The state ranked forty-sixth for public health spending, and the budget declined between 2010 and 2018.

But what was true for Ohio was true for the country as a whole. After decades of health improvement, the tide was receding. Something was making America sick to death.

▌▌▌

You could see it in the county and in Bryan: something was seriously wrong. The public health workers, the social workers, the do-gooders at the YMCA, the churches, the local cancer society, the county and municipal court officials, the cops, and a few local politicians in Bryan and Williams County all knew it. And they talked about it often. All through the fall of 2018—and for a long time after—they gathered at early morning meetings in the Eagles lodge, or in the hospital's Bard conference room, before going to their regular jobs. They sipped watery coffee out of styrofoam cups and nibbled on breakfast Danish as they tried to figure out what was going on.

They all wanted to improve "outcomes." For the health people, that meant physical and mental well-being. For the cops, that meant less crime—especially less dumbass crime: the meth busts, the fighting inside Club Bentley's, the smashing of chairs against the doors out at the Colonial Manor Motel. Having to arrest people for those acts just led to a useless drain on resources for everyone, from cops to court personnel to the perps themselves. For the local pols, improved outcomes meant a few more steps down the long path toward community rejuvenation.

On the morning they met in the Bard conference room of the hospital to review the questions for the upcoming Community Health Needs Assessment (a survey required of all nonprofit hospitals under the Affordable Care Act of 2010 that's meant to guide public health initiatives), they spoke of the trends they saw as concrete and obvious, but also mysterious and unfathomable.

There was so much depression. Every three years, when the results of the health needs assessment were tabulated, the percentage of teenagers and adults who said they'd been so depressed for at least two weeks during the past year that they were unable to do normal activities increased. Sixteen percent of young people said they seriously considered suicide; 5 percent of adults said so.

Les McCaslin saw the shift firsthand. McCaslin ran the Four County Alcohol, Drug Addiction, and Mental Health Services (ADAMhs) board for Williams, Fulton, Henry, and Defiance counties. Over the past few years, he watched as the number of people in Northwest Ohio needing aid for mental health soared.

"Oh, my God!" he exclaimed. "We saw four thousand more patients in 2017 than we did in 2016. We had twelve thousand people! So we start looking because we said, 'No, that's gotta be wrong; where's the mistake?' But no. It was twelve thousand people."

The rising suicide rate alarmed him. Fewer than four thousand people lived in the village of Montpelier, for example, yet the Montpelier police department responded to thirty-two attempted suicides in its service area (which included some outlying sections) in 2017. It was called to twenty-eight attempted suicides in 2018. Most of those attempts would not result in a death, but too many did.

Six days after Keith's buddy Chad killed himself, Brandon Jondreau sucked carbon monoxide into his lungs until he died. He was twenty. A few days after that, Sheila Cottrell hung herself. She was fifty-three. It was a bad start to the year. Again, the problem wasn't unique to Williams County. Between 1999 and 2017, the American suicide rate increased by 33 percent. Americans were killing themselves in larger numbers than ever.

Ennen saw it in the hospital. Some people killed themselves quickly—usually with guns—but many more did it slowly. "Customers come in heavier all the time," he said. "So we need more ceiling lift systems" just to get people into and out of beds. Nearly three-quarters of Williams County residents were overweight or obese. Nearly half of all people ages thirty to sixty-four were obese, and 61 percent of adults under thirty were.

While declarations of war against cancer might temporarily ignite a flame in a lunchtime audience, the enthusiasm for doing big things to improve the health of all residents soon dimmed. "Nobody cares!" McCaslin said. He meant that he cared—and professional public health workers and social workers cared, and so did a few cops—but the general public remained unaware, often willfully so.

McCaslin may not have liked that, but he understood. So did Ennen. The causes of poor health, both mental and physical, were murky. The professionals themselves groped in the dark for explanations. Tonie Long, of the ADAMhs board, cited "a crisis of loneliness in our communities." Rob Imber, the executive director of the YMCA, said, "We know our men are not entirely okay." A Montpelier police officer pointed out that his village witnessed enormous turnovers of residents. Sometimes it seemed that half a school class would disappear from one year to the next.

The kids were doing something called vaping. School administrators only had a vague idea of what it was, but they knew for sure it was "huge." They hadn't yet heard of Juul, the biggest vaping company in the United States. Juul was just about to announce a deal to sell more than a third of itself to tobacco giant Altria (formerly Philip Morris), an $80 billion company, for $12.8 billion.

Excavating for root causes of the disquieting trends could also prove uncomfortable, because digging around too much cracked open taboo territory. When it came time to discuss the questions to be asked of the county's youth, school administrators sat tensed and wary, their lips drawn back as they listened to the items and the multiple-choice answers. Sometimes they'd squirm in their chairs and nudge the health experts for deletions.

"This won't be well accepted in some communities," one administrator said of a question about youth sex practices. Yet chlamydia was a serious problem in the county; Williams had a higher rate of infections of the sexually transmitted disease, which could cause infertility, than did most other Ohio locations. Samar Hassouneh said the chlamydia rate among young women was "awful! It's embarrassing. Huge!" The lack of comprehensive sex education led to unwanted pregnancies and infertility. Hassouneh would refer patients to Toledo for abortions because nobody would do one in Williams County. "I have learned here that I have to tiptoe around that a bit," she said.

Another official wanted to know if an option to select transgender or "other" as a sexual identity was absolutely necessary. He wanted it cut. For a moment nobody said anything. Then Tonie Long, sitting at the middle of the table, straightened and protested that it should remain. "These kids are already invisible in our community," Long said, insisting that they existed but hid in fear. The option was deleted from the survey.

The school officials pictured irate parents storming their offices over condoms, homosexuality, and anal sex because it had happened before. "The last time, when the report got out, it got ugly," Watkins explained.

Long next found herself defending a question on guns: "Are any firearms now kept in or around your home?" was followed by choices that included information about whether any guns were locked up or not. (Ohio law did not mandate that firearms be so secured.) She lost that argument, too.

■■■

Marc Tingle didn't know about the cancer symposium, or about any of the county health meetings. He was too busy enjoying his own good health—by working, mostly. He worked just about all the time. You had to if you ran a one-man-one-daughter contracting firm in a rural county. Marc would do anything, from pulling a toilet to building a whole house.

He was always one of the roughnecks, a bravo with the vigor of a bull, so when he climbed atop a house out in the village of Stryker on a "stupid-cold" late February day in 2018 to start a roofing job, he filled his lungs with the frozen air and reveled in the good fortune of his well-being. His daughter, Summer, a small, pretty thirty-year-old, stayed on the ground to gather up the shingles and debris Tingle would tear from the roof and toss down.

Tingle appreciated the day all the more because he had recently gained insight into life as an invalid. In his case it was voluntary, but still, his time in recuperation made being on the roof feel as much like a celebration as a tough, cold job.

The previous November, Tingle had donated a kidney to a relative. He hadn't set out to donate. His wife, Cindy, had intended to be the donor, but Cindy was taking three blood pressure medications. One drug wouldn't disqualify her from donating, but three was unacceptable. Then Summer was tested. She and Marc stood in the garage of the small wood-frame house the Tingles shared in Edgerton when the phone rang and the transplant coordinator in Ann Arbor explained that Summer had small kidney stones. She didn't know she had them—she'd never felt a twinge—but they disqualified her, too. She hung up the phone and wept. Marc stood there in the garage, watching his daughter's tears, when he heard the Lord speak to him and say, Guess whose turn it is.

When the compatibility tests came back, Marc was surprised to learn he'd make a suitable kidney donor. He reckoned the Lord was having His way with him, seeing as how he was proud—even a little cheeky—about his robust constitution. He'd smoked a pack and a half of cigarettes every day for the past thirty-five years, and there was all that beer and all those drugs—coke, meth, you name it—back before he'd surrendered to Jesus, so friends would fret over his forgoing health insurance for those years after he started his little contracting business. But he'd laugh and say he liked to live dangerously, not that he couldn't afford insurance.

Even after Obamacare arrived in 2010, he found it was cheaper to pay the penalty for not having insurance than it was to have it. It wasn't until Cindy took a job with the county, working at a senior center in Edgerton, that he was covered. She only made about $11,000 a year, but the wages weren't the point: the health insurance was. She and Marc were aging, after all, and Marc could laugh off insurance all he wanted, but Cindy was determined they'd finally get some.

Still, he had never developed the habit of visiting doctors, and he didn't see why he should start now. He hadn't even had a physical exam since, oh, maybe the eighth grade, or sometime in high school when he played sports, and you could hardly call those physicals, with a doctor poking his finger up his scrotum to check for a hernia and listening to him breathe and declaring him fit. Marc couldn't remember a time since then that he'd seen a doctor, and as far as he could recall, until an episode with his front tooth neither he nor Cindy had visited a dentist since they were married out of high school.

Normally, Marc would lose a tooth and just keep going. More recently, though, after he'd reformed and repented and taken up sermonizing, becoming a church leader and meeting more people around the county through his work as the contractor for the county's annual Habitat for Humanity project house, he'd begun to worry about his appearance. Then, one evening, about fifteen minutes before he was supposed to give a sermon, a cap that had been placed on a front tooth when he was a kid (Marc was a bit of a brawler in his youth) fell off. Marc, being handy, found some superglue and jammed it back into place, but he knew that was no solution. So he had the remaining teeth pulled—first the uppers and then the lowers—and had himself fitted for dentures.

Cindy's insurance covered about half the cost of Marc's new teeth. Paying the other half was tough, but the teeth were becoming. Marc was a handsome fellow. She'd thought so since they first met in high school. She was a good girl—Marc liked to joke that Cindy hadn't been allowed to walk around the block until she was thirteen years old—while Marc was the bad boy with the mean, hard-drinking stepfather who ran a bulldozer out at the landfill. He grew up poor on Township Road H, just north of Bryan, in a house where feelings were expressed by the buckle end of a belt. But he was tall and strong, gray-eyed, with a gold hoop earring and a swagger, and Cindy found him irresistible. He still wore an earring in his left ear, a leather band around one wrist, and a turquoise ring on his right hand. He was bald now, but he covered his head with a flat leather cowboy hat and was still fit-looking and lean.

After the tumultuous years—when Marc was drinking and snorting and smoking meth, and when Cindy had kicked him out of the house and he'd stayed with his mother for a while and then at a motel, where loneliness and desperation nudged him to talk to God and read the Bible and then promise God he'd dedicate his life to the Lord so as not to lose his family—she and Marc had been happy. Now she feared losing him in a different way, from a kidney transplant, which nobody could have ever seen coming.

Hospitals were not pleasant places for the Tingles. Both had spent a lot of time in them because their son was born with spina bifida. Over the years, the boy had undergone a number of medical procedures, including surgery, which were mostly paid for by a program in Ohio called Children with Medical Handicaps. Marc figured they had run up about a million dollars in costs so far. But Marc was only ever a hospital visitor. Now, though, he was about to travel up to Ann Arbor, to the University of Michigan, to have a kidney cut out of his body.

The surgery unfolded just the way textbooks said it should. He spent all of November and December 2017 at home recovering, under strict orders not to swing a hammer. Then, finally, on January 2, 2018, the first day doctors said he could, Marc and Summer worked a simple toilet replacement job. When Marc stood on the roof and breathed the cold air deep into his lungs on that cold February day, he finally felt just like his old self.

That was good, because he had a lot going on. The year's Habitat for Humanity House was being planned. The excavation was about to begin, and the foundation would be poured. He had meetings with potential clients, trying to line up his spring and summer work. As an elder, Marc attended three services at Life Changing Realities Fellowship (LCRF) every weekend as well as a group Bible study on Thursday nights. Every Sunday night, he attended an LCRF meeting to plan for an event called the Great Banquet.

Once the weather warmed up, he and Cindy took all four kids and the grandchildren on an annual family vacation to a campground not too far away. By September, the Habitat house, out in Pioneer, was complete, and Marc and Cindy took some time for themselves. They rode the Harley down to Savannah, Georgia, stayed in some motels on the way, and pulled the bike's wheels onto the sand at Tybee Island because Marc believed the Harley had ridden a long way, too, and deserved the feel of the sand in her treads. They rode the Harley back. He picked up his hammer, and he and Summer went back to work. By late fall, everything was normal again.

Ennen attended many of the meetings aimed at improving the community's health and deciphering its social problems. The hospital was the center of gravity in Bryan—one reason so many of the conferences were held there. He also funded the health needs assessment (another requirement of the Affordable Care Act), paid for mental health counselors placed in schools, organized the cancer symposium, and hosted other gatherings. But because he hated meetings, he tended to do much more listening than speaking, and when it came to public health, Jim Watkins usually ran the show.

About half an hour into one such morning meeting with local officials, Ennen, as was his habit, sat near the end of the conference table with his head bowed, saying nothing. He scribbled on a pad. The rest of the group, not yet fully caffeinated, was trying to figure out who would be in charge of filing the appropriate paperwork to start a new anti-drug organization and act as the responsible contacts. They joked about who was the busiest, and therefore the best person to take on one more duty. Just as a court official shrugged his surrender, the hospital's PA system cackled open and blared an announcement: "Members of the Joint Commission will be arriving." Ennen's head snapped up. The blood rushed to his face.

The other attendees didn't notice, and the meeting carried on. But Ennen, now filled with anxiety and a surge of pique, mentally checked out.

The Joint Commission was a private body with roots stretching back to 1913. That was when the newly formed American College of Surgeons created a committee to answer the question of what good hospital care—mainly surgical care and facilities—should look like. By 1952, several organizations agreed to carve out a stand-alone hospital standards group under the governance of a board that included representatives from the American College of Surgeons, the AMA, the American College of Physicians, and the American Hospital Association. By the time of the PA announcement that morning in Bryan, it was known simply as the Joint Commission, and it included the American Dental Association.

Though a private organization, the Joint Commission wielded enormous power. It was by far the largest (if measured by the number of hospitals subscribing to it) of several businesses that were authorized by the government's Centers for Medicare and Medicaid Services to "deem," or accredit, hospitals. (States could also deem hospitals via state agencies approved by CMS, though few hospitals used this option.) Hospitals spent tens of thousands of dollars to submit themselves to inspections because CMS required the seal of accreditation before it would issue Medicare reimbursements. So being deemed was a life-or-death matter for hospitals like

CHWC, which depended upon government payouts—a requirement that fostered a new hospital inspection industry.

The 2018 edition of *Hospital Accreditation Standards*, a book published each year by the Joint Commission, was a massive 518 pages. Entries listed everything from "openings in vision panels or doors in corridor walls (other than in smoke compartments containing patient sleeping rooms) are installed at or below one half the distance from the floor to the ceiling" to what should go into a medical record.

The Joint Commission inspection team had arrived in Bryan the night before and had announced their imminent arrival at the hospital just minutes prior to the PA announcement. As the meeting continued in the Bard Room on the first floor, department heads were alerted to go to the fourth-floor conference room. The moment his meeting broke up, Ennen rushed to the elevators.

He was furious. Joint Commission accreditation is good for three years. While inspections are not announced ahead of time, they typically occur near the end of the three-year cycle so a hospital can get its full money's worth out of the three-year period. For weeks CHWC staff had been receiving reminders that 2019 would be an inspection year, so they figured they had about five months—well into Ennen's twelve-to-eighteen-month "glide path"—to prepare. They should always be inspection-ready, Ennen and compliance officer Cathy Day said, but in the lead-up to the predicted survey window, they should check themselves and their departments in case any technique, habit, or physical or equipment condition had been allowed to slide.

Everyone remembered what it had been like in 2007, just before the renovation and additions to the building began. The Joint Commission found so many violations of standards it had nearly revoked CHWC's accreditation. Now Ennen was being blindsided with an early survey. He wasn't so worried about possible findings, because he believed CHWC was ready. Instead, he resented the five months he'd lose from the three-year cycle. The Joint Commission survey would cost the hospital about $65,000, he figured, and tens of thousands extra would be lost because he wouldn't get the full three-year benefit from the previous inspection.

And for what? Like many hospitals, CHWC regarded a Joint Commission survey as, on balance, a waste. It was a hurdle standing in the way of CMS money. Patients had no idea what the Joint Commission was, and they didn't make any decisions about becoming CHWC customers based on a survey's results.

Nobody mentioned the built-in conflict of interest in this system, which was a relic from the days when medicine was allowed to govern itself. The Joint Commission was a side business of large medical associations. It collected fees from the institutions it inspected. CMS could—and did—follow up on surveys by conducting spot checks of its own to examine the work of the Joint Commission and the other businesses authorized to deem hospitals, but the surveys were inside-the-fraternity jobs.

Compliance officer Cathy Day, a short, stocky, flush-faced woman who projected a drill-sergeant competence, had just minutes to talk to the assembled leaders in the conference room before the surveyors appeared. Cancel all other meetings, she said. Other than regular duties and patient care, the inspection took priority. On Friday, when it was all over, she announced, there'd be drinks at Jackie Blu's, a bar and restaurant on the town square. Until then, everybody was to be on their best behavior.

The surveyors entered moments later. An ophthalmologist who was also a risk management expert led the team. He introduced himself and gave a brief biography, then the other two members of his team did the same. They asked the eighteen staff leaders assembled in the room to introduce themselves, describe their jobs, and state how long they'd been with the hospital.

Ennen sat in a chair he'd shoved against a side wall, away from the conference room table. His chin rested on his chest. He took a couple of notes but said nothing until it was his turn to identify himself. "Phil Ennen, chief executive officer," he said. And that was all he said. The lead surveyor stared for a moment, as if trying to think of some sort of follow-up comment or question before the next department head picked up the conversational baton.

After the team outlined how the inspections would unfold, they left to orient themselves with the help of a couple of staff members. Once they'd gone, Day, who would escort the chief surveyor, explained how she planned to approach the next four days. "My job is to bond," she said. "What are your interests? What do we have in common? By the time he leaves Friday, he should be hugging me goodbye because we've become so close." Obsequious cooperation was to be the default pose.

Ennen stood. "This'll cost us $3,500 per day for eighteen surveyor days," he told the room. "This is the kind of thing that kills small, independent hospitals, another example of the federal government's inability to bend." The hospital in Findlay, Ohio, he pointed out, was much bigger but would pay about the same amount as Bryan would. And because Bryan was a smaller target, the surveyors would be sure to find more faults.

In the end, though, the inspectors found very few problems. At the conclusion of the first day, the team and the department heads gathered in the conference room for a debriefing. The report card was good, with minor dings. The time of some medical orders had not been properly logged. A member of the cleaning staff wasn't wearing goggles while working with a caustic chemical. A fire extinguisher was placed six inches too high on a wall. A blood compatibility error in the lab was the only finding that elicited a "red" critical notation.

The staff exhaled, but Ennen fumed. At first he said nothing. Then one member of the survey team asked about the Montpelier facility, referring to it as a separate hospital—an easy mistake to make since it was about twelve miles away, was built and used as a separate hospital, and had its own small ER (though the Montpelier site was now mainly used as the rehabilitation center for CHWC patients). And the inspector could not have known about the fraught history of the hospitals' merger under Brunicardi, the century-old rivalry between Montpelier and Bryan (which town would get the courthouse? Which would get the fairgrounds?), and the many efforts at smoothing feathers in both Montpelier and the county that Brunicardi and Ennen employed over the decades.

But Ennen snapped: "Could we just stop referring to them as separate hospitals? They're *one* hospital. It's all CHWC. *One* hospital." The mouths of several department heads fell open. Their eyes flashed to Ennen, then back to the surveyor. After an uncomfortable pause, the moment passed. The team congratulated the staff on a good first day and left to return to their motel in Holiday City, up by the Ohio Turnpike. Ennen was still angry. He couldn't get the money out of his head. "That'll be our big takeaway: lowering our fire extinguishers by two inches. So it cost $10,000 to have that moron nitpick us."

The remaining survey days began and ended with the same kinds of briefings that contained the same kinds of mostly minor nicks. A negative pressure gradient between a sterile room and a nonsterile room could allow air to flow in the wrong direction; that had to be fixed. A patient in Montpelier who had overdosed on heroin had become combative, and the doctor ordered twenty-four-hour restraints, which seemed excessive. The nurses removed them after three hours, and that worked fine, but it created a conflict between the orders and the action. That led to a discussion about how the hospital monitored patients at risk of suicide. Ideally, they'd be placed in a special room stripped of anything that could be used to harm themselves, and a nurse would keep watch. But a nurse's time was expensive. Maybe CHWC could use student nurses.

By Friday, the Joint Commission's inspection team was effusive. "One of the cleanest I've ever seen," one surveyor said. "Very well run," said another. "Some of your facilities are surprisingly good here." "You should be proud of yourselves," the team leader said. The lab inspector chimed in: "Most of my surveys are about fifteen findings, and I only have three here." One of the survey team said he'd return in forty-five days to check that a particular fix involving doors had been made—"And we'll pay $4,000 for it," Ennen muttered to himself—but otherwise CHWC would be accredited for another three years.

Members of the hospital board attended the final meeting—part of the inspection covers governance—and had a conversation with the surveyors. The team commiserated with the board over how difficult the terrain had become for small, independent community hospitals.

Dave Swanson, a board member and the owner of Daavlin, a small manufacturing company that assembled lights used for dermatological treatment, said, "We don't want to be one of those that closes. I feel the government does not want us to succeed." Swanson was a friend of Ennen's. He'd entertained Ennen and Mary at his house in Manistee, Michigan, and occasionally they had dinner together.

Chris Cullis, the third-generation owner and editor of the *Bryan Times*—and the chairman of the board—was a friend of Ennen's, too. Cullis had given rare books, including an early edition of Mark Twain, to Ennen's daughter, who'd studied literature at Wellesley. "The government wants consolidation," Cullis said.

"I was chief medical officer of a hospital that closed," the head inspector replied. "And we were winning awards. I'm rooting for you, but I'm not telling you about what's fair. I'm telling you about how it is."

The surveyors left, the board members left, the staff's blood pressure dropped. A few of them were giddy. But Mike Culler, the chief operating officer, was still simmering about an inspector's insistence that there was no eye-wash station within fifty-five feet of the women's clinic, where Bazzi and Hassouneh worked.

"An eye-wash station!" he yelled in his country accent. "Eye wash! There *is* one!" The inspector just walked in the wrong direction, he said. That got him on the fire extinguisher height issue from the first day. "Fifty inches is *not* five feet!" he said, referring to a misunderstanding about just how high the extinguisher was. "I've been here eleven years," he said, rubbing the top of his bald head. "I used to have hair."

Still, Culler was proud of the survey results. "Ya know," he said, "we don't do brain surgery here. We don't do open-heart. We don't do transplants. But for itty-bitty Bryan, it's amazing what we do here." Even so, he said, "people in Bryan have no idea what they've got."

The staff leadership drifted out of the conference room to finish whatever they needed to finish for the day. It was Friday, the survey was over, and Cathy Day had promised drinks at Jackie Blu's. She looked around the room. Ennen had disappeared. "Where's Phil?" she asked. Nobody knew. "Well," she joked, "did he leave his credit card?"

Ennen would not go to Jackie Blu's. Chad Tinkle would. Angelia Foster would. Everybody would have a few drinks, and then Day would hold hers up and shout, "Let 'em call us a Band-Aid station *now*!" The others would then chug their drinks and make mild sex-related comments they didn't mean but that were purposely loud enough for Foster—the human resources vice president who drilled them on inappropriate work conversations and harassment—to hear, and then they'd crack up as Foster covered her ears and sang "lalalalalala," pretending not to hear, and everyone would have a good time because, as they said, they'd helped to create the best damn hospital in northwest Ohio.

Whether or not that was true, it was true that the CHWC staff worked like a well-practiced pit crew. They managed some of the most complex gadgetry and processes dreamed up by twenty-first-century America. Yet most of them were small-town people, many of them born and raised in Bryan.

A few were self-described oddballs. "We're all misfits here," pathologist Shannon Keil said. She meant that some of them had attended the "wrong" colleges and med schools, had lived the "wrong" personal histories, and had earned the "wrong" exam scores. Keil described herself as a white Toledo "ghetto" girl from a family in which nobody had ever received a college degree. She had slugged her way through medical school as a single mother on food stamps and welfare. Underdogs like Keil, foreign-born and -educated doctors like Kesireddy, the few native Bryanites like cardiologist Jodi Tinkle, and the smart-but-young beginners like Bazzi and Hassouneh composed the pool from which small rural hospitals could fish for medical talent. Lab techs, nurses, cleaning crews, back-office staff: most mastered their jobs on the job. Everybody at Jackie Blu's was aware of all that, and they were a little defiant about it.

Ennen had reason to blow some steam, too. Not only had the Joint Commission survey gone well, but Mike DeWine had won the Ohio guber-natorial election that week. Ennen may have been more in sympathy with the Democrat Richard Cordray, but DeWine's victory meant the Republican legislature would have little incentive to repeal Medicaid expansion—at least in the short term.

And Sherrod Brown had been reelected to his U.S. Senate seat in a walk over a sad-sack Republican named Jim Renacci. This also pleased Ennen. Ennen had connected with Brown's staff a few times over the past several years—since his time as president of the Ohio Hospital Association—and had found that Brown's philosophy of expanding healthcare access, as well as his support of favorable rules for rural hospitals, aligned with Ennen's and CHWC's needs. For Brown, Ennen was an ear in a rural, conservative county. So they spoke once in a while by phone.

Williams County voted for Renacci, of course, but Brown won many more votes there than Cordray did in his governor's race—a measure of the small reservoir of goodwill toward Brown in the county that was not enjoyed by any other Democrat at any level. He'd won that affection by showing up, by listening to what people in the county had to say, and by often acting upon what they said. It could be uncanny how many Williams County residents had a Sha-ROD story. Sha-ROD had helped an aunt. Sha-ROD knew a cousin. Sha-ROD understood working people. Sha-ROD *got* them.

The old political animal in Ennen—and the small-town boy in him, too—always felt charged after speaking to Brown. He would explain to Brown that, in his view from the fourth floor in Bryan, healthcare was a "yellow vest moment." The reference to the populist protests in France that were sparked by fuel prices and that saw strikers wearing yellow hazard vests was a little exaggerated. But it was true that Bryanites, as anti-government as they could be, seemed to treasure their Medicare and Medicaid.

Les McCaslin, the Alcohol, Drug Addiction, and Mental Health Services chief, liked to tell the story of "an incredibly conservative person who came into my office and was just ripping Obamacare. 'We gotta do something about this Obamacare!' And I said, 'Darrell, where do you get your insurance?' He said 'Oh, well, I get it on the exchange, and it's good insurance.' I said, 'Well, what do you think Obamacare is? Read a newspaper!'"

So Ennen was feeling vindicated on multiple fronts. The health of Williams County residents may not have been good, or equitable, but his hospital's buildings and procedures were first-rate. Even so, he didn't believe in partying with the staff. His presence might make them uncomfortable, he thought, and anyway, he didn't want to see or hear things he didn't want to see or hear. So he walked back across Garver Park and had a Friday night cocktail with Mary, relieved he had a little less to worry about.

The hospital's operational health had just checked out as excellent, but less than a mile away, Keith's health was failing. He knew nothing about the work of the agencies whose job it was to look out for residents like him. He thought the Bryan hospital was owned by Parkview. All such conversation and debate flew over him like the planes overflying Bryan on their way from New York to Chicago. And, now, despite his perpetual optimistic reply, he wasn't doin' good. Not at all.

During Stephanie's last days, some of her relatives had helped Keith look after Caleb while he tried to pack as many hours in at Ashley Industrial as he could. He'd work twelve-hour shifts sometimes. But he took a couple of weeks off after Stephanie died and, while her relatives helped out, Keith spent those sad days arranging that memorial headstone for her grave. He bought side-by-side plots in the Fountain Grove Cemetery out by the Arby's so he'd never have to be without her. He watched racing on TV. He drank a little.

The headstone and plots were expensive. To pay for them, and for some medical bills and general living expenses, he emptied his 401(k) account of the little that was left. There wasn't much money to pay for anything else. He tried to figure out what he owed for rent and utilities, and to tally and sort the medical charges, but with all that had happened, he'd fallen far behind. The best he could guess, he owed somewhere around $35,000, but he didn't know. The bills were confusing. They came from so many people and outfits he'd never heard of.

The dealer who'd sold him his used Ford Flex wagon was quick on the draw to repossess it. Keith was sorry to see the wagon go, but he didn't hold a grudge. He hadn't made the payments, and so the guy took it back. Fair was fair. He'd just have to make do with an old Jeep he'd worked on in spurts over the years.

Doctors and hospitals couldn't repossess Stephanie, but they were persistent. "This is the final notice on your account," the statement for $695 from Consulting Pathologists Corporation of Toledo said. "We require payment in 10 days or we may refer your account to a collection agency." "Final request for payment," the invoice for $852.84 from Mercy Health announced.

In late August, Keith started at the distribution center owned by Menards, the big midwestern hardware and building chain, at Holiday City. He worked a 4-PM-to-12:30-AM shift, standing for hours sorting boxes, paletting them, and moving them onto a big conveyor, repackaging their contents so they could be sent to Menards stores all over the Midwest. He didn't love it—he missed Ashley—but the job allowed him to spend part of the day with Caleb, and once the school year began, he could greet his son when he got off the bus from his Bryan public schools kindergarten classes. Stephanie's niece helped pull Caleb duty at night.

And Menards wasn't so bad, really. Keith, being his congenial self, didn't complain much about the working conditions. He even made a couple of friends there, like Zach Rhinard. Zach was younger than Keith—just twenty—but he was into cars and, being a country boy, shooting and fishing. He was also a reservist in the Marines. Keith respected that sort of thing.

One day at work—possibly sometime in September; he wasn't sure exactly when—Keith stepped on something. He didn't feel anything at the time because his toes had been a little numb. Anyway, after what must have been some days after whatever had happened, he saw a wound on his right big toe. The wound didn't hurt, either. Still, he put a bandage on the toe, padded up his work shoe, and went back to Menards the next day.

Keith didn't feel the initial injury, nor the wound it left, because he'd developed diabetic neuropathy—he had little sensation in parts of his feet.

Now that he was aware of the damage, he kept an eye on the toe. A week later, the sore looked bigger and meaner. "All a sudden, my toe got big, and the red started coming up across the leg," he recalled, referring to the scarlet streaks that spread over his foot and inched up his leg. He thought the streaks were some sort of rash, and he figured it would go away. He didn't connect them to the toe at first.

Keith didn't think long about going to a doctor. For one thing, he now had no health insurance. He'd started at Menards just over a month before, and you had to work there for sixty days before they'd cover you with an insurance plan. But even if he did have it, he probably wouldn't have gone. "I was trying to work. I had to support a five-year-old. I didn't know what to do, because I have to take care of stuff. And I knew, if I went to a doctor, they were going to take me off work."

But the toe continued to swell until it became a large, angry-red bulge. On Tuesday, October 2, after he sent Caleb off to school, Keith finally gave in and drove himself to the Bryan emergency room. The doctor on duty had no trouble with a diagnosis—he saw a lot of diabetic foot ulcers. Diabetic ulcers were the main reason Ennen had opened the wound care clinic in the hospital. Not only were diabetic wounds difficult to heal, but Ennen also knew a growth market when he saw it. In fact, George Magill, the doctor who ran the wound clinic, had become so sensitized to seeing the effects of diabetes on the feet of Williams County residents, he could spot the diabetics in Walmart with their slight shuffle, the foot slide, a gait that seemed a little off because people couldn't feel their feet. Twelve percent of adults—including 16 percent of all men and 27 percent of all people over age sixty-five—in Williams County had been diagnosed with diabetes. More probably had it but didn't know.

Keith's wound was infected—that much was obvious. He'd been afraid to miss work, but now he was going to miss a lot of it. The ER doctor admitted him to the hospital. There he was seen by Carolyn Sharrock-Dorsten, a podiatric surgeon from the Parkview group across the street. It was too late, she told Keith. The only thing she could do was cut out the infection by amputating much of his big toe. He resisted the surgery. "The thing is, I didn't wanna do it. I didn't wanna be off work." But most of the toe came off. Keith left the hospital after two days. More bills would follow him home. The ER bill alone, just for the doctor's time, was $1,250.

On that Friday, October 5, Keith hobbled into the Bryan Community

Health Center on Main Street, just off the town square. The center, a new addition to Bryan that was located in what once had been a grocery store, was operated by Health Partners of Western Ohio, a nonprofit system of sixteen federally qualified health centers spread throughout the region. Though accessible to anyone, the centers were designed for low-income and poor people whose health needs were not being met by traditional medical practitioners. Health Partners billed on a sliding scale that depended upon income. Keith didn't know all the ins and outs of how it worked or how it was funded. People at the hospital had told him about it since they knew he no longer had insurance.

Barb Purvis, the nurse practitioner at the community health center, saw Keith. She soon realized that although he looked healthy enough from the outside, his innards were in turmoil. A PICC line (peripherally inserted central catheter) that had been placed in his arm at the hospital was still there so he could receive intravenous infusions of antibiotics to combat what was left of the infection and to prevent any new infection from invading the amputation wound. Keith said his A1C—a measurement indicating blood sugar levels over a longer period of time than the usual instant glucose readings—had been 11.9 in the hospital, meaning that his blood sugar had probably been up around 300 over the past ninety days or so. He didn't know what the A1C had been before, because he'd never had it checked. And he hadn't checked his blood sugar levels himself for the past couple of years.

Purvis could tell Keith hadn't seen a dentist recently, either—he told her "it had been a while." In fact, it had been a long while. He couldn't remember how long.

Keith told Purvis what he told everybody whenever they asked about him: He was feeling pretty good. He slept fine. He wasn't depressed, and he didn't have anxiety. He said he'd taken his insulin, a drug called Levemir, made by the Danish company Novo Nordisk, after breakfast. But when Purvis tested him, his blood sugar was 391. His A1C was 12.1. And Purvis noted that Keith was "under multiple different stressors currently related to his wife recently passing away and having a special needs child." He was also taking a fistful of drugs, most of them prescribed while he was in the Bryan hospital for his toe.

Purvis loaded him up with vaccines—flu, pneumonia, diphtheria-tetanus-pertussis (whooping cough)—and with medications: a baby aspirin, a statin, an anti-clotting drug to improve leg circulation, a blood pressure drug, and metformin for his blood sugar.

She also made sure Keith spent time with the clinic's behavioral health consultant, a social worker. The social worker found the obvious: Keith had a number of risk factors. He was depressed and anxious, though he'd denied it to Purvis. Keith admitted to the social worker that he'd been drinking lately, so she counseled him about limits and cautions. But when she offered him some grief support counseling, he refused it. He was doin' good, he said.

Before he left, the clinic's staff helped Keith apply for Medicaid through a plan in Ohio called Paramount Advantage, a subsidiary of the ProMedica health system. They tried to make it effective October 1, the day before he first walked into the Bryan ER.

A week later, Keith returned to the clinic for a follow-up. Purvis had recommended that he get some exercise, but with his right foot in a plastic boot to prevent any injury to his amputation wound, Keith found moving difficult. His blood pressure was up, and his blood sugar was still high—at between 200 and 300—but he was testing more often. So he asked for more test strips. Purvis told him she'd give him some from the clinic's supplies, but she warned him that they wouldn't be covered by Medicaid once he got it—he'd have to buy them with his own money.

▌▌▌

A week after the Joint Commission survey, Ennen typed a memo about the hospital's financial health. He sent it to all employees. He announced a fiscal year loss of $1.647 million and wrote, "It's not the end of the world by any means . . . but it is a clear message that we gotta start making some changes. It will be much better to start now. There's no point in kicking the can down the road."

The hospital's "Achilles heel," he wrote, "was the spending in our health plan. We planned to spend $8.8 million on benefits. We actually spent $10.1 million. We were over budget by $1.3 million. That's an almost 15% increase." The cost of health insurance for people who worked in the health-care industry was just too high, and it was growing.

So, beginning in January, employees would have to pay between 4 and 6 percent more for insurance. But there'd be no layoffs, he said. "I really don't think that will be necessary and it's for sure not what anyone wants. We did that in 2009 and 2010, and I don't ever want to do that again."

Ennen enlisted the help and cooperation of all employees: "If we're not willing to do this work . . . then CHWC will continue to struggle. We will weaken over time and we won't be able to stay independent. Then new owners will take over. What I can totally promise you is the new owners WILL make the changes that we SHOULD HAVE made. I just think we can make these changes ourselves and stay in control of our destiny."

A sign soon went up in the cafeteria. The food subsidy was ending. Don't take it out on the cashiers, the sign said. The hospital's cafeteria was the best meal bargain in town, by far. Whatever the cooks there made was tastier than what half the restaurants in Bryan served. And the prices were absurdly low. Ennen took pride in those prices. Some people in Bryan patronized the cafeteria just to eat dinner. A group of older men came one or two mornings every week to have breakfast, drink coffee, and talk the talk of middle-aged regret and disgruntlement over local events, national politics, and college sports. Ennen knew that some patrons, including some of his own employees—like the women who cooked the food and the people who cleaned the floors—needed the subsidized food. Even after the new prices took effect, $9 would still buy a full dinner of fish, mashed potatoes, a vegetable, and a visit to the salad bar. Still, he hated raising the prices.

He also had a board meeting to gird for, at which he planned to force a "showdown" with one of the board members. Bragging about the survey results would help justify his attack—he ran a good hospital—but the discussion was about money, as always seemed to be the case. He thought the board member harped unnecessarily on the bank loan covenant breaches. He wanted to tell her to stop, that he might break the loan covenant again, maybe more than once, on the way to stabilizing his shop. Preempting criticism about it now might save him some grief later.

So before the meeting he pulled Chris Cullis aside and warned him of his plan. Cullis, the board chair, told him to go ahead and that he'd support him. But Tinkel had just heard from Fifth Third Bank, which had signed off on the latest breach. Tinkel was joyful about the reprieve, and the crisis evaporated, at least temporarily, as Ennen had said it would. There was no breach discussion.

One thing Ennen did not say to either the board or to his employees (to whom he'd promised no layoffs) was that he'd already decided on one layoff. He wasn't sure exactly when, but before the year was over, he planned to tell Mike Culler that CHWC just couldn't afford so many vice presidents. Eliminating Culler's job would save $237,000 a year in pay and insurance and

other benefits costs. The duties of the chief operating officer would be div-
vied up among the remaining VPs. That Culler's wife, Dina, worked two feet
away from Ennen's office wouldn't make his decision any easier to carry out.

Nor did he ask for any discussion about Kim Owen's new job. By the
time of the board meeting, Owen was fed up with the contract doctor's
constant advances. She'd also been offered a job working for Parkview in
Fort Wayne. She decided to accept it, not only because it was a good offer
but also because she figured that, given CHWC's financial performance,
the pressure from the big systems, and the fact that the doctors belonged
to Parkview, there was a good chance she'd wind up working for Parkview
sooner or later anyway. But when she told Ennen about the offer (without mentioning Parkview), he made one of his own. Negotiations with
Parkview about creating a cancer care joint venture had progressed. Owen
was smart, talented, a community native. She already ran radiation oncology. With the prospect of expanded cancer care at CHWC, he said, she
could assume a new position: corporate director of all cancer care, with a
hike in pay. A surprised Owen accepted. Ennen thus solved his problem.
He kept his radiation oncology director and found a lead person for the
expanded cancer program. He didn't speak to Foster, his human resources
director, about the job. He didn't post the job to the wider CHWC staff. He
just did it the way he'd made many big moves over the years, the way Rusty
Brunicardi had, the way he was taught.

▌▌▌

The night after the end of the Joint Commission inspection and the celebration at Jackie Blu's was as typical as ER nights went in Bryan. It was even
a little quiet, though the ER nurses would never say "quiet." They called it
"the Q word" because saying it out loud would jinx a quiet night. They'd be
sharing cookies and completing paperwork and telling stories about their
days off, and somebody would say, "Pretty quiet night." Minutes later, the
Williams County ambulance scanner would beep and honk, and there'd be
a car wreck, and people would arrive out of nowhere in the lobby of the
hospital and pick up the red phone outside the ER security doors and say
their little girl had fainted, or their father was slurring his words, or they
had the weirdest growth on their foot and maybe it was cancer.

Eventually a forty-six-year-old woman with chest pain did pick up the
red phone. And a few minutes after that, a man with a puncture wound on

his thumb asked to come in. His dog had bitten him, he said, though the dog didn't mean to bite him—it was just that the dog ran into the street and was hit by a car, and the man ran after it, and the dog, in its pain, snapped and caught the man's thumb. He cared a lot more about the dog than the thumb, but he thought he ought to have it looked at.

A constipated three-year-old, bundled in her mother's arms, needed some attention, too, and so did a ninety-eight-year-old woman who had fallen and bruised her hip and might have fractured her wrist. She argued she didn't need any doctor's exam, that she was just fine, but her daughter insisted. (She had indeed fractured her wrist.)

A mental-health patient was being monitored, too: a young nurse sat and watched. Nurses hated mental-health cases. They weren't psychiatrists or counselors, and neither were any of the doctors who rotated ER shifts. Medicaid, Medicare, private insurance: none of them paid well for watching mental-health patients. Transferring such a person out of the ER and into a specialized facility was nearly impossible because there was no money in mental health and thus few mental-health beds anywhere from the Indiana state line all the way through Toledo. "They can wind up here for three or four days," a nurse said.

The thing was, every year they saw more such cases. People just didn't know how to cope anymore, the nurses concluded. Or they had a mental illness that had been incubating for years—maybe since childhood—and now they were middle-aged adults with ongoing dysfunction that could have been avoided had there just been an intervention way back. The nurses were expected to do something. But there wasn't much for them to do, aside from calming and soothing and watching.

The brief flurry of activity paused. The nurses returned to their paper-work and their talk. They had plans for the coming week—nothing too significant, except, one said, a gun handling and safety class. After thinking about it a while, she'd decided it was time to get her concealed-carry permit. You just never knew.

■■■

As challenging as it could be, running a hospital was easier and simpler by far than trying to turn a community's health problems into "better outcomes." Chris Spielman's cheerleading at the Bard Cancer Symposium made it sound simple: be a warrior. But it was complicated.

Bryan may have been small, and its hospital may have been small, and the county may have been rural, but "the world's changed in the last couple of years," a school principal said at one of the many meetings to discuss community health. He could tell anybody who wanted to know what he saw change. Just for example, kids sometimes took guns to school; only a few years back, he'd never encountered pistol-packing sophomores. But he couldn't tell what had happened to create those changes.

After one meeting, health department director Jim Watkins and I chatted while others filed out of the room. What, I asked him, did he think the healthcare system could do to alter some of what worried the others? How could it make "better outcomes"? He laughed out loud and looked at me the way an old cowboy might look at a greenhorn wearing shiny new trousers and an unstained hat. "System?" he asked. "What system? There is no system!"

Some months later, in yet another meeting—this one in the basement of the little house that served as the Montpelier headquarters for the county health department—Fred Lord listened to an expert from Ohio University talk a little about mental health and addiction and how Williams County might look for community solutions. Lord, director of the Williams County office of the Ohio Department of Jobs and Family Services, had been a cop before turning to social work. He knew trouble when he saw it.

As the discussion about steps to take and whom to enlist in the effort bounced around the table, Lord appeared skeptical. He thought the health needs assessment and all the other meetings and organizations and efforts were fine ideas. But they seemed to be circling something he could almost see the outlines of, yet couldn't quite bring into focus. He and his staff touched erosion—health, family, social—every day, so he saw the concrete manifestations of dysfunction more clearly than most of his colleagues who attended the meetings. Still, the sharp outlines of their structure eluded him. He knew, though, these efforts felt doomed to fall short. CHWC could indeed be the "best damn hospital in northwest Ohio," and the health needs assessment could be comprehensive, and all the concern could be real, but somehow that didn't help the many people who needed his agency. He looked up, put his note-taking pen down, sighed, and, apropos of nothing, said, "I think we're chasing a symptom."

4

Powers Beyond Us

The Contagion of
the New Capitalism

NOW HIRING ADULTS UP TO $11.50 AN HOUR. The sign on the little marquee under the cheerful Taco Bell, with its balloon-soft edges and candy-colored aura, rang out the news. Day and night, rain and sun, snow and wind: the sign was a beacon on Bryan's Main Street—U.S. 127, a road once traveled by laborers from as far south as Tennessee. Those economic refugees had crossed the Ohio River on journeys up toward the factories and mills of northern Ohio and Michigan. Now the logos for Kentucky Fried Chicken, Sonic, McDonald's, Burger King, and Arby's stood sentinel along Main, guarding the path to the Walmart Supercenter and the Fountain Grove Cemetery, where Stephanie Swihart's body lay underground. With each passing day, the Taco Bell seemed most insistent. Back in May 2018, the sign had read: $9.50 AN HOUR, $50 HIRING BONUS. As winter approached— the trees bare, the wind cutting—the Bell offered adults $2 an hour more to fill taco shells with ground meat and cheese and shredded lettuce.

The $2-an-hour bump replaced the signing bonus, but that wasn't any more effective. The sign had come to seem permanent. Nobody wanted to work. Just about everybody said so: "Nobody wants to work!" "You can't get people to work!" And the applicants who did walk through employers' doors couldn't pass a drug test. Everybody said that, too: "You can't get anybody who can pass a drug test!" The nurses in the ER said it. So did the doctors.

Business owners said it. So did politicians. "You can't get people to work," Brian Davis, a county commissioner, told me. "Or they can't pass a drug test."

The idea that the old Bryan work ethic had disappeared had become a gospel truth held with the same fervor as the gospel of Jesus, and it was just as unshakable. The government had so coddled the working class and the poor that they'd decided to give up on work altogether so they could collect their government cash and sit on their rent-a-couches and watch their giant flat-screen rent-a-TVs and shoot heroin and snort meth. And then when they felt sick, when their teeth fell out, when they got diabetes and bad hearts and fevers, they'd call an ambulance to bring them to the ER and then rack up bad debt or bill Medicaid.

The freeloading and subsidized services were damn unfair, and the people who worked for a living—the nurses and the injection molders, the farmers and the county commissioners, the business owners and the retirees (as well as the near-retirees) at the hospital cafeteria's morning coffee klatch—resented the hell out of it. Everybody had a grandpa or a mother or an uncle who'd worked until they dropped dead in the field or at the lathe. What had happened since those days to the drive and sense of responsibility that had made America great was a damn shame.

Few considered that something inherent in the way America had come to function was to blame. The notion seemed almost treasonous. There were many voices bolstering that view, from performers on Fox News, to local business owners and politicians, to elders who recalled a different time and for whom the true underminers of American drive were faint and unknowable shadows. The idea of American failure was no more acceptable than the idea of God failing. The only explanation had to be personal sin.

This belief left Bryan with a terrible paradox. On the one hand, the chamber of commerce types and the economic development people championed the local workforce to prospective employers. A new Williams County Economic Development Corporation brochure featured Ron Ernsberger, president of 20/20 Custom Molded Plastics, saying, "We have good, hardworking people, and they are the reason for our continued growth." Bryan's promoters didn't tell companies looking to move into the area that nobody wanted to work; they talked instead about how Bryan and the wider county had made a dramatic comeback after the Great Recession nearly squeezed the life out of the place. Now the Fountain City was on the move again and eager for even more business growth.

Yet within Bryan and Williams County, there was constant grumbling about lousy workers. And despite the cheery message to the outside world, there was no "Happy Days Are Here Again" vibe in Bryan's few cafés, bars, or shops. "The sense I get is that people look at Bryan as 'our best days are behind us,'" Kevin Maynard, director of Bryan Municipal Utilities and the city's unofficial historian, said as we sat in Kora's, the little wine-and-coffee bistro he and his wife, Theresa, had opened in 2018 on the town square. Maynard, who had worked elsewhere before returning to take over the city's utilities, understood the sentiment, but he didn't agree with it. Instead, he thought there were two Bryans: the one people remembered—the Bryan of ARO and Etch-A-Sketch and those Buicks and thriving stores and good jobs—and the one they lived in now. The one they remembered was dead. Its death was so slow that, if you had chosen to, you could have ignored the signs of it. And then, with unavoidable clarity, it died all at once with the coming of the Great Recession.

A few thought Bryan had survived the recession just fine. It was a little dinged, maybe, but okay. These people had decent jobs and lived in decent houses. The houses around Garver Park, like the Ennens', were spacious and tidy, and fine—an idyll of Cape Cod and Federal styles. You could drive along Townline Road on the western edge of the city and see some grand homes, some of which belonged to doctors. Behind those was a nice housing development around a nice park equipped with an ice arena and a community center. There were kids' soccer games, and the families reveled in small-town life.

Others despaired. Some turned sullen and angry. Some left. The county's population declined. "We lost a whole generation of people," Maynard said. He couldn't think of any reason an educated, skilled young person would come to live in Bryan unless they worked for the hospital. Few did. Only three permits to build new houses would be issued in the city of Bryan in 2018, while there'd be 567 permits issued to carry a concealed gun in Williams County.

Boosters were convinced—or maybe they just hoped—that some magical intervention would arrive, but Maynard knew it wasn't coming. During the recession, a man named C. David Snyder parachuted in and promised Bryan five hundred jobs in a new technology company he called Ruralogic, a name meant to defy the image of rural places as technology deserts. Bryan embraced the idea. Phil Ennen personally lobbied officials to provide Snyder with financial aid to start the data processing outfit. Snyder was a local north-west Ohio boy, after all, raised in Napoleon in next-door Henry County. Though he lived near Cleveland, he'd never forgotten his roots. He could revive Williams County, he said, by linking it to the modern digital economy.

The city, the county, and the state of Ohio all opened their pockets and granted loans to the fledgling enterprise. In 2010, a Ruralogic executive appeared at a Bryan Rotary meeting and credited Ennen and his friend Dean Spangler, of the candy family, for helping to bring the company to town. Ruralogic, he said, was setting up its headquarters in some old ARO offices: the new economy would repurpose what was left of the old.

But the jobs never came. Ruralogic was a con. Snyder was sentenced to two years in prison and ordered to pay back $781,000. Everybody who'd been taken in—Ennen and the other local leaders, the city, the county—were embarrassed and bitter. Years later, when Ennen spoke of the episode, he'd say, "He was a local guy!" Which made Snyder's betrayal seem all the more despicable.

No, Maynard realized, there'd be no dramatic rescue. Still, to him, the good news was that some Bryan people were tired of being down. They were starting to think about the future in new ways. Since Maynard was an amateur historian who knew better than most how Bryan had built itself from the wilderness of the swamp, he believed the town still had the power to create that future.

Kora's was his family's one small contribution. He and Theresa hoped to make money, but they were also intent on providing an anchor of life in the town square. And they weren't the only ones. John Trippy, a for-mer oral surgeon, bought an old church off the square and turned it into a restaurant and brewhouse called Father John's. The movie theater in the square had been taken over by a youngish couple, and it now showed first-run films. Maynard wasn't naive enough to think such amenities would rejuvenate Bryan by themselves, but they were signs—a stirring of mojo, a recognition—that Bryan's salvation was going to have to come from within.

Yet many still believed that forces far bigger than Bryan or Williams County were conspiring against success. Some of these forces were social and cultural. Parents no longer allowed children to fail—"Everybody gets a trophy!"—so the kids never learned to cope with disappointment. Social media was poisoning youth and too many adults. Girls got pregnant at sev-enteen and eighteen. When births at CHWC were listed in the *Bryan Times*, the father always seemed to have a different last name from the mother. Children needed fathers, not baby daddies.

Some argued that religion—by which they meant the Christian version—had been systematically attacked by the teaching of evolution and by squishy multiculturalism until, as one hospital employee insisted, "It's against the law to pray in public or say the Pledge of Allegiance." Without Jesus, society was doomed. "The only thing that can save our community is Jesus," Chris Kannel, a hospital board member and councilman for the village of Montpelier, said. Without Jesus, without people "looking up" and forming a loving relationship with Christ, "we cannot provide enough therapy to overcome this community's heart problems."

Some forces were political. The federal government, in cahoots with softhearted (and softheaded) liberals, was broadcasting the message that people no longer had to take care of themselves: Old Uncle Sam and buckets of taxpayer money would provide life's necessities. And the "elite," Brian Davis, the county commissioner, said—the big-city smarty-pants people, the coastal wealthy, the long-entrenched politicians of both parties—felt "entitled" to dictate such principles without regard to communities like Bryan and their values. And so American gumption had turned weak-kneed. Nobody wanted to work.

But when I asked Dave Swanson, the hospital board member who owned Daavlin, the dermatological light company, about the mantra, his face flushed red. "Bullshit!" he half-shouted. He had no trouble attracting good employees. "You just gotta pay them something!" And health department chief Jim Watkins didn't buy the notion that nobody could pass a drug test or that nobody wanted to work, though he'd heard that a hundred times. Just maybe, he said, smiling, it was "convenient to think so" because the truth behind the paradox—not to mention the cause of the symptoms Fred Lord, the Jobs and Family Services director, believed the local organizations were chasing—was a lot bigger and a lot more complicated than a collective failure of personal responsibility.

░ ░ ░

Valerie Moreno did nothing *but* work. Short, plump, dark-haired, with a direct, no-nonsense manner, she sat in her sweatshirt and jeans at a small table in the basement of the First Lutheran Church on Cherry Street, a couple of blocks from Keith Swihart's house, and talked about medical care—which was funny, she said, because she had the sniffles. No big deal: a runny nose wouldn't slow her down. Not much did. It was late on a Monday afternoon, so she'd just knocked off from her job as a school-bus monitor. She kept a close watch on her phone, though, because the junior high had a basketball game that afternoon. Her daughter was cheerleading, so Valerie would play taxi driver. Her older daughter was out of the house now, but Valerie tried to stay as involved as she could in the life of her younger one, the cheerleader.

After the game, Valerie would drive to her full-time job making furniture at Sauder Manufacturing Company, over in the village of Stryker. She'd just started at Sauder, where she worked the third shift. Tomorrow morning at about sunrise she'd drive from Sauder to the school-bus depot for the morning shift of her monitor job. Then she'd go home for three or four hours of sleep. After that, she'd report to her third job, which was providing care for the elderly retired pastor of the church. Then she'd monitor the bus for the after-school shift before heading back to Stryker and Sauder.

It was cold outside, and as she put down her phone and picked up her checkbook, the pipes over her head ticked and crackled as the heat switched on and off. The church was an old east-side Bryan institution, its pews once filled with worshippers. But not now; people had drifted away, either because they weren't churchgoers or because they'd shifted their allegiance to one of the newer, fancier evangelical outfits. The room, a basement that was sealed tight against the coming winter, marinated in a cloud of mustiness.

Valerie looked up from her checkbook ledger. "I have $65 in the checking account," she said. That was lower than usual, but not by much. This was why, she said, the Morenos almost never saw doctors. "Oh, my gosh, no!" she said, laughing. "We have to be dying before we see a doctor!" The problem this time, Valerie explained, was that she was between paychecks. Her husband of twenty-nine years still had his full-time job, and she had her new one at Sauder plus her two part-time jobs, but she hadn't yet received her first paycheck from Sauder.

Money had been a little less scarce back in 2010, when she worked at Bryan Metal Systems—now known as Global Suspension Systems since being taken over by Global Automotive Systems. The Bryan factory made suspensions for Chrysler, most of which were trucked over to Toledo and installed in Jeeps at the huge assembly complex there. The United Steelworkers represented the 144 Bryan workers. She made good money.

One day on the job, Valerie, who worked as a metal stamper, tried to empty a big hopper full of scrap, about 17,000 pounds of it. The hopper was supposed to tilt when she flipped a release lever, but this time it didn't. Valerie figured she'd give it a heave with her body and the thing would tip.

That was just like her. She'd been raised in the country, out by West Unity, near a hamlet called Alvordton. Her father worked at Mohawk Tools in Montpelier, but when that company disappeared in the wave of consolidation among auto suppliers, he moved over to Fayette Tubular in the village of Fayette, across the Fulton County line. Fayette Tubular was sold to a French conglomerate that shut the plant and moved the jobs to Tennessee, so her dad wound up working maintenance at Allied Moulded, a company that made plastic electrical-outlet boxes. He was retired now—but because of all those employer changes his retirement income wasn't great, so he still worked part-time to afford his share of Medicare. Anyway, when Valerie was growing up, her dad also raised a few chickens, a cow, some pigs, and vegetables on an acre and a half of land. Of course he couldn't do all that by himself, so Valerie and her siblings had to help butcher pigs, weed the garden, and tend to the animals. In her family, you didn't whine about work. That's why she didn't think twice about trying to tip over 17,000 pounds of metal.

So she heaved and strained, but it was just too heavy and too stuck. Finally her foreman had to bring in a tow motor. Valerie thought she felt a pain in her back afterward, but she figured she was "just bein' a girl," so she didn't mention it. By the end of the day, though, the pain was worse. She told her supervisor about it. Still, she kept coming into work until about six weeks later, when she found she could barely get out of bed. X-rays showed two blown discs in her lower back.

Workers' compensation covered her vertebrae-fusion surgery and physical therapy afterward. She didn't use the Bryan hospital for those procedures, because, she said, it was "more of a Band-Aid station." But then the recession hit. In 2010, Global Automotive Systems closed the Bryan factory as part of its "global optimization strategy" and moved the machines to Michigan. Valerie went with them, for a time, to train her replacements.

As part of her layoff, Valerie received some funding to retrain for new work. She attended Northwest State Community College to study electrical engineering. While she studied, she worked four part-time jobs. That was why the two-year AA degree took her over three years to earn. But the degree wasn't as valuable as she'd hoped.

"I get this degree, and this education, but it does me no good because I can't get somebody to give me that little bit of a leg up," she said. "And there's a lot of men who don't like to work with a woman in their field. That was discouraging."

She wound up working at the fastener company where her husband worked. There she learned CNC and other machines and was put in charge of the toolshed. She made $14 an hour. With her two part-time jobs, she and her husband earned roughly $45,000 a year—after health insurance premiums, but before taxes. With those accounted for, her budget was always tight.

"I do anything. If there's somebody who needs a ride to the doctor's office, I do that. If they need something cleaned, I do that. Need your yard raked? I do that. I am one of these individuals—I do just about anything I need to do to make ends meet. I delivered pizzas."

Valerie was forty-six years old. She had every reason to be resentful, even bitter. And yet even after she was fired from the fastener company over a seemingly minor error involving a security key fob and had to cash out her 401(k) while she worked a series of temp jobs through an agency before finding work at Sauder, where she attached the foam and upholstery to sofas—many of which wound up in the dorms of fancy universities all over America—she was not resentful. "I have learned that God puts me where I need to be at that time, and I can't dwell on it. There's nothing I can do about it. I have to move on, find where I need to be. I hope I found my home over at Sauder's. I have to look for the silver lining in everything. That's just how I look at my life." If she kept working hard, she said, she might be able to take her younger daughter to Disney World.

But there was that matter of the $65 in her checking account. She was, she admitted, one dead car battery away from being broke, and winter was about to make life difficult for car batteries. Her back injury still bothered her—her leg was becoming numb—and she might require more imaging and surgery. Thank God, she said, workers' compensation was still paying for that.

There were many Valerie Morenos in Bryan and in Williams County. The unemployment rate approached historical lows at about 3.2 percent, and just about every person considered a member of the labor force had a job. Contrary to the gospel, five families in the entire county received government cash assistance. The numbers, Jim Watkins said, also did not bear out the notion that nobody could pass a drug test. But "people say, 'I don't care what the data says!'"

People were working, all right: they just weren't making much money. The median household income—that is, half the households made more, and half made less—in Williams County was $47,593 (about what Valerie said she and her husband earned).

If "recovery" implied a return to the previous state of affairs, there'd been no recovery from the recession in Bryan, nor in the county. About 13.5 percent of Williams County residents lived in poverty. That was average for Ohio, and just one percentage point more than for the United States overall. But in both number and percentage, more people in the county were in poverty than had been during the worst of the Great Recession—and many people were struggling to stay out of poverty. Over 36 percent of the county's residents earned incomes of less than 200 percent above the poverty line. Statewide, that number was 28 percent, the same as in the nation. About 40 percent of Bryan's elementary schoolchildren qualified for free or reduced-price lunches.

The local United Way had a name for situations like Valerie's: ALICE, or "asset limited, income constrained, employed." First coined by the United Way in New Jersey, the term referred to people who were working, often in full-time jobs, yet were still short of cash. Williams County, with a population of about 37,000 people, had about 4,600 ALICE households and over 1,900 households in poverty. Obituaries in the Bryan Times often included appeals for donations to help families defray funeral costs.

Yet many in Bryan didn't make the connection between the birth announcements citing unmarried parents and the money asks in the obits. They regarded its struggling community members with the same suspicion and loathing with which Donald Cameron had regarded them sixty years earlier. There was a broad streak of the intrinsic generosity and public spirit of the rural Midwest in Bryan. Hold a fund drive for some good cause, and people would buy the pies and cookies, run the half marathons, and eat the pancakes at the pancake breakfasts. But the instinct for generosity clashed with disgust over the decline of the town and, because they were among the most visible evidence of that decline, with disgust over those who suffered the most from that. When Les McCaslin worked with Health Partners of Western Ohio to open the clinic where Keith was treated, some in Bryan opposed it. The clinic, they said, was just for lowlifes and drug addicts.

Even the director of the local chapter of the United Way suspected a moocher culture. "I've heard people come to this area because it's one of the most giving areas," Chastity Yoder said. "It makes you wonder if [the poor] are coming here because there are so many ways to get help, and if they really need it." Younger people said they couldn't afford health coverage, but they all seemed to have cellphones and big TVs. "People talk about that all the time," she said of Bryanites.

Just as Yoder talked of moochers, she checked herself. "You know," she said, putting her hand to her cheek, her memory clicking, "now that I think about it, maybe it was a little bit tougher than I first . . . because . . . yeah." As it happened, her husband lost his health insurance in the wake of the recession. "Then I ended up getting pregnant," she recalled. "So it was . . . yeah, now I remember going, 'How are we gonna be able to afford insurance?' And I had never . . . I mean, my parents were blue-collar. Worked in factories." Her parents were frugal and self-reliant, so asking for help was difficult for Yoder. "I went to my church, and my church said, 'You know, there is help out there,' and I had no idea. I got insurance just for me . . . what do they call it? Medicaid. And I was able to because I was pregnant, and that ended up covering all my doctor bills and I didn't owe anything! I was, like, 'What's my portion?' and they were, like, 'Nothing,' and I was, like, 'What?'" Yoder paused and thought of other people she knew—some in her own family— who had almost no savings. "I've been there. I know there's a need."

"If you ask the average person," Fred Lord said, "they would think our population [of clients] is people sitting around watching Jerry Springer, cashing checks, eating filet mignons. It's not true. The majority of people we serve, even three-quarters of the ones on food stamps, are working."

You could hear it at the 7:00 AM coffee klatch in the hospital cafeteria. The men had gathered around their usual table in the middle of the room, two tables over from a Mennonite mother in a black bonnet and her little girl in a white one. The mother and daughter sat quietly, looking concerned, while the ten men covered the important topics of the day.

The previous weekend's late-season football games were analyzed and the home maintenance chores reviewed, most having to do with winterizing rain gutters and readying chimneys and furnaces. They ribbed each other. "We went to a Hooters," one said, referring to the burger joint more famous for its waitresses in tight shorts and T-shirts than for its burgers. "And every time this one waitress walked by him, she snapped his suspenders! I think she was just tryin' to wake him up!" They all howled.

The conversation turned to investments and retirement funds. One man mentioned that he'd "made out" on U.S. Surgical Corp., a maker of sutures and surgical instruments. "I got in on that at the right time," he said. U.S. Surgical, then based in Connecticut, had been taken over by Tyco International for $3.3 billion in 1998 as part of a campaign of takeovers by Tyco chairman and CEO L. Dennis Kozlowski. Four years later, Kozlowski was indicted for skimming about $100 million out of Tyco to fund a life so extreme that a $6,000 shower curtain was among the least of his expenditures. He was convicted in 2005.

Two years after that, Tyco spun off its medical products division, renamed Covidien. Covidien incorporated in Ireland to protect itself from American taxes. In 2014, Medtronic, the world's largest medical device maker, bought Covidien for $42.9 billion in an "inversion" so that it could move its own official headquarters from Seattle to Ireland.

A member of the group entered in a bright yellow jacket. "You one of those yellow vest protesters?" somebody said to general laughter. And so they talked about the demonstrations and riots in France. "It's all the fallout of socialism," one said. "If you give everybody everything they want, and then try to take it away, that's what you get."

■ ■ ■

"I can't afford an ambulance," Ann Metzger* said, a few hours after the coffee group adjourned. She stood over her husband, Roger*, who was lying on a gurney, an oxygen mask on his face, a spaghetti maze of tubes and wires connecting his body to monitors and IV bags in the ER's intensive care room. ER doc Marv Stalter had asked her how she'd gotten her husband to the hospital. "I brought him in the car," Ann told him. ER supervisor Buddy Moreland raised his eyes from Roger's body to exchange a glance with the doctor. Stalter repeated, "In a *car*?" even though he'd heard her the first time. He just couldn't believe it. Her husband, in his early sixties, was ravaged by cancer and in acute renal failure, with heart failure and pneumonia. Yet somehow his wife had managed to get him in the car, and her husband had survived the short trip to the hospital. She couldn't afford an ambulance. "I always bring him by car," she said.

Stalter leaned over the gurney, weaving around the wires and tubes until his lips were near Roger's oxygen mask. "If your heart were to stop," Stalter said in a clear, slow cadence that was gentle but direct, "and you were to stop breathing, would you want me to put a tube down your throat and revive ya?" The husband nodded against the pillow. "You want me to put the tube down your throat and revive ya," Stalter said again, not asking, but declaring. Stalter heard a muffled "yeah" from under the mask. So now Stalter, Moreland, and the nurses had work to do to keep him alive. Stalter asked Ann to list Roger's medications. She looked up with a wrung-out face and blank eyes. "He's on so many meds, I can't remember them all anymore."

Roger's heart rate dropped to thirty-two beats per minute. Stalter frowned. He walked out of the room to call another doctor. "This is the end of life," he muttered, glancing up at a monitor. The husband's heart fought, rallying to do its job. The rate rose to fifty-one, then dropped again to twenty-five. "He's a young guy," Stalter said.

Roger had been diagnosed with his cancer only weeks before. On that day he'd stopped smoking. He'd had his first chemotherapy treatments six days ago, and though Stalter didn't say so, his expression implied that he was wondering why he had been given chemotherapy at all. Then, as if to answer his own unasked question, he said that although Roger was going to die—maybe in minutes, maybe in hours—"he was just diagnosed, and it's too soon to tell him that."

He'd been a laborer. He'd spent his life working hard with his hands. His wife worked the third shift. She wondered if she should go to work tonight. She worried about her job. "I have no more sick time," she said. She shouldn't have been working at all. She was spent, wan, wispy. A home health aide had been helping, but for most of the intense sprint since the diagnosis, Ann had tended to Roger, trying to keep him comfortable. "Our house is old and cold and drafty," she said. "And we have him in the living room because that's the only place the hospital bed will fit, and we pile on the blankets. But we can't use the electric blanket because of the oxygen."

Stalter admitted Roger to the hospital's intensive care unit. He would be warm there and tended by nurses—until, about fifty hours later, he would die.

███

Ennen couldn't be sure his shop would be paid for Roger Metzger's care. His uncertainty was also part of the paradox. With nearly all the workforce employed, a lot more people had employer-sponsored health insurance. But that insurance came with high deductibles, sometimes as much as $5,000.

And because pay was often low, people didn't have $5,000—or $500, for that matter—to cover the deductibles. But sure as the sun rose every day, misfortune visited some people, and they wound up in the ER. Or they developed an odd pain they couldn't figure out that proved to be something serious. Or they came down with pneumonia.

With so many people in poverty or just above poverty, nurses and doctors often held meetings about how to evade strict interpretations of payment schemes so they could care for their patients. Could they hold the eighty-year-old with kidney failure for an extra day by insisting she could not yet walk fifty feet? Could they load up the old man with enough drug samples to get him through the week? "Insurance often says they don't need to be here," one nurse told me, even when the nurses and doctors thought they did. "We look at it as playing a game." One patient needed a ramp to navigate a wheelchair into her home before being released, but there was no money for a ramp. "Can you imagine how many people don't have the means?" the nurse asked.

Even for a small hospital like CHWC, "bad debt" and "charity care" were complex concepts, as they were for all ostensibly nonprofit hospitals. The old Hill-Burton law mandated that hospitals receiving federal money provide charity care to people who couldn't pay. But how much, and how to define that, was left to the hospitals. Some flouted the law for decades.

Bad debt sounded straightforward—a person with the ability to pay wouldn't pay—but, like almost everything to do with American healthcare, it wasn't straightforward at all. And because hospitals could often receive government payments designed to offset some "uncompensated care," and also because many depended upon the government for income—and therefore wanted hikes in Medicare and Medicaid reimbursements—there was an incentive for hospitals to plead poverty to the government and report lots of uncompensated care.

Still, there was no doubt that CHWC's uncompensated care expense was rising, even though unemployment in Williams County was low. For the previous fiscal year, CHWC reported nearly $3 million in bad debt expense, and by the end of November it was clear the hospital would surpass that figure in the new fiscal year, which had begun the previous month. That October the hospital incurred $320,720 in bad debt, about $109,000 more than in the previous October. In November, CHWC tallied $363,000 more than Tinkel had budgeted for uncompensated care.

The Bryan hospital wasn't the only one suffering. Henry County Hospital, over in Napoleon, was losing money every month, too, and seeing more bad debt and more discounted charity care.

Keith was a source of bad debt. He rested in his black recliner inside his east-side rental house. A young woman, a relative of Stephanie's, fussed in the kitchen, trying to straighten up after breakfast. It was 10:00 AM. Caleb had gone to school, and though the house was a shambles, it was peaceful.

The quiet gave Keith a few moments to think. So much had happened. Now Christmas was coming, and with it the anniversary of his first date with Stephanie. Thanksgiving had been rough, as had Halloween before that. Stephanie had been a Halloween fanatic. He'd missed her an awful lot that day. Keith wasn't sure what he'd do about Christmas, or where he'd go. There wasn't any money. He wasn't sure how Caleb would feel about a sparse Christmas, but Caleb could be inscrutable about lots of things.

He was annoyed about the headstone guys, too. He'd given them the $3,000 a long time ago, but the headstone still hadn't been placed on Stephanie's grave. He'd called them up and said, "Come on, guys!" They'd reassured him. They put a wooden stake in the ground and poured a concrete pedestal. Once in a while he'd drive into the Fountain Grove Cemetery and park. He'd sit in the car and look at the piece of ground. The wooden stake and the bare rectangle of concrete insulted him. ("*So* angry," he'd said to me one day as we sat parked next to her grave. "I can't represent . . ." His voice faded. He stared at the blankness. "I wish it was there. It hurts.") And the next day he had to go back to Toledo for another surgery—this time on his left eye.

The eye problem was another bad surprise. Keith could deal with the toe. A big toe wasn't such a lot of real estate to lose. Without it, his balance would be off a little, the doctors said. But he'd get used to it and compensate, and then barely notice it was gone. There was no reason he couldn't return to work at Menards after the amputation wound healed up.

But on November 1, he'd pulled into the parking lot of the Community Health Center for a follow-up visit to check his blood sugar numbers. Maybe it was the sun in his eyes or something, but he sneezed—a normal, one-off kind of sneeze—and in an instant it was as if a translucent red curtain fell over his left eye. Barb Purvis, the nurse practitioner, called the Bryan office of Specialty Eye Institute, a corporate chain of ophthalmology clinics based in Jackson, Michigan. Though it was only 10:15 in the morning and Purvis had described Keith's situation as an emergency, the Bryan outlet said it had no time for Keith. He'd have to drive to one of the chain's Toledo offices. Keith could see nothing but red out of his left eye. Driving all the way to Toledo was out of the question. Purvis made an appointment in Bryan for the next day.

The Specialty Eye Institute doctor told Keith that blood vessels in his left eye had ruptured. Keith had developed diabetic retinopathy. The sugar in his blood had blocked the tiny blood vessels to the retina, and to compensate, his body grew more vessels. These were weak, so when Keith sneezed, one or more of them burst. He'd need a surgery called a vitrectomy if he was to have any hope of seeing out of it again. And his right eye was also at risk.

The Community Health Center assigned an outreach worker to help Keith. On November 27, when he reported to St. Vincent's, the Mercy chain outlet in Toledo, he named her as his contact person. She, in turn, coordinated with Williams County Jobs and Family Services, Fred Lord's agency, to give Keith a ride back to Bryan after the surgery.

During the surgery, the doctor drained the blood and some vitreous fluid, then installed a gas bubble to hold Keith's retina in place. The surgery didn't hurt, and Keith felt fine afterward. But there was no surgery for his worry, and this latest setback with his eye triggered a cascade of it.

He worried about food. There wasn't enough food in the house for himself, Caleb, and Stephanie's relative, even though the community outreach worker had helped him get on food stamps and he'd used them. He didn't like using them, but he hadn't been working, so he wasn't getting paid. He worried about money. Caleb received a little Social Security payment because of Stephanie's death and his autism, so Keith tried to live on that. He worried about driving. He couldn't now. He no longer had a phone. He hadn't paid the utility bill and thought his power might be shut off. He couldn't see well enough to give himself his insulin shots. His blood sugar was still high at 270. Over at the CHWC wound care clinic, George Magill wasn't happy with how Keith's toe amputation was healing. And Keith still had one more eye surgery to go, the Toledo doctors told him—the one he'd go in for tomorrow.

Keith couldn't sleep when he returned home from that first eye surgery. And he was depressed. But he would say none of these things out loud. As he sat in the recliner, Liz, a nurse from St. Vincent's, called Keith. She asked a few basic questions in preparation for his surgery the next day to drain more fluid from his eye. "That should improve the vision," he said when he hung up. Keith always grabbed for the most optimistic interpretation.

"I mean, I want to get back to kind of a normal life," he said. "It's one of them things. I look around. I see that my house is a mess. I want to try to get it cleaned up. The problem is they don't want me doing that much, 'cause I can't really lift anything 'cause they're scared I'll have more bleeding. So that's why they've had me off work. They're worried about my eyes. You lift up, you strain your muscles, you strain everything, you bleed."

His Menards job wasn't much to go back to. Fourteen bucks an hour wasn't great. But it was work, and he'd always worked. Working felt normal. Now he feared that even that was being taken away.

Some people might give up, he said. He handed a picture of Caleb with Stephanie to me. "It's him," he said—Caleb gave him courage.

▮▮▮

The dim view of socialism held by the old men in the CHWC cafeteria ignored the fact that government payouts stood between the hospital and closure. Meanwhile, the language of the modern healthcare economy was all capitalism, but it described a world that sounded nothing like the one Keith, Valerie, and Ann Metzger inhabited. That was the world where Ennen and the vice presidents now found themselves as they listened to consultants they were auditioning to help create a strategic plan. "Transformational changes dictate that leaders within the physician enterprise focus on enterprise sustainability." So they drove. They drove at "solutions." The consultants offered entire suites of solutions. The solutions could be "leveraged" toward "accelerating the journey to risk capability." There'd be "applied analytics" in "the Achieve solution set," which was "purposely designed to assist physician enterprise leaders to align compensation models and strategic priorities, maximize productivity."

"The Achieve solution set not only drives current performance improvement but also establishes the forward-looking strategic, financial and operational structures to provide for the future risk capable physician enterprise." Change was driven. Results were driven. Everything was "forward-looking" and "dynamic."

Zoom!

Most people couldn't get rid of the fading image of the doctor as a selfless, wise grandfather or as a science saint like Joseph Lister or Louis Pasteur. But to the healthcare MBAs, physicians were entrepreneurs and enterprise leaders. The executive collective—Ennen, CIO Wade Patrick, vice president of patient care Jan David, CFO Chad Tinkel, vice president of human resources Angelia Foster, and COO Mike Culler—sat around a table in the boardroom staring at a speaker through which the voices of the experts from Dixon Hughes Goodman spoke of "drivers," "disruptors," "data analytics." DHG was pitching itself as CHWC's guide into the bigger, winner-take-all healthcare economy. There was mention of an "Excel model" and "strategic initiatives."

The management seminar mishmash was so meaningless it defied satire, but it sounded impressive and necessary. It also sounded expensive. Such language had never been CHWC's way, and it was not Ennen's way, either. Once in a while he'd use a word like "commoditization," "leverage," or "proactive." He did, after all, have a master's degree in public administration, and he'd done a training sojourn at Stanford University's business school. Most of the time, though, he spoke like a smart guy from Bryan, Ohio, who used clear, plain, language. When he gave a presentation about the state of CHWC to the community in May 2018, he used PowerPoint slides, all right, but the headings included "OK . . . What Are You Doing About It?" That was followed not by "Strategic Initiatives" but by "Trying to Grow."

It wasn't just about style. Ennen thought the world—and especially the world of medical care—was complicated enough without further obscuring meaning and understanding by spouting terms of the business dark arts. Such terms were deliberate obfuscations, thrown up as fortress walls to keep the uninitiated outside and throwing cash over the walls to the mysterious magicians inside so they'd shout down their wisdom. Now, though, like it or not (and he didn't), Ennen and the others were knocking on the gates of the consultants. That moment had been two years in the making.

For decades, CHWC's strategic planning, such as it was, arrived whole from the burning bush of the CEO's office. But as younger members began to appear on CHWC's board, and as the financial woes and the threats from the big health systems stacked up, a few board members hankered for a more formal process.

Ennen's strategic plans were pretty simple documents: staying solvent and independent were the goals. CHWC could attain the goals by growing—adding Bazzi's women's clinic, for example—rather than by retreating, as some other community independents had done. He wanted people in Williams County to choose CHWC over hospitals farther away.

CHWC, like many hospitals, was often forced to be more reactive than proactive. After all, the government, its biggest payer, could change a rule at any time. So creating an expensive, detailed, consultant-driven strategic plan had never struck Ennen as worthwhile.

So far, this more casual method of planning had worked—mostly. But there were notable missteps. Brunicardi's effort to fend off ProMedica's incursion into Fulton County by building the stand-alone CHWC clinic in Archbold was costing the hospital half a million dollars a year, sometimes more. And when Ennen first hired a gastroenterologist to create a GI clinic, the doctor came with a reputation for being difficult to work with and to manage. Ennen insisted CHWC's family culture would mold the new doc into an agreeable team player. It didn't, and Ennen, without consulting the board, paid for his mistake with a million-dollar buyout of the physician's contract.

The board looked askance at such developments, seeing them as the result of Ennen's risky swashbuckling. So, gradually, it came to believe that a real strategic plan, created with guidance from professional consultants, could rein him in and position the hospital to escape from the financial handcuffs that so worried them.

While that sounded reasonable and logical and efficient, Ennen was suspicious of "efficient." He liked to say that America was built on inefficiency. Amazon was efficient: you could make a couple of clicks on a computer, and, the next day, there'd be a book or a hedge trimmer or a baseball glove sitting on your front porch. The price for that efficiency was paid by the bookstore, the hardware store, the sporting goods store that closed on Bryan's town square as well as on the main streets of communities like Bryan all over America. These stores had helped to build their towns. But, compared with Amazon, they were all inefficient.

The hard fact was that CHWC was inefficient, too. The board knew it, the executives knew it, and Ennen knew it. It was not "efficient" to hire pricey specialists and establish in-hospital clinics when elaborate facilities and other pricey specialists were an hour away. It would be more efficient to allow CHWC to be taken over—reduced to primary care, the ER, and baby deliveries—and then send everybody else to Toledo or Fort Wayne.

The consultants from Dixon Hughes Goodman knew this, too, saying they could help CHWC navigate the inherent inefficiency of being a small, unaffiliated community hospital. DHG would "address the desire to stay independent in a landscape of consolidation" and help CHWC identify "potential partners." "Partners" could mean anything, from the kinds of joint ventures Ennen was beginning to explore with Parkview and ProMedica to an outright takeover.

DHG employed about three hundred people in its healthcare practice, some of whom were niche specialists in things like Medicare reimbursement. These experts, it claimed, could implement its "solutions sets" to "holistically drive a strategic reimbursement playbook." The company earned about $500 million annually. It had offices in thirteen states and—via an association with Praxity, an international consortium of accounting consultancies—access to the world.

As the DHG consultants explained their services, a faint smile edged across Ennen's face. DHG would provide a baseline image of where CHWC stood, the voice on the speaker said. And as their experts worked inside CHWC to assess its status, certain opportunities would present themselves. Based on this information, models would be created, and new inputs would be plugged into those models representing different possible changes. These would tell CHWC what its five-year future might look like. What if CHWC built a freestanding emergency department, for example? By knowing where all CHWC's possible patients lived and where those people went for medical services, DHG could tell the hospital "where the organization needs to head," and if the market was big enough to support the suggested changes.

"We don't have that data," Ennen told them.

The lead DHG executive paused. Then he asked how the leadership team saw itself as a hospital. He expected a grand vision. But before anybody else could reply, Ennen said, "We care tremendously about not making our patients sicker than they were when they came into the hospital."

This wasn't a glib crack. Every chance he got, Ennen bragged about the fact that CHWC had an excellent record of preventing hospital-acquired infections and sepsis. Kesireddy could work on a heart, Bazzi could deliver a baby, Stalter could set a broken arm, but if the patient died or got sicker because of some mistake in hygiene, the most sophisticated procedures would have been worthless. Ennen lived in the world of the basics.

The consultants, however, talked data. They wanted a lot of data from CHWC. "The honest answer is that we've never done a business plan like you'd expect to see," Ennen replied.

In the forty-minute call, DHG never mentioned sick people. As a quick aside, however, the consultants did add that they could help with "wealth advisory."

Ennen aimed his voice at the speaker on the table and said, "Look, it's difficult to think what we might want, because we've never done this before. We're on such new ground." He told DHG that he and his team would huddle and confer.

Ennen and the others had heard from three firms: DHG; Root, a healthcare consultancy headquartered in Sylvania, a suburb of Toledo; and Atlanta-based Warbird, a group founded as Callaway Partners in 2003 by former Arthur Andersen consultants after Andersen collapsed following the Enron scandal.

COO Mike Culler had a dictum. "As soon as they hear 'healthcare,'" he liked to say, "the price goes up." It didn't matter what the object was: a generator for Montpelier, a piece of metal for a door fix, an electric conduit. If a vendor knew the shopper was a hospital, an item you could buy for twenty bucks at a hardware store would suddenly cost three hundred.

The board had figured that the services of an outside consulting firm would cost around $50,000—a lot of money—but they also figured the product would be worth the price. DHG estimated its price at about $170,000. Root would charge about $125,000. Warbird wanted $175,000. Those numbers didn't count expenses. Healthcare consulting was an extremely lucrative business.

Ennen knew there was no way the board would approve spending that much money at a time when CHWC was trying to shed employees and had just cut the cafeteria subsidy. But he didn't take the numbers as bad news. Though he agreed that an outside consultant could perhaps teach them a few things, he viewed the entire exercise of auditioning the firms as a waste of time, and hiring one as a waste of money. He also feared that CHWC staff would wind up feeding a data-consuming beast. "People like working for us because they don't have to meet a bunch of metrics," he said.

For decades—through Bryan's cozy years and through its decline—the hospital had existed as a scrappy hybrid, a community asset devoted to the people's health that used some methods of business to stay afloat. First Brunicardi and then Ennen spent much of their time figuring out how to get what they needed from the system.

The cath lab, the hospital's big moneymaker, was the prime example.

Hospitals that placed cardiac stents in people's bodies had always also been able to perform open-heart surgery—cracking open a patient's chest—in case a stent wasn't the right answer after all, or if something happened while performing a cardiac catheterization. Surgery was the safety net. But CHWC didn't perform such surgeries, so it couldn't install stents.

Kesireddy, ever the workhorse, insisted he was capable of inserting stents if Brunicardi could somehow figure out a way to get permission from the state of Ohio. As it happened, a Johns Hopkins physician named Thomas Aversano was leading a study comparing results between hospitals that placed stents and also performed open cardiac surgeries and those that placed stents but did not perform the surgeries. Kesireddy and Brunicardi convinced Aversano to let CHWC take part in the study. CHWC took his approval to the state authorities and said, "See? We're in, and we'll be monitored the whole time."

The state's approval annoyed big hospitals. They feared they'd lose profitable heart cath business if little guys like CHWC could horn in on the market.

There was a hitch, though. According to the rules, all hospitals in the study were supposed to keep the cath lab operational every hour of every day for the sixteen years of monitoring. But Kesireddy was the only interventional cardiologist for fifty miles, and though he worked like a demon, even he couldn't work every hour of every day. If a heart attack patient arrived at CHWC when Kesireddy wasn't there, CHWC would find a reason (aside from the cath lab being closed) to send the patient off to Toledo. In other words, CHWC should never have had a cath lab.

"I figured, and Rusty before me, 'Okay, let 'em come in and make an issue of that," Ennen recalled of regulators. If the state tried to shut down the cath lab, "we know how the community will react: 'Kesireddy saved my life!' Plus he was still working 350 days a year." (This was true. During a conversation with the owner of a bar and restaurant in Montpelier, the man volunteered, "Dr. Kesireddy saved my father." That exact sentence, save for substituting a different person—"my grandpa," "my mom," "me"—was spoken all over Williams County.)

CHWC wasn't the only hospital to fudge. They all wanted cath money, Ennen said. "The other hospitals in the study would bitch about each other, saying, 'They are not following all the rules!' But they'd leave Bryan alone, because of its isolation, and we weren't competitive."

By 2018, the lab was open all the time. CHWC paid "an enormous amount" for two Toledo doctors to fill in when Kesireddy wasn't available.

So CHWC had survived thus far—when other small, independent hospitals had not—by playing by its own rules. But now some board members, (like Chris Kannel, the Montpelier council member), and some of the vice presidents (mainly Angelia Foster) believed this view was far too parochial. Change had to come. They all had to adapt. It was a business now, wholly and completely. A business with a mission, maybe, but a business.

The vice presidents and Ennen discussed the DHG call and compared it with what they'd heard from Warbird and Root. It was obvious that CHWC couldn't afford to hire any of them. Foster was disappointed. If they couldn't take on an outside firm, they'd have to construct a strategic plan themselves in order to satisfy the board. She feared that, under Ennen's guidance, any plan would amount to more of the same. She wanted a quantitative investigation to show how the hospital could "make it to the next base path of life. If we're not looking three to five years ahead, then what's the point? We will continue to struggle and struggle." It was time to transform the hospital. She didn't believe the hidebound board, filled with locals who were insistent on remaining fully independent, nor the rest of the executive leadership, had the skills to be "transformational."

"I am confused because I don't even know what we're doing anymore," Ennen countered. "I did not see [a strategic plan] as a quantitative process. We don't have the skill set to do a quantitative process. Cost is the number one thing we need to worry about."

"If it's 'What will make us lose our independence?,' I agree," Tinkel added. Without cost control, they'd have to seek a merger. It was only a matter of time.

Foster argued for growth as the top priority. "We are only a 38,000-population county," Tinkel said, overestimating the population a bit. Ennen had already grown the in-house specialties—including the women's, ear, nose and throat, wound care, pain, and GI clinics. There wasn't much more growing they could do.

There was also the problem of uncompensated care. If the local economy were different, Ennen said, "we wouldn't even be having this conversation," because his shop would be making more money.

"But have we looked beyond our primary service area?" Foster asked.

"We have Bazzi and Hassouneh, who are making inroads for us" by drawing patients from neighboring counties.

To grow again would imply that CHWC would have to partner with a big system for more services, Tinkel pointed out. And "board members wouldn't let Parkview come in."

"Our position on affiliation may change," Foster countered.

"That would be very personal" for the board, Ennen said.

Foster's face flushed with frustration. The way she saw it, Ennen was looking for excuses to retain the status quo. She tossed her pen down on the table in front of her, folded her arms, and said, "I am terrified that in two years I'm going to people to say, 'You don't have a job because we didn't do this!'"

Ennen proposed a compromise. Given the price of consultants, why didn't they all increase their focus on cutting costs to soothe the board, start a strategic planning process on their own, and maybe create "benchmarks"? Then in a year, with any luck, they could budget for an outside consulting agency to build on what they'd accomplished.

The board held its monthly meeting a few days later, just before Christmas. Ennen choreographed a presentation on the executives' experience auditioning the firms. The message from the leadership was clear: We hear the board. You want us to hire outside eyes. But the cost to CHWC would be about $185,000.

Some attendees gulped. The board of directors from Bryan and Montpelier, Ohio, were learning just how expensive a proposition it could be to walk through the doors of American healthcare's economic superstructure.

The board members and the executives talked for about twenty minutes. Ennen assured the board—as he had in the past—that he not only was aware of the need to cut costs, but had already implemented plans to reduce expenses in food service and janitorial. He would cut staff via attrition. Foster pushed her view for transformation. Kannel said he wanted to hire the outside consultants now, regardless of the cost. But in the end, the plan Ennen favored—letting the C-suite try to do its own strategic planning analysis, then building money for an outside firm into the next budget, swayed most members. Only Kannel and Dave Swanson opposed it.

That final meeting of the calendar year also represented an end of an era. A week before the meeting, and in anticipation of the cost-cutting discussion he knew he'd have, Ennen had informed Mike Culler he'd be laid off. It was a difficult moment for both men. Culler was angry and disappointed, but he behaved like a pro. At the board meeting, he carried out his role in the consultant presentation without a hint of rancor. Ennen requested that, for the time being, Culler not tell any other employees. With all the other trims and cuts going on, Ennen didn't want to spook them.

Two longtime board members, Jim Rupp—a local industrial real estate developer—and Swanson, announced they'd be leaving the board at the end of 2019. Both men were well over sixty. The board would get younger still.

Most profound, however, was Dr. Nick Walz's goodbye. His retirement was effective that day.

Walz was revered throughout Williams County. At seventy, he was a short, round-faced man with a ring of white hair framing his bald head. His eyes and voice were gentle, and he smiled easily and often. He was the Norman Rockwell image of a family doctor, which was how he'd spent his career since moving to Bryan in 1984.

He'd come from a busy practice in Toledo, where he'd also taught at the Medical College of Ohio (now the University of Toledo College of Medicine and Life Sciences). He moved to Bryan because he and his wife wanted to raise their children in a small town. He'd grown up in Defiance, so he knew that in places like Bryan doctors' kids could never get into trouble without parents knowing about it.

Family doctors were already becoming a rare species by 1984. They didn't make nearly as much as specialists, and Walz sometimes complained that, whenever he referred a patient to a specialist in Toledo, he never saw the patient again and lost income as a result. Still, he enjoyed his work.

Then medicine changed. Perhaps it would be more accurate to say that medicine was already changing when Walz moved to Bryan, but that those changes finally began infiltrating there. Digital technology invaded his practice—and, while there were positives to the new computerized records and charts, there were big negatives, too. Computers interfered with doctor-patient interaction. Country people tended to be stoic about their health, especially about mental or emotional stress. He found he had to spend time looking a farmer or a factory worker in the eye, chatting about nothing much in particular—the weather, high school sports, local gossip— before turning the conversation to his patient's well-being. Clicking on lists of boxes on a screen wrecked all that. Now, he said, "when I go to a doctor, they do not maintain eye contact. They are in that box."

Younger doctors, he thought, were preoccupied with money. He under-stood why; two of his children were doctors. His tuition per quarter at the Medical College of Ohio had been $100. Now, medical students left school carting around the weight of hundreds of thousands of dollars in student loan debt. Young doctors didn't want to be on call and have to see a patient in the middle of the night or on a weekend. He remembered feeling like he was always on call. When he started in the county, he worked at a practice in Montpelier. There were doctors' offices in the villages of West Unity, Pioneer, Edon, and Edgerton. Except for Montpelier, none of those villages had a doctor now.

After a few years, his little practice was absorbed into the Bryan Medical Group. As time passed, the Bryan Medical Group faced decisions about its own future. Should it invest the money for an MRI machine? Should it start an ambulatory surgery center of its own? Those kinds of changes could cost millions. Partners in their fifties and older wondered if they'd ever recoup the money. But they had to do something to compete. Other, bigger groups, and hospitals in neighboring counties—some affiliated with healthcare systems—could siphon away patients with jazzy technology and more outpatient services.

Rusty Brunicardi and the group held talks about merging the doctors into the hospital, where they'd become salaried employees. "The psyche wasn't right at the time," Walz recalled. Then Ennen made his approach after becoming CEO. By then, though, the hospital's future looked shaky, so the doctors chose to sell to Parkview. Ennen offered Walz the job as the hospital's chief medical officer, or CMO. He accepted. Upon retiring from the CMO job, Walz took a regular seat on the board.

Walz believed the sale of the medical group to Parkview was good for the partners, but not necessarily good for patients—and certainly not good for Bryan. Medically, he believed, the care was fine. And the changes—less personal interaction, more insistence that patients go to the Parkview corporate "mother ship" in Fort Wayne, for example—weren't unique to Parkview. Such was life in America's new, more consolidated medical ge-ography.

But, he said, Parkview was now "a big power in our community. "You have a large hospital corporation who has a satellite facility in Bryan, Ohio. So, all a sudden, you now have a corporation saying, 'Use us. Stop sending [patients] to Toledo. You need to use us.'"

He pointed to the world of "hospital pay versus physician's pay." When a patient had surgery at CHWC, the Parkview surgeon was paid a fee and the hospital was paid a fee for rental of the surgery suite, for use of the instruments, for disposable supplies, and so on. Since Parkview owned the surgeon, the company kept the surgeon's fee *and* the facility fees when surgeries happened in Fort Wayne. Money left the community.

"The patient will get great care at Parkview in Fort Wayne and in the Bryan hospital in Bryan," he said. "But they will get better social care in Bryan because the family is here."

Voices like Walz's were diminishing around Bryan, so everyone in the board meeting was aware they were witnessing an important passage. As the meeting wound up, Ennen paused to thank Walz for his years of service, both as CMO and as a member of the board. He asked him to say a few words. Walz glanced down at a piece of paper on which he'd written a farewell. He didn't want to ad-lib his goodbye. He knew there was no way he'd make it through even a short speech without breaking down.

After recalling his decision to move to Bryan and praising Brunicardi, he said, "Maintaining our independence and maintaining the high quality of ancillary services . . . is imperative. The message," he said, choking back tears, "is, without question, stay independent as long as you can. Unfortunately, we all know we're at the mercy of powers beyond us." He praised Ennen. "I remember Phil coming in as a young protégé under Rusty, and what great insight Rusty had."

Walz's farewell was the most emotional moment Ennen had witnessed at a board meeting in his thirty-two years of attending them.

None of the people in the room—not even Ennen—could have guessed that as they adjourned for the Christmas holiday, the forces Walz alluded to, along with friction within the hospital itself, would make them all confront a new era much sooner than they expected.

5

Pray

"Praise to God," the man in the back said as he rose from his pew inside the West Unity United Methodist Church. "Linda's back home from a hospitalization." He no sooner sat down than another man stood to announce, "My brother, his gallbladder is being taken out." One by one, half a dozen of the fifty or so worshippers rose either to give thanks for a recovery or to beseech Jesus and their fellow congregants to pray for them or for a family member afflicted by some disorder.

Then it was Pastor Greg Coleman's turn. He stood under Jesus, whose stained-glass arms were outstretched in welcome and love. At his best, Coleman looked like a former high school fullback: a short, solid build and crew cut. But now he was diminished and ashen as he croaked out the story of how he'd been down with a bad cold, and then the cold had turned into pneumonia. He'd only just begun feeling well enough to lead services, he said. Then he asked everyone to bow their heads and pray for health.

Coleman wanted them to pray for something bigger than their own bodies or those of their friends and families. He wanted them to pray for the health of the body politic. "We lift up before you, our nation, that our hearts and minds should be lifted up to you. That we move back to being a Christian nation and not a polarized one."

America was sick. The nation's symptoms were many and varied, and they all troubled him. He'd been troubled for a long time—ever since, without setting out to, he'd made his own diagnostic tour of the country's midsection, emerging frightened.

Before the Great Recession, Coleman had run his own little contracting company up in Michigan. Business was good because he was building houses that sold for $1 million, or $2 million, or $3 million. The people who could afford the houses weren't like normal people with normal money. They could plunk down a couple of million bucks in cash—money they had lying around.

But then the contracting business slowed. He was still managing at first, because the rich had all that money to insulate themselves against troubles, but he knew a storm was coming: he'd watched friends fight to save their businesses and fail. Ford and GM laid off hundreds, then thousands. Homes were sold in foreclosures. By then, Coleman had heard God calling him to ministry.

After his training, he was sent down to Martinsville, Ohio—northeast of Cincinnati and just south of Wilmington. As it happened, there was an old Air Force base at Wilmington. When DHL, the international delivery service owned by Germany's Deutsche Post, bought its much smaller rival Airborne Express in 2003 for $1.05 billion, the state of Ohio induced DHL to expand there. Local authorities, backed by the state, issued $270 million in bonds to finance DHL's construction at the airport so the company wouldn't have to borrow money at higher interest rates. DHL got another $122 million in state-paid road construction and tax breaks. But four years later, none of that mattered. In November 2008, DHL announced it would shut down most of its operations in Wilmington. About 7,500 people worked there. The mayor of Wilmington called the closure "catastrophic."

Just about everybody in Coleman's Martinsville congregation once worked for DHL, but they didn't anymore. Just about everybody in Coleman's congregation outside Lansing, Michigan, had some sort of relationship with the auto industry, but they'd lost their jobs, too. He'd gone from one formerly thriving place to another in Michigan and Ohio, learning a lot about America in the process of trying to help both the people who knocked on his office door and those who never did.

He'd arrived in West Unity four years before, assigned there by higher-ups because he'd earned a reputation as a guy who could splint up a church on its last legs. West Unity's church wasn't as badly off as his previous assignments had been, so it was supposed to be a respite. It wasn't.

The village turned out to have a lot in common with Martinsville and Coleman's other stops. It was once reputed to be the egg capital of Ohio. Starting in 1972, and into the 1980s, West Unity held the annual Egg-N-Fest celebration as the kickoff to summer. Its egg-processing plants were long gone, though. Now the biggest employer was a small factory just outside the village where Kamco made injection-molded plastics and formed metal for car interiors. Kamco was owned by Kumi Kasei Co., Ltd., of Tokyo. Like every other employer in Williams County, Kamco needed workers. A sign in the Jobs and Family Services office in Bryan announced starting wages of $11.50 an hour, the same as Taco Bell's.

Bad news had arrived on the Friday before this Sunday service. Arcelor-Mittal, the Indian steel giant, had just announced it would close its small plant in Pioneer, the village north of West Unity where Phil Ennen's father once ran his own small factory. The biggest customer for the factory's steel blanks (steel that is later machined into parts) was GM's plant in Lordstown, Ohio, where the company made the Chevy Cruze. GM had announced that the Lordstown factory would close. Hundreds would lose jobs there, so fifty people in Williams County would lose theirs, too.

Most of the laid-off workers would probably find work. There was Kamco, for example. Some people in the West Unity area worked for Sauder, the furniture company that employed Valerie Moreno. And Menards, of course, was always hiring. For people from Bryan on up into Hillsdale, Michigan, Menards had become the one place you could count on to get a job.

But the presence of such a safety net didn't comfort Phil Ennen, and it didn't comfort Coleman. For a couple of decades, Ennen had witnessed one stable, well-paying employer after another lay off workers, move, or go out of business. The employees who worked at those places found other jobs, but those jobs were often nonunion and paid low wages. Many people made do by combining some form of government payout with the new jobs to cobble together a hybrid income, and that meant CHWC made less money. As for Coleman, he worried about communities and souls as well as bodies—and, since he'd gotten a glimpse of the Big Picture, he knew that a job did not necessarily mean what it once did.

As he began his sermon, he spoke in a quiet, mournful cadence. The social health of America, he said, was "collapsing." The nation was "falling apart."

███

The nation may have been falling apart around Coleman, but the low-wage economy worked just fine for John Menard Jr. A billionaire close to twelve times over, Menard, like many other big business leaders and financiers, reaped handsome rewards from it. He founded what became Menards in 1958 in Wisconsin and grew it to three hundred stores selling lumber, tools, and home products by keeping it off the stock market and running it like a cranky lord of the manor.

In the 1990s, Wisconsin authorities obtained video of old John Menard himself dumping arsenic-tainted toxic waste. He didn't believe in environmental laws, he told investigators. State regulators did, however, and levied a $1.7 million fine. In 2005, the state of Wisconsin found that Menards had been routinely discharging toxic chemicals down a drain that ultimately led to the Chippewa River. The company paid $2 million in fines.

Wisconsin lightened up on Menard when Republican Scott Walker was elected to the governorship. The billionaire had given $1.5 million in "dark" money to a group supporting Walker's campaign.

Perhaps even more than he hated environmental laws, Menard hated labor unions. "The Manager's income shall be automatically reduced by sixty percent (60%) of what it would have been if a union of any type is recognized within your particular operation during the term of this Agreement," read an employment contract managers were required to sign. "If a union wins an election during this time, your income will automatically be reduced by sixty percent (60%)."

The ways in which the Menard family treated employees was the stuff of Victorian melodramas. In 2015, the company paid a $1 million settlement in a race discrimination case. The following year, the National Labor Relations Board found that Menards had illegally required regular line workers to sign away their right to band together or join in class action lawsuits against the company. And when employees did file grievances with the required arbitration panel, they had to pay for their own lawyers as well as half the cost of the arbitration process, even if Menards was found to be at fault. The company spied on its employees, forced even low-level workers to sign noncompete contracts (so they couldn't quit and go to work for Home Depot, for example), and forbade them to build their own houses (Menard feared they'd steal supplies from his stores). The company fired one longtime executive after he modified his home to accommodate his daughter's wheelchair.

Though Menard believed himself a self-made man, he and the company he controlled craved corporate welfare. After Walker was elected in Wisconsin, the state, via a committee chaired by the new governor, gave Menards $1.8 million in tax breaks. Wherever it went, the company demanded payments and incentives from towns and counties. In 2015, it wrote to the commissioners of Kansas's Douglas County: "Menards is requesting that the Commission consider a $200,000 grant to be paid over a 10-year period, which combined with City assistance, would help to offset a portion of the development costs of the project." Since 2002, but mostly since the Great Recession, Menards lapped up $23,321,779 in subsidies.

When Menards came to Holiday City, in Williams County, it found local leaders eager to open the public purse. Hundreds of thousands of dollars' worth of infrastructure—including a road, water and sewer systems, and power systems—were used to build what Menards wanted built. On top of all that largesse, the county established the Menards site—a rural tract of mostly empty land—as an enterprise zone. Thanks to the enterprise zone designation, by 2016, Menards was enjoying nearly $600,000 in tax abatements every year. Other businesses in the county took the breaks, too, for a total of $1,512,956, but Menards was by far the biggest beneficiary. The outlays were so generous that hospital board member and Montpelier village councilman Chris Kannel worried about how the old wealthy families like the Spanglers (of the candy company) and the Steeles and Bards (of the cooling and heating company), who were constantly tapped for donations, would feel about the giveaways to Menards.

Meanwhile, the hamlets of Kunkle, where the median income was about $14,000 per year, and nearby Alvordton, where Valerie grew up, did not have sanitary sewer systems. Both were polluting streams that eventually flowed into the Maumee River and, in turn, Lake Erie.

Still, all this welfare for Menards, local officials said, was to help the company employ Williams County workers. And Menards did. It was the largest employer in the county, beating out the hospital (which was the largest employer in Bryan). Roughly nine hundred people worked at Menards.

In 2012, the average Menards wage was $11.30 an hour. When Keith started in 2018, he made $14. With wages so low, many employees felt they couldn't afford the Menards health plan, which was administered by Anthem Blue Cross and Blue Shield. Some people working full-time at Menards made so little money that they qualified for Medicaid, making it the unofficial backup health plan for Menards. Others played roulette with insurance in an effort to save money.

Shari and Jason Temple,* ages twenty-eight and twenty-seven, both worked at Menards. Their combined wages were enough to make a decent living. But they didn't sign on with the Menards health insurance at first, because the plan was expensive and had high deductibles. In 2018, a single employee had to pay $83.37 a week, or $333 a month, for an "A" plan. An employee with one dependent paid $151.01 a week, or $604.04 a month. If they tried to lower those premiums by enrolling in a "B" plan, their deductibles could rise into the thousands. (The 2019–2020 "B" plan deductible for a single Menards employee was $5,750 for an in-network provider. For many workers, that might as well have been $5 million.)

When Shari became pregnant, the Temples decided to pay up and enroll in the health plan, making it effective January 1, 2019: in plenty of time, they thought, for the insurance to cover the costs of delivering the baby. But late in her pregnancy something went wrong, and, still uninsured, they found themselves in the ER. They were taken upstairs, where Shari gave birth prematurely. Because the baby was so premature, it had to be taken to the neonatal intensive care unit at Toledo Hospital, owned by ProMedica. Many thousands of dollars in ProMedica billings later, baby, mother, and father were okay. But not counting the ProMedica bills, they owed CHWC $17,028. They had $26.35 in a checking account and $660 in a savings account. So the Temples asked CHWC for a discount based on need. CHWC cut their bill in half and wrote off $8,500 as charity.

Ennen often railed against what he called the "Menards effect." Every time he drove up Ohio Route 15 and passed its intersection with Traxler Drive—the road the county built for Menards—he'd grumble, "We built them that road!" Big companies owned by multibillionaires were supposed to build their own damn roads and pay their taxes. But the wooing of corporate manufacturing plants, distribution centers, and offices had become an extortion racket as one beaten-down county, town, or state competed with all the other ones to see which could prostrate itself most by offering the juiciest tax breaks and payoffs—and by passing the most anti-union legislation. Meanwhile, the community assets of such places, like CHWC, were left to clean up the fallout.

Ennen thought there were other healthcare chiselers in the county, too. Some manufacturers, he said, manipulated employee hours to avoid giving overtime or the health insurance benefits mandated by the Affordable Care Act to employees who worked 30 hours or more per week or 130 hours per month. Unique-Chardon, for example, was a Bryan supplier of formed parts to the auto industry—part of Michigan-based Unique Fabricating. A private equity firm, Taglich Private Equity LLC, had created Unique Fabricating, and Unique's chairman was a Taglich employee. Half the workforce at Unique-Chardon was classed as "temporary." In November 2019, Unique Fabricating decided to close the Bryan plant—though Bryan didn't hear about it until January 2020—and send the work to Mexico and LaFayette, Georgia.

But Menards, Ennen said, was "a real problem for us—the worst in the county. Seventy-five percent of Menards [employee] accounts with us are Medicaid, charity, or some sort of self-pay," and that meant low reimbursement, no reimbursement, or bad debt. "From a healthcare perspective, they are a horrible employer."

"We are seeing more bad debt than we were before [the passage of the Affordable Care Act and Medicaid expansion] from people who do have health insurance," said CHWC's CFO, Chad Tinkel. "Too many jobs do not offer benefits, and low wages qualify them for Medicaid."

Some of Hassouneh's patients made just enough money to be excluded from Medicaid, but not enough to live on and pay medical bills, too. Several times, when a patient appeared in her office complaining of abnormal bleeding, the doctor prescribed birth control pills to regulate the patients' periods. "And they'd say, 'I'll pick up the pills when I get my paycheck Thursday.' And I'd say, 'But you're bleeding right now!' So I'd give them $10 and say, 'Don't tell anybody. But go get your pills.'" One woman had severe chronic pelvic pain so bad she couldn't work. Finally the pain became so severe she broke down and visited Hassouneh, who diagnosed an early, treatable cancer. "Then she started crying, and said, 'But I don't know if I have enough gas to get back to Van Wert.' So I'm, like, 'Here. Here's ten bucks.'" Hassouneh continued to see the woman—who, now pain free, was able to get a job and begin pulling herself out of debt.

ER nurse Heather Gaylord found herself fighting the urge to judge. Most of the patients who swept through the ER weren't having an emergency at all: "People come in when they could spend $5 or $6 for some over-the-counter medication, which seems asinine to some of us," Gaylord said. "But lots of people don't have $5 or $6 to spend. I had one specifically ask for a prescription for ibuprofen, and I said, 'You can go to the vitamin store. It's, like, a dollar.' She said, 'We do not have a dollar.'" Such people sometimes exhausted Gaylord's patience. They were abusing the Medicaid system, the ER, her. When she felt grumpy about them, she'd try to imagine walking in their shoes for a while: What must that be like?

With high deductibles, no insurance, or sketchy insurance, people often tried to save money, sacrificing their health in the process. Marc Tingle's earnings varied, of course, but he netted about $37,000 a year, and Cindy Tingle's county job brought in another $11,000. So they were living, but it was never easy, and going to doctors was one more expense they didn't need.

Some—like Marc and like the husband with cancer in the ER—were critically ill before they visited doctors. "I had one guy, had pancreatic cancer," one of the ER docs working in the small Montpelier branch of CHWC said. The patient was a farmer, and "he didn't come in until he got his crops in, and then he came in because he had an infection. He had pain before, [but he ignored it]."

Pathologist Shannon Keil recalled a man who lived with a scrotal hernia for years before he was able to find insurance and have it repaired. "It came to me in a bucket!" she said. "It was five pounds! This guy's gut was in his nutsack."

"When I first started [at the CHWC women's clinic]," Hanan Bazzi recalled, "I had patients who hadn't had an exam for, like, ten, fifteen, twenty years. We found a lot of precancers and cancers. And it's because patients never actually came to see their doctor." The low incomes of many of her patients changed the way she practiced medicine.

"I am used to, like, you know, 'This is the differential diagnosis.' You order a slew of things, and you do not think necessarily about what it is going to cost your patient. You do that to rule out all the potential things that could happen. But I feel with these people, 'okay, let's see how much this is going to cost.' Or I try to answer things over the phone, or via my chart, via the [computer] portal so they don't have to pay a clinic visit. I try my best for these patients because, yes, it's horrible!" Several times, she said, she, like Hassouneh, reached into her purse to fish out a few dollars so patients could get a prescription filled.

"Diabetes emergencies are big," Jim Hicks, the EMS director, said of the number of calls for his ambulance crews. He figured lots of those calls came from poor people: they were more likely to have diabetes in the first place, and second, "they're not keepin' it controlled because they can't afford the meds and the services." (As a seizure patient told the Montpelier ER doctor to explain why he wasn't taking his drugs, "Doc, they're expensive. I gotta pay for food. And the TV.")

The wound where Keith's big toe used to be was healing, so he returned to work at Menards in late December. He was glad to be back in the warehouse. It was pretty cold in there—about fifty degrees with the big doors closed—and then, when they'd open up the bays to dock an incoming trailer encrusted with icicles, all that below-zero air would rush in. But Keith wore layers he could put on and peel off as necessary, so it wasn't so bad. He was just happy to be out of the recliner. He could talk to his buddy Zach Rhinard and his other coworkers, and he could feel productive again. That was the main thing. If his health held up, he figured he could dig his way out of the hole into which he'd fallen.

He knew it'd be a tough slog. He owed tens of thousands of dollars to Parkview for Stephanie's medical care, to CHWC for his care and hers, and to the various physician groups and pathology labs. But now that he was working again, he called up Fort Wayne and asked them to consolidate all those different bills and explain them to him—and then put him on some sort of payment plan. "They said it'd be a long process, a couple months maybe, and I was like, 'Fine. You guys wanna get paid, and I don't want my credit ruined.'" It was too late for that. Keith's credit score was already ruined: below 500, which was considered "very poor." But Keith set a goal of raising it over time by paying off a little debt every month.

He was grateful his landlord had a heart. She'd agreed to wait for some back rent, so that helped. He was behind on his child support for the son he'd had with his first wife. He was talking to the authorities up in Michigan, and had sent documentation of his recent medical troubles, so if they were reasonable, he'd be able to work that out, too.

His expenses worried him, but less than before, when he hadn't been sure he could feed Caleb. Now that real winter had descended on Bryan, he was paying about $360 a month for heat, power, and cable to Bryan Municipal Utilities. And since he was still technically employed by Menards during the period when he had to take leave to tend to his toe amputation and his eye, he'd met the sixty-day requirement to obtain health insurance, so he signed up. Once it kicked in, he would pay about $60 a week for a plan that carried a $5,000 deductible. He couldn't be sure if the insurance was active yet or not, or whether he really had Medicaid. The whole thing seemed complicated.

After accounting for insurance, utilities, and rent, Keith was left with about $1,000 a month from his gross salary—and that was without the deductions for taxes and Social Security. After those amounts were taken out, food and gas for the drive up to Holiday City chewed up a good portion of what was left. Still, with the addition of Caleb's Social Security money, Keith thought he could just make it. In fact, he said, "I'm tryin' to get my finances rearranged to help out [a relative of Stephanie's]." Helping other people made him feel good.

Though money would be tight for as long as he could see into the future, he'd been knocked down so far that every step he took felt like a step back up. He'd done it before when he lost his job at Hi-Lex in Michigan. He'd been low then, too, but he came to Bryan, stayed with Chad, met Stephanie, found a job at Ashley, and had Caleb. That was the way American life was supposed to work, and it had.

He also made a new friend, a woman named Bobbi. She lived up in Hillsdale and had a son Caleb's age, Gabe, with a chromosomal disorder that mimicked autism. She was broke, too. Her place in Hillsdale had sketchy heat and no washer or dryer. Since there'd been some trouble with the boyfriend of Stephanie's relative who'd been helping Keith (Keith accused him of using meth and stealing a few things), Keith figured Bobbi could come live with Caleb and him and take the place of the young woman who'd been helping out. Caleb would have another boy to play with, and Bobbi would have reliable heat and some companionship. It'd be a mutually beneficial friendship. He was still grieving the loss of Stephanie, so he couldn't tell if it would ever become more than a friendship, but he was willing to think about such a future.

A trip up to Grand Rapids for an RC car event also lifted Keith's mood.

(He and Bobbi and the two boys drove up in a snowstorm.) He had fun talking to guys he knew from RC car events. "They were givin' me hugs," he said. The RC car clan was a big family, and Keith liked feeling part of it. Come June, maybe he'd go to Lebanon, Ohio—maybe even out to California after that—for big RC car meets.

His health improved, too. He could see shadows out of his bad eye, which was better than nothing. He was hopeful another surgery would restore some more vision. The cost would take his whole deductible, he reckoned, so he wasn't sure how the finances would work, but he'd just put it on his growing personal tab, keep his head down, and plink what money he could at the bills. His toe amputation site looked a little better, too, and it seemed to be holding up to the pressure of his work at Menards.

To others, Keith's plans and hopes may have seemed dreamy. But Keith believed he lived in an America where only those people who'd messed up their own lives with drugs or by doing bad things—by being unkind and untrue—found themselves caught in the flypaper of despair.

He believed in Barack Obama, and had voted for him because he said he could get the country out of the recession. Then he believed in Donald Trump, and had voted for him because he said he would make all the other countries be fair to America because America was getting a raw deal, and because Keith was feeling beaten up, too, and looked upon Trump as a surrogate who could change what he could not. He didn't like Trump much as a man. Trump behaved in ways Keith never would. Keith tried to be nice to people. He liked doing favors for people. Trump was a little scummy, and that made Keith uncomfortable, but the economy seemed to be doing okay, and Keith figured he would now be able to catch the trailing breeze of the expansion.

But as the winter transitioned from the Christmas season and the new year came, Keith was being forced to conclude that his world wasn't what he'd hoped. He'd begun to say that "lots of people these days, their word doesn't mean anything. Being stand-up doesn't mean anything." He'd think back to a time maybe twenty years ago—before the recession, for sure—and how people had been back then. Now everything seemed meaner and lonelier.

Keith lived in Pastor Greg Coleman's America now. One event after another, minor and major, proved it. Not long after he started back at Menards, another of Stephanie's relatives fell ill with the flu and was prescribed Tamiflu, a drug manufactured by the Swiss company Roche, which had a gross profit of about $20.7 billion in 2018. Keith gave the relative $40 to buy the Tamiflu, even though he couldn't afford it. She drove to the drugstore, then sent a text. She'd need three times as much: $120. Such a price seemed so incredible, Keith didn't believe her. Maybe she was trying to weasel more money out of him. So she sent another text with a photo of the Tamiflu with the $120 price.

Not long after that, Keith got in the old Jeep he'd partially rebuilt himself and started driving home from Menards. A big Chevy truck approached a turn near the Menards entrance from the other side of Traxler Drive. The truck began to slide on the ice. Keith stopped the Jeep and watched, helpless, as the truck skated with slow-motion inevitability into his Jeep and jammed it against a curb. Nobody was hurt, but the force damaged Keith's suspension, killing the Jeep for good. He wasn't angry at the other driver, who was apologetic. But it was all he could do to not cry in front of him.

The insurance company paid Keith $2,500. Keith needed wheels to get to work, of course, but $2,500 wouldn't buy him much. So he went to a "buy-here-pay-here" (BHPH) used car dealer in Bryan, where his shattered credit and dim prospects wouldn't matter.

The buy-here-pay-here dealers' trade organization, the National Independent Automobile Dealers Association (NIADA), viewed buy-here-pay-here dealers as the mobility saviors of low-income working-class people like Keith, who had no place else to turn. At their dealerships, the customer bought the car at the lot with some money down and borrowed the rest, usually from the dealer. The customer then made payments at the lot (buy-here-pay-here), typically weekly or biweekly.

The number of deep subprime auto loans given to people with bad credit soared after the Great Recession and continued to remain high, especially in communities like Bryan and in counties like Williams, where people worked for low wages. A lot of people in such places had bad credit and low incomes.

As an accounting consultant to the industry wrote to buy-here-pay-here dealers, they were "selling money, not cars." And there was a lot of money to be made selling money to poor people. Buy-here-pay-here dealerships made net profits of about 12 percent, while new car sales netted profits of between 2 and 4 percent. The dealers typically bought high-mileage cars from auto auctions. ("In BHPH one fact of life is vehicle breakdowns," a consultant advised dealers in 2019.) Operators spruced the cars up a little and then sold them—often at double the wholesale price they paid for them. NIADA dealers like the one Keith turned to charged, on average, 20 percent interest for a car loan. (Regular auto loans at the time of Keith's accident could be had for about 3.5 percent from credit unions by customers with good credit.) Buy-here-pay-here businesses expected a lot of their customers to default, so they installed GPS tracking devices, and often "kill switches." That way the dealers knew just where the car was at all times and could disable it if the customer was late with a payment. "Lenders [are] repossessing at a record pace," the same consultant wrote. Once they repossessed the car, they could sell it again. And again.

The buy-here-pay-here industry was jubilant at the election of Donald Trump in 2016. For years the trade group had fought regulation by the new Consumer Financial Protection Bureau (CFPB), which in 2013 banned forced arbitration of disputes and allowed borrowers to seek redress in courts. The CFPB had also asserted it could regulate the dealers' financing schemes. But in 2018, at the time Stephanie Swihart's symptoms were worsening, congressional Republicans, to whom the NIADA made generous campaign contributions (NIADA also donated to Democrat Nancy Pelosi), passed a joint resolution calling on Trump to nullify the CFPB's assertion of jurisdiction. Trump signed it into law on May 21.

So Keith found himself negotiating with a newly unleashed buy-here-pay-here dealer who sold him a 2007 Saturn Outlook SUV with 140,000 miles on it for $15,000. Keith handed over the $2,500 insurance money and drove out owing $12,500 he had no hope of repaying (though he insisted he could): $110 every week, at 21 percent interest.

He thought about the rusty clunkers he might have bought for $2,500. The math made more sense, but to a man who had nothing, sitting high up in the Outlook—its shiny cream color brightened by the dealer's polish, its interior leather seats soft—the SUV had a tonic effect. He was somebody again.

There was another reason he'd bought the car: he'd just had another reminder of just how short life could be. Three days before the accident that wrecked the Jeep, Keith's best friend at Menards, Zach Rhinard, pressed a gun to his head and pulled the trigger. Zach shot himself almost two years to the day after Chad had put the barrel of a rifle in his mouth during that final phone conversation with Stephanie.

Jim Hicks took the call for EMS because both squads were already out. He hadn't had a day off in a week, but he stayed on the scene while a squad arrived. He left on another call, then returned. It was three hours before they could carry Zach's body away.

Keith was crushed. He couldn't figure it out. People were killing themselves all around him—if not with guns, by hanging, or in a car, then with drugs. Not long after Zach shot himself, Roger Mann, a sixty-seven-year-old from up around Lake Seneca, walked into his bathroom, pressed a handgun to his head, and pulled the trigger. A few days after that, Latasha Currence, a thirty-seven-year-old homemaker who loved to fish, cook, and help her friends, took fentanyl and some amphetamines and some other drugs and died in the home she'd made. Zach had cheered up Keith at a time when Keith was hungry for cheer, and if Zach thought there was no point in living, how was Keith supposed to regard his own life?

"I had a guy at work—he made the comment—he looked at me and said, 'That shoulda been you, all the crap you been through,' and I looked at him, like, laughing, and smiling, but I felt like slapping him. I mean, that's not even funny, you know? Look what happened to me in the last year. Last two years! I mean, it takes something to drive somebody to that point, you know? Like, 'I can't take it.'"

Keith had liked hearing about Zach's time in the service. He had joined the Marines right out of high school, like a lot of young men in Williams County. The Marines helped Zach add a few pounds of beef onto his tall, skinny frame, and he tried to fill the gung-ho jarhead role. He had his last name tattooed across his back in big black Gothic letters. He posed for a social media post with his best jutted-jaw, steely-eyed face as he knelt beside an 81-millimeter mortar in his green camos: "81mm of death, pain and destruction. ususus." But Zach's soft eyes betrayed him. He wasn't cut out to stay in the Marines for good. He was honorably discharged, became a reservist, headed back home, and took the job at Menards.

Zach didn't love Menards. It was just a job. He goofed off once in a while, trying to have some fun in the cavernous warehouse by hiding behind tall stacks of big boxes with barcode labels pasted to their sides and "Holiday City" inked onto them. He even built a little "fort" out of boxes in a dark section of the building. Zach posted a photo for his Instagram followers of himself behind the wall of cardboard in a hoodie and knit hat against the cold of the warehouse with a big grin on his face: a mischievous child playing hooky.

When he wasn't working, Zach liked to go fishing for catfish at night, hang out with his bros, drive his car with the stereo blasting, and go target shooting. He had a necklace made out of a chain similar to those used to hold dog tags. A brass-colored, rocket-shaped bullet hung from it. As far as Keith could see, Zach was like a hundred other fellas. That's why Keith couldn't figure out what had happened. Zach was just twenty. He was "a good friend. He asked me questions. We talked a lot. I didn't know things were that bad for him. He didn't show it."

There wasn't an obvious answer. Zach had been bored: "Boring day today, boring days to come," he'd said. But a lot of young men in Williams County were bored. There wasn't all that much to do other than the things Zach was already doing. Something wore on him—that was for sure.

Zach had copied and sent an image of a cartoon by artist Kristian Nygard to his Instagram followers. It depicted a black, faceless wraith struggling to get out of bed to start his day. The wraith staggered to his closet, which was full of human suits. He zipped himself into the human suit of a smiling, happy young man with glasses. Nygard had titled this "Dressing Up."

Not long before he picked up the gun, Zach sent out a selfie with a caption: "If we go our separate ways just know it's all love." Another selfie followed with Zach in a backward baseball cap and hoodie. Its caption read: "*Ich bin innerlich tot*"—German for "I'm dead inside." And then there was another self-portrait, a little blurry, hatless, a thin smile: "I don't know."

There was no alcohol in his body, no drugs of any kind. The Williams County coroner, Kevin Park, a Parkview doctor, entered "reactive depression" (also called "situational depression"), meaning depression triggered by events in one's life, on Zach's death record.

"I can't believe it," Keith said. "He had so much to live for. It's sad. It's very sad. The thing I'm tryin' to wrap my head around is: What was the trigger? I don't understand it."

We happened to be sitting in a booth at the Four Seasons diner on Main Street when he said this. It was a Saturday morning. He'd ordered the Dixie Breakfast: a split biscuit with sausage gravy, three eggs, hash browns, two strips of bacon, and two sausage links. All for $8.95.

After breakfast, Keith drove to the cemetery to visit Stephanie. We sat in the Outlook, high above her grave. Keith was still steamed the headstone wasn't in place. He'd driven up to Montpelier, to the workshop, and seen it. The company told him that now that winter had settled and frozen the ground, it might be spring before it was installed. "I was so angry," he said. "But I sat there nice and quietly and walked away. Because if I get angry and mad, what will that solve?" He was silent for a long time.

"You okay?" I asked.

"Doin' good, buddy. Doin' good."

███

That same week, Judy Hartman drove the ambulance as fast as she dared, with Misty Dean beside her and the siren screaming, over an icy Ohio Route 15. Cars slowed to a tiptoe as they pulled over onto the berm, trying to stay out of the high piles made by the plows but get far enough over so the ambulance could pass. The temperature had dropped to –8 the night before, and it was just above zero now, at 1:15 in the afternoon, and breezy, too. The cold sliced through you. With the ambulance's heater blasting, Dean and Hartman were too hot in their layers, but they knew they wouldn't be for long.

Hartman made it to the corner of Route 15 and Traxler Drive in about nine minutes. She took another minute to cover the distance between there and the guard shack where a NOW HIRING sign offered jobs at Menards. The guard waved her through, and she crawled over what had turned into acres of snow-covered ice, passing rank upon rank of semitruck trailers until she spotted a man waving her down. She pulled into a row of trailers where a group of men huddled, surrounding another man who lay on the ice. He was shaking like a can of paint getting mixed at a hardware store.

Brad Stoner*—in his forties—wasn't sure how long he'd been down. He wasn't a good judge of the time because he was in agonizing pain and so cold his body temperature had dropped by three degrees. He wore a sweatshirt, a pair of jeans, and work boots—but no jacket, no hat, no gloves.

He'd been driving doubles: two trailers hooked together and towed by a tractor. He climbed out of his cab to break apart the doubles, thinking it would take just a couple of minutes. He was trying to position the jiff—the four-wheel axle equipped with the greased disc that connects to a trailer—when he slipped on the ice. Stoner fell under the jiff, and weight equal to a small car landed with a sickening thud on his ankle and lower leg, crushing them.

He screamed, but he was alone. He screamed again. No reply. The shivering started right away. Every shake triggered a fresh bolt of pain. He tried to remain still, but he couldn't. He screamed some more. He'd started out from his home in Michigan that morning to drop a load at Menards and pick one up at Spangler Candy, and now he imagined freezing to death on a patch of ice-covered blacktop in Holiday City, Ohio. It could happen. Just the other day, a ninety-four-year-old woman had frozen to death in Alvordton.

Was it ten minutes? Fifteen minutes? Longer? Maybe. Finally a UPS driver pulled in and heard Stoner's shouts. Somebody called Williams County EMS.

The call would be one of four hundred runs Jim Hicks's EMS crews would make in January. That was a new record. The volume just kept rising, month after month, but more business didn't mean EMS was flush. Hicks, like the hospital, struggled with payments. Unlike in most Ohio counties, the system was not supported by a tax levy. It operated on insurance reimbursements by billing the people its ambulances carried—about $800 for a standard run, $1,200 for a transfer to Fort Wayne or Toledo, plus $14 a mile—then trying to recoup the charges after the patient's insurance company paid off. But with deductibles so high, and with so many living so close to poverty, Hicks couldn't be sure he'd ever see the money.

Widows would come to his office to plead their cases after their husbands died following an ambulance trip; perhaps the widows had to move in with an elderly mother and had to find a job themselves. Or maybe a woman was a wife who couldn't work because she had multiple sclerosis and, sometimes, while her husband was away at his job, she'd fall and couldn't get back up, and because they couldn't afford a health aide, the EMS would come to put her back in the wheelchair—a run not covered by any insurance—and if they couldn't afford a health aide, how were they going to afford to pay for that run? So Hicks did his best to make deals. He often accepted whatever an insurance company paid the customer and forgave the rest of the bill. Sometimes he set up payment plans. Sometimes he just wrote it off. "I'm grateful," he said, "that I have the freedom to do that."

The helicopters that flew into Bryan to pick up emergency transfer patients weren't so understanding. A ProMedica flight to Toledo, a Parkview flight to Fort Wayne, or to either from any of the other companies that flew around northwest Ohio cost between $47,000 and $55,000 depending upon the level of care needed in flight. Insurance covered some patients, but others found themselves in life-altering debt.

The county commissioners did pay the EMS health insurance bill of about $230,000 a year, so that didn't have to come out of Hicks's budget, but without the support of a levy, he had to run EMS on a diet of about $1.4 million a year. He hoped to earn about $1.5 million a year in the "eat-what-you-kill" billing system. Whatever profit he made had to be saved for future expenses. A heart monitor cost $27,000. A new ambulance cost about $140,000, and Hicks needed new ambulances.

As it was, he said, Obamacare and Medicaid expansion saved Williams County EMS. "People thought nobody would survive Obamacare, but they found out different."

A fully qualified emergency medical technician for Williams County EMS earned $13.50 an hour. Top-line veterans made $15. Some Williams County EMS personnel made $11. Brock Zuver, a young EMT, earned $9.50, so he lived with his mother and worked other jobs: he farmed and worked part-time for the village of Pioneer's fire department as well as for an auction company. The lousy wages for his crews frustrated Hicks. Crews in Archbold, across the county line, made just over $19 an hour. Hicks lost staff. He'd get them trained and working well, and then they'd light out for some other service. In the twelve years he'd been full-time with Williams County, he'd gone through about fifty people. He didn't blame them for leaving.

The county's 421 square miles was a lot of territory to cover—other than Montpelier, there were no doctors' offices in outlying villages since Parkview took over the medical group—and he could maintain only two full-time crews and ambulances to cover them. That meant that if somebody was having a heart attack in Walmart and there was a car accident on County Road 13, the person having a stroke at Lake Seneca was out of luck. That was a big reason he wanted to stop long-distance transfers out of the county: they tied up an ambulance for two hours.

Hicks wanted a levy. The way he figured it, EMS was a community function like police and fire. He could make that case to voters, he thought, many of whom already believed the EMS ran off tax money. But the county commissioners resisted. They didn't like taxes.

Hicks loved his job, though. He'd worked for an ambulance outfit in Toledo and found that in a smaller community "You get rewarded for it. You save somebody's life, and boy, you hear about it."

▌▌▌

In the Menards truck lot, Dean, Hartman, and an EMS volunteer from the township rolled Brad Stoner onto a blanket, then picked him up as if handling a Tiffany vase. He screamed. They laid him down on the squad's gurney, covered him with another blanket, and rolled the gurney a couple of feet to the electric hoist in the back of the ambulance. Stoner, half frozen, shook with epileptic fury.

The heater in the squad was still pumping out hot air, but, with that kind of cold, Dean knew that a person had to be warmed from the inside, too. She and Hartman scissored off parts of his sweatshirt and pants leg. Hartman held down his arm while Dean inserted a needle to start an IV of warm fluid. Then Dean pushed 50 micrograms of fentanyl into the line.

His shivering didn't stop right away, making it tough to get a blood pressure reading. The electrodes on patches stuck to his chest told the EKG machine that his heart was triggering premature ventricular contractions—his heart was fluttering. Maybe it was the cold, or the adrenaline, or maybe he had a heart condition. They asked Stoner about it: "All I know was I was screamin' and screamin'!"

Hartman drove while Dean tended their patient. His shivering began to calm a little. "How's the pain?" Dean asked. "Awful," he answered. She pushed another 50 micrograms of fentanyl and alerted CHWC to the patient's status, his vital signs, and their estimated arrival.

"I was supposed to go to Spangler Candy to pick up another load," Stoner said. Dean told him Spangler Candy was just a block or two away from the hospital. "Guess I'll make it there," he said.

The fentanyl began to work. Dean looked at Stoner's pupils. They'd turned into black saucers. "I think you're feelin' a little better," she said.

"Yeah," he answered. He became talkative. He was surprised Dean had heard of a jiff, but she explained she had an ex who drove, and so she knew all about trucks. He relaxed a little—whether from the opioid or from the conversation was hard to tell—so Dean asked again about his heart.

"I don't go to the doctor much. My wife keeps tellin' me I should go." He'd driven tankers hauling gas and diesel for three years, he said. This was the first winter he'd driven doubles for the trucking company, and he didn't like it. "You gotta do what you gotta do to make a living," Dean said.

Making a living in the United States wasn't easy for people like Valerie and Brad Stoner—nor for people like Dean and Hartman. If you were a police and fire dispatcher in Bryan, you started at $11.76 an hour, about what Taco Bell offered.

Minimum wage in Ohio was $8.30 per hour (it would rise to $8.55 in 2019)—lower than it was in 1968, when adjusted for inflation. Some other states mandated even lower minimums by matching the federal minimum wage of $7.25.

Working-class wages in the United States just about flatlined from 1979 to 2017. Over that thirty-seven years, the bottom 10 percent of earners saw a 4.1 percent rise in wages. Meanwhile, economic productivity rose 70 percent. Most of the reward for that productivity was scooped up by the top 5 percent of earners, who enjoyed a 69.3 percent rise in real wages. The top 0.1 percent increased their haul by over 343 percent.

From 2000 through 2018, the average hourly wages of a white high school graduate in the United States, as expressed in 2018 dollars, rose $1.75—from $18.60 to $19.75. Wages for African American high school graduates dropped during that period: from $15.75 to $15.57. Most workers in Williams County were high school graduates. Only 14.6 percent had a bachelor's degree.

Insecurity had percolated through the working and middle classes for over a generation. Then the recession hit, and one generation turned into two. Long after it was over and many Americans had moved on, many others remained anxious—always—even people who seemed to have no reason to be. George Magill, Keith's doctor at the CHWC wound care clinic, had a brother-in-law who worked at the big Whirlpool washing machine factory in Clyde, Ohio, outside of Toledo. He'd risen through the ranks over his long career and made good money: $30 an hour. But when he got sick, coughing so hard he passed out on the factory floor, he didn't go to a doctor. "Man, I'm workin' three jobs!" he said. "I couldn't afford to take the time to be sick, to see a doctor. Turned out I had pneumonia." Luckily for him, there was a doctor in the family—he called Magill, who prescribed an antibiotic.

He didn't have any big complaints about Whirlpool. And he didn't have to work three jobs. But he was scared. He remembered when Whirlpool bought out Maytag of Newton, Iowa, closed the Newton plant, and sent the jobs to Mexico. That was a "bad deal," he said. It made him wonder what could happen to him.

That was the thing: you never could know. Anything could happen at any time. There was nothing you could count on, and the insecurity bred by that knowledge had now been indelibly etched into the minds—and often the bodies—of every working person for the past forty years.

Tonie Long, with her decades of experience as a social worker, had come to believe this was part of the American sickness. "You wanna know what's going on in our country?" she asked, referring to Pastor Greg Coleman's diagnosis. Long, the woman from the Alcohol, Drug Addiction and Mental Health Services board who'd sparked discomfort among the school administrators by insisting the health needs assessment include questions about gays and lesbians and trans kids, had a few ideas that had germinated over her thirty-year career: "There's nothing you can really believe in. We say we hold these American ideals, but then we don't live by them." The ideals, she said, are fake. "They are like clothes," she said. "We put this stuff on the outside, but inside—who we are? Who are we?

"We say we believe in people working hard, and people being true and honest, but we don't really believe that. We have set up a society in which people are not paid enough wages to buy the products they are producing. Companies want more and more profit and less and less well-being for their workers" while simultaneously projecting "impossible standards of what a successful life in this country looks like. But [people] are not paid enough to achieve it. . . .

"We were built on the idea of the American Dream. You pull yourself up by bootstraps. You work hard—and that's all true—but people must have opportunities to work hard, and I mean work hard so you get ahead and things get better for you. But then they don't.

"If you are a person who does not have any means—you're poor, living in Williams County, and that is your whole experience—what are your options? We say in America anything is possible. Well, how? If you've got babies? Have you seen the price of childcare? And you wanna work where? And for how much?" Many say "'choices have to be made and sacrifices made,' but why should only poor people have to make sacrifices and choices?"

She used words that evoked those of hospital board member Chris

Kannel, who said Williams County had to lift its eyes to Jesus to cure its heart problem, but she had a different target in mind. "They keep us looking down. If we looked up, where the real crime and greed is going on, and people are raking in enormous amounts of money and power and rigging the system so people cannot get ahead . . . ?" She raised her eyebrows at the prospect of what might happen if people looked up.

Failure to thrive, and the constant nagging pressure to conform to what constitutes a successful American life, could, and did, lead to spirit-sapping disappointment. You didn't have to be poor or working-class to feel it. As part of her job, Long coordinated Local Outreach to Suicide Survivors (LOSS) teams in the four counties. She had as much experience with suicide and suicide survivors as anybody in northwest Ohio. In one week, she had served the family of a wealthy man who flew his own airplane as well as the family of a man who was broke. The lie, she said, victimized both the haves and the have-nots. Both were told there was one version of a successful American life, and it was the consumerist ideal. Those who succeeded in aping that version were seen not only as successful and smarter but also as good. Only flawed people failed to achieve it. But even those who seemed to have won the American race could suffer, because "when the storm comes—and it comes to all of us—they find out having that perfect pair of jeans and the right manicure doesn't help you in this situation. That can be devastating. That's one reason why suicide cuts across everything. That is really a dark place to be, to make the decision you want to end your life."

America had turned its dream into a formula for disappointment. Disappointment led to anxiety, and anxiety could lead to the erosion of health; if twisted and deliberately manipulated, it could lead to fear, hate, paranoia, and self-loathing. Those people who were a rung or two higher on the well-being ladder and still had something to lose feared losing it, while despising those they thought were dragging them down due to their lack of self-control, their inability to act like responsible, conformist citizens. Their poor health was their own fault. And the poor—many of them, anyway—had come to believe all that, too. Something had to be wrong with them—inside their heads, inside their bones, inside their hearts—so what was the use of trying so hard anymore? "If you have people who are impoverished, and do not have a way out of that poverty," Long continued, "at some point, it becomes this learned helplessness in terms of being able to control their own health. It never gets better, so why try? How long would *you* try," she asked, "before you say, 'You know what? I'm tired.'"

It was common in Williams County for people to say that the poor and working-class complained they had no money but owned or rented giant flat-screen TVs. And it was true, too. Long thought it was "crazy" that so many homes she entered had the TVs. But as CHWC social worker Linda Trausch liked to point out, "If you were never going to take a vacation, never go anywhere, maybe never go to the movies—that TV is your entertainment." With rewards so long delayed, or with no chance of a reward at all, a "bad" choice could seem like the most reasonable, desirable choice, whether it was a Dixie Breakfast, an SUV, or a TV.

Given enough time, defeat could become a culture. Your parents were disappointed and defeated. They struggled for the very basics: a roof, food, clean water, some clothes. They had no time to read to you, to nurture and mentor you, to help you do homework. They couldn't put you in soccer or on the swim team because they had no cash to buy the shoes or the goggles. And so you learned from disappointment and defeat.

Montpelier police chief Dan Magee arrested generations of the same families. "If you're lucky enough to have longevity [in the job], you'll deal with grandkids," he said. "See, they have the same plights in life. Living underprivileged, living in the same sort of economic group, doing the same types of jobs, making the same decisions. And you see what happened with the grandfather—healthwise, actionwise, decisionwise—is happening with young kids."

Sarah Vashaw often witnessed the dynamic. "For instance, this mom today," she began. "I went to see her because her child missed 132 hours of school." Vashaw was one of the social workers/psychologists Ennen helped place in the schools. She also happened to be the wife of Kurt Vashaw, a scion of the Spangler clan and the current CEO of the candy company. "She had no lights. It was freezing, because her electricity had been turned off. The place was a disaster. But she welcomed me into her home. She was obviously depressed. She'd been in and out of jail due to drugs, she'd been the victim of domestic violence, and was the victim of something growing up, and I am sure this is trauma playing out before my eyes. She'd been working at [a fast-food franchise] but they just closed without any warning. She found out the day before the closing she was losing her job. No phone. No car."

She defended Spangler, which had a reputation in town for trying to pay well (a candy packer made $14.15 per hour), but "well" in Williams County wasn't great. "Gosh, I think, could I make it on $32,000 a year? I could, but it would be hard. And some other people make less, and they have kids. That's stressful."

Constant stress, trauma, and depression molded the psyches of people like the woman Vashaw was trying to help, affecting everything in their lives. "They don't have the ability to cope with regular stress. They can't self-regulate enough to maintain for eight hours to get through boring, menial tasks like working on a line. They don't have the psychological flexibility to persevere. The cycle of poverty is traumatizing: the domestic violence, witnessing parents using drugs and everything that goes with that. It's snowballing. It's not getting better. I'm pretty pessimistic."

Even suicide could become part of a culture. "If somebody you know, or in your family, has ever taken their life," Long said, "it is another huge risk factor. It breaks a taboo. It becomes a solution to look at."

Long, who grew up eating government cheese, believed many all over the United States had been tossed aside. But they still existed—lived and breathed—and they not only triggered anxiety in themselves but also in those above them. They were the "lowlifes" and "drug addicts" cited by opponents of the Community Health Center. They were the people like Keith who needed Medicaid. They were the people who stood patiently in line at the charity food pantry held by the Methodist church across the street from the YMCA on the west side of Bryan.

"Didya hear my sister's pregnant?" "No!" "Yep. Four months." "From Jeff?" "Yeah." "She still usin'?" A nod. "Heavy?" A nod. "That baby'll . . . won't make it. If it does, it'll be born addicted fer sure. They'll take it away, give it to Child Protective or whatever it's called now. She been to a doctor?" "No." "That's maybe a good thing. If she gets tested, she'll get arrested." "She's got fourteen months hanging over her head in Indiana. She needs to stay out of there."

Another woman in line complained about her husband who worked as a janitor. He came home for lunch while she was out chopping wood for heat, but "he don't wanna help. He wants to complain about his job. We're takin' bets how long he has it. He won't get no more jobs if he keeps quittin' 'em." Though the husband worked full-time, they qualified for food stamps. She was in line because the government had shut down over Trump's insistence on money to build a border wall, and she was stocking up, worried the benefits would stop "'cause Trump, he don't get his way."

A regular, a military veteran about sixty, wearing a tattered topcoat that had once been dapper and shoes that had once held a shine, had appointed himself the advice-giver and helper to others. To an older man, also a veteran, who said he didn't go to doctors because of the expense, he said he got on a bus and went to Toledo, to the VA, though the trip took all day. The old man should, too.

He turned to a younger woman, maybe thirty-three: scrawny, hair in disarray, fright in her eyes, a cast on her wrist. She'd just been released from jail. This was her first trip to the pantry. She was married, she told the older man. She and her husband were living in an old trailer—without heat or plumbing—on somebody's property. "I got to keep running into [the nearby] house to get water and use the toilet," she told the man, who was explaining how to use the pantry. "And my husband, he just sez, 'I'll get a bucket,' and I'm like, 'I ain't usin' no bucket,' and he's like, 'I'll empty it!' And so I said, 'You empty it, okay.'"

A seventy-nine-year-old woman with a walker and a life-monitor button hanging around her neck, where, it seemed, a string of pearls should have been, couldn't manage her boxes. They were filled with chili, noodles, ramen, instant beans and rice, off-brand imitations of Cheerios and cornflakes, expired desserts like cupcakes and cheesecake, black bananas, a bag of spinach, and cucumbers. She was hoarding the food in her old station wagon, already full of junk and papers. It was parked next to the Buicks and Pontiacs of a generation ago, now patched with Bondo and held together by rust.

Nobody regarded the pantry and the people waiting in line as medical symptoms, but they were. They were symptoms of a deeply rooted American disease incubated by a brutal economy that left them, and, in some cases their parents, behind. Over years—over two generations—they'd become part of a culture of defeat, what doctors liked to call "noncompliant." When doctors used the term they meant somebody who didn't take prescribed medications or didn't exercise as recommended. These people were noncompliant in a bigger sense. They no longer complied with society's prescriptions. They were either unable or unwilling to obey. Maybe some of them had tried to obey, once, but obeying didn't lead anywhere better, or obeying was just too difficult because everything cost so much, or was so hard to achieve, and so they said to hell with it.

"I think, with [money], you have the ability to cope a little more than someone who is always trying to cover their bills with that one paycheck," Bryan mayor Carrie Schlade said. "Because there's so many factors in their life that they can't control if that paycheck doesn't come through."

The world Dan Magee policed in Montpelier was not a world where the mother was home to greet the children rushing in from school. There were no Swiffers and Fords and Nature Valley granola bars and Ralph Lauren school clothes. His world was not the one on the west side of Bryan, where most people were clean and smiled with bright, white, straight teeth. "When people tell you to do something," Long said, "and if you're not able to do that, something is broken in you. You cannot follow these instructions. We've told you you need to exercise! We've told you you need to eat differently! We've told you you need to go to the doctor! The information is out there."

The inability to comply was the worst of the character flaws. Many in Bryan were convinced a lot of noncompliant people had seeped into their town. Almost nobody really needed to get food from food pantries, they said. People wanted something for nothing. No doubt some people *did* want something for nothing, Long said. People did abuse charity and what remained of the public safety net. "But those assholes stand out," she said.

And the better-off people who complained about the "everybody-gets-a-trophy" culture as a cause of the lack of coping skills in children weren't wrong, either. But Long believed that the middle- and upper-class obsessions with trophy-giving—the catering, the hovering—were driven by fear. Not only were parents terrified their children wouldn't have everything they saw in America's consumer paradise—implicating them as parental failures—but the pressure to accumulate trophies and inflated school grades were arrows in their quiver in the great American battle to rack up childhood "achievement" as a way to assure that their children had a future chance in a society obsessed by rank: academic rank, athletic rank, beauty rank. You didn't want to wind up working at Menards, but Menards was a safety net if you didn't get into the right college.

There was fear everywhere. People had convinced themselves, or had been convinced, that the world was an unsafe place. But though Williams County had a meth problem and some theft, the crime rate was low. Some people in Bryan still left their doors unlocked.

Crime was far from West Unity's biggest problem. Yet the Mill

Creek–West Unity School District, which covered fifty square miles and educated about 630 students from kindergarten through high school in one school building—and where 38.6 percent of the children qualified for free or reduced-price school lunch—had equipped that school with forty-eight security cameras. "School resource officers"—police and sheriff's deputies—were assigned to schools around the county.

There was fear of difference. "Even the Williams County health assessment!" Long recalled of the autumn meeting at the hospital. "You saw the reaction when I said we shouldn't take out questions around LGBT identity. You could have heard a pin drop. It's not a pie! It's not like, if I give you rights and dignity, it takes away from me."

There was a corrosive strain of such fear in Williams County. "As I watch these Democrats asking for votes while giving these illegals everything free, it's very disgusting," Bryan resident Rochelle Lee wrote to the *Bryan Times*. "These people are not supposed to be here and get everything for free. How about taking care of our own. We have seniors trying to live on less than $1,000 a month. Take a look at how we're being treated now—just imagine how we'd be treated if these people had full power. No thanks!"

The east side had always been the working-class side. Before it was torn down and all the city's elementary schools unified into one building on the west side, the wealthier west-side kids called the east-side school "Stinkin' Lincoln." But there were some nice homes there, too, and vibrant churches like Valerie's Lutheran, and there was Miller's grocery store. People on the east side walked to Miller's for provisions. When Miller's installed gas pumps, you could earn points for buying groceries there and then turn them into big gas discounts. A lot of people counted on the cut-rate gas in a region where, if you didn't walk to work—and many did, to ARO and Spangler—you could wind up driving twenty miles each way to your job.

But, especially since the recession, the east side felt dumped upon. Home ownership dropped. Local investors bought houses on the cheap and rented them out. Many of those houses just kept crumbling. The low rents attracted people who had trouble affording housing in other, more well-to-do communities like Toledo's suburbs, or who had lost jobs in villages like Fayette, as Valerie's father had lost his. An east-side low-income apartment complex, Meadow Creek, built by an out-of-town development company with help from federal tax credits and a federally funded state and local grant program, came to be known as "Ghetto Creek." Miller's closed.

The church pews emptied. The old rivalry between east side and west side turned bitter.

"I had one guy chase me on a lawn mower, calling me every kind of name because I was a west-side snob, and I needed to get off of his property," Mayor Schlade recalled of a time when she was helping to campaign door-to-door for a school levy. "So there's some anger with that. It was something that I hadn't wrapped my head around."

Tonie Long's view was that of a secular professional, a social worker, but it wasn't much different from that held by Pastor Greg Coleman, a man who believed that "hell is the default" and that we lived in a broken, sinful world and were all going there unless we adopted God's rescue plan. Like Long, Coleman believed that a culture of defeat had sprouted and spread. Some old, established families in grand homes, and a few landowning farmers, lived in the area around West Unity, giving the village and its immediate surroundings a lower poverty rate than those of most other county census tracts. But now there were also a lot of semi-nomads, driven on by low incomes. They'd move into an apartment or a ramshackle house, and a few months later they'd be forced to seek even lower rents. A few lived in the Dodge Hotel, a dilapidated two-story redbrick structure built in the 1880s. It had iffy heat and shared bathrooms. Coleman's church sometimes gave those residents food, but they were unable to cook it because there were no stoves, or because they had only an electric skillet. Others lived in single-wides or Section 8 apartments and houses.

Coleman's church distributed between $5,000 and $15,000 annually in utility-bill assistance. In some months, it provided $400 in gasoline vouchers so people could get to jobs. Transportation was difficult for many: they either didn't have a car or didn't have one that worked. A few drove without licenses and insurance.

Coleman was stumped about what to do about all of this. He was torn between loving small communities (a little more than 1,600 people lived in West Unity), feeling they were necessary to America's social fabric, and recognizing that many had been turned into zombie places where the old and established finished out their lives, the young escaped if they could, and the nomads passed through. Anxiety and depression—and the self-medication that came with them—were now among his biggest pastoral concerns. (A member of his own family had acted out suicidal behaviors.) The inaccessibility and unaffordability of care only aggravated the damage.

Though he didn't claim to have solutions, he knew how this had happened and how it had affected the health of his people. When he diagnosed it, he sounded like Tonie Long. Of course people didn't make long-term goals and think far ahead. In his village, people just hoped they could make it to the end of the week with the last dollar in their pocket so they could wake up Monday and do it all again.

Employers didn't want to pay people enough to live dignified lives. Yet they demanded fully trained workers who were drug tested, credentialed, and free of any criminal record. Employers didn't teach people anymore, the way they once had, and as unions died away union training programs went with them. "Workforce development" became a government responsibility: its benefits spilled from the lips of public officials, economic boosters, school administrators. Educating young people in civic life, history, the arts, how to be a responsible and empathetic citizen in a democracy, and how to live the rich life of a human being seemed secondary to feeding the need of employers for human capital. (In 2015, Wisconsin governor Scott Walker tried to change the state university's mission statement to exclude "search for truth" and "improve the human condition" in favor of "meet the state's workforce needs." In February 2020, Ohio's state superintendent of schools, Paolo DeMaria, would change the requirements for high school graduation: students would no longer have to achieve a proficient rating in either math or English to graduate. DeMaria set the standard in consultation with industry as a way to tailor the "workforce" to its needs.) Kid jobs had disappeared. Adults needed that work now, and yet people complained that teenagers had no work ethic and sat around all day playing with the apps on their phones.

The glue that formed community had become brittle. During the Great Depression, many people in small places like West Unity were carried by family-owned grocery stores, hardware stores, gas stations. Those owners lived in the communities and helped their neighbors. During the recession, Coleman watched people approach big chain stores with hopeless expressions in their eyes. One store in West Unity, Handyman Hardware, stood out because it was run by the family that owned it. They floated more people than they should have, sometimes even offering to fix whatever it was a customer was struggling to repair. Handyman Hardware was the exception that underscored the change. Menards wasn't about to let a customer walk out of a store without paying.

The sum of all these changes, he thought, had helped cultivate a feeling of helplessness and passivity. He called it "the impoverished mindset." With the impoverished mindset, one's only capital was social, invested in other people. The impoverished mindset was the code Keith believed in. He wanted to help the people who'd been close to him, even though he could barely help himself. But Coleman learned that the ability to help others had become a luxury in twenty-first-century America because it might mean taking a leave from a job and from health insurance. The working people he knew couldn't do that. He saw the beauty of people struggling to help one another, but it saddened him because he'd seen such people wind up pulling each other down instead of lifting each other up.

He came to believe his role was no longer just one of turning the hearts and minds of people toward Jesus, but of shifting the culture created by the economic forces that had changed places like West Unity and the people in them. He found that task daunting and knew of only one way to go about it. So he continued his sermon by posing a question: "How do I live honestly as a Christian, and live in this environment?" Things weren't working in the nation, he said. His worshippers could all see that. What was the correct response for Christians?

The answer, he said, was an uncomfortable one. It could be found in the words of the Apostle Peter: "Submit yourselves for the Lord's sake to every authority instituted among men." God, in His wisdom, allowed harmful institutions and policies to exist. People could not always understand why. God was like the surgeon who once removed a tumor from Coleman's arm. The surgeon had to cut through good flesh to remove the corrupting tumor. Maybe, he said, that was what was happening now. So be compliant. And pray. Pray hard.

Part II

Winter/Spring,
2018–2019

6

What Free Market?

The Myth of
Free-Market Medicine

The question sank like a balloon losing helium: "Who are we?" It was the same question social worker Tonie Long had asked, but she'd been asking about the collective everybody—America itself—and didn't expect an answer. Angelia Foster's question was limited to the hospital, so she did expect an answer. She tried again. "Who should we become? Where should we go in the future?" After a few beats of silence, Jan David, vice president of patient care, volunteered, "We are a vital, well-respected, independent rural hospital." Foster tightened a corner of her mouth. Strategic planning was proving to be a frustrating exercise.

She, Chad Tinkel, Wade Patrick, Jan David, and Phil Ennen had decided to meet for two hours every two weeks to begin constructing a homemade strategic plan to satisfy the board. (The Joint Commission required hospitals to have strategic plans, but it was liberal when defining what constituted one.) The meetings started on January 11. Since Foster and Patrick had been at hospitals that used a systematic process to create such plans, they'd been assigned by consensus to lead the others through the early stages. They chose two standard, buzzy-sounding business analysis techniques, known, of course, by acronyms: SWOT (strengths, weaknesses, opportunities, and threats) and SOAR (strengths, opportunities, aspirations, results).

The idea of both was to help participants organize thoughts into categories rather than to spew a slurry of unconnected notions. Despite the structure imposed by the acronyms, the meetings were agonizing—not least because tensions that had little to do with strategic planning continued to build between the occupants of the fourth-floor offices.

All the letters of both acronyms revolved around a single central question: What was the economic geography in which CHWC existed, and how could it navigate that geography? As Patrick explained when he called the first meeting to order, there were pillars and big rocks, leakages and threats, strengths and weaknesses in relation to the medical economy existing outside the walls of CHWC. Their job, he said, was to figure out how to turn those relative variables to CHWC's advantage. And so he tried to channel his inner consultant, using what he'd been able to scrape together from the pitches the three agencies had given before the executives concluded CHWC couldn't afford any of them.

Patrick was game, and Foster tried to nudge him and the others on, but the meeting had the feel of a high school homework project concocted by an overenthusiastic teacher for a bored class. Aside from Foster, nobody in the room would have received an A for participation.

Ennen still harbored doubts about the entire assignment. The kind of planning Patrick and Foster were asking them to do was a lot like the ones introduced to the industry by corporate, for-profit hospital companies and subsequently adopted by nonprofits. Foster believed Ennen was uneasy with anything that smacked of the corporatization of the community hospital. She, on the other hand, was not only an extrovert prone to thinking aloud, but also comfortable pushing the others into the trappings and lingo of corporate culture. Ennen was happy to have Patrick and Foster act as meeting coaches, but he couldn't help thinking that both hospitals from which he'd hired them had been taken over: The acronyms hadn't saved them. Meanwhile, he'd kept CHWC independent. Tinkel and David weren't much help, either—both were reticent by nature. When Foster had insisted that the hospital leadership take a Myers-Briggs personality test, over 80 percent of the CHWC staff turned out to be (or so said the test results) "introverted, thinking, judging." Now she was witnessing those traits in action.

Patrick slogged through, with an occasional assist from Foster. They spent two hours placing sticky notes on easel-mounted flip charts, each headlined with "Strengths," "Weaknesses," and so on. They began by repeating the obvious. It didn't take business school training or a six-figure consultant to see what CHWC faced. "Aging population" was a weakness, though it could also be an opportunity to, say, establish a geriatric service. "Government reimbursement" was a weakness because CHWC was so reliant on it. Kesireddy was a strength—the cath lab was a profit center—but also a weakness because no replacement for him appeared on the horizon. The radiation oncology center was a strength because it, too, made money. The inability to give raises or increase contributions to the employee 403(b) retirement plan was a weakness, because they risked losing valuable staff.

The group was mixed about the Parkview doctors across the street. On the one hand, they believed they had a good relationship with most of them. On the other, while the Parkview doctors sent business to CHWC, they also sent a lot of business to Fort Wayne. And they took business away. The group had bought a CT scanner and an ultrasound machine, both of which cut into CHWC's imaging revenue.

That a town of 8,500 people—or even a county of 37,000 people—hosted two CT scanners within fifty yards of each other might seem a waste of resources. But American medical care existed in an arena in which Morris Fishbein's idea of the "free market" placed profit and loss at the top of the decision pyramid. CT scanners made money. Imaging created cash flow. Parkview charged much higher rates for CT scans than CHWC did. "At CHWC, for a CT we charge $900 for," Ennen said, "Parkview charges probably $2,600." The highest price listed for a CT scan at Parkview's flagship hospital in Fort Wayne was over $4,000. The highest list price for a CT scan at CHWC was $1,400. A wide range of pricing was normal in the United States, but even the lower prices were higher than the prices in almost any other peer country in the world.

Such price disparities were common. The price to receive a lower-limb MRI in the United States could vary by a factor of twelve. Even within the same market region, the price in one hospital could be double the price in another.

They knew all this. But Foster saw herself as a "change agitator," and so she scribbled sticky note after sticky note and peppered the sheets on the easels with thoughts. She envisioned CHWC playing the role of Parkview and ProMedica to the even smaller hospitals in surrounding counties—like the facilities in Hicksville and Napoleon—and nipping customers away from them. She wanted to grow, and to one day be in charge of it all as CEO. "I'm driven," she said, "sometimes to my detriment."

She'd come to believe that the hospital's leadership, including the board, had become hidebound and complacent. Incremental change wasn't good enough. She wanted a revolution, and the sooner, the better. But she had concluded that the other members of the team were not ready to have the difficult conversations necessary for revolution—for instance, about who stayed and who went. Ennen, for example, was physically affected by his struggle with the decision to fire Mike Culler, though he knew it was right for the hospital. Ennen, Foster believed, had "conflict avoidance."

She cited the flu vaccine as an example. Unlike some states, Ohio didn't require hospital workers to have a flu shot. In past years, CHWC had strongly encouraged all employees to get it, but many didn't, part of an anti-vax, libertarian strain within Williams County, including among healthcare workers. (The county commissioners even refused to require EMS crews to get the flu shot, though they were often in contact with fragile people, like those in the Genesis HealthCare nursing home.) In the fall of 2018, Ennen considered making the shots mandatory for all, but knew he'd face strong protests. So he decided on a compromise used by some other hospitals: any employee who refused to get a shot would have to wear a surgical mask at all times. Though aggrieved, vaccine objectors acquiesced. And so Ennen's own administrative assistant, Kathy Davis, the wife of county commissioner Brian Davis, sat day after day at her desk, her face covered by a mask, and some nurses walked the halls wearing masks, too. But Ennen avoided what he considered an unnecessary showdown.

"When I got here," Foster said of the weeks after her arrival in 2017, "we had an ER nurse they had written up at least ten times in the last five years, and she was still employed here. She wouldn't show up for half of her shifts. We were suspicious that she had a drug or alcohol issue. She was hateful to all the patients. And I said, 'Phil, let's get rid of her.' You would've thought I asked them to murder their own child. And maybe that's how it feels for them."

Ennen was a creative thinker, she thought, and smart as hell, but a slow mover. She judged Tinkel to be rigid. Jan David preferred to shrink into the background, and Foster questioned her endurance after her decades at the hospital. Patrick was good at being a CIO, but she sometimes wanted to shout at him, "Get a backbone!" For strategic planning to succeed, she decided, she'd have to drive the rest of them.

She wanted to use the Community Health Needs Assessment results to target new services for the problems identified in the survey. The obvious pothole, though, was that CHWC had just started women's and GI clinics, hiring doctors to run them and equipping and staffing them. Those efforts soaked up CHWC's limited supply of money. While they hoped the investments would pay off soon, they hadn't yet. And the needs identified by the Health Department's survey were not the ones that made money. Pediatrics, primary care, obesity, mental health, and dentistry all affected a lot more people, but none of them were big moneymakers like a cath lab or radiation oncology were. They didn't spin off lots of lab tests, either. Good dental care could prevent heart attacks, but treating heart attacks, and placing the stents used to prevent another one, made profits.

Five days after the first strategic planning meeting, Ennen called the hospital's larger leadership group—the people in charge of the various departments—to a gathering in the Bard Dining Room on the first floor. It was time to announce results for the first quarter of the fiscal year.

After a quick opening, Ennen handed the floor to Tinkel. "First, I want to say, congratulations!" Tinkel began. "We made the first quarter with a 0.9 percent positive operating margin!" Whoops, applause, and obvious relief filled the room. "We budgeted for a very small loss, –0.1 percent," Tinkel added.

As he began to break out the details, he tempered the good news about pinching a small margin out of the revenue with the fact that the world in which CHWC lived wasn't becoming any friendlier to small independent community hospitals. People no longer stayed overnight in hospitals like they once did because more procedures were performed on an outpatient basis. Inpatient revenue was way down. Outpatient revenue was up. But Medicaid, Medicare, and private insurance paid less for outpatient procedures. Hospitals everywhere reported the same phenomenon, and so all had to create budgets for an outpatient world in which each customer yielded less money.

Wages had come in $323,000 below budget, thanks partly to Ennen's program of "self-firing" and not replacing the workers who quit. And, with fewer employees, the benefits tab shrank by $139,000.

Supplies cost $157,000 more than budgeted. Tinkel explained that the new services, like the GI clinic and Bazzi and Hassouneh's office, required additional supplies—but there was more to it than that. Supplies in general just cost more, and so did repairs and equipment service agreements.

Outside wages—paying temp workers and "locums" (temp doctors)—cost $141,000 more than planned. (Not every self-fired employee's job was expendable.)

Radiology revenues came in at $657,000 below budget. "Keep in mind," Tinkel said, "that this is a really good example of consumerism."

Tinkel had developed a deep faith in "consumerism." Patients weren't patients: they were consumers—the same consumers who bought oven cleaner, shoes, and digital assistants. As consumers, they had choices. And in a free market, CHWC was going to have to compete for their dollars. This was as true for radiology as it was for Snickers bars. "So, PPG Ohio [Parkview Physicians Group of Ohio, the offices across the street] went and bought an ultrasound machine. So they have been taking some of our ultrasound business. We didn't budget for that. They bought a CT scanner a year ago, and I did not correctly budget our reduced volumes from CT based on that. I thought we would be able to maintain more than we did. So, this is a perfect example that we need to make sure that patient experience is *a*-mazing!"

Cath lab revenue and radiation oncology revenue, the two big profit centers, both earned more than budgeted. Radiation oncology outperformed by nearly $800,000. The Joint Commission survey took an unexpected bite out of the quarter. The $212,000 bottom-line margin wasn't much; it depended upon some government money that had come in after Medicare and Medicaid billing appeals, and it wouldn't add to the hospital's days of cash on hand. But it was something.

"We still have more to accomplish," Tinkel said. "We need to continue down this path."

If anybody needed a reminder of what could happen if they didn't continue down this path, all they had to do was look a few miles to the north and east, to Sturgis, Michigan. At that moment, the board of Sturgis Hospital was deciding to fire its CEO.

Sturgis Hospital was in crisis. It had already closed its wound care clinic, home healthcare service, pain clinic, and an urgent care center. But cutting its way out of financial distress wasn't working. Over 80 percent of its customers were outpatients. Medicaid and Medicare paid less than private insurance, and most of the hospital's business came from Medicaid and Medicare patients. Bad debt was running about $275,000 a month because Sturgis had become a low-income area since the Great Recession. As the population aged, younger people moved away, and those who remained earned less money. Seventy percent of babies, and 55 percent of their mothers, were on Medicaid—and people weren't having as many babies in the first place. Meanwhile, labor, supply, and drug costs all rose.

In late November, the Sturgis CEO announced more cuts. Hospice would close. He was shuttering the obstetrics department. Two weeks before Tinkel spoke to the leadership about the financial results at CHWC, Emilia Pearl Miller became the last baby born in Sturgis Hospital. Sturgis slashed medical-surgical services. The oncology treatment center closed entirely. About sixty people would lose their jobs. Sturgis-area residents were furious. The CEO would be fired, but Sturgis's financial crisis would continue.

After Tinkel's presentation, Wade Patrick took the floor to brief them all on strategic planning. The fourth floor, he told them, aimed to "create a road map for success." The meetings were tough going, he said, though he didn't reference the team tension. "When you are in that room and talking about 'Are we really strong in this area? Are we really weak in this area?' and you have differing points of view, it forces you to have those hard conversations"—the exact "hard conversations" that Foster believed weren't happening at all.

Ennen wound up the meeting by quoting Abraham Lincoln's 1862 annual address to Congress: "The dogmas of the quiet past, are inadequate to the stormy present. The occasion is piled high with difficulty, and we must rise with the occasion. As our case is new, so we must think anew, and act anew."

Foster had misread Ennen. Change was part of his agenda, and it had been since he assumed the CEO job. But he believed that, like an experienced comic, he knew his audience. Abrupt change was neither the Bryan way nor the CHWC way. It was certainly not in keeping with the hospital's family ethos. So, as with the vaccine policy, Ennen preferred to execute change gradually whenever possible, in a person-to-person way, and with a minimum of drama. Foster viewed this as conflict avoidance; Ennen viewed it as tactical prudence.

░░░

Sheila Carpentar* didn't have much say about what was happening to her or where she'd take her business. The Genesis nursing home made the call, and

Misty Dean and Brock Zuver climbed into their ambulance. Since it was a transfer, Dean left the siren off and stopped at traffic lights until she pulled into the Genesis parking lot. She and Zuver placed surgical masks over their noses and mouths—Dean hadn't had a flu shot, and she had gotten the flu—to protect the people inside, some of whom sat, listless and silent, in wheelchairs in the empty lobby as they stared through the glass doors.

Dean and Zuver walked their gurney through the doors, past the wheelchairs, and down a gloomy hallway. When they came to a tiny, dark room with cinder-block walls, they tried to wedge the gurney inside. A curtain divided the room: half was for a lady who sat on the edge of her rack-like single bed, watching a picture-tube TV that stood on a small stand, and the other half contained Sheila on her own rack. "She hasn't been good," the TV-watcher said of her neighbor.

No, Sheila had not been good. She was only sixty-eight, but she was plagued by a number of conditions: heart failure, kidney failure, lung cancer—all of them fatal, and some of them rooted in diabetes. She took twenty-three different drugs. Her fingers were purple. She was swollen with retained fluid. Dean could hear fluid in her lungs, plain as day. You could stand several feet away and hear the fluid. Yet she was lying flat in the bed. She couldn't get air. Sheila was drowning.

"Why is she laying down?" Dean asked a Genesis employee who was standing over Sheila's bed. "She shouldn't be laying down."

Dean, Zuver, and the employee sat her up in the bed. "Now, I think you could use some CPAP," Dean said to Sheila, referring to the assisted breathing device. "You can't tolerate it, let me know."

"Do whatever," Sheila replied. Dean had seen her before—several times. She'd been noncompliant.

Once Sheila was loaded into the ambulance, Dean tried to start an IV but had a tough time finding a vein. CHWC was just a short drive away through Bryan, Dean figured, so she considered waiting on the IV. At the hospital, she knew, the ER could drill into a bone to place the needle.

"Now," Dean said to Sheila, "you don't want anything done if your heart stops, correct?" Sheila had had enough. Her nod may have been weak and ambiguous, but Dean interpreted it as strong and definite.

At the hospital, the ER team discussed drilling her. They discussed intubation and comfort care and intervention. They wanted to do the right things in Sheila's last hours, which, as it turned out, totaled ten.

When Kesireddy put a stent into a person's coronary artery, it was like installing fourteen $100 bills. That wasn't how much the stent would cost that man or woman but how much it would cost CHWC. That price was not, however, what many other hospitals paid. Some paid about $750. A few paid $1,600. That the same stent could cost 100 percent more at one hospital than at another went a long way toward explaining why independent community hospitals struggled.

"It's implants—orthopedics, cardio. The price we pay compared to Toledo or Fort Wayne is dramatically different," Tinkel said. "We pay anywhere from three times as much as they might."

A ProMedica or a Parkview or a Mercy could pay, say, $4,200 for an artificial knee. That same knee could cost CHWC $7,000 to $8,000. "I had that conversation with a vendor," John Rymer, the director of CHWC's supply chain (purchasing), said. "It was Biomet. They were in my office, and at that time we were paying about three times what ProMedica was paying for a knee. I said, 'Do you realize that, if you keep this up, we will be a ProMedica hospital? And just a switch overnight, you'll cut our rates by 66 [percent]. And they were, like, 'We know. We have to be within our tiered structure.' And that doesn't make any sense." By tiered structure, the sales rep meant volumes. CHWC might perform a hundred joint replacements a year. The Cleveland Clinic performed thousands. With volume came clout.

Kim Bordenkircher, CEO of Henry County Hospital in Napoleon, fought the same battles. They didn't make any sense to her, either. "Hip replacements is an example," she said. "We have great outcomes, but I pay twice what ProMedica pays for their elements. When insurance companies direct patients, they might direct them away from us because our costs are higher. And our costs are higher because I pay more for the implantable device than what we get reimbursed by Medicare. Every hip replacement I do, I lose money, but my revision rate is almost zero, and my infection rate is zero, and patients have unbelievably good outcomes. But I don't have the volume."

Because medical economics don't work like regular economics, the big hospitals did not pass along the cost savings of their lower implant prices to their patients (even if insurance companies paid a little less). Instead, they used much of the money they saved on the cost of goods to pad their margins.

Device makers could get away with charging one hospital one price and another a much lower one because hospitals didn't have much choice about where they obtained devices. The Biomet sales rep who called on CHWC worked for Zimmer Biomet Holdings, based nearby in Warsaw, Indiana. The company was created through a series of consolidating mergers, including a $14 billion deal between Zimmer and Biomet in 2015, until it had become an implant behemoth with a greater market share of knee and hip implants than any other company: 35 percent of the knee market and 31 percent of the hip market. CHWC paid it about $800,000 a year. (CHWC paid stent maker Boston Scientific about $1.2 million a year.)

In 2018, Zimmer Biomet CEO Bryan C. Hanson made about $9.7 million. The ratio of his salary to his median employee's salary was 148 to 1. Hanson's earnings were about 25 times what Phil Ennen earned, 215 times what Valerie Moreno and her husband took home each year, and 334 times Keith's Menards wages. As large as that was, though, it was a drop from the $16,334,356 in compensation given to Hanson (not counting the $200,000 allowance for personal use of the company jet) in 2017 when he first joined the company. In 2018, the firm spent nearly $1 billion buying back its own shares.

Zimmer Biomet also had a history of corruption. In 2017, the company paid $30 million to the government for repeatedly violating the Foreign Corrupt Practices Act. In 2007, Zimmer Holdings, Biomet, and the other big makers of joint replacements—DePuy Orthopaedics and Smith & Nephew—entered into deferred prosecution agreements after they were found to have paid orthopedic surgeons "consulting fees" of between tens and hundreds of thousands of dollars per physician, including expensive trips and meals, in return for their brand loyalty. (Another big maker, Stryker Orthopedics, made a side deal in return for cooperating with the government.) Zimmer had to pay $169.5 million for violating anti-kickback laws. Even as Zimmer Biomet (as it was known after the merger) was paying the government for its corrupt foreign operations, the company received a subpoena from the Office of Inspector General for the U.S Department of Health and Human Services demanding the company produce additional records related to consulting arrangements.

Consolidation gave manufacturers oligopoly pricing power. Everything from syringes to bags of saline solution was controlled by a diminishing number of corporations—some of them among the most profitable ones in the United States. This meant that they could raise their prices with impunity. In 2019, B. Braun Medical, a Germany-based (its American division was located in Pennsylvania) manufacturer of saline bags—plastic bags of salt water—would raise its price for them by 100 percent. In addition, it boosted by over 50 percent the price of a decades-old, off-patent antibiotic used in many hospitals.

Other drugmakers routinely hiked prices by double-digit percentages. Drug companies raised the median prices of their products by about 26 percent over just one year, from 2017 to 2018. Insulin medications like the ones Keith needed ballooned in cost by 700 percent—from about $35 to nearly $300 per vial—over the previous twenty years. The U.S. Justice Department spent years investigating price-fixing among big drugmakers and imposed hundreds of millions of dollars in penalties. For example, two former Heritage Pharmaceuticals executives pleaded guilty to federal charges, and the company, a supplier of a diabetes drug called glyburide, was forced to pay $7 million to buy its way out of price-fixing accusations. Back in 1922, when University of Toronto researchers Frederick Banting and Charles Best purified cow insulin and used it to treat diabetics, they sold their patent rights to the university for $1 as a way to benefit humankind. But drug discovery had since become the drug business. Even old drugs, like insulin, were slightly tweaked or made in new ways so that companies could patent them and charge high prices.

In 2007, a dose of the Celgene cancer drug Revlimid cost $247. The price rose over the years, but after Bristol-Myers Squibb agreed to take over Celgene in early 2019 in a $74 billion acquisition, Celgene raised the price of Revlimid by 3.5 percent, to $719.82—doing so on the day it broke the news of the buyout. Since people using the drug to treat cancers like multiple myeloma require many doses, the drug would now cost them nearly $200,000 per year.

Jim Hicks faced the same price hike problems running EMS. His crews used Narcan—an opioid blocker that can revive overdose patients—to save lives. In 2008, a dose of Narcan cost Hicks about $14.50. It cost $78 now. Albuterol, used to treat asthma, shot up 3,400 percent. Saline bags used to cost $5.95. Now they were $22. A drug for cardiac arrhythmias that was first marketed more than fifty years ago and should cost only a dollar or two inexplicably rose to $180 a vial. Hicks waited two years to get morphine after companies stopped making the generic version. When he finally did get some, it cost $12 for a 1 cc vial. He used to buy twenty-five of them for $43.

In response, small hospitals like CHWC joined—or formed—group purchasing organizations, GPOs. (New York City hospitals pioneered the strategy in 1910.) CHWC joined the Independent Hospital Network (IHN), a collection of Ohio hospitals. It also helped form a smaller group of hospitals in the region called Vantage Ohio with facilities like Henry County in Napoleon and St. Luke's in Maumee in Lucas County as a way of cooperating to buy goods and services like laundry and malpractice insurance. The strength-in-unity tactic helped. IHN was able to jaw down the prices of some supplies—like implants—by doing the purchasing itself on behalf of all the hospitals collectively. In its shareholder proxy statements, Zimmer Biomet identified such GPOs as a danger to its revenues.

While the ability of working people to join together to increase their own power via unions or by class action lawsuits had been under attack for decades by corporations like Menards, by state laws dubbed "right to work," and by the evisceration of federal bodies like the National Labor Relations Board, the business of health in America had become a race to consolidate: to get as big possible. Each industry within the healthcare octagon bulked up to combat every other industry in it.

This was another way in which the medical economy existed in a parallel realm completely separate from the economy where Keith, Valerie, Marc, and hospitals like CHWC existed. They weren't able to consolidate; they were on their own. When the universe of patients, small hospitals in rural places, urban hospitals in poor neighborhoods intersected with the universe of the healthcare industrial complex, they were squashed.

This reality caused every hospital to reassess its future. When Henry County Hospital looked ahead, its board decided to do just what CHWC's board had asked Ennen and his crew to do: it hired a consultant. After a long strategic planning process, Henry County sent out requests for proposals, announcing it was willing to entertain mergers. In the end, Henry County decided not to merge but to form an affiliation with Cincinnati-based Mercy. Mercy's buying power, especially the deals available through its pharmacy GPO, was a motivating factor.

Ennen had a similar thought. ProMedica and Mercy both had hospitals in Defiance. The city didn't need two hospitals—to say nothing of two hospitals about a mile apart from each other—but neither of the big systems was willing to cede Defiance to the other. In early 2017, ProMedica had a vacancy in the Defiance CEO's office. Randy Oostra, ProMedica's CEO, began a conversation with Ennen about somehow linking CHWC and ProMedica Defiance. Eventually Ennen and Tinkel drove to ProMedica's Toledo headquarters to sign a nondisclosure agreement and to talk about a deal.

As the conversation developed, Oostra made an offer. ProMedica would give CHWC a 10 percent stake in the ProMedica Defiance hospital in exchange for 10 percent of Bryan. Ennen would be CEO of both. For ProMedica, the deal would help block Parkview from acquiring an Ohio hospital on the edge of ProMedica's home turf. And since some CHWC patients were transferred to Defiance already, ProMedica could nab more of that business from Mercy. Ennen believed the advantage to CHWC was obvious: CHWC would come under ProMedica's purchasing umbrella. Vendors would have to give CHWC the ProMedica price for syringes, knees, stents, IV bags—everything. "That is real cash," Ennen told the CHWC board. Oostra himself drove out to Bryan to pitch the idea.

The board would have none of it. A couple of the members questioned Ennen's personal motivation—did he just want to be a bigger wheel?—and were angry with him for even entertaining the idea. Some questioned his ability to run two hospitals, though Ennen pointed out that Brunicardi had done exactly that when he became CEO of the Montpelier hospital while remaining in charge at Bryan, before the two of them merged. The biggest obstacle, though, was that the offer had come from ProMedica. "'I'm not even sure I wanna shake his hand when he walks in!'" board member Chris Kannel quoted another board member as saying. "'Why is the enemy coming here? Why are we even talking to him? It sounds like a bad idea.'"

Independence—and a fear of losing it—had animated the hospital, the community, and the board for decades. Bryan had been pushed around since the ARO debacle. But the hospital was Bryan's homegrown institution, as well as Williams County's, and though Ennen wasn't talking about ceding that independence and Oostra tried to reassure the board he wasn't asking for it, even 10 percent (and that in exchange for influence in Defiance) wasn't enough to soothe the minds of the board's majority.

There was more to the board's rejection than just stubbornness. The board didn't trust Parkview or ProMedica. ProMedica, though, had earned an extra measure of suspicion. Every small hospital in the region, and many across the country, knew what it had done to St. Luke's.

███

The story of ProMedica's attack on St. Luke's begins with the story of industrial decay. Grand mansions once lined the bank of the Maumee River in Toledo near the spot where the river flowed into Lake Erie. But they were relics now, some with boarded-up windows and weedy yards, others long ago chopped into low-rent apartments. All of them testified to Toledo's glory days, when the founders and operators of Libbey Glass, Willys-Overland, Acklin Stamping, and other big-industry companies displayed their wealth in their homes, as well as via the institutions—art museums and orchestras, for instance—that they'd helped to establish. As the 1960s gave way to the 1970s, followed by the industrial collapse of the late 1970s into the early 1980s, corporate offices and Toledo's well-off left the city for suburbs like Perrysburg and Maumee to the south, where they built new grand homes on the banks of the river.

St. Luke's Hospital was there, waiting for the refugees from Toledo's decline. Established in 1906, when the region first began to boom, St. Luke's, an independent, stand-alone hospital like CHWC, was a southern Lucas County keystone. By the time of the Great Recession, it had a reputation for providing good care at lower prices than some of the other regional hospitals. But the twenty-first century had been unkind. In 2000, before the recession of 2001, it had 358 days of cash on hand. In 2008, before the Great Recession, St. Luke's had 135 days of cash. By August 31, 2010, it had 104 days, or $65 million. The Moody's bond rating agency downgraded its debt.

The very things local people liked about St. Luke's—its smaller size, lower charges, good quality, community focus, and independence—were also the main sources of its financial problems. They were the same problems that plagued CHWC and every other hospital like it: St. Luke's didn't have the market power to stand up to suppliers for lower prices, or to insurers for higher reimbursement rates.

So, like CHWC, St. Luke's struggled in the pre-Obamacare, pre-Medicaid expansion days of the Great Recession. But the hospital also faced another problem: it was being deliberately strangled.

The demographics of Maumee and Perrysburg, in addition to that area's resurgence during the recovery, meant that more residents had more
money, and that many of them were covered by higher-paying private insurers. Hospitals want to go where the money is, which is why so many
abandoned inner cities in favor of suburbs. Already Mercy, a big Ohio chain
and a ProMedica rival, had plans to build facilities in the area. ProMedica
bought land near St. Luke's in anticipation of building a new hospital. But
a new hospital would cost ProMedica scores of millions. St. Luke's, meanwhile, was already built, and it was weakening.

ProMedica wanted it. As early as 2000, St. Luke's CEO, Dan Wakeman,
accused ProMedica of pursuing "an aggressive strategy to take over St.
Luke's or put us out of business."

That strategy used ProMedica's market power. First, it blackballed St.
Luke's from its for-profit insurance business, Paramount. Paramount was
one of the largest insurers in the region, so being in-network with Paramount could make or break a medical practice or a hospital. Before 2001,
St. Luke's was part of the Paramount network, but then, at the behest of Pro-
Medica, Paramount refused to give St. Luke's a contract, costing St. Luke's
about three hundred admissions per year, and forcing the leadership at St.
Luke's to conclude that Paramount would "only let us back in when we give
them [ProMedica] the keys."

ProMedica also strong-armed Anthem Blue Cross Blue Shield. Anthem
was one of the biggest insurers in Ohio, but from 2005 through 2009, Pro-
Medica threatened Anthem with higher rates for services at all ProMedica
hospitals if Anthem included St. Luke's in its network. Anthem feared Pro-
Medica's market power more than it wanted St. Luke's business, so Anthem
capitulated. (ProMedica preferred to say that it gave Anthem discounts on
services in return for shutting out St. Luke's.)

St. Luke's leaders thought the plan was obvious: "ProMedica will continue to starve St. Luke's through exclusive managed care contracts and
owned physicians," they concluded. St. Luke's was so troubled by ProMedica's tactics, it considered mounting an antitrust lawsuit.

Finally, in July 2009, after years of trying to negotiate with Anthem, and
as the recession squeezed the nation, ProMedica relented—but on terms
favorable to itself. If Anthem added St. Luke's to its network, ProMedica's
director of managed care contracts stated, "Anthem will have to pay PHS
[ProMedica Health System] for the privilege" by paying ProMedica higher

reimbursements to make up for income ProMedica would lose to St. Luke's, an amount ProMedica estimated at $2.5 million a year.

Anthem laid conditions of its own on St. Luke's. It demanded what's known in the American healthcare industry as a most-favored-nation (MFN) clause: St. Luke's could not charge Anthem a price for any procedure or service that was higher than the lowest price charged to any other insurer. MFN clauses were viewed by some economists and regulators as being anti-competitive and as encouraging cartel pricing. Ohio banned them two years later. But despite feeling "miserable" about having to sign such a deal, Wakeman did so because he knew St. Luke's was a minnow compared to its two consolidated predators, ProMedica and Anthem.

As CHWC would later do, St. Luke's breached covenants on its debt in 2008 and 2009. Still, under Wakeman's leadership, the financial picture began to improve. He even made a margin—just $7,000 in the black, but a good sign. And St. Luke's began hard negotiations with insurers to raise reimbursement rates, using the same argument that CHWC's buyer, John Rymer, had used on Biomet: pay us a little more now, or you'll have to pay us a lot more later when we become a ProMedica hospital.

Facing an uncertain future, though, St. Luke's considered its options. It could affiliate with a big system, as Kim Bordenkircher's Henry County Hospital had; it could try joint ventures with big systems, as CHWC was considering; or it could submit to an outright merger or takeover. When the St. Luke's team charged with exploring the options reported its conclusions, it used bitter language. Affiliating with either ProMedica or Mercy would "stick it to employers, that is, to continue forcing high rates on employers and insurance companies." "Going over to the dark green side," referring to ProMedica's corporate color branding, "we may pick up as much as $12 million to $15 million in additional payments from three health plans." St. Luke's could raise prices significantly because ProMedica, thanks to its size and market domination, negotiated favorable reimbursement contracts with insurers, making it the highest-priced medical provider in the region and one of the highest in the state, despite its reputation for lower quality.

Like CHWC's board, much of St. Luke's board clung to the hospital's independence. But Wakeman and several board members realized that the end of their independence was inevitable—likely sooner rather than later. If they had to affiliate or merge, ProMedica, then a "nonprofit" corporation with about $1.6 billion in revenues, would make the most powerful ally.

Wakeman changed his tune, at least in public. In 2008, he'd accused ProMedica of taking "the greatest resources from the community" and performing "poorly in terms of costs of outcomes." But by the fall of 2009, Wakeman nodded toward ProMedica's "incredible access to outstanding pricing on managed care agreements." True, he wrote in an internal memo, an affiliation with ProMedica "may not be the best thing for the community in the long run," but it "sure would make life much easier right now, though."

On May 25, 2010, ProMedica and St. Luke's signed a deal for ProMedica to take control of St. Luke's. Like a small-time Chicago bootlegger who'd been nibbling at the big boss's turf, St. Luke's was faced with the choice of continuing to fight—and lose—or joining Capone's outfit. So it joined.

The Federal Trade Commission and the state of Ohio immediately attacked the joinder. Six months later, they took ProMedica to court. The FTC charged that ProMedica's takeover of St. Luke's was anti-competitive—a violation of the Clayton Act, a foundational document of U.S. antitrust law. ProMedica, the FTC argued, would dominate far too much of the market for hospital services if it could get away with absorbing St. Luke's into the "dark green side."

Area employers, employees, and insurance companies would all suffer the financial consequences of ProMedica's power to raise rates—a fact recognized by St. Luke's leadership: "The reason [insurance companies] should care," it said before the deal, "is that an independent St. Luke's Hospital keeps the systems a little more honest. The [companies] lose clout if St. Luke's is no longer independent."

If ProMedica charged an insurance company more to treat a broken leg, the insurance company would pass that extra fee to the businesses that covered their workers. The companies would then charge the workers higher premiums and deductibles.

ProMedica argued that it wasn't so dominant after all, even with the addition of St. Luke's—an argument belied by its representations to debt investors. "ProMedica Health System has market dominance in the Toledo MSA [metropolitan statistical area]," it had declared. And when it did its own SWOT analysis like the one Ennen and his vice presidents were trying to complete as part of CHWC's strategic planning, ProMedica concluded that "dominant market share" was a strength.

There were other, lower-cost options for Lucas County residents,

ProMedica insisted. And doctors could steer patients to these lower-cost hospitals—like to the University of Toledo Medical Center (UTMC), a state-supported teaching hospital. In other words, ProMedica appealed to the free market.

"*What* free market?" Henry County's Kim Bordenkircher wanted to know. Politicians, businesspeople, and ideological conservatives "assumed healthcare is a free-market economy. It's not!" This was the flaw in Tinkel's push for a consumerist approach. There was no such thing as a free market for medicine in the United States, and there hadn't been for some time. Asking patients to become consumers burdened them with the responsibility to shop wisely in an opaque economy, even as hospitals introduced high-cost, hotel-like extras to lure them through the doors. The idea that doctors could or would steer patients to low-cost hospitals or to high-quality ones was laughable. Doctors had no idea what hospitals—even hospitals where they worked—charged for services, and neither did most other people. Hospitals and insurers kept their pricing and their insurance contract negotiations confidential. So a broken leg for one patient could wind up costing much more—or much less—than the exact same break would cost someone else.

ProMedica's hypocrisy in suggesting that doctors were free to steer patients was revealed by its own contracts with insurers. ProMedica had a policy of discouraging steering by offering financial incentives not to, and by using anti-steering language in its deals with payers. (In 2018, Atrium Health, a North Carolina "nonprofit" system, was forced by the FTC to eliminate language in its insurer contracts that forbade insurers from steering patients to lower-cost providers.) And, as it would turn out, University of Toledo Medical Center wouldn't be much of an alternative, anyway: some of UTMC's services would wind up being taken over by ProMedica, to the point that by the summer of 2020, UTMC, in danger of closing, would entertain a ProMedica offer to take over the operation of the hospital.

The appeal to the free market also papered over another inconvenient reality of the medical economy: doctors were consolidating, too. Just as Parkview bought out the Bryan Medical Group, practices were selling themselves to health systems, hedge funds, private equity (PE) firms. And every one of those investors had the expectation—and sometimes the requirement—that doctors would send patients to a hospital preferred by the investors. That's one reason hospitals wanted staff doctors—and why Ennen wanted to open the specialty clinics.

While doctors couldn't steer patients, insurance companies could, to the detriment of small hospitals. "I see 'em in Walmart," Bordenkircher said. "They say, 'Kim, I wanted to get my MRI in Henry County, but my insurance company called me and said I have to go to XYZ.' Well, I know they don't have to go there, but the manner in which that is communicated to the patient makes them feel like they had no choice."

That's why everybody wanted to get big. ProMedica craved bigness to stand up to insurers and suppliers—and because power and money accrued to bigness. Insurers wanted to get big to stand up to ProMedica and the other consolidating systems. Device makers and drug companies wanted to get big to stand up to hospitals and the insurers. Meanwhile, bigness in chain systems (even if "nonprofit") seeking maximum revenue clobbered everybody who needed medical care.

"Everybody knows that when St. Luke's merged with ProMedica, the costs went up," Bordenkircher said. "It goes back to what we know about monopolies." Even under the eye of the FTC, the rates St. Luke's negotiated rose under the ownership of ProMedica—and one expert predicted double-digit percentage rate increases to come.

In the end, after six years, multiple court hearings, thousands of documents, and mounds of money, ProMedica was forced to surrender to the FTC. It divested itself of St. Luke's in July 2016.

The tactics used by ProMedica in the St. Luke's affair weren't unheard of. Other hospital systems tried to undermine smaller hospitals or the big physician groups with which they competed. But even as big health systems swallowed one small hospital after another all over the United States, the FTC almost never challenged the takeovers. The agency had tried, back in the 1990s, to block hospital mergers it deemed damaging to consumers, but it often lost in court. Stung, the FTC retreated while economists and other experts conducted research to build a more solid foundation from which to request injunctions. By the time the research demonstrated the anti-competitive—and health—effects of consolidation, the FTC was swamped with mergers occurring in industries across the American economy, even as it faced inflation-adjusted budget cuts that eviscerated its power. So, though armed with new knowledge, it still challenged few hospital takeovers. The injunction action it brought against ProMedica was only the second one in the previous dozen years, even as hundreds of other hospital mergers, affiliations, and buyouts were allowed to proceed.

Since 2000, the American hospital landscape had come to be dominated by regional oligopolies in a struggle for pricing power. The phenomenon puzzled a judge who presided over the ProMedica case. "And this appears to me counterintuitive," he said. "But increased concentration and therefore power through the use of market share can lead to the ability to negotiate better prices as between the institution and the insurer, the [health] plan. The institution then has, do they not, two alternatives, assuming they achieve better pricing: One, pass it on to the public; two, increase the bottom line?"

One might have thought that a nonprofit hospital system like Pro-Medica would pass it on to the public. ProMedica, Parkview, OhioHealth, Mercy: most of the consolidated regional systems in the United States, including the state university systems, were all officially nonprofit. They were supposed to serve charitable functions, receiving 501(c)(3) tax-free status from the Internal Revenue Service. That was why their profits were officially called "operating surpluses." But there was no meaningful difference between the behaviors of for-profit giants like Hospital Corporation of America and those of the big "nonprofit" systems. Michigan's Spectrum Health, for example, took in $6.9 billion in operating revenue in fiscal year 2019 (for a 14.7 percent total margin), while providing only $6 million in charity care. They were all big corporations. They all acted with the same goal in mind: to increase market share.

And so, in Fort Wayne, you could watch the Class A Tin Caps baseball team play in Parkview Field. (Parkview, which had paid $3 million for the right to name the stadium, wasn't the only nonprofit to jump into the stadium-naming business. In Texas, Children's Health paid $2.5 million for the naming rights to a high school football stadium in Prosper, near Dallas. Some thought the notion of a children's hospital system paying millions to name a school football stadium was strange, given the growing concerns over serious injuries—especially head trauma—caused by the sport.) In Toledo, you could visit the ProMedica Museum of Natural History at the Toledo Zoo. (ProMedica had paid $3.5 million for those naming rights.) ProMedica was a sponsor of the Toledo Symphony's Masterworks Series so that those who could afford tickets could hear Mahler and Dvořák. In the

name of branding, hospital systems had become the new industrial benefactors, the post-manufacturing sheikhs.

Some people in Fort Wayne and Toledo groused about the donations,
arguing that those millions would have been better spent doing what the
medical giants were supposed to do: take care of sick people, and charge
them less to do so. But those dollars were tiny drops when compared with
the overall income of both conglomerates.

Big hospitals had become machines spewing wealth. For tax year 2017,
Parkview Health System reported gross receipts of $2,130,554,741. It ended
the year with net assets of about $1.2 billion. (That amount would rise by the
end of 2018 to $1.28 billion.) It paid its CEO, Michael Packnett, $2,335,046.
Parkview orthopedic surgeon Matthew Grothaus, who often operated at
CHWC in Bryan, made $1,747,260 in 2017. Other Parkview doctors made
well over $1 million. And like other big systems, Parkview owned a number
of for-profit entities, like MRI leasing operations, condominiums, various
real estate development outfits, and, of course, doctors' offices like the one
in Bryan. It provided $27.4 million in charity care, or 1.2 percent of its gross
receipts, which is about what other big systems, including ProMedica, provided. For the same year, ProMedica reported net assets of $2,467,501,418.
It paid CEO Randy Oostra $2,233,034. ProMedica's chief medical officer
made $2,083,877. (As big as these compensation packages were, they were
tiny compared to that paid to R. Milton Johnson, CEO of for-profit hospital
operator Hospital Corporation of America: $109,050,692.)

"Nonprofit" Parkview was profitable. It and its fellow hospital systems
were so profitable that a coalition of Indiana employers and medical professionals called Employers Forum of Indiana asked the Rand Corporation to
study Indiana hospitals. The Rand team noted that in a typical free market,
buyers of a product or service could steer consumers toward lower-cost,
higher-quality providers, but that a "lack of transparency in contracting
and negotiated prices undermines the ability of self-insured employers to
demand value from providers and from health plans. . . . Despite spending
more than half a billion dollars on hospital care over a three-year period,
the employers participating in this study have limited or no information
about the prices they are paying for that care."

Rand used Medicare pricing as a benchmark to measure the relative
prices charged by the largest Indiana hospital systems. During the three
years from July 2013 through June 2016, the employers who took part in

the Rand study paid $695 million to Indiana "community" hospitals like the ones in Parkview's system. Medicare's payments to the same hospitals, for the same care services, would have been $255 million—a $440 million difference. Parkview Health was by far the most expensive. Overall, the Rand team found, "relative prices have been rising over the period of the study, with particularly steep increases for Parkview Health and Community Health Network. . . . [T]he flagship hospital in the Parkview system had an operating margin of 16.4 percent in 2015, which is remarkably high among community hospitals."

What was true for Parkview and other hospitals in Indiana was true for hospitals in Ohio and everywhere else. The bigger Parkview got, the more it charged the insurance companies that covered people like Marc Tingle, who obtained insurance through his wife's job with Williams County. And, of course, those insurance companies charged Williams County—and, ultimately, Marc—more. Though Parkview's dominance of the northeast Indiana region allowed it to charge more, relative to Medicare, than any other system, those other systems were different only by degree. In 1998, Indiana patients paid less annually for medical care than the national average. In 2017, following consolidation, they paid $819 more, even as Indiana's health outcomes fell. "By 2017," a Ball State University study found, "Indiana's five largest not-for-profit hospital systems have accrued profits that exceed $27.74 billion, or roughly 8 percent of Indiana's total Gross Domestic Product in 2017." But even the Parkviews and ProMedicas of America were themselves small in comparison with some of the new consolidated giants. At about the time Angelia Foster was cajoling Ennen and the other executives into embracing a more corporate ethos, hospital operators Catholic Health Initiatives and Dignity Health (which bought naming rights to the former StubHub Center in Carson, California, adjacent to Los Angeles) consummated their union, forming CommonSpirit Health. The new company had 142 nationwide hospitals, 150,000 employees, and $30 billion in revenue. It was the biggest of the 1,162 hospital mergers announced in 2018, and it was "nonprofit."

There was little resistance to the consolidation. In California, the state attorney general sued Sutter Health, a chain with twenty-four hospitals, dozens of surgery centers, and, in 2018, $13 billion in operating revenue. Sutter so dominated the Northern California market for medical care that a heart attack costing about $15,000 in Los Angeles could cost $25,000 in

San Francisco. Sutter was also "nonprofit." The attorney general charged Sutter with doing the same thing ProMedica did to St. Luke's. Sutter, while denying any guilt, caved and made a deal to pay $575 million to the state as a settlement. But Sutter remained dominant.

Prices rose—not just in Indiana or in California, but everywhere. From 1998 through mid-2019, the United States experienced 57.6 percent inflation for all goods and services above the 1998 baseline. Hospital services rose over 200 percent.

To anybody who asked, hospital executives—from Ennen and Tinkel at CWHC to the CEOs at the biggest of health conglomerates—would explain that charging higher prices to the privately insured, the self-insured, and the uninsured only helped to recoup the costs of providing medical treatment to recipients of Medicare and Medicaid. The government programs, they insisted, did not begin to cover their costs. The insurance payments subsidized the government programs.

The natural follow-up question, of course, was whether their costs were too high in the first place. It was possible that hospitals, at least those with dominant market share, were able to use their power to extract more money from insurance companies and then use that money to increase their own costs by raising physician and administrator wages and building unnecessary buildings—in other words, by gold-plating their operations in the name of "consumerism."

The big "nonprofit" systems, which often advertised increased efficiencies as justifications for their mergers, didn't lower rates, they raised them. In 2015, the average margin made by "nonprofit" hospitals in the United States was 3.4 percent, a margin CHWC would celebrate. Parkview's Wabash Hospital made 49 percent, the highest in Indiana. In Colorado, hospital profits increased 280 percent from 2009 through 2018, from $538 per patient to $1,518. They then took those profits and, instead of distributing the cash to shareholders as a for-profit might, paid big salaries and stored dollars—billions of them—away in cash hoards and investments. (ProMedica parked money in "Central America and the Caribbean.")

They bought physician groups and built new facilities with fancy technologies like proton beam therapy centers. A proton beam setup cost many millions but would result in enormous billings. When experts began to argue that the benefits of proton machines had been overhyped by device and therapy companies, insurers grew reluctant to reimburse for the treatments, and the rush to build the centers waned. Indiana University's center closed in 2014. ProMedica bought HCR ManorCare, a nationwide chain of senior living and care facilities, in a $3.3 billion deal. The University of Pittsburgh Medical Center opened two hospitals in Italy, and in 2020 it would announce that its UPMC Enterprises arm, a venture capital outfit, would invest $1 billion in a drugs, devices, and diagnostics business. Nationwide Children's Hospital in Columbus would join the rush to start for-profit drug companies in 2020 by creating one of its own, and then asking for a city schools tax abatement of nearly $20 million on the for-profit drug company. After Mercy merged with Bon Secours, another big system based in Maryland, Mercy became the biggest private hospital operator in Ireland. Cleveland Clinic planned to open an outlet in London even as it took over hospitals in Florida.

Hospitals had ventured far afield from fixing sick or injured bodies. They acquired real estate and became developers. Mercy Health announced that St. Vincent's, in Toledo, would build a block of apartments and retail stores. Michigan's Beaumont Health developed a new shopping center and hotel complex. Sanford Health, of South Dakota, went into the golf business. ProMedica announced plans to build a hotel, apartments, and a restaurant on land near its Toledo campus.

The consolidation of hospitals into big systems not only failed to reduce costs, it diminished quality and access. This was true for both rural and urban residents. The argument that a takeover of CHWC by a Parkview or a ProMedica would necessarily bring all sorts of health benefits was contradicted by reams of economic and health research. While it was possible that a takeover *could* improve the health of Williams County residents, such acquisitions often raised prices and reduced the quality of care.

Insurance companies, drugmakers, and suppliers were not going to stand by and watch as hospitals formed giant corporations without responding. So drug giant CVS—which, in addition to its omnipresent stores, ran the nation's largest pharmacy benefit manager (PBM) operation, CVS Caremark—bought out insurance giant Aetna for $69 billion. Aetna had earlier acquired Prudential Healthcare. As a *Columbus Dispatch* investigation showed, CVS Caremark used its consolidated power against small pharmacies in much the same way ProMedica did against St. Luke's. CVS, which ran the prescription operations for three of Ohio's managed care plans, reduced plan reimbursements for drugs sold by smaller stores. CVS then sent those stores letters warning of impending financial distress due to the lower reimbursements CVS itself was handing out. CVS offered to relieve that distress by buying out the small stores. (In response to the *Columbus Dispatch* investigation, CVS and another PBM, OptumRx—part of the Optum insurance giant—sued Ohio Medicaid to prevent the release of information showing they'd charged the Medicaid program $224 million more for dispensed drugs than they had actually paid out to pharmacies.)

Not to be outdone, Cigna acquired the second-largest pharmacy benefits manager, ExpressScripts, for $67 billion. Anthem had tried earlier to take over Cigna, but in 2016 the Department of Justice and attorneys general from several states sued to block the merger and succeeded. The department also blocked Aetna's acquisition of Humana. But the insurance industry was furiously trying to figure out ways to get bigger and more dominating. In 2019, Centene announced that it would try to take over WellCare Health Plans for $17.3 billion.

Meanwhile, physicians began to respond to the insurance companies. The AMA issued regular reports on competition in metropolitan statistical areas. In 2018, it concluded that "it appears that consolidation has resulted in the possession and exercise of health insurer *monopoly power*—the ability to raise and maintain premiums above competitive levels—instead of the passing of any benefits obtained through to consumers."

To better compete, many doctors sold their practices to hospitals—as the Parkview doctors in Bryan did, giving them a near-monopoly in Williams County. (Only the few doctors who worked for CHWC provided any competition.) Those who didn't already work for hospitals started to consolidate among themselves, with one large practice buying up smaller practices in a region. The Bryan branch of the Specialty Eye Institute, where Barb Purvis sent Keith, was part of a ten-office chain in Ohio and Michigan.

Some joined with private equity firms to create "platforms"—multipractice juggernauts—in almost every medical specialty. Private equity had a well-earned reputation for using borrowed money to finance buyouts, raising prices, skimping on services, gutting the companies, and then walking away with the proceeds. That didn't stop doctors from selling out. Hundreds of private-equity healthcare deals worth billions of dollars dotted the financial pages.

The strategy was to scoop up many practices—sometimes in multiple states—by targeting the most lucrative specialties, including GI, orthopedics, dentistry, dermatology, urology, and infertility. New York Spine and Pain, for example, was bought out by private equity in 2011 and sold to another PE firm in 2017, becoming part of National Pain and Spine Centers with offices in seven states. Advanced Dermatology and Cosmetic Surgery became the country's largest provider in its specialty. Kohlberg Kravis Roberts (KKR) bought a controlling stake in Heartland Dental. A consortium that included Bain Capital, Summit Partners, and Revelstoke Capital bought U.S. Renal Care, the number three dialysis and kidney care company in the country.

With enough heft and the billings for cash flow, the consolidated platforms could demand higher reimbursements. Most patients wouldn't know that their doctor had been absorbed into such a platform unless they asked.

Emergency rooms were especially lucrative because people didn't shop for ER care; they just went. Many hospitals, especially small ones, contracted with ER doctor staffing companies because staffing their own ERs with their own employee-doctors could be so daunting: you had to hire four or five to run a 24/7 operation, and pay their salaries and benefits. And so people often wound up going to a hospital that was in their insurer's network, but whose ER was staffed by doctors who were out of network. Out-of-network doctors were not held to a contract price—they set their own prices, at an average of 637 percent of what Medicare would charge. So the PE-controlled companies could count on that extra revenue. KKR bought out a company called Envision, the parent of an emergency physician staffing outfit called EmCare, for $9.9 billion. Kim Bordenkircher's Henry County Hospital contracted with Envision to staff the hospital's ER. Blackstone took over TeamHealth, another ER staffing company. (On the day of the takeover, TeamHealth agreed to settle Justice Department charges that the company used fake billings to defraud the government. It paid $60 million.) Brown Brothers Harriman gained control of American Physician Partners, doubling its size in a year.

Private equity took over ambulance companies, prison medical care companies, mammography companies, nursing homes, electronic medical records companies, autism treatment and addiction treatment companies, and home health companies. Big for-profit hospital chains were controlled by private equity. In 2018 alone, private equity made 855 deals into which it invested $100 billion. The private equity healthcare feeding frenzy was so great that after Joseph Swedish retired as Anthem's CEO, he started his own private equity outfit, Concord Health Partners. Attendees of the biggest confab for medical wheeler-dealers, the J. P. Morgan Healthcare Conference in San Francisco, paid $1,000 per night for hotel rooms that normally cost $200.

Because the PE firms used borrowed money to finance these transactions, they needed to have a lot of cash spewing from the other end. They tried to maximize that cash by cutting costs and stripping assets. They sold off hospital real estate and kept those proceeds, then had the hospitals they controlled lease back the same real estate. After a few years, the firms would "exit" by selling the chain to some other party—if it hadn't gone bankrupt first. Apollo Global Management paid $5.6 billion for LifePoint, a chain of hospitals whose outlets were located mainly in smaller southern towns. It then merged that chain with one it already owned, RCCH HealthCare Partners. The new company had hospitals in twenty-two states. The CEO of LifePoint walked away with nearly $70 million. In late 2019, Apollo had LifePoint sell ten hospitals to a real estate investment trust for $700 million and then lease them back.

New LifeCare Hospitals (not to be confused with LifePoint), a chain of seventeen facilities in nine states, declared bankruptcy in the spring of 2019. Controlled by a private equity consortium, it had sold its hospital's real estate and leased it back.

While the PE takeovers may have been lucrative for the principals, they didn't always work out for patients. Private equity–owned dental practices were suspected of performing unnecessary but expensive procedures to up their revenue. When a University of Florida dermatologist named Sailesh Konda studied his field, he found that PE-owned dermatology practices submitted big-number bills to Medicare, performed lots of high-dollar procedures, and tended to open their own pathology labs that could bill for checking skin samples for diseases like cancer. When he and some colleagues wrote a peer-reviewed research paper reporting this information, it was accepted by the nation's leading dermatology publication, the *Journal of the American Academy of Dermatology*. Then Dr. George Hruza, the incoming president of the academy, disputed the paper's findings to the journal's editors. Hruza's own practice had been bought out by United Skin Specialists, a PE-created company, and he served on its board. A lawyer for another PE-backed dermatology company demanded that the paper be censored. The journal removed it from its website.

When Bain Capital and J. H. Whitney Capital Partners created a company called Aveanna Healthcare—a nursing provider, mainly serving children requiring at-home care—it was accused of lousy performance in the name of cutting costs. As Bloomberg News reported, "More than a dozen former Aveanna employees described how the pressure to meet financial goals jeopardized the quality of care for children. . . . [I]n Texas, Aveanna's biggest market, the company accounted for 85 percent of what the state calls 'deficiencies' at the ten largest pediatric home health agencies from September 2016 through May 2019, even though the company served only 23 percent of those organizations' patients." Seven children died over three states.

HCR ManorCare was available for ProMedica to purchase because it had declared bankruptcy after being strapped with debt, soaked by fees, and forced to sell off its real estate in sale-leaseback deals by its former private equity owner, Carlyle Group. Under Carlyle's ownership, code violations considered serious enough to lead to "more than minimal harm," "immediate jeopardy," and "actual harm" rose 29 percent.

After Blackstone acquired TeamHealth for $6.1 billion in 2017, its subsidiary, Southeastern Emergency Physicians, a Tennessee-based ER staffing company, began an aggressive program to sue patients over billings. As news organizations ProPublica and MLK50 found, Southeastern had filed 4,800 lawsuits in Shelby County (Memphis) in about two years—more than three big Memphis hospitals combined. The firm's bills did not tell patients, many of whom were poor, that they may have been eligible for charity care. In response to the reporting, TeamHealth backed off the lawsuits.

For a time, EmCare held a contract with CHWC. Ennen considered it a "disaster." The Genesis facility where Sheila Carpentar lay struggling for air had once been controlled by a Canadian PE firm, Onex Partners. Onex also controlled Schumacher, an emergency physician staffing company it had purchased for $323 million in 2015. In 2016, Schumacher rolled up another ER staffing company, ECI, for $140 million—and, as it did for its purchase of Schumacher (now called Schumacher Clinical Partners), it used lots of debt to finance the buy. Ennen had brought in ECI to replace EmCare, so, with Schumacher's purchase of ECI, CHWC's ER was now staffed by a PE-owned company. It was Schumacher that billed Keith for his visits to the CHWC ER.

As emergency department services consolidated under the reign of investor groups, patients paid more. Out-of-network billings rose, and patient cash liability jumped. ER company revenues rose 21.9 percent over just five years.

During the fall and winter of 2019, the issue of surprise medical bills gained the attention of Congress. In a rare bipartisan move, Congress tried to cap out-of-network charges. Just when new legislation seemed imminent, KKR and Blackstone ran a $53.8 million advertising and PR blitz meant to frighten viewers and listeners into believing emergency care would not be available for their traumas and illnesses. The bill stalled.

█ █ █

Finance, lobbying, and corporate consolidation mattered a lot to the lives of people in Bryan, Ohio, though few realized just how and how much. Their concerns were far more immediate and pedestrian.

About ninety minutes after Zuver and Dean had dropped nursing home resident Sheila Carpentar off at the CHWC ER, EMS chief Jim Hicks and Zuver approached a residence in Bryan. Once a single-family house, the structure had been turned into three small, sagging apartments unified by what had been a front porch.

Inside one of the units, fading color photos of a smiling family rested on a crowded table: brothers in turtlenecks, checked flared trousers, and belts as wide as their sideburns, their hair just over their ears; Father in his suit, his sideburns a little bushy, too; Mother in a dress, her hair lacquered into sculpture. In a corner of the tiny living room, a TV set tuned to a nostalgia station displayed Lee J. Cobb standing stern and honorable as the Judge on an old episode of *The Virginian*.

One of the brothers from the photos lay on the floor, on his side. He was about seventy, and obese; he was weak, his breathing was labored, and he was a little disoriented. He'd rolled out of his bed by accident and couldn't get up. The bed was in the living room. He lived in the bed most of the time. A plastic tube ran from his nose to an oxygen generator.

Mail—bills and notices, mostly—was spread on the bed. There were piles of them on the floor, too, on a corner of the kitchen counter, on the seat of a chair. Mounds of clothing slumped on the floor. An aluminum-frame walker stood ready to help him, but he couldn't pull himself up on the rocking chair he'd tried to use as a brace.

Hicks and Zuver wrestled the man into a sitting position, the first step toward wrangling him into a chair Hicks had cleaned off. But before they tried to maneuver him into the chair, Hicks asked some questions.

"What year is it?"

"Uh, 2016." The wrong year, but close.

"Who's the president?"

He thought for a beat. "Trump." Then he corrected himself about the year. "No, 2019."

Hicks asked if he wanted to go to the hospital. "No," the man said. "I go there about every week."

Hicks and Zuver levered the man into the chair and then placed his walker before him. Hicks moved furniture out of a doorway. "How'd you expect to get to the bathroom with these chairs?" The man shrugged.

In Hicks's judgment, the man was okay to be left alone. The apartment was in disarray, but it wasn't filthy. The man was a little confused, but he came around all right. Hicks had seen a lot worse. In a couple of weeks, Williams County EMS would send a bill for $100—the response fee. Because the man hadn't been taken anyplace, Medicare wouldn't pay anything for the run, and so the hundred bucks would be the man's responsibility to pay. Hicks wasn't under any illusion he'd pay it.

7

The Crap End of the Stick

The Hospital
as Hope

Joe Brooks had worked at Dow Automotive, up in Hillsdale, where the company made adhesives and other chemical products for the auto industry. He'd been a supervisor. His health wasn't the best, though he wasn't yet even forty-six years old. He had a mother, a wife, six children, and three siblings. Money was scarce.

He owned a piece of ground on Territorial Road, a couple of hundred yards across the Ohio-Michigan state line. Land was cheap there because there wasn't much else around. Brooks knew how to handle saws, drills, screwdrivers, and a carpenter's pencil. He'd built two other homes pretty much by himself, so he set to turning the land into a home for his family— when he could, and when he had a little cash. The house wasn't yet finished, but they were living in it. The yard was a goo of mud, especially after a thaw. Brooks put down long planks over the land to make a path to the door. Most Sundays, he attended services at a Pentecostal church.

Earlier that January Wednesday, he drove to the Home Depot up in Coldwater, Michigan, for supplies. He took his fourteen-year-old son with him. Brooks was on his way back—they were almost home—driving west on Territorial Road, at about a quarter to four in the afternoon, when he watched twenty-six-year-old Brian George's car veer across the center line.

Brooks swerved, but there wasn't much he could do about it. George hit him head-on.

Down at CHWC in Bryan, Dr. Brian Campbell, the night's ER doc, settled into his duties. He'd driven up from his home in southern Ohio for his rotation, rooming at a motel up in Holiday City by the turnpike. He expected a typical shift. The temperature had dropped below zero the night before, so the roads had iced up again, but that Wednesday was warmer: 41 degrees, cloudy, and misty, with most of the roads pretty clear. So there probably wouldn't be any serious accidents. The flu had sunk its teeth into Williams County, so he anticipated a couple of cases of that. Campbell, a portly man, was genial and competent, but he had a reputation among the nurses for being a slow mover. This wasn't going to be his night.

At about three-thirty in the afternoon, people started picking up the red phone in the lobby. Then EMS arrived with a forty-two-year-old man with a mental disability. They suspected he'd broken his leg. He was in pain, agitated, fighting the nurses. He bit one. When Barb Rash, the ER director, arrived to help, he bit her, too. The commotion took everybody's attention. More people picked up the red phone.

Back up in Michigan, EMS from Waldron, a village in Hillsdale County, responded to the accident on Territorial Road. A firefighter-paramedic arrived first. He found three injured. Michigan deputies pulled up. So did another squad from a neighboring township. Brooks remained trapped in the car with severe wounds. The crews unholstered their jaws of life rescue tool and set to work freeing him.

The rescuers faced another problem: where to take the victims. Bryan was twenty-three miles to the south. Montpelier, north of Bryan, was closer, but its ER was small and not as well equipped. Hillsdale's hospital had an ER, too, about fourteen miles away, the same distance as Montpelier.

By the time they extracted Brooks from the vehicle, the winter sky had darkened. The temperature fell. The emergency crews decided to head for Bryan. Though it was farther away, the roads in that direction were bigger, wider, and straighter, which meant the squad could drive faster.

A series of beeps and electronic honks sounded over the radio mounted at the central station in the CHWC ER. A voice announced that there'd been an accident across the Michigan state line, on Territorial Road. Two vehicles. Multiple injuries. Squads were headed for Bryan. Buddy Moreland and some other nurses prepped the intensive care room.

Then EMS notified CHWC by radio that although Brooks had seemed to be talking when he was first being pried out of the vehicle, now paramedics were pumping his chest. "Respiratory," the CHWC intercom announced. A team gathered its equipment and hustled toward the emergency department.

Overcast skies kept the temperature above freezing, but those low clouds and the mist grounded the Parkview helicopters out of Fort Wayne. St. Vincent's, the Mercy hospital in Toledo, was full up, so it halted incoming emergency transfers. CHWC's ER was not a trauma center, but Campbell and the ER team were going to have to do the best they could.

People in the hospital lobby kept picking up the red phone. A mother said her son had cut himself in the webbing between his index finger and his thumb: a small cut, sure, but somebody ought to look at it, she insisted. A seventy-one-year-old man with chest pains wanted help. A dozen more people sat in the chairs near the red phone, waiting for admittance.

The ambulance carrying Brooks rolled up at about four-thirty. The EMS crew pushed his gurney through the ER and directly into the intensive care room, pumping his chest all the way. Campbell and the nurses shifted a mechanical compression device over Brooks's torso and activated it. A steel piston drove down onto his chest over and over to mimic a heart's rhythm while another device forced air into his lungs. Brooks flatlined—no pulse— but they continued to work, trying one thing after another while Brooks's body quaked with each compression, a tangle of tubes and wires linking that body to a century of medical technology progress. Muscle bulged from a gaping wound in his thigh, but there was no point in addressing that yet.

The phone at the station desk rang. A voice on the other end wanted to know if Joe Brooks was there. In reply to the answering nurse's question, Moreland shook his head. They all knew that Joe Brooks lay on the table behind them, but they didn't have any official identification—and even if they did, this was not the time to answer questions or give out any information. For now, Joe Brooks was John Doe.

Another EMS team pushed through the ER doors with a belligerent Brian George, who shouted, "Fuck this! Fucking give me something!" from his own gurney. George was followed by another EMS pushing a boy in a wheelchair, his ear and neck bloody, a small gash on his face. Though his injuries were not critical, he sat, bare-chested and staring, in the aisle next to the nurses' station, saying nothing, not even blinking.

EMS personnel, all wearing the different winter uniforms of their jurisdictions, crammed themselves into the ER, joined by Michigan police, patients, and the respiratory team. "Let's move this wheelchair," Moreland said. Janice Bearer, Wade Patrick's partner, realized the boy was sitting eight feet from his father. She reproached a cop who was loudly discussing the accident, then leaned over the boy, said hello, and told him—as if it were a gentle suggestion—that she'd take him to a more comfortable place. She wrapped a blanket around his shoulders and rolled him away, out of the commotion.

Minutes ticked by—ten, then fifteen—as nurses in other exam rooms tried to tend to their full house of patients, and as Moreland, Campbell, and several nurses tried to save Joe Brooks's life. Moreland looked up at the clock on the room's wall. He exchanged a glance with Campbell. "Call it?" Moreland asked. Campbell grimaced. He paused as if he were running every procedure, technique, and treatment he knew through his mind. Had they tried everything? He looked up at the clock, then at Moreland, then at the piston pumping up and down, up and down, then back at the clock. The room froze into a tableau: the rhythmic pumping the only motion, the only sound.

"Okay," Campbell said. "Four fifty."

"Four fifty," Moreland repeated. And Joe Brooks, who was dead before the EMS had pushed him through the door—who was probably dead before he was pulled from his vehicle—was now dead officially.

Just because human tragedy played out in one room did not mean the still-living stopped picking up the red phone. Fourteen people waited. All the exam rooms were occupied. A woman had been vomiting for two hours. "Where do you want this one?" somebody shouted. EMS and Michigan cops milled about, too, because there was an investigation to be done. Rash went out into the lobby to triage waiting patients. One sat with an IV in her arm.

A nurse wheeled the mentally handicapped man, now restrained on a gurney, out of the psych room. He was headed upstairs to have his leg examined. As the bed rolled by, Rash, who'd returned to the ER, smiled at him and waved goodbye. He smiled and wiggled his fingers to wave back.

Meanwhile, Brian George received a chest X-ray as nurses tried to stabilize him. The fourteen-year-old boy waited. Moreland picked up a ringing phone. "We have no information on Joe Brooks," he said into the handset. He wasn't being cruel. A positive, legal identification had yet to be made. If, by some bizarre happenstance, the dead man in the room eight feet behind Moreland was not Joe Brooks . . . well, you can't make that mistake. But the family member on the phone knew. They'd checked Hillsdale. They'd checked Montpelier. "We do have *him* here," Moreland said of the fourteen-year-old. "I can confirm that."

The family was already on the road. They'd arrive any minute with questions and demands and emotions. "His family's gonna need support when they finally find him," a voice said. CHWC's social worker, Linda Trausch, was gone by now. Phone calls went unanswered. "Check with Dr. Keil," another voice said. "See if she's still in the building."

Shannon Keil filled in as coroner when Kevin Park was unavailable. She believed her medical degree and specialty knowledge carried an obligation to use her training for the civic good, but she hated subbing for Park. She spent her days looking at the gore taken from bodies—at miscarried fetuses, at cancerous tumors, at bits of innards—but she went queasy at the prospect of speaking to people whose loved ones had been turned by fate into "remains."

People would not stop picking up the red phone. Seventeen of them waited in the lobby. Patients still occupied every exam room. Campbell thumped down into the chair at the doctors' workstation while the medical scribe charged with taking notes typed furiously on a laptop. Campbell glanced up at the overhead flat-screen monitor that listed every patient in every room, as well as those waiting in the lobby. "What now?" he asked.

"What is *happening*?" the scribe asked back by way of an answer, without looking up from her computer.

Keil arrived. She stopped by the corner of the central desk and stood silently, wishing away the duty. She felt like throwing up. Brooks's body had to go someplace—they needed the room, and she needed an appropriate place for a preliminary examination—and CHWC didn't have a morgue.

Campbell asked a nurse to put out a call to the entire hospital for nurses. Anybody who could pitch in should come down to the emergency department. A nurse who'd been part of the respiratory team called up to her floor: "If it's okay, I'll stay down here and help for a little while."

Keil and Moreland decided to roll Brooks's body into an unused radiology room. Once there, Keil uncovered Brooks's face. She stepped back in shock: he looked a lot like one of her exes. But she carried on, while Moreland wrote down the observations she dictated.

Back in the ER, a voice said, "I need help."

"Who needs help?" Rash asked.

Two patients were ready to be admitted to the hospital, but the nurse in charge of them had more patients waiting. So she handed charts to Rash, who phoned upstairs to arrange for the two rooms. "I'm trying to get your guy shipped," Rash called out.

Joe Brooks's family arrived. The volume in the room dropped. Everyone but them already knew the terrible truth. Staff attended to their work with deliberate intent to avoid eye contact. Brooks's wife wanted to know the whereabouts of her husband. She wanted to see him. She demanded to know why she could not see him. Other family members became insistent, too. The scene inside the ER, already threatening to crumble into chaos, was about to tip over the edge.

Rash, who knew of Keil's phobia, took charge. She directed the family, including the injured son, into another, quieter room. After Keil finished dictating her observations, she and a Michigan deputy joined them there. Then Rash said, "I'm sorry. Your husband did not survive his injuries." Keil thought that Rash's words were the best possible way to give such news. Rash was direct, but "did not survive his injuries" sounded a lot softer to Keil than "died" or "is dead."

Rash asked if they would like to see his body. Keil remembered escorting Brooks's wife and one of his older sons to the radiology room. She uncovered Joe Brooks's face. "Why? God!" his son moaned. "Why?" Joe Brooks's wife leaned over her man for a last moment of intimacy. Keil couldn't stop staring at her hair: it was long, and beautiful as spun silk, and it fell over his face. His wife held it back with her hand as she kissed him. Keil imagined that Brooks loved that hair, and so, though she wasn't a teenager anymore, his wife kept it long to please him, and Joe Brooks would never see it again. (Six months later, Brian George would be arrested for driving a motor vehicle without insurance and operating a motor vehicle while intoxicated, causing the death of Joe Lee Brooks.)

There wasn't any time to ruminate on Joe Brooks, his family, or Brian George: the night hurried on for the ER staff. The red phone did stop ringing at about eleven, but some staff worked long past the end of their shifts, into the small hours of the morning. Nurse Shayla Carlisle, about seven months pregnant, left at 10:00 PM, but she might as well have stayed, because she couldn't sleep—there was too much adrenaline. Once in bed, she replayed her shift over and over. The whole night had been a sprint. *So many patients.* Had she forgotten to chart this, to chart that?

Two days later, after the ER staff members discovered that the vehicle Brooks drove was the only one the family owned—their only means of transportation—they started a collection. In subsequent days, just about everybody donated. They wrote out a card. Janice Bearer, who had bonded with the injured son, and Wade Patrick drove up to Territorial Road, walked over the planks, and knocked on the door to hand over the money. Brooks's wife and some of the children were there. It was an emotional scene for everybody.

That wasn't the first time the staff had taken up a collection. A while back, a father—poor and Native American—had reversed his vehicle without noticing his four-year-old son and had run over him. The son and the distraught father found themselves in the CHWC emergency room. The son died. Overcome by the pathos of it, nurses and doctors paid to have the little boy's body prepared for transport to Native land out west for a traditional burial.

After some sleep, Barb Rash would return to work and applaud her crew. She would pose a question to them: "What if this hospital wasn't here?"

███

Early the next morning, the executives were back in the fourth-floor conference room for another planning session to talk about how to survive in the consolidating medico-economic world. By now, though, the tensions among them had risen further, and the awkward silences and contentious exchanges were stained with anger.

There'd been a board meeting during the intervening days. As he always did, Ennen prepared packets in advance of the meeting, sending them to members, who could then identify any topics they wanted to raise. Since it was the January meeting, he included his annual boilerplate statement outlining a succession plan in case he required an extended absence. For ten years, the succession plan had amounted to one word: "Tinkel." If Ennen were to fall ill, or if he had to be away from Bryan for three months, or six months, then Tinkel would fill in. If Ennen died or was fired, Tinkel would be named interim CEO until the board decided on a successor.

Tinkel wanted to be that successor. But not all the board members thought his longevity at CHWC, his local ties, and his skill as CFO made him a shoo-in to take over Ennen's job. Tinkel was a black-and-white guy in a gray world, they said. "I told Chad, 'Show me you've got some heart,'" Dave Swanson explained. "You are running a business. A lot of it is analytics, but most of it is spirit, dreaming: the intangible crap that you cannot touch with mathematics. That's what makes the difference between great and so-so." Swanson thought Ennen had that creative quality—that Ennen was, in fact, a little nutty. On balance, he regarded those attributes as pluses for the hospital, though Ennen's tendency to freelance had begun to worry him.

Swanson also questioned Tinkel's devotion to the hospital. Tinkel sometimes moonlighted by looking over the books of Swanson's company, and he had asked Swanson, who was over seventy, if he would sell the company to him. Swanson didn't mind Tinkel's ambition, but he harbored a thought that Tinkel might be too willing to put CHWC in the hands of Parkview or ProMedica as a means of corporate ladder-climbing.

Foster, meanwhile, believed Ennen had hired her with the understanding that she would one day have a shot at succeeding him. She'd been disappointed that the board at her last hospital didn't consider her for the top job when hiring a new CEO. So, though she didn't expect to occupy Ennen's chair by default, she did expect to be considered.

This year, Ennen included an addendum to the annual succession plan in the board packet. To be sure neither Tinkel nor Foster was blindsided by it, Ennen briefed them both before the meeting. Cuts were necessary, Ennen told them. So he'd made the difficult decision to fire Mike Culler—a decision that Culler knew about but which would remain secret from the rest of the staff for now. But if the financial situation had not stabilized by 2020, and "if we wanna stay independent, and getting rid of the COO is not enough, then it's my job that needs to go next. Because if Chad leaves, I have to find a talented finance guy. If Angelia leaves, a talented HR person. If Jan leaves, a clinical leader. If Wade leaves, an IT guy. So it's my job."

Ennen made about $390,000 a year in salary. With that pay, and with his benefits, firing him would save close to half a million dollars. Many doctors—at CHWC and around the country, having never given up on the old idea that hospitals were doctors' domains—believed administration was a top-heavy money drain, and that executives were often more of a problem than a solution. Ennen didn't agree with that point of view, but his plan acknowledged that in a severe financial pinch, medical services trumped civilian jobs.

But Tinkel, Ennen said, should not become the new CEO under that scenario. Instead, Tinkel and Foster should share the position. "Chad has the skill set to be CEO," Ennen explained. "But he does have weaknesses. Everything he is weak at, Angelia is really good at. And vice versa. So the two of them together can figure out how to keep it independent." He wasn't blind to the obvious potential for trouble in naming two ambitious people, both in their late forties, as co-CEOs, but he trusted in their professionalism and reckoned the relationship would last long enough—a couple of years, maybe—for one or the other, or an outsider, to become a clear choice for CEO.

When Ennen met with Foster and Tinkel to explain this reasoning, he told Tinkel that Foster could help him see the gray and consider the uncomfortable. Tinkel felt stung. "He is angry but won't say that he is," Foster said. "It rocked his world." (Tinkel declined to be interviewed on these topics.) Tinkel confronted Foster after the meeting with Ennen to ask if Foster was trying to usurp the CEO spot from him. Now it was Foster's turn to be stung. "If I wanted the spot, I would have already taken it from you," she snarled.

Ennen's attempt at pragmatic self-sacrifice didn't go over any better at the board meeting. When some members read his addendum, they concluded that Ennen must have been diagnosed with a terrible illness. "I thought you were going to tell us it was stage IV and only a matter of time!" Swanson said. Once Ennen reassured them of his good health, some expressed irritation. A few felt the need to defend Tinkel, so Ennen explained he hadn't intended to denigrate Tinkel. Others accused Ennen of devaluing his own contributions to CHWC's survival.

"If it makes you feel better," Ennen answered, "I will say it out loud: the number one reason we are still independent is me. But what that means is I get 11 percent of the credit, and the closest person gets 8." In the current economic environment of hospitals like CHWC, he said, none of that mattered. The hospital was at an inflection point. The past was not as relevant as the near-term future. They'd given him time, he said, to stem the losses, and so far he was on track. Nobody had told him he had to do better than break even. If he could do it by making incremental change—not as fast as

Foster or Tinkel or some board members might prefer—he'd uphold his end of the bargain.

More criticism followed. Some said that maybe he wasn't moving fast enough. But a few department directors were already leaving, Ennen told the board. "I believe we are having some leaders who are looking at how CHWC is changing in response to our fiscal challenges and making their own decision to find an alternative career path. . . . For some of our leaders, the amount and pace of change is not what they seek for themselves.

"I said, 'I will hit the budget,' and you said, 'Okay,' " Ennen argued. "Things Chad describes might get us to a 3 percent margin, but I was supposed to hit the budget. We better get this cleared up."

Meanwhile, the harassment situation with Kim Owen, the radiation oncology center director, had turned bitter. Avoiding drama was Ennen's way. He figured that since the contract for radiation oncology coverage was coming up for renewal, he could take out the offending doctor permanently, without making the harassment public. As part of the tentative talks with Parkview about creating a joint venture for cancer care, he broached the subject of radiation oncology coverage with them. He also sent out a request for proposals to other groups, including the one the doctor worked for, but specifically excluded the doctor himself.

That, Ennen admitted, was a mistake. The doctor, angry, began retaliating against the center's staff. The atmosphere in the clinic soured, though Ennen was not aware of just how sour it got. Despite accepting Ennen's offer to elevate her to the cancer care coordinator position, Owen now wondered if she'd made a mistake. Ennen's tactic with the doctor hadn't worked (in some ways it seemed to make matters worse), and recruiters contacted her all the time. She decided to bite on the bait.

Ennen had always had tetchy moments. But under the stress of recent months, he more often wore his emotions like a battered shirt for the world to see. The baked-in tension broke out within minutes of the strategic planning meeting's start as Foster pushed for more enthusiastic brainstorming. The more she pushed, the more Ennen recoiled. When she asked the group to imagine goals, she insisted they should try to make CHWC a "world-class" healthcare facility, not just Jan David's "vital, well-respected, independent rural hospital."

"Nothing's 'world-class,' " Ennen said flatly.

Tinkel agreed. "World-class implies academic research, too, and we don't do that," Tinkel said. They were a small rural hospital—good at what they did—but they weren't going to fool anybody by saying they could turn CHWC into the Mayo Clinic.

"Okay, best in class," Foster conceded.

Well, they agreed, the cath lab could be best in class.

"So, how about regionally?" Foster tried, still pushing.

The radiation oncology center, cath lab, and maybe surgery could each be best in the region, Tinkel answered, depending on how they defined the region.

"And how do we know that?" Foster prodded, trying to establish criteria and data points against which they could measure themselves in the future.

"I wanna know why you're being so emotional when we push back about not being world-class," Tinkle asked Foster.

"I think you're reading more into it, Chad."

"I thought I saw you tearing up."

"No. No. But we are saying the community does not expect world-class if we don't expect it for ourselves. People need to see why we are the best. It does surprise me we do not have aspirations to be world-class."

"We want reasonable expectations," Tinkle countered.

The room went quiet.

"Having a heart attack and being able to come here and get it fixed is a big deal," Jan David volunteered at last. "But maybe others don't think that. Having the ability to get cancer treatment here rather than drive an hour each way when they don't feel well already . . ." She trailed off. The room went silent again.

Foster looked directly at Ennen. "Any thoughts?"

"Nope!" he barked.

"That was a resounding no. Tell me why."

Ennen leaned back in his chair and crossed his arms over his chest. "I don't like being called out. If I would have had something to say, I woulda said it."

All of them were good people. All of them were good at their jobs, and all of them wanted CHWC to thrive. But each had a different idea of how to make it thrive because they were all trying to figure out how to play the economic game of American medicine. If they were to meet with success, it would be in spite of that economy, not because of it. Every strategic move, every change, every SOAR or SWOT data point they dreamed up had as much to do—and often more to do—with how to wring money out of the great soaking sponge that was the medical economy than it did with how to fix people's bodies. The pressure of trying to do both, while also preserving or advancing their own careers, freighted everything they did, just as it freighted everything ProMedica, Parkview, Mercy—every hospital, big or small, chain or independent—did. Hospital executives all over America were having the same conversations because the hospital industry had become a cutthroat business.

Even though CHWC had made that small margin in the last quarter, all around them the danger seemed to be growing, not diminishing, Down in Circleville, Ohio, OhioHealth, a twelve-hospital chain, absorbed Berger, a community hospital founded in 1929. Around the country, fourteen rural hospitals closed in 2018, and there were already reports of more closings in 2019. Eighteen would ultimately shutter that year, including Ellwood City Hospital in Ellwood, Pennsylvania, just across the border with northeast Ohio.

As Ennen and the others sat in the boardroom, arguing over the strategic plan, Ellwood stiffed its employees by missing payroll. More than a hundred years earlier, Ellwood City had started with a few beds in what had been a private house. In 1938, two years after Cameron opened his hospital in Bryan, local big shots formed the nonprofit Ellwood City Hospital Association to run what had become a fifty-five-bed acute-care facility. In 1996, the hospital—by then up to ninety-nine beds, but facing the same turbulence as other community independents—affiliated itself with the University of Pittsburgh Medical Center (UPMC). That deal blew up in 1998, and the hospital limped into the twenty-first century. UPMC acquired a nearby hospital and brought the full weight of its system into the market. Next it bought out three medical practices in Ellwood City itself. Those doctors then sent their patients to the UPMC hospital.

In 2017, Ellwood City agreed to sell itself to a for-profit outfit, called Americore Health LLC, which was snapping up distressed community hospitals. Americore promised a bright future, but Ellwood City would struggle until it shut down in December 2019, idling employees who once totaled about four hundred. "We desperately need this hospital to prosper," the mayor would say of his community.

Mayor Carrie Schlade felt the same way about Bryan. "For Bryan—economically and socially—if we lose that hospital, I'm afraid of what the town's going to look like. Because they have so many important services for our community. And they really do try to be a community partner." All the CHWC executives felt the responsibility and the pressure, but Ennen, the hometown boy who'd put in thirty-two years, carried most of it.

Four days after the second strategic planning meeting, Ennen broke the news of Culler's firing to CHWC's broader leadership council. "In these final days, I ask you to keep this information as confidential as is possible. . . . If staff have questions, please direct them to me. . . . We are dealing with difficult times. If we try to live our values, then we'll make the best of a difficult situation."

Ennen knew that, despite his request, word would spread—and it did. Culler was a local guy, not to mention Dina's husband, and while some expressed a satisfaction that the fourth-floor honchos were taking a hit after the peons hadn't had a raise in a long time, most were surprised. "I didn't think Phil would have the balls to do it," one leader said. That Ennen *did* have the balls served as further evidence that times were indeed difficult: Ennen wasn't kidding about that. Over wine at Kora's and burgers at Father John's, a few began to wonder if they'd be next.

■ ■ ■

Twenty-four hours later, nobody was talking about Culler or finances or possible job losses. The polar vortex descended on Bryan, dropping temperatures down to the minus teens. Ennen issued instructions to delay courier runs—for lab samples, for example—and for nonessential or off-duty personnel to call into any scheduled meetings from home. Air handlers for the operating rooms failed in the arctic cold, forcing CHWC to cancel one surgery and institute a tracking protocol for infections for those people who were being operated on when the handlers seized.

Away from the hospital, the poor and the ill-housed faced difficult decisions. In a trailer park on Bryan's eastern edge, people in single-wides cranked up their kerosene heaters. In West Unity, a few huddled up with friends blessed with reliable heat. Dad's Place, a charity near the Bryan town square, admitted everybody who showed up. The charge nurse in the Montpelier ER instructed staff that nobody was to be turned away, no matter how dubious their complaint. People often sought refuge in the ER there but generally were booted out after being allowed to loiter for a while: not now, though. Pastor Greg Coleman got in his truck and cruised the county.

When he spotted somebody outside, he checked to see if they needed help. If they did, he drove them to a church in Bryan that opened its doors. One homeless guy wandered around Walmart before Coleman found him. A man appeared in the Bryan ER with blackened toes from frostbite. He wasn't sure just how that had happened.

Work didn't stop at Menards just because Williams County froze. Keith made the drive up to Holiday City every afternoon. On the day the vortex released the county and the temperature rose all the way to 3 degrees, Keith woke up with a rumble in his belly and aches in his joints. He thought he might have a fever. Lots of people around the county were sick with the flu, but the Health Partners clinic on Main Street had given him a flu shot back in October. The vaccine wasn't a guarantee, he knew, but he sure hoped he didn't have it. He couldn't afford a day off work.

With every mile of his commute to Menards that afternoon, Keith felt worse. But he clocked in and walked to the end of his station. A couple of minutes later, he grabbed a trash can and threw up in it. Go home, his supervisor told him. Keith made the drive all the way back to Bryan, walked in the house, sat on the edge of his bed, and doubled over with fever, nausea, and aches. "You better go to the hospital," Bobbi said.

By evening, as the temperature dropped back to zero, Keith Swihart was dying. He drove himself the half-mile across Main onto High Street, parked, and walked into the lobby. There he picked up the red phone for admittance into the ER. Marv Stalter was on duty.

When Stalter looked at Keith's right foot, he knew right away that Keith was in trouble. The tips of Keith's remaining toes were black—and black ran down the outside of his foot, from his little toe to the arch. Keith's blood sugar had spiked to 900, about 300 points above the usual threshold that could induce a diabetic coma. His blood was turning to syrup. Stalter drove his blood sugar down, but he suspected it was so high not only because Keith had been incorrectly monitoring it but because Keith was also fighting osteomyelitis, a bacterial bone infection, and part of his foot had turned gangrenous.

Stalter and the nurses were nice to Keith, but he knew what they thought: How could this guy let this go for so long? Why won't he comply?

They didn't get it.

Keith thought he *was* complying. He'd noticed some black on his foot, but he thought it was a bruise. His feet weren't painful because he didn't have a lot of feeling left in them—more like a tingle—so he didn't think much of the bruise. That stuff just came with the job. When you worked in the Menards warehouse, on your feet for eight hours, you came home with bruises all the time. Infections can push blood sugar to high levels, especially in diabetics, but Keith didn't know that. And, yeah, he wasn't being as diligent as he should have been about his diet or about his testing. (He *did* check his sugars, but the numbers on his device maxed out at 400, so he didn't know it was as bad as it had become.) It wasn't like he was ignoring the fact that he'd already lost most of his big toe and most of the sight in one eye.

Over the next two days, doctors pumped high doses of antibiotics into Keith's veins, but with so little blood supply circulating through the rotting areas of his foot, the drugs couldn't kill the bacteria. Carolyn Sharrock-Dorsten, the Parkview podiatric surgeon who'd removed most of his big toe, told him she would have to amputate the rest.

Keith objected at first. He didn't want his toes cut off. He didn't want to be crippled, to be needy. He wanted to work, to enjoy his son, to be in control of his life. But, in the end, Keith Swihart complied. He obeyed.

And so, at just about the time when much of America settled in with nachos and pizza and beer to watch the New England Patriots receive the opening kickoff from the Los Angeles Rams on Super Bowl Sunday, Sharrock-Dorsten cut off a third of Keith Swihart's right foot. She cut away the rest of his big toe, and all the other toes, down into the metatarsals, also cutting away most of the little toe's metatarsal—the bone running along the outside edge of the foot—all the way to the arch. She sliced through his skin and muscle and nerves and snipped away more of Keith's life. His toes and part of his foot wound up in a small clear plastic container, like a grocery store tub of cottage cheese, in Shannon Keil's pathology lab.

At CHWC, Keith recovered in room 2131—an isolation room—his foot wrapped and taped with so much dressing it looked like a gag from a silent-film comedy. The room, super-clean, large, and silent as an empty church, had an anteroom where visitors had to wash their hands before opening the door to Keith. His bed moved up and down. A flat-screen TV on a swing arm adjusted to any height he desired. A nurse brought lunch: a small sandwich, some soup, and a little salad.

For a man who'd had much of his foot separated from his body, Keith seemed happy. Or, if not happy, then perhaps not distressed. Maybe the

painkillers and the anti-anxiety drug were *that* good—or maybe it was because he was out of the chaos of his home and in a quiet, sterile haven where
smiling nurses brought lunches on trays. Keith—most recently of Menards,
of being broke, and broken, sick, and grieving—was now the center of attention, an object of concern, a man of importance.

Of course, he couldn't help thinking about his foot. But from the vantage point of his bed in the big room and its attentive staff, all the disin-
tegration within Keith's world outside of CHWC seemed far away. In the
hospital, order ruled.

A young woman carrying a folder entered the room. She opened it
in front of Keith and showed him some papers. His new guide for living
was all laid out in black and white: there was a paper for a follow-up appointment with Sharrock-Dorsten, a paper about drugs (lots and lots of
drugs—ceftriaxone, insulin, Percocet, pantoprazole, sodium chloride, aspirin, atorvastatin, cilostazol, Paxil, lisinopril, metoprolol, acetaminophen),
a paper about his leave of absence from Menards. "Dr. Dorsten will have to
fill that out," she explained.

Keith paused. He said he'd looked at his Social Security records recently
and had realized he'd been working for twenty-five years—since 1993—and
that didn't count detasseling corn at thirteen, or helping his mother at the
nursing home where she worked, or hauling and pulling for farmers around
Burr Oak with his three-quarter-ton Chevy.

"Lotta them farmers were older—like fifty and sixty—and some Amish,
and, you know, Amish can't drive, so they needed our help," he said, adding in
his friends. "Don't get me wrong: We had fun mud-boggin', drinkin', hootin'
'n' hollerin'. But, at the end of the day, it was that we helped them farmers out."

The work wasn't always steady or fancy or well-paid, but he always did
it: the tool and die shop, Hi-Lex (where he'd fainted and then gotten his diabetes diagnosis), Ashley, Menards. But he was never able to get ahead of his
disease. At first, with his insurance, the drugs he was supposed to take cost
him about thirty bucks a week, he figured. But then they started costing
more and more, "and it just got to be too much." So sometimes he skipped
the medications. He never skipped work, though.

He understood that some people lived lives far different from his. He
recalled stepping into another world once, as if visiting a new planet, back
when he worked as a marketer for Pepsi, a title that meant he stocked shelves
and filled vending machines. He delivered to Michigan State University in

Lansing. "I never been in a big college like that. Michigan State's a big college. Seeing the stuff going on there, seeing stuff around there was mind-blowing, you know? I was awestruck. I mean, it's unbelievable how they get research money from the state to do stuff and see how everything works. We had access to all the vending machines in the labs all over the place. It was shocking.

"The other thing was, they have this big Muslim community on the doorstep of that college. That was different. I never saw that, either. I felt like I was in Dearborn." He was uncomfortable seeing so many Muslims in one place, "but I have Muslim friends I talk to here and there. Again, it's one of them things: people get angry about race and things, but it's just understanding somebody's culture, where they come from, their background. I mean, knowledge is everything. Ignorance is nothing."

Keith once dated a black girl. Her parents were upset she was seeing a white guy. That taught him why no one wants to be judged by something like skin color.

Though his world wasn't the world of the students at Michigan State, he still believed he had his destiny in his own hands, just like they did. But now he didn't. After looking at his Social Security records, he reckoned he might collect $1,600 a month if he was unable to work again. That amount didn't seem so bad—maybe he could spend more time with Caleb—but he hated the idea of it. And besides, how could he enjoy life with Caleb if he was going to be laid up all the time? Keith's mood darkened. "For me to get the crap end of the stick—it makes me wonder sometimes."

One floor below, Shannon Keil opened the cottage cheese tub containing Keith's toes and part of his foot. She arranged the toes and flesh in the proper order in her gloved hand. Corruption had invaded the tissue, seeped into the bones, oozed its way up the metatarsals until they became pliable, decayed, and no longer able to support a man.

Three days after the amputation, doctors released Keith from the hospital. It was almost evening. He had another PICC line in his arm, a folder full of papers, a walker, and the promise that a home health nurse would call on him to administer IV antibiotics through the PICC line.

Nobody, including Keith, knew just who would pay for all of this: the surgery, the drugs, the testing. Had his Menards insurance taken effect? It seemed like an open question whether Medicaid would cover what had just happened. What if the Menards insurance and the Medicaid fouled each other up? Keith still had a trash bag full of white envelopes from Parkview,

ProMedica, CHWC, PPG Ohio, lab testing companies, Schumacher, and pathology labs sitting under the workbench that held his RC cars. Ennen knew Keith's six days in the hospital would cost CHWC a lot of money. If Medicaid paid the bill, there was no way that the reimbursement would come close to the charges.

Bobbi drove the big Saturn, with the two boys in the back, to the hospital. A nurse wheeled Keith out and helped load him and his walker into the truck. Instead of crossing Main to reach Cherry Street, they turned right onto Main—in the direction of the cemetery—and then pulled into McDonald's. When they finally rolled onto the little driveway on Cherry, Keith couldn't figure out how to juggle the Happy Meals—dinner for the kids— and the big drink he'd bought for himself and fumble for the walker, too.

Five days after his release, Keith shuffled behind the walker into one of Sharrock-Dorsten's exam rooms and sat down on the edge of the padded table. His dressing needed changing. A nurse asked Keith if he wanted to watch her do it. If not, she could recline the table. Recline it, please, Keith said. He didn't want to see his foot. He hadn't seen it since the operation.

She lowered the top half of the bed and removed all the bandaging and dressing. Keith's right foot was now a stump—and narrower, since the outside had been carved away. The sutures across the top, where toes should have been, were neat and straight, precise as a tailor's seam. Keith kept his eyes closed.

The nurse left the room to gather a few supplies. Keith stared at the ceiling. The foot gnawed at him. It hung out there: at the end of the table, off the edge. Keith raised his chest a little, strained his neck, and looked down. The unreality of it stunned him for a moment. His foot now looked alien—not of his body at all. But the longer he examined it, the clearer the transformation became. That was his foot, all right, or what was left of it. He frowned with disgust. The frown deepened and grew severe, until he lay back, closed his eyes, and pushed away a tear.

He smiled when the nurse returned. She kept up a chatter of talk— about children, about the Betadine she slathered over the stitches, about the Aquacel material meant to keep Keith's wound dry and sterile. As she wrapped the wound, she said she was happy to see there was no red streaking that could indicate infection. Keith seemed relieved once the foot was again encased in wrappings. He could imagine it was all there, whole under the Aquacel and cotton and gauze.

Keith remembered to ask about all the forms that would give him permission to live his new life. He needed a signed document from Sharrock-Dorsten testifying that he was now handicapped so that the Ohio Bureau of Motor Vehicles would issue one of those blue placards for his dashboard. He asked if the office could fax the form describing his surgery and disability to Menards to extend his leave of absence. And he needed testimony sent to the child support people in Michigan explaining that he wasn't going to be able to work for a while—maybe not ever again.

Because Keith mentioned that he'd had some swelling in his leg, the nurses at Sharrock-Dorsten's office ordered a Doppler scan of his thigh and calf to be sure a clot hadn't formed. They called across the street to CHWC's imaging department and arranged for Keith to head over.

Jonda Borck welcomed Keith into the dark ultrasound room. In a few months, Borck would win CHWC employee of the month honors and perks like a front-row parking spot, a pin, a custom-made dessert to share with the crew, and a day off with pay. It was easy to see why. She'd been giving vascular ultrasounds for nearly nineteen years and had a way of connecting with people who lay down on her table. She and Keith talked about motorcycles and ATVs. Her husband had once raced ATVs as a pro—and still did sometimes, though Borck didn't approve because it was dangerous. But whattaya gonna do? Keith laughed and said he'd been up to Red Bud, in Buchanan, Michigan, where they hold pro motocross races.

The conversation took Keith's mind off his foot—so much so that as Borck slid the ultrasound handset on a cushion of gel over and over Keith's leg, he fell asleep. When the test ended, Borck asked a number of questions meant to ID Keith. He agreed on his date of birth, and that he was thirty-nine years old.

"Oh, we're almost the same age," Borck said. "I just turned forty."

Keith looked at her, and then at me: "I'm the youngest one in this room, but I'm in the worst shape."

I drove Keith home. He sat down in the recliner, turned on the TV, and tuned in to some racing action.

███

At about the time Keith's leg veins were being sounded by Jonda Borck, Marc Tingle and his daughter, Summer, stood in a bathroom they were tearing apart over in Fayette in Fulton County. They had a problem: you can rip out a sink, tear the walls down to the studs, and pull up a floor easy, but taking a cast-iron bathtub out of a room that had been built around the tub was a tactical nightmare. You could disconnect it from the plumbing, upend it, wheedle it upright onto a dolly, and—if the doorway was wide enough (a big if)—roll it out. Or you could break it up and take it out in pieces. Breaking it made one helluva racket, but with just himself and Summer as crew, Marc decided to beat on the tub with his 30-pound sledgehammer to crack it apart.

Marc did that kind of labor all the time. But, after about twenty minutes, he turned to Summer and said, "You know, this is kinda tuckerin' me out."

"What do you mean, Dad?" Summer said.

"I don't know," Marc answered. "I think I might be comin' down with somethin'." Marc knelt in a corner of the bathroom and removed his leather hat. Sweat trickled down his face and neck. Then he said, "Honey, I'm gonna go out and set in the truck for a few minutes. I don't want the client to see me like this." He walked outside into the cold, sat down in the driver's seat, and took some deep breaths.

Summer picked up the sledge and hammered on the tub for about ten minutes. Then she walked outside to check on her father.

"Honey," he said, "I wanna go home. I don't feel very good. I must be comin' down with somethin'." With every breath, Marc's chest felt heavier, as if he had to force air into his lungs. He'd felt like this before, when a solid chest cold had hit him, and he was a little grumpy that he'd be knocked out of work for a day or so. This cold must be a doozy, he thought. It came on so fast. He hoped it wasn't the flu. Whatever it was, he just wanted to get home, take a cold shower, and retreat to his recliner.

Summer drove. At a certain point, they had a choice to make. Fayette was just across the eastern border of Williams County. Edgerton was on the far west side of the county. They could use the more country route (which would take about an hour), or they could turn and head toward Bryan to travel along the main roads. Partway into the trip, Marc turned to Summer and said, "Honey, something isn't right. Let's head to Bryan." Five minutes later, about five miles outside of Bryan, he felt better. "Nah," he said. "Let's just go home."

But within seconds, Marc felt his arm go numb. He'd heard about heart attack symptoms and arm numbness. He told Summer about it.

"We're going to the hospital, Dad," she said, pressing her foot hard on the accelerator. Marc warned her about getting pulled over by a deputy. She ignored him.

By the time they rolled into the CHWC parking lot by the front doors, Marc was struggling for air. He eased out of the truck and walked as fast as he could through the lobby, with Summer trailing behind, and then picked up the red phone. "Hello," he said. "My name is Marc Tingle, and I think I'm having a heart attack." The security doors swung open, and Heather Gaylord showed them to Room 7. "Take off your shirt," she said, and handed Marc a small nitroglycerin tablet, which he swallowed just before his mind turned to fog.

Commotion, rushing, shouting, he himself screaming in pain, a white machine, and then the walking. Walking, and there was somebody beside him walking, too—a pair of hands and feet. He didn't know who it was, but he believed in Jesus and wanted to think it was Jesus. But he didn't turn to look: he just kept walking in green grass and red-yellow-blue and thinking how nice this place is. But then he heard female voices, and somebody was holding his hand, and one voice said, "Marc! Marc!" so he opened his eyes, and she said, "Stop doing that! Listen to my voice!" But now he heard himself screaming again, saw the white machine, and heard a man with an Indian accent saying, "This is going to hurt," and he felt a sharp pain in his groin, and then he woke up to his pastor's face.

For Gaylord, Marc Tingle's V-fib was an oh-shit moment of indelible clarity. After twelve years of nursing—two and a half in the ER—she knew what to do. The ER staff, headed by Moreland this shift, was a veteran bunch. So she was confident. But people don't go into V-fib every day in the Bryan ER, and now her patient had gone and done it.

After Stalter yelled, "Call the cath lab!" Kesireddy walked out of the med/surg department and took the elevator downstairs. In his suit and tie, he stood at the end of Marc Tingle's bed in Room 7 and watched impassively as Stalter and the nurses issued another shock to Tingle's chest. He ordered an injection.

"Are you with me, Marc?" he said. "Marc?" He moved to stand over Tingle, close to his face, and said, "Take some deep breaths here." Marc coughed and choked on fluid from under his oxygen mask. "In through your nose. Out through your mouth." Marc gasped in pain.

"Everyone clear!" Another shock quaked Marc's body: "Arrggghhh!" That shock seemed to work. "Amiodarone, please," Kesireddy instructed.

"Shock again, please. Push Ativan, please." One more pulse of electricity shot through Marc's chest.

Marc groaned again, and his eyes opened. He asked for Summer.

"Your daughter's here, hon," ER director Barb Rash, in her pink and purple workout wear, said. Summer held her father's hand, placing her other hand on his chest.

"You're working too hard for a Monday," he said (though later he wouldn't remember saying it), and everyone laughed, even though they didn't know it was an inside joke between father and daughter. Summer cried and laughed, and then they rolled Marc Tingle out of the room, into the elevator, and on to the cath lab. There, Kesireddy would thread a wire through his groin and place a stent that cost CHWC $1,400 into Marc's coronary artery to prop it open. It was completely blocked: what ER docs like Stalter call a widow-maker.

As Kesireddy operated, the ER cleaned up. Heather Gaylord pushed a cart out of the room. Her eyes were moist. But she wasn't crying, she insisted, because nurses don't cry. And why would she cry? She was happy. Call it relief: a release after the pressure.

Just five days before, she had worked the Montpelier ER when a fifty-four-year-old man appeared in full arrest. His wife had just been diagnosed with stage IV cancer. Gaylord and the others in Montpelier worked on him for a long time, with his wife screaming, "Don't stop! Don't stop! Don't stop!" But after ten rounds of epi, of bicarb, of the shocks, there was no point in continuing. The thing was, he'd felt lousy the day before. But he didn't come in.

This time, Gaylord had witnessed a happier ending. She would think about Marc's case for weeks afterward, rehashing it in her mind.

Marc would go to church that Saturday, and his pastor would point out Shayla Carlisle, the nurse who'd given him CPR, whom he'd never met and didn't remember from the ER. Marc would tap her on the shoulder, and she'd spin around, see him, start to cry, and slap Marc on his arm and say, "You really scared me!" The Monday after that, Marc and Summer would go back to work: they had the bathroom remodel to finish in Fayette. Marc gave up smoking. He and Cindy bought a lifetime supply of nicotine patches and made sure to pay the $550 county insurance premium every month. Summer would start a GoFundMe campaign (over Marc's objections; "I'm very prideful," he said) to help with his deductibles and co-pays, and the people at church would kick in money, too.

Half an hour after taking Marc to the cath lab, Kesireddy, with his white doctor's coat over his shirt and tie, filled a dinner plate before the medical staff meeting. Marc was upstairs, waking up from his surgery, but Kesireddy was certain Marc would "be fine and live a long life." There was no way Kesireddy was going to miss the staff dinner—the best dining-out experience in Bryan, Ohio.

The monthly meetings, run by Ennen or by the chief medical officer, were open to all physicians with CHWC privileges, but they didn't always show up until Ennen realized you had to put out a good spread to entice them. The idea of the meetings was to keep physicians apprised of CHWC news, developments, and policies.

For example, drug and supply shortages plagued CHWC and every other hospital. Hurricane Maria didn't just take out saline bags, it cut production of things like vial adapters and some generic drugs that were also manufactured in Puerto Rico. Many other generics just weren't being made anymore—not in sufficient quantities, anyway—because profits on generics stank. Lidocaine and dextrose, diazepam injections, injections for imaging, morphine, silver nitrate, a slate of antibiotics, ketamine, liquid vitamins, cancer drugs, atropine: all these were staples of modern medicine, but all were either in short supply or not available at any price.

The market failed, over and over. With the profit motive supreme and prices for old but critical generics low, companies left the market, and nobody was telling them they couldn't. So patients suffered. Shortages of drugs cost money—hundreds of millions of dollars per year by some estimates, though the U.S. Food and Drug Administration suggested the harms from the shortages were "drastically underestimated."

The doctors sped through this meeting's agenda, perhaps because it had been a long day. They approved two applications for staff privileges, and received briefings on infection control and some data on flu cases. When the floor opened for new discussion, Kevin Park, the Parkview physician who was also the county coroner, stood to say something about prescription drugs. Doctors should be aware, he said, that drug prices varied by wider amounts than most of them realized. They had little idea what their prescriptions cost patients unless they were a patient themselves. One of Park's

had told him that Walmart charged $217 for a month's worth of a choles-
terol drug called Crestor—thirty pills. "Two hundred and seventeen dollars!" Park shouted. He let that hang in the air for a moment. The patient,
he continued, decided to do a little research and found an equal amount of
Crestor for $17 at another pharmacy. "My patients are being ripped off by
Walmart!" he said, his face reddening. Doctors ought to know that. They
ought to do something about it.

After the meeting ended, Cathy Day, the compliance chief, said she'd
been talking to Dr. Mike Liu, a young Parkview general surgeon who was
still somewhat new to Bryan. Liu had told Day it seemed to him that he
was seeing a lot of colorectal cancer cases. She and Liu were working on a
theory.

"We are just now seeing the effects of the recession," she said. "People
have jobs, but they're not paying the twenty-five an hour. They're making
twelve, thirteen an hour, and have insurance with $5,000 deductibles, and
so they stopped screening, stopped going to the doctor." She also meant that
ten years before, as the local economy crashed, people stopped spending
any money they didn't have to spend, including for medical exams.

"Lots of people here were self-employed," Liu said, agreeing. "The prospect of paying for a colonoscopy is a huge expense. A single medical problem or medical bill could destroy their entire month's budget—maybe their
entire year's budget." Just as Valerie Moreno and her family did, Williams
County people weighed every ache and pain against the cost of seeing a
doctor, which was how you got young men with their guts in their nutsacks,
and what would have been a small colon polyp ten years ago showing up as
cancer now. The relationship between dollars and care troubled Liu. "How
can you tell yourself healthcare shouldn't be a right? That is another human
being you are sitting in front of, and because of the costs they tell you, 'I am
going to choose to die.'"

In the context of the state of Ohio, Williams County didn't have a high
rate of cancer. But it did have a problem. Williams had a relatively low incidence of bladder cancer, but one of the highest rates of death from bladder
cancer. The same was true for pancreatic and prostate cancers, for leukemia
and lymphoma, for oral and pharyngeal cancers. Ovarian cancer incidence
and death rates were both high. It was cervical cancer that killed Stephanie
Swihart; other than one county in Appalachia, Williams had the highest
proportion of cervical cancer cases detected at a late stage, as Stephanie's

had been. It had a moderate rate of colon and rectal cancers, but a higher rate of death from both. It also had the lowest rate of meeting colorectal screening guidelines in the state.

Studies linked hundreds of thousands of cancer deaths around the world to the effects of the Great Recession. An estimated ten thousand American and European suicides were attributed to it. Blood pressure and blood sugar measures worsened in American adults. And, as Day and Liu implied, Williams County hadn't ever recovered from it.

By the end of the meeting, Ennen was exhausted—and not just because of this one day. Everything was grinding on him. He was no closer to solving the puzzle of Kesireddy's replacement. The hospital needed a new phone system, and Patrick was still trying to solve the problem of how to upgrade the electronic medical records system without bankrupting the hospital and without falling deeper into Parkview's web. Negotiations with Parkview over the new cancer care joint venture dragged on. Jim Hicks informed Ennen that as of midnight on September 28—nine months from now—Williams County EMS would stop making the long transfers from CHWC to Fort Wayne and Toledo. Ennen and Hicks had been discussing such a move for a while. Ennen had ideas for replacing the transfers, but they were still just ideas. He had nine months to come up with a solution.

Marc Tingle rested comfortably in Ennen's shop, his life saved. Keith rested in his recliner, his life uncertain. In nine days there'd be another board meeting. It was only Monday. But as Ennen walked home through the park, he felt like it had already been a long week. He'd seen a lot in his thirty-two years at CHWC, but he didn't see how they would end.

8

Puppies Are Drowning

Janis Sunderhaus was a walking contradiction. She was a "terrible" Catholic who attended mass most every Sunday. She swore like a thirteen-year-old street tough and claimed to "never cry" but went weepy at stories about the kindness of nurses. She built and ran one of the biggest healthcare operations in the state, but collected a long list of medical enemies and relished any chance to verbally punch them in the nose by throwing rhetorical jabs like "I was like a raging, friggin' lunatic! I get in this doctor's face, and I'm, like, 'You take my patient or I'm fucking calling Medicaid. And I'm calling fraud lines'" and "They always say that shit! Doctors say whatever they want to say. Listen, listen: I've seen doctors fuck people up unbelievably, and then say, 'We found it.' And people are, like, 'Thank you, Doctor.' Oh my God!"

But belief embodied her most profound contradiction. She was as cynical as a film noir private eye, and yet Sunderhaus *believed*. She believed in inspiration and faith and justice, and when any of these beliefs were violated, she couldn't help but be outraged and then try to do something about it.

Nursing had made her that way ("I'm a crazy nurse. I have two daughters who are nurses. Nursing is my identity"), and her experiences nursing in the poorest neighborhoods of Lima, Ohio, as well as her life since, had taught her a hard truth about the American medical economy and how it had evolved.

Sunderhaus was part of a Lima tradition of nurses creating new ways to care for the city's people. Nursing nuns from the Sisters of Mercy founded St. Rita's, one of the two big hospitals in Lima. The nuns came to town in 1918 to minister to the sick among Lima's industrializing workers during the ravages of the same influenza epidemic that had once prompted Bryan to seek its own hospital. St. Rita's became Mercy Health St. Rita's Medical Center. Its crosstown rival, Memorial, began life as a tax-supported community hospital. Now it was Lima Memorial Health System, a ProMedica affiliate with the big green signage beckoning from atop its buildings.

Sunderhaus, a Lima native who had watched the transformations from the inside, developed a dark view of big nonprofit hospitals. "Nonprofits all began for a mission. There's a reason it's a nonprofit. You know, you believe in puppies, or whatever. People are committed to that. And you work hard, and you're committed, and you build this organization that then takes care of all the puppies. And then you've got all these people that are now committed to taking care of puppies that now are this big organization. And at some point, you say, 'Oh my God, if we don't get more money in here, we can't pay for everyone to take care of the puppies.' And then pretty soon the conversation becomes more about the organization and less about the puppies. And *then*, pretty soon, you don't even know there are puppies around. The puppies are drowning in the river right next to you, and you're worried about keeping everyone employed. That's what happens to nonprofits."

Sunderhaus ran a nonprofit, Health Partners of Western Ohio, that operated the Bryan Community Health Center, the clinic that helped Keith Swihart. She didn't see any contradictions in being a mass-attending terrible Catholic who cussed her way through life and viewed nonprofits with cynicism while running one.

Lima, the seat of Allen County, boomed with the rest of northwest Ohio during the first half of the twentieth century. European immigrants, whites from Appalachia, and African Americans from the South traveled north to work in foundries, to build battle tanks, to manufacture auto parts. By 1950, nearly 50,000 people lived there. Allen County's population peaked in 1980 at 112,000—and then slid, year by year, as the American middle deindustrialized. By 1990, Lima's population had dropped to about 45,000. (In 2019, it stood at just over 37,000.) Lima found itself with two large hospitals, Memorial and St. Rita's, trying to survive on a diminishing population. The city didn't need both. There was talk of a merger.

As one experiment among several in how such a merger might operate, the two hospitals supported a free clinic to serve the city's growing population of poor people. At the time, Sunderhaus worked as a nurse at St. Rita's. She also had four young children and was studying for her master's degree in nursing administration. Her husband taught at a Catholic school. She thought the proposed clinic, slated for operation from six to ten each night, could be an opportunity to escape her impossible schedule. Her husband could be home with the children on those nights, and she'd have weekends off.

She worked as a behavioral health nurse, not as a public health nurse or as a primary care nurse. But once she started working in the free clinic, she realized how blind she'd been to her own patients' needs. "All of a sudden, I'm dealing with high blood pressure, diabetes, and all this shit. And I just immediately fell in love with it, because it was my mental health patients now seeking medical care. And I was, like, 'Now I've got the full picture.'"

The people she saw for mental health problems also required help with their hearts, their teeth, their weight, their budgets, their diets, their homes. The medical system, whatever that meant, had failed them. Hospitals like St. Rita's and Memorial, doctors, nurses like her, public officials, and whoever it was who dealt in money had all failed them. Everybody said they cared about the young pregnant woman living in Victory Village, the barracks-like housing built by the federal government during World War II to accommodate segregated African American workers. But there was no place for that young woman to go for prenatal care aside from an emergency room, where she'd sit and wait with other scared pregnant young women to see a doctor she didn't know and who didn't know her. If you valued that young woman and her baby, that's not what you'd do.

The clinic experiment didn't last long because relations between the hospitals floundered. Then, during the Clinton administration, the city of Lima applied for and received a grant for neighborhood policing. Storefront police stations opened around the city. St. Rita's suggested placing nurses in some of those storefronts with the neighborhood cop. After an African American minister in Lima's south end badgered the hospital to assign a nurse to his neighborhood, Sunderhaus, who'd grown up there, requested the job.

She arrived to find an office, a computer, a cop who was rarely there, and a mandate to take charge of the neighborhood's health. She had no idea just how to do that. "I was, like, 'What the fuck?'"

She received some schooling when a fifty-eight-year-old woman walked into the office complaining that she didn't feel well. Sunderhaus took her blood pressure. It was around 240/120. "I was, like, 'Yee! She's gonna stroke out on me. I'm a little psych nurse. Threaten to kill yourself, jump out a window: that doesn't bother me. Threaten to stroke out in my office, and I'm, like, 'Ehh, I really don't want you to die here.'"

She closed up her office, put the woman in her car, and drove to the St. Rita's ER. Treatment there forced down the blood pressure, and, that night, Sunderhaus bragged to her children over dinner that Mommy had saved a woman's life.

Her self-congratulation proved premature. Three weeks later, the woman returned. What's wrong? Sunderhaus asked. The woman's blood pressure had spiked again, back to where it was. The hospital, the woman explained, "'gave me this list of people. I called every one of them, and nobody would take me. They gave me two weeks of meds, and I ran out.'" Well, Sunderhaus told herself, you didn't save a life. You did pretty much nothing.

Doctors didn't want to take Medicaid patients. Hospital ERs were too busy to follow up with patients, and they weren't the right place to seek care for a chronic condition like high blood pressure, anyway. So Sunderhaus started walking the neighborhood, including Victory Village, knocking on doors. Sunderhaus became the crazy white-lady nurse in sneakers who chatted up pregnant teen girls, old men, women working multiple low-wage jobs. When her friends expressed alarm she was walking around a neighborhood that had a reputation for crime, she'd say, "If I want to be loved, I go out in the neighborhood. If I wanna be beaten up, I go to the hospital."

"I saw a glimpse of the healthcare system from a poor black perspective that very few white people get to see," she recalled. People were getting pushed around. Doctors would use any excuse, like a missed appointment, to kick a Medicaid patient off the practice's rolls. They'd charge money to get back on the rolls, or charge money up front to see the patient in the first place—money many didn't have. There was no preventive care. Then, when people became sicker, they wound up being admitted to the hospital, costing Medicaid and Medicare many more thousands.

Sunderhaus envisioned a comprehensive, one-stop medical clinic where nobody would be turned away. Patients would be assessed for their overall health, receiving primary care, dental care, mental health counseling, and prescription drugs—all at an affordable price.

Such places already existed, and had for a long time. "Dispensaries" were as old as the United States. They were often founded for a specific group, like workers in one factory or residents of one neighborhood, and they could be affiliated with a nearby hospital or with a charity or social service organization. The concept expanded during the Great Depression—some served tens of thousands of people annually—then faded, then surged again during Lyndon Johnson's Great Society push with the Community Health Centers program. These clinics (somewhat reminiscent of Frank Dresser's proposal for "consulting stations" made during the early twentieth-century battles over government healthcare) aspired to be what Sunderhaus wanted for Lima: one-stop primary care providers servicing poorer neighborhoods for free or on a sliding scale. Support came from the federal government. They became "federally qualified" for aid.

George W. Bush reinvigorated federally qualified health centers by pouring money into an effort to open twelve hundred of them during his first five years in office. Sunderhaus believed a single-payer national health plan was probably a better answer to America's medical care needs, and that Bush's advocacy for the centers was a way to deflect comprehensive health-care reform. But as long as the money was out there, she saw a way to open the kind of service she'd hoped for since she first worked in the free clinic.

Sunderhaus established the South Side Planning Committee in 2002, with representatives from the Red Cross, United Way, both hospitals, city hall, and local neighborhoods. They held meetings. Soon the hospitals stopped coming. The Red Cross and United Way dropped out. The health department abandoned the committee, too. Then she went to mass.

The priest told a dramatic parable about a young boy who ventured deep into a canyon his elders had been afraid to explore but where they'd hoped a treasure awaited them. The boy reached the end of his rope. On faith, he let go, dropping onto a soft landing, where he found himself surrounded by jewels. "And that priest looked directly at me, and he says, 'Sometimes you have to trust that the Lord will have a soft landing.' And my husband looked over at me, and he's, like, 'Hee-hee-hee.' I quit my job the next day. It was Martin Luther King Day."

In July 2003, Sunderhaus opened a space—borrowed from the local Head Start program—with a used exam table, some boxes, a staff member she'd pried loose from the CEO of St. Rita's, and a young doctor who'd been moonlighting at Memorial's ER. They saw eight patients their first day even though they had no phone, no advertising, no news coverage. By the end of the week between twenty and twenty-five patients were coming to the clinic every day. Each uninsured patient paid $4, with Medicare or Medicaid covering the rest. A few neighborhood people donated money. "We had a little old lady, her name was Alice. She started sending us $2 a month. She was ninety-three. I've kept all the letters she sent me. We would be ready to drop, and we would get a letter from Alice with $2."

By the time Keith walked into the clinic in Bryan that previous fall, Health Partners of Western Ohio had fifteen clinical outlets and a budget of $34 million, and was serving 37,000 patients—including Pastor Greg Coleman and his family. Fifteen percent of the patients had no insurance. About 60 percent were covered by Medicaid, 12 percent by Medicare, and the rest by private insurers imposing high deductibles. Health Partners worked on a sliding scale, with a $10 minimum fee. Sunderhaus, who went unpaid for the first six months she was in business, now earned $228,000. Her doctors and nurse practitioners made median national wages for their jobs. (Barb Purvis, the nurse practitioner who cared for Keith, made $120,000 a year, plus a bonus that was dependent upon her patient volume.)

Sunderhaus managed all that by applying for grant money and subsidies, and by going into the drug business. Health Partners ran a 340B drug program. Under 340B—a federal rule—drug manufacturers who wanted their products approved for reimbursement by the Centers for Medicare and Medicaid Services had to agree to sell "outpatient" drugs at a steep discount to federally qualified services like Health Partners. On average, such entities received about a 22 percent discount off the wholesale price of the drugs. CMS would then reimburse the centers for dispensed drugs at the same price as non-340B providers. Health centers could keep that profit to fund themselves, and still save their patients money. During the first week in operation in Lima, Sunderhaus recalled, "we had a lady who came to get her blood pressure medicine. It was like $58. And she probably lived on $800 a month. And Jenny said, 'I'm gonna try to put it through [the new system] and see what happens,' and it came through, and it rang up $22. That was the savings from the 340B price. And the patient cried. The patient *cried*. That's thirty bucks. If you're living on $700 or $800, that's big."

The pharmacy business brought Health Partners to Bryan. The Four County Alcohol Drug Abuse and Mental Health Services board, where Tonie Long worked and Les McCaslin was chief, had made a commitment to provide psychiatric drugs to patients who could not otherwise afford them. But the drugs were costing the board a fortune. Sunderhaus offered McCaslin the benefits of her 340B discount.

But, she told McCaslin, "'your psychiatrists don't know what the fuck they want.' And a report came out, and mentally ill people were dying twenty-five years earlier, based on high blood pressure, diabetes—all that. Crazy people need primary care stuff, too." The more they talked, the more convinced McCaslin became that Health Partners should just open a facility in the area. At first the fledgling clinic worked out of McCaslin's offices, but McCaslin provided $200,000 out of his budget for a place of their own.

Sunderhaus and McCaslin scouted Defiance, but they faced the Mercy-ProMedica battle for patients there. The hospitals "didn't want us," Sunderhaus said. Then they found an empty building just off Bryan's town square. McCaslin provided $1.2 million for building out the interior to accommodate a medical operation and to pay for bright, sunny decor and professional-looking furnishings (Sunderhaus was adamant that her facilities look spiffy: "It says, 'I value you as a person, and you deserve this. You deserve it, no matter what. Because you're human. You just deserve it'").

The Health Partners clinic wasn't the only or the first alternative provider in Bryan. A local minister opened the Compassion Clinic on the east side for limited hours in 2005, with different volunteer doctors taking turns at providing care. Spangler Candy contracted with Activate Healthcare, a private equity–backed corporation, to give basic primary care to its Bryan employees at a cost of about $31 per enrolled employee. The city of Bryan followed suit not long after Spangler. (Such on-site company clinics were once common in the United States.) Activate was bought out in 2019 by Paladina Health, another private equity–backed outfit that promised to deliver "value-based" primary medicine and to "transform healthcare in America."

From the earliest days of the dispensaries, doctors moaned about free and discounted care. During the rise of the Great Society clinics, AMA president Milton Rouse called them "unnecessary" and "wasteful." Some local medical societies pressured hospitals to refuse admitting privileges to doctors who worked for the clinics. When the Bryan Community Health Center opened in January 2016, there was opposition in Bryan, too—from both doctors and dentists. "They don't like the competition," Sunderhaus said. "You have to be willing to piss off a few." When the center bought a dental van with help from the ADAMhs board, and when the van began visiting the county's schools, there was more blowback from the local dentists, who accused the health center of stealing patients from them. Yet not a single private-practice dentist in Williams County accepted Medicaid patients—in a county where a lot of children were on Medicaid, even if their parents were not, and where far too many suffered from "Mountain Dew mouth," if not meth mouth. The need was so great that the dental clinic in the Health Partners building had a six-month waiting list.

And Parkview doctors weren't much happier with the center, Sunderhaus believed, "because they're charging hospital outpatients for everything. And their job in Bryan is to refer those patients to big services in Fort Wayne. Their job is merely as a feeder site for testing. And for their specialists. That is their only purpose for having family practice there, to feed their beast. Feed the beast of the MRI, the CAT scan machine. They keep track of those docs: how much they prescribe, how many tests they ordered. That's how they decide who gets bonuses and who gets big bucks. Yeah! We piss everybody off!"

Ennen figured the new Health Partners clinic was like the Spangler Activate clinic: one more primary care site that could feed *his* beast, send patients his way for more advanced procedures, specialty services, imaging, tests. And he was happy some people who wouldn't walk through the doors of his shop were at least receiving some care—what Sunderhaus called "a hug of services."

The Bryan clinic's medical staff consisted of one physician, two nurse practitioners, a medical technician, a chiropractor, a full-time dentist, three dental hygienists, three pharmacists, and two mental health counselors. They were all very busy. "We are so far behind!" center director Ronda Muehlfeld said one morning shortly after the doors opened.

They saw a lot of people like Keith. Rationing of insulin was common, and so the effects of rationing insulin were common, too. Insulin could cost a diabetic $500 to $600 a month. "That's rent," Muehlfeld said. A vial of Levemir could cost over $300 in a regular pharmacy. Their patients could get it for $10.

A young woman in her late teens and wearing a Team Jesus camo T-shirt approached the reception desk with other members of her family. She was new to the clinic and hoped to establish care there, because she wanted to see a dentist. She'd never seen one. It would be a long wait, the intake clerk told her—months, maybe. The young woman said she'd waited this long, she could wait until then.

Customer after customer checked in: another young woman, who'd missed a Pap smear and dental appointments because she didn't have a way to get to them; an old lady who'd arrived from Mexico to live with her son; a woman, about sixty, who'd had a stroke and could no longer speak; a bronchitis case; a flu case; a mother pushing her wheelchair-bound epileptic daughter, who received Medicaid, and so could not find any other doctor in town who would take her. A clerk phoned a thirty-two-year-old woman who wanted to start Vivitrol, a drug used to treat opiate addiction. She'd missed two earlier appointments and was now late for another. No transportation, she said. Many other doctors would write her off as noncompliant and un- reliable. It's very important you start, the clerk said. How about one-fifteen?

The Smiths* were married, in their late thirties. Belle was obese, dia- betic, and had not had her insulin lately. John was dressed in a ball cap and camo pants and was missing a front tooth. Both worked as cleaners at the service plaza on the Ohio Turnpike, out by West Unity, for a turnpike contractor called Any Domestic Work, or ADW.

John was originally from Tennessee. Belle lived in Williams County. They had met through Plenty of Fish, an online dating service. She came down to Tennessee for a visit, and then they moved together up to Williams County. John found a job at Rassini Chassis in Montpelier for a while, mak- ing $11 an hour, then did a stint at Kamco, and after that worked security at Menards for over $11, but his sciatica got worse. After some time off, they both started with ADW so John could save up money to fix his vehicle—or to get it good enough, at least, to make it to New Jersey, where, he said, a buddy might have a job for him that paid $20 an hour. ADW offered health insurance, but it didn't kick in for ninety days, and, anyway, they each made only $9 an hour. He handed over a paycheck to prove it. The Ohio Turnpike Commission paid ADW $342,000 a year to keep that plaza clean.

▦

As the Smiths were starting care at the Health Partners clinic, in the fourth- floor boardroom, the CHWC executives held another strategic planning meeting. As part of the "current state analysis" they were all trying to create, Patrick had been assigned to collect Ohio Hospital Association data on geo- graphical hospital market share. All of them were concerned about "leak- age." How many people in their core market (Williams County, mainly) were leaving to buy services from competitors? That could mean Henry County in Napoleon, Hillsdale, Hicksville, the Mercy and ProMedica hospitals in Defiance, and the hospitals in Toledo and Fort Wayne, among others. Conversely, they wanted to know how much opportunity there was to nip some business away from those facilities, and, if so, what "service lines"—ob-gyn, radiology, cancer, wound healing, lab testing, and so on—they'd need to promote or establish in order to do so.

Angelia Foster favored creating a psychiatry service line. Nobody in any position to know—Jim Watkins at the health department, the mayor of Bryan, leaders at the ADAMhs board, Jim Hicks at EMS—had any doubt that Williams County's mental health was a shambles. The county's crisis wasn't any more or less severe than a hundred other counties in the United States, urban or rural, but, being rural, Williams lacked for diagnosis, treatment, and care.

Foster also mentioned geriatrics. Like many other rural areas, the county was aging but had no geriatrician—no geriatrics program at all. CHWC could capture Medicare payments by starting such a service line. Ennen added that perhaps they could put that service line in Montpelier, the critical access hospital (CAH), so CHWC could reap the 101 percent of "reasonable costs" Medicare paid to CAH facilities.

Tinkel suggested that more marketing and advertising might be necessary: an appeal to consumerism. The big for-profits advertised, marketed, and then hired paid greeters and patient escorts. They redecorated rooms and made them all private. The big nonprofits followed suit. The elderly volunteers who said good morning as you walked in the front doors of CHWC were sweet, but maybe it was time to make CHWC a bit more like the Ritz and then market the high-touch "concierge" service.

The message Ennen took away from the data wasn't so much about what new services CHWC could offer as it was about how well CHWC already performed. Despite the "Band-Aid station" rep, CHWC took close to 70 percent of the market share. "The same market share we had in the nineties," he said—before Parkview bought out the doctors, before the big systems had grown so big, before the Affordable Care Act, before two recessions.

At the much larger hospitals where Foster and Wade Patrick had worked, CEOs and boards considered 70 percent market share the best they could achieve. "And I'm just saying, a more fair comparison of CHWC and Williams County, versus where you guys came from, would be CHWC owning the docs in Williams County. That is the more fair comparison."

Parkview owned the docs in Williams County, but CHWC still wasn't suffering much leakage. Ennen didn't say so outright, but the undercurrent was clear: he hadn't done such a bad job on the last strategic plan, back in 2016, and he didn't need fancy consultants and a monthslong process, or any acronymed business-school techniques.

Foster pushed anyway. "Can we talk about Plante?" she asked. Plante Moran, CHWC's auditors, had offered the services of one of their rural hospital specialists to help "facilitate" the strategic planning meetings. What that meant wasn't clear, but Plante would charge nothing for the help, and Foster thought a third-party referee in the room could prevent tortured sessions in the future. "It is very difficult to be a participant and also facilitate, especially given our group dynamics," she said. "If I challenge your assumptions, I still have to deal with you all the next day."

Ennen was skeptical. He foresaw a conflict of interest when an independent auditor would also be serving as a consultant. Besides, he noted, the "free" offer was probably a wedge to tempt CHWC into signing a consulting deal. To Foster and Patrick, Ennen's skepticism sounded like opposition, but that wasn't necessarily so. Ennen understood the value of outside eyes that had seen hospitals face many kinds of dilemmas. But the idea of bringing in another professional smacked of expanding the strategic planning mandate beyond what he thought they'd all agreed to do. For this iteration, the point was to get something done by August that would satisfy the board, and then set the stage for paying the big dollars a year or two down the line for Root—their preferred consultancy—to take over the job next time.

"I can tell you this much: if you guys turn this over to me, we will have a strategic plan by August," Ennen said, "because I will make sure we have one by August. But I'm not sure it will accomplish what we want to accomplish."

"For me, it's the ability to have the difficult conversations we need to have that, in previous sessions, were very difficult to have—which is why I would like to have someone facilitate," Foster added. "Because I am not gonna do it again."

After some back-and-forth, Foster lost this round. Tinkel agreed with Ennen that once they'd decided against hiring an outside consultancy, it was foreordained that deep analysis and a new, profound vision for the hospital's future would have to wait. Meanwhile, Tinkel said, they could still make headway: "Whatever we accomplish is better than not trying at all."

Ennen tried to soothe Foster, but she still wanted a facilitator: "Last time, I left really defeated."

"I'm sorry you felt that way," Ennen replied. "I am really sorry you felt that way. Because we made it through. It wasn't pretty, but we made it through."

This was CHWC as a business—but as a business being run by people who also claimed to abide by a mission, people struggling not to lose sight of the puppies. But how to apply the new American religion of corporate efficiency and return on investment metrics to a "community asset"? This inherent contradiction made for tortured conversations.

How, for example, to address the bad debt? Ennen mentioned billings to self-pay patients as a way to curb the problem. In the past, CHWC hadn't often sued people for overdue payments; records from courts in Williams and nearby counties did not contain many entries. CHWC preferred to work out payment plans, offer grace periods, or, if all else failed, write off an unpaid bill as bad debt, take the government credit, and move on.

But maybe they should start talking money up front. Ennen suggested a prescreening of customers—what some in the industry called a "wallet biopsy": a meeting to "confront the patient about how much they will be responsible for, and how they will take care of it." Perhaps CHWC should work out a payment plan *before* any procedure. The hospital had done such a thing on a small scale. But now, Ennen said, maybe the hospital should require a deposit before every single elective or nonemergency surgery, as some other hospitals did.

"My ex-wife had to pay her $2,500 up front before they even scheduled her elective surgery," Patrick said, "and that was at the hospital she works at."

Like any other business, CHWC employed people, and there, too, they struggled to juggle their mandates. Ennen felt both a collective responsibility—to Bryan, to keep people on the rolls—and a responsibility to individuals, the employees. He hated that some of his own workers made so little money in full-time labor that they qualified for Medicaid, just like some at Menards. And now he'd fired Culler—the first time in thirty-five years the hospital had cut loose a vice president.

Culler's firing had spooked the staff, Foster told Ennen. Some thought it meant more layoffs were coming. Ennen had taken great care to craft his memo about Culler to avoid that very situation, but now he worried he'd mis-fired by asking leadership not to talk about it to other employees. Of course everybody found out anyway—this was Bryan, Ohio—and then wondered why their bosses hadn't explained. In the absence of information, they made up stories, most of them conjecture that CHWC's finances had collapsed and that Tinkel's cheerleading the tiny margin last quarter was just pablum.

"I dunno," Ennen said. "How do you [fire people] well?" He thought about 2009, when he'd had to lay off so many as the recession pounded the county. The experience left a scar. "I guess I hope we don't get good at it," he told the others.

They suggested Ennen address Culler's departure in more detail in an upcoming leadership meeting. But Dina Culler would be at the meeting, too, and Ennen worried about her feelings.

Ennen's concern illustrated the yin and the yang of his role at CHWC, and why the board had supported him all those years—but also why that same board now worried about his leadership. Both the board and the community wanted—demanded—a community and a family focus. The hospital was special. It wasn't only a community asset in the legal sense; it was a community glue, a community economic powerhouse, a community source of employment, a community lifeline.

People in Bryan often talked about the hospital. Nurses and patients told stories about running into each other in Walmart, just as Shayla had run into Marc Tingle in church. "We were in bed together once," a man told one of the veteran nurses upon being introduced to her at the Bryan bowling lanes. "You didn't recognize me 'cause you never seen me with my clothes on!" Any mention of CHWC in any café or bar in Bryan would produce a comment from somebody who had a relative who worked there.

In November 2011, as the county's recession dragged on while other parts of the country recovered, Ennen sent one of his "fiscal watch" memos. Continued government payments were at risk, he wrote. The composition of the Congress had changed after the 2010 midterms, and the new Republican-led body—still angry over the passage of the Affordable Care Act—was going to fight President Obama all the way. "CHWC is today staring at $2.7 million in Medicare cuts over the next two years," he wrote. "That is almost $1 million more than our budgeted margin for this year.

"There is no reason to panic. There is every reason to plan. So that's what we will continue to do. . : . We don't get nasty and rude. We just find a way to make it work. We cope. We provide excellent service. We treat each other with respect. We bond with the communities we serve. We support them. They support us. . . . If we all make a commitment to one another, if we build a culture of resilience against the negative—if we do that, then we can find ways to cope with the bad times and rejoice in the good times. But we have to make a total family decision."

These weren't phony platitudes. Ennen recalled times when Bryan had fought to keep its local character—not out of insularity, but because the local relationships and the local ownership mattered. His father once tried to keep a bank from being absorbed by a bigger, regional outfit. "My dad was part of lots of conversations about 'we need to keep this bank solvent and independent, because it's gonna be better for all of us if it is,'" Ennen recalled. "'Because if we don't, all the decision-making is going to go someplace else.'" The bank was swallowed up anyway, and his father's prediction came true.

Some other CEO—say, one brought in by a Parkview or a ProMedica—wouldn't hesitate to fire people. They'd cut and meet the numbers. Some board members, after the loan covenant breaches, were asking for that kind of cold corporate calculation.

To soothe the nerves jangled over Culler's firing, on the day of the planning session Ennen sent an unexpected message (full of ellipses, as was his manner) to all the staff: "I know that we had planned to share financial information quarterly . . . but all of us in senior leadership believe you need to see our most recent data . . . that now includes January. What you will see is that we continue to perform ahead of budget. This is our 3rd month in a row with a positive operating margin. We are busier while maintaining our costs. Net revenues are up 8% . . . while operating expenses are up 3%. You . . . we . . . us . . . we've done really excellent work . . . and it is showing in our financial performance.

"I know this is not easy work . . . especially for certain department[s] where we have been focusing . . . but the effort is worthwhile. I'm sorry that things feel so confusing . . . I wish I could always give everyone more clarity."

The talk of the personnel change at the top sparked a conversation about others who might be leaving. The potential losses could prove disastrous, yet Ennen—and to a lesser degree the others as well—visibly relaxed when they talked about them, as if the near-term problems were easier to confront than the long-term vision.

Nobody knew when Kesireddy—it was always Kesireddy—would retire. "One thing we have to be honest about is, when he is done, the cath lab is done," Ennen said. "That is the way we would have to forecast it, and then we could try to keep it going. I wanna try to be pragmatic about it," he added. "Getting three interventional cardiologists to try to see the value of an emergent interventional cath lab in Bryan is gonna be really hard. And I think it is gonna take three to replace his three-hundred-some days, and we'd still have to bring in locums coverage for probably as much or more than we do now."

To some prospective Bryan doctors, the number of Marc Tingles spread over Williams County was less important than how much money there was to be made by setting up shop in the city. This was true not only for interventional cardiologists, but for all kinds of physicians. Recruiting doctors to rural communities was never easy and grew more difficult every year.

Back in the 1980s, Brunicardi had targeted foreign doctors eager to find a place in the U.S. When he thought he'd hooked one, he reeled the doctor in by treating them like royalty. For Zoher Vasi, originally from Gujarat, India, and then practicing in Halifax, Nova Scotia, it began with a phone call.

"He said, 'I like your voice. I want you to come,'" Vasi marveled. Vasi had arranged to visit a brother in Cincinnati. "He said, 'No problem. We will come and get you in Cincinnati.'" Brunicardi, the chairman of the hospital board, and the mayor of the village of Sherwood (south of Bryan, across the Defiance County line) all piled into the chairman's private plane, picked up Vasi, and flew him back to Bryan. In the hospital's boardroom, they introduced Vasi to local officials, a school principal, and other board members. Brunicardi promised to transform an old Sherwood motel into a fully equipped office for Vasi. He loaned a personal car to Vasi's wife.

Immigrants like Kesireddy and Vasi made up a significant portion of Bryan's medical community. "We have been blessed with talented people from Iraq, Jordan, Israel, India, Pakistan, Mexico, the Philippines, Jamaica, Egypt and Canada," Ennen wrote to the area's federal legislators in the wake of Donald Trump's 2017 anti-Muslim travel ban. Doctors from foreign countries often had a difficult time finding positions in desirable metro areas, so they turned to rural places and small towns as a way to gain a foothold in the American medical economy.

Some, like Vasi and Kesireddy, grew to love the places and stayed. Ennen valued them. "The actions of the Trump Administration to further restrict immigration is having a direct and negative impact on our hospital," he wrote in a challenge to local sentiment. "Please know that rural America is quite often the place where medical professionals of foreign descent (both U.S. citizens and non-U.S. citizens) choose to practice their craft. . . . They each made a commitment to our community and we returned that commitment to them."

He invoked the experience of Hanan Bazzi. Though born and raised in the United States, Bazzi had family in Lebanon. "In celebration of completing her long medical training, the family was planning a summer trip to Lebanon, to visit with all of their Lebanese family. They wanted to celebrate the start of their new life in Bryan. But now there is great concern about whether they would be able to safely get back into the United States. The entire trip has been canceled. What should be a happy family celebration has been crushed. . . . The clear fact is that rural America needs immigrants to serve our communities."

Other doctors came to Bryan for the money. "Nobody will lie about that," the Parkview surgeon Mike Liu said. Rural areas were forced to pay a premium to attract talent, so much so that doctors could make a third more in Bryan than they could in many metro areas of the United States. Bryan doctors were rich—a vast change from the 1930s, when a doctor in the region could expect to take home about $45,000 in 2019 dollars—not only because of the high salaries, but because the cost of living in Bryan was so low. That attracted young doctors like Liu, who were carting around a couple of hundred thousand dollars in medical school debt.

When Liu first thought of coming to Bryan, he saw job postings for both the hospital and the Parkview Physicians Group. Because he'd worked at Cleveland Clinic, where surgeons were hospital employees, he spoke to Ennen in addition to the group across the street. Ennen offered $350,000. Parkview offered about $500,000. "So I said to Phil, 'Why aren't you able to meet what Parkview was going to offer, to make it more enticing for me to sign with you?' He said, 'That's the limit of what I can do.'" What's more, CHWC had no family doctors in its employ. All the family docs worked for Parkview. Liu could count on those family doctors feeding their patients to him. "They will keep everyone in-house, in the system," Liu said. "They are well aware of where that revenue is going. I am actually very surprised at how business-oriented they were."

With such competition for doctors, CHWC sometimes had no choice but to offer top salaries. Chad Tinkel's wife, Jodi Tinkel, the hospital's medical cardiologist, made $616,489 for the fiscal year ending in September 2018—higher than the 75th percentile for nonsurgical cardiologists

($563,130) in the United States. Michael Nosanov, who ran CHWC's ear, nose, and throat clinic, made $546,519.

Both the medical group and the hospital paid signing bonuses, too. When Keil hired on as CHWC's pathologist, Brunicardi paid her a bonus of $50,000. Years later, in 2018, the average signing bonus for all physicians across the United States was still only $33,707. This competition for doctors occurred at a time when doctors—with the exceptions of family and general practitioners—were making more money all the time. Taken as a whole, with all fields of practice combined, physician compensation rose over 16 percent in the four years between 2013 and 2017—a period when wages for hourly workers remained flat.

As it turned out, Kesireddy's probable departure wasn't the only one Ennen and his team would face sooner rather than later. A Parkview oncologist was about to retire, too. If the cancer joint venture with Parkview was to become reality, CHWC might have to hire an oncologist of their own. The medical group was also losing an ob-gyn to retirement, leaving a shortage in the community. Parkview had known of the retirement for months, but corporate didn't seem to be in a hurry to find a replacement. That would mean busier days and nights for Bazzi and Hassouneh—which might be good for the hospital's bottom line, but not for their lives. "Bazzi's contract comes up first, and she could say, 'This quality of life thing he gave me is going away,'" Ennen said. He wanted to keep both of them happy so they'd stay. "I want them to solve this problem," Ennen told the others, referring to Parkview. But if Parkview didn't, Ennen might have to hire another ob-gyn of his own. Nosanov was probably leaving soon, too. If they couldn't find another ENT specialist, that clinic might have to shutter.

Kim Owen, the radiation oncology center chief, had also announced that she was quitting. Ennen's instinct had failed him. He'd wanted to protect both Owen and the hospital by keeping his handling of Owen's alleged harassment off the books. Thinking the problem had disappeared, he'd planned an announcement of Owen's new position as cancer care coordinator to the staff. He had not, however, clued in Foster or Chad Tinkel.

In January, Owen spoke to Foster. She told Foster how the doctor had made working conditions inside the center intolerable. New job or no new job, Owen had had enough.

Upon hearing the details of the doctor's actions from Owen, Foster decided that, as the hospital's human resources boss, she was compelled to conduct an investigation, and that she should have been informed the first time Owen mentioned the harassment. She also worried that any lawyer looking in would match Owen's complaint and the new job offer from Ennen, and think quid pro quo. "If I'm a lawyer, I would run wild," she said. Elevating Owen made sense, but it looked bad. "I said, 'As chief HR officer, I need to protect the organization,'" Foster told Ennen, "'and remove you from [the situation].' You can't talk to the doc, [the contracted group], Kim. No more emails. This is to protect you and the organization."

Ennen resisted. He felt he had acted in the best interests of all concerned. But Foster, well aware of the new Me Too movement blazing hot amid allegations of assault swirling around high-profile men like Harvey Weinstein, believed Ennen's way of trying to protect Owen by warning off the doc and easing out the group hadn't been sufficiently aggressive. "The law doesn't care about your intent. The law holds you culpable as CEO to take action when a woman says she's been harassed."

Foster also worried Owen would sue; Owen had, in fact, consulted a lawyer. Reasoning that Owen would be less likely to pursue legal action if she still worked for CHWC, Foster tried to get her to rescind her resignation. As of the strategic planning meeting, Owen had not, though Foster believed she was making progress. "I think I can salvage it," she said, "and can say to attorneys that we've done all we're supposed to."

After her investigation, Foster concluded that Ennen's initial instinct to avoid a medical staff meeting was the correct one. She planned to recommend to the board that the doctor not be allowed on the CHWC campus, but that the hospital not formally rescind his privileges. "He could mount a defense. That could get very public. I told [the doctor], if he really wants what's best for [the group], CHWC, patients, he can't be in our building anymore. The financial incentive to figure this out is in his best interest." But one thing Ennen wanted to avoid—telling the board, which was scheduled to meet one week after the strategic planning session—became unavoidable the moment Foster began the investigation.

His handling of the Owen situation rippled outward. Word of Owen's new position infuriated another staff leader, who felt wronged that Ennen did not post the job and give other employees a shot at it. CHWC may have been the biggest employer in Bryan, with about five hundred at the main campus and another two hundred between Montpelier and Archbold, but it was, as Ennen liked to call it, a "family." Now the family was upset.

Ennen could be both reactive and thoughtful. He sometimes appeared to reject a suggestion or comment out of hand, only to come back to it fifteen minutes or half an hour later, having considered it anew. He thought over the planning session the rest of the day and through the night. The following day, he sent a memo to the vice presidents that was at once contrite for leaving the impression he wanted to assume control and write the plan himself—and for how difficult the group's relationship had become—but also defensive about the value of his previous strategic plan. "I agree it is not specific, not targeted . . . there is no SWOT . . . there is no SOAR . . . there is no 'Current State' . . . there is no 'Future State.' . . . It was a good plan." He apologized to Patrick and Foster, who'd tried to coach them all through the process, for anything he'd said or done that made their work more difficult, but insisted he was not opposed to strategic planning. "I do work at the behest of the Board . . . I'm fully aware of that . . . and I have no desire to lose my job."

Rather, he knew that in this business you couldn't count on anything. Perhaps everyone would stay in their jobs, and perhaps Ennen could find replacements for Kesireddy, and maybe the government's payouts would remain the same, but you never knew. You could spend much precious time and money laying out the most sophisticated multiyear projections and strategic plans, but they wouldn't necessarily be worth much in the real world of a small, independent community hospital.

Henry County hospital, down in Napoleon, had a consultant-driven strategic plan, and they lost money all through 2018, too. Every little indie hospital in the region lost money in 2018. Foster's and Patrick's old employers had SOAR and SWOT, and they were taken over. Since at least 1973, when Brunicardi arrived at the failing institution, the leadership of CHWC had avoided that fate through seat-of-the-pants opportunism to build what the community needed. That culture now clashed with the culture of the twenty-first-century corporation. But CHWC wasn't making injection-molded parts for cars. They were trying to take care of human beings, to be an economic lifeline for the town, to survive.

███

That afternoon in West Unity, Shilo* and Jimmy* settled into their new home. They'd started in Toledo, back when they fell in love—when she was just seventeen, when she dropped out of high school. That was 2003. He bought an engagement ring for her. It was nice; she looked at it often. Then he bought a big pickup truck. By 2007, they had a baby boy.

The engagement was a long one and still ongoing because the relationship was pretty turbulent. He had a child with another woman, a heroin addict; the boy now lived with him and Shilo. And there was the time she had sex with the man who was dating his mother—the mother who'd abandoned Jimmy before he was two years old. She wished he'd just get over that and forgive her, but he carried a grudge about it. She was pretty sure he needed a counselor.

Jimmy had had possibilities once. He went to community college, but after two years he had too much student loan debt. So he took a job driving. Then he screwed up and got slapped with a grand theft auto charge. He lost his job in Toledo, so they moved to Wauseon, where it was cheaper. He got a job there, in a machine shop, but that ended, and so they and the two boys moved into an apartment in West Unity, where the rent was cheaper still, and where a sign out front said NO SMOKING. Their apartment reeked of tobacco smoke.

The truck held up just long enough to get them there. Often it didn't work at all. The lack of transportation made it difficult for Shilo to get into Bryan, so for now her world was limited to West Unity. Her anxiety meds needed refilling, though. She was already climbing the walls. She skittered around the apartment in her yoga pants and an old T-shirt, burning calories she couldn't spare off her wispy frame. A doctor wanted her to go on Lexapro, the antidepressant, but she said there was no way she would. The son they had together had anxiety, too, and the son Jimmy had with the addict was already taking Zoloft and Adderall. Shilo hadn't seen a dentist since she was a kid. She received her drugs through mental health service agencies, paid for through her Medicaid.

She planned to start interviewing for jobs. But since the truck rarely worked, her options were limited to what she could find within walking distance. That wasn't a rare thing in West Unity; Greg Coleman often watched people without transportation walk by the church to go to work at Kamco and other employers.

Feeding Jimmy, herself, and the two boys was another matter. She received food stamps (Supplemental Nutrition Assistance Program, or SNAP) in addition to her Medicaid, but in West Unity, buying groceries wasn't as simple as driving to the neighborhood supermarket. Williams County had one supermarket, Chief, as well as the giant Walmart across the street from Chief. Both were in Bryan, twelve miles away.

Without the truck and the gas money to make the 24-mile round trip, Dollar General was Shilo's only grocery option. There'd once been an IGA. When she was a girl, Valerie Moreno and her family could buy groceries there, including fruits and vegetables they didn't grow on their own. About 200 yards down the road from the Dollar General, the empty shell of the IGA slumped into what had been its parking lot.

When the private equity giant Kohlberg Kravis Roberts bought Dollar General for about $7 billion just as the Great Recession snuck up on America, some experts wondered why: it was a chain of roughly sixty-five hundred stores that sold cheap stuff to poor people. But soon the recession created lots of poor people. Under KKR's ownership, Dollar General exploded, spawning more than a thousand additional little concrete-block shotgun-shack stores in one small town after another and in the poor neighborhoods of cities. By 2009, when KKR relisted the stock on the public markets, more than eight thousand Dollar Generals had metastasized across the United States. When KKR sold all of its stake in 2013, the company was worth three times what KKR had paid for it, and the financial press hailed the play's success.

Two other chains, Family Dollar and Dollar Tree (Dollar Tree acquired Family Dollar in 2013), sprinted to catch up. By 2019, all three chains combined had opened around twenty thousand stores, often wiping out small-town grocers and preventing any new independent stores from ever opening. By the time Shilo and Jimmy arrived in West Unity, the IGA was out of business.

They, and everybody else who couldn't easily reach the Chief in Bryan, were left with meager pickings. She could use her food stamps at the West Unity Dollar General ("SNAP and EBT accepted here," the sign on the store read), but if she were to walk in on the day I did, she'd find a tiny section of shelving—about four feet of it—dotted with a few bananas, some garlic, a couple of heads of lettuce, half a dozen tomatoes, four cucumbers, and a couple of green peppers. Some canned vegetables—green peas and green beans, mainly—sat on another shelf.

On the other hand, she could choose from almost any popular soft drink made in America. Their red, blue, orange, and green hues lit up an entire aisle, from the front of the store all the way to the back: Red Bull,

Monster, Mountain Dew, sugared teas, flavored waters, Pepsis, Cokes. She could also buy any number of salty snacks and chips. Another entire row offered cheap toys from China.

Stores in the SNAP program were supposed to abide by certain minimum stocking requirements established by the Department of Agriculture. Those requirements were enhanced in 2014 as a way to provide more nutritional options and variety to shoppers, and in late 2016, the Obama administration issued a rule implementing the change. But in 2017, the new Republican-controlled Congress passed legislation: "None of the funds made available by this Act may be used to implement, administer, or enforce the 'variety' requirements of the final rule entitled 'Enhancing Retailer Standards in the Supplemental Nutrition Assistance Program (SNAP)' published by the Department of Agriculture in the Federal Register on December 15, 2016."

Lobbyists for the convenience-store industry convinced legislators that requiring more fresh fruits and vegetables—and more varieties of other foods—was too burdensome. The Trump administration agriculture department agreed. So a can of ravioli in tomato sauce counted as a vegetable. The Dollar General offered the bare minimum of the even more relaxed food menu, and yet a long aisle of sugary drinks, because the drinks produced high profit margins and were also eligible for purchase with food stamps. The SNAP program paid billions of dollars a year—about $4 billion, by one estimate—to the soft drink industry, to the stores, and, by extension, to the sugar and corn syrup industries, via SNAP recipients. In other words, taxpayers were subsidizing the promotion of diabetes and obesity.

A cornfield just across the road—Route 20A—lay fallow, ready for the next season's planting. There was a chance that a product of the corn that grew there would wind up right back in West Unity, on the Dollar General shelf, in the form of the high-fructose corn syrup used to sweeten drinks.

Many in Williams County were poorly nourished. In a county with square mile upon square mile of some of the best farmland in the world, that seemed unbelievable—but it was true. Most of the farmland was covered with corn destined to become feed for animals, fodder for ethanol plants (encouraged by a Byzantine system of government incentives), or high-fructose corn syrup. If they didn't grow corn, farmers planted soybeans—but most of them weren't for people, either. The beans would be processed for feed and for industrial products. Corn and soy had long dominated Williams County agriculture, but farmers once also grew sweet corn for people, as well as tomatoes, oats, tree fruits, and vegetables. But fresh vegetables had become a luxury item accessible only to those with reliable cars and the money to pay for the produce.

"We have a lotta people who go there instead of driving back and forth [to Bryan]," Greg Coleman said. Often, he said, he'd look out his office window and see people walk by, toting bags in their hands, even in the deepest cold. "People walk from their homes to Dollar General to pick up what they can, and walk back."

"Stryker, Edon," Jim Hicks said, referring to villages in the county, "tried tax incentives to get a grocery store, but it didn't work. But you got Family Dollar and Dollar General come in. And the first thing you see in those first rows? Chips and snacks and pop." The dollar-store CEOs knew their market. As Dollar Tree's chief said, his customers were "one doctor bill or one car repair bill away from not being in such good shape."

The people at Coleman's United Methodist did what they could to help. Led by office manager Jane Short, they put on a free dinner every Wednesday. Short and the other volunteers started the dinners in 2010, as the recession dragged on in Williams County, because everybody knew people who were out of work and suffering. They served about ninety people back then. Times were better now, so the number had dropped to about forty-five. About a third of those people were older and living on whatever money they received from Social Security. Another third were church members. A final third were what Short called "your true down-and-outers."

The volunteers managed to keep the cost down to about $1.25 per meal by providing main courses that hinted of meat, and by using lots of potatoes and noodles. On an evening when they served "stuffed baked potato in casserole form," the diners ate pieces of potato in a creamy sauce speckled with diced ham, white bread, canned corn, a mini salad of head lettuce with some shredded carrot and cucumber and a cherry tomato, and a square of angel food cake with canned jellied cherries on top—all presented on small styrofoam plates and bowls. They ate with plastic forks and drank water out of paper cups.

A woman over sixty, wearing a Tweety and Sylvester sweatshirt, sat down next to a woman with a walker parked next to her chair and a man with few remaining teeth. "I can't eat with my left hand," she said.

"Oh?" said the other woman. "I can't eat with my right." They laughed.

"I can't hold a spoon," the first woman explained.

They complained about the cold, snow, and ice. "I ain't been outside in six weeks."

Younger men and women sat with adolescent children at other tables. Every one of them rushed through their meal, saying nothing, as if in a hurry to escape the future.

∎∎∎

Just days later, Ennen prepped for the monthly 8:30 AM board meeting. It looked to be pretty routine. CMS had visited the labs to verify the work of the Joint Commission, and, sure enough, the labs checked out fine. They'd have a conversation about the ongoing negotiations with Parkview for a cancer care joint venture. Kim Owen had agreed not to resign, so that seemed to have blown over. Foster, who'd concluded her investigation into Owen's allegations and found them credible, told Ennen to go ahead and formally announce Owen's new job. Ennen figured he'd be out by lunch-time.

Ninety minutes into the meeting, the board went into executive session in order to hear from Foster. As was customary, they excused Ennen, who retreated to his office, figuring he could do a little work for ten minutes or so. Ten minutes became thirty, then forty-five. Foster left the boardroom.

Eventually Ennen's old friend Chris Cullis, the chairman of the board and the owner and editor of the *Bryan Times*, walked into Ennen's office. He looked miserable. The board, he said, was starting a formal investigation into Ennen's handling of the harassment of Kim Owen with the help of CHWC's law firm, Bricker & Eckler, in Columbus.

"I think that's enough for today," Ennen cracked. "I think it's in every-body's best interest if I reduce my role. I don't want to be here, anyway." He walked out of the building, across the park, and into his house.

Mary Ennen was out of town, having a girls' weekend with a friend, so Ennen was alone. A thousand thoughts bounced around in his head. He opened his laptop and began sending emails that amounted to "I don't understand what is going on." Meanwhile, the board, turning to the short-term succession plan, appointed Tinkel, who was about to leave for a ski vacation, as interim CEO. "I'm worried I'm about to be suspended," Ennen wrote to Tinkel. He received no reply. He tried to do a little work, but now found himself frozen out of the hospital's computer system. He emailed

Tinkel, asking if his inability to sign in was deliberate. Tinkel replied that it was. Ennen "freaked out." He sent a couple of intemperate emails.

The following day, the board held a special session during the lunch hour. At 2:00 PM Cullis called Ennen. The board, Cullis said, had formally suspended Ennen as CEO of CHWC, pending the outcome of the investigation. The only two people affiliated with CHWC with whom he could communicate would be Cullis and Chad Tinkel. A formal letter of suspension arrived the following day, banning Ennen from the CHWC campus. He called Cullis. "Are you shittin' me?" he yelled.

Cullis now found himself in the most uncomfortable spot of his life. His friendship with Ennen was a strong one. Mary's mother had worked for the paper. He held the entire family in high regard and considered Ennen "probably the smartest guy I know. When you listen to him talk about healthcare, and the various visions for the hospital, it is just really remarkable. When you talk to him about things not a part of the hospital, he is still that way." Ennen, the local guy, not only participated in the civic life of the community at large, "he took care of people as well. He will go over to the optometrist and pay somebody's bill out of his own pocket if that is a need he sees. And I don't mean one time. He did that a lot, and people don't know about that."

And yet Cullis served as the chairman of the board of CHWC and had a duty to the institution. The board itself had Foster talking about legal risks to the hospital, and the big Columbus law firm weighed in via the speakerphone in the middle of the board table. It all seemed pretty serious. In the old days, if such a thing had happened, they would have met over lunch in a closed room and hammered out a solution and moved on. But it wasn't the old days.

Ennen called his friend Dean Spangler. He sent a text to Dave Swanson, who, in reply, asked about the community play Ennen had been rehearsing as if nothing at all happened, saying he'd like to go. To Ennen—alone, pacing in his house, his thoughts running away with his reason—that sounded incredible. "My career is shredded! It's a fragile house of cards!" And he believed the board had just done more to risk the independence of the hospital than any loan covenant breach could have. CHWC would spend a fortune in legal fees to Bricker.

Then he thought of his children and wept. "My daughters will have a Me Too dad! I'm one more male trying to cover it up." He felt humiliated, embarrassed, abandoned after thirty-two years—stunned that not a single member of the board would say, "Fuck the attorney."

Yet he was still only suspended. He tried to take solace in that. The investigation would show what he had done to make the doctor back off. And he hadn't even thought of any quid pro quo when he offered the job to Owen: he'd been thinking of the next move for the hospital. Even some of his detractors on the board nodded to Ennen's tactical mind. "He has things on back burners behind back burners," marveled Chris Kannel. So maybe it would all blow over. Probably it would. Speaking to his brother on the phone helped. Calling upon the old Ennen sarcasm, his brother pointed out that their mother had been fired back in 1972, so he wouldn't be the first Ennen to get the sack from the hospital. It could be a family tradition.

The board made no announcement of Ennen's suspension to the staff, though it did issue a confidential memo to the top department leaders. The story became that Ennen had put himself on administrative leave, which wasn't false, exactly—Ennen did walk out—but wasn't the whole truth, either.

"All I could discover is that it's not health-related," George Magill, the wound care clinic director, said. "They are keeping this very quiet. Clearly, something major has happened." Telling people not to speculate, he added, would just make them speculate all the more. And they did.

Ennen had an emotional breakdown under all the stress. Ennen embezzled. "Somebody just told me, 'He must have used drugs.' Or he was 'diddling a staff member,'" one department head said. "And I thought about that and said, 'Nah, Phil's way too straight and boring for that.'" Some suggested to the vice presidents that they'd better come up with some more information, because myths were tearing through the ranks, but anyone in a position to know the truth had been warned to say nothing.

Mike Culler's firing had set off anxiety, but Ennen's suspension blasted it into the stratosphere. Things must be much worse financially. A Parkview takeover was imminent, and Ennen opposed it. No, a ProMedica takeover was more likely—ProMedica being an Ohio company—and Ennen must have engineered it. No, no: Foster had staged a coup. Whatever happened, surely people would lose jobs. "What a shitshow," Shannon Keil said. The Ennens weren't around to hear the gossip. They'd packed up their car and left town.

In response to the rampant speculation, Cullis finally sent a confidential memo on CHWC letterhead to the entire staff. Ennen had been placed on administrative leave, it said. Tinkel was now interim CEO. The board had confidence in senior leadership. It requested "your support and assistance to Chad, Jan, Wade and Angelia during this time. We will update as we can." This told them nothing they didn't already know.

Fear was more consequential than the rumors, though the rumors contributed to the fear. Not everybody loved Ennen. When annoyed, he could be abrupt, cranky, and impolitic. But he also inspired loyalty and appreciation for his big-picture vision. Magill, for example, had agreed to open the wound care clinic because Ennen asked him to. Before that, he'd been an ER doc who'd also spent time flying on the choppers out of Toledo. Whatever Ennen did to be suspended, he thought, must have been in the best interest of the hospital. He couldn't imagine Ennen doing anything wrong—at least not deliberately.

And what now? The family atmosphere, the caring—that would all go. There'd be no collections for survivors from ER staff because, surely, without Ennen, CHWC would be absorbed into some bigger system all the quicker, and Magill had no desire to work in the kind of atmosphere that would result. He'd done it before, in the big Toledo outfits where he'd practiced in ERs: "It's meet 'em and street 'em. Get 'em in, get 'em out."

With ProMedica, he said, you might have one interventional cardiologist covering four hospitals, and so heart attack patients might wind up waiting an hour—and that "golden hour" window was so important. As for flying everybody to Toledo, well, that took at least fifty minutes from the time the call came in to the chopper's arrival in Bryan and then the flight back. Marc Tingle would have died.

"I would like to know what's going on," Hanan Bazzi said. Both Bazzi and Hassouneh weren't sure if they'd stay. "Phil's been an employee for, what, twenty years? Ten as CEO?" Hassouneh said, underestimating Ennen's employ by a dozen years. "And they just said goodbye? What makes you think any of us are safe in this hospital?"

Bazzi had come to CHWC because of Ennen. Back at the University of Michigan, when a boss left and was replaced, everything crumbled—and she had no intention of waiting around to experience the same thing in Bryan, Ohio. As the months had passed, she'd grown exhausted by the looks and the awkward conversations resulting from her religion. She still loved her patients, and they still loved her, but relatives of patients sometimes needled her about the hijab: "Why are you wearing that hat? Are you cold?" When she, her husband, and their children went to a community event, she could feel the stares. The scrutiny had grown worse since the election of Minnesota congresswoman Ilhan Omar and Trump's subsequent rhetoric targeting her, telling her to go back to her native land, Somalia, and the crowds at Trump rallies chanting, "Send her back!"

"It's more every time, even at the Y," and if the news showed violence from "Saudi Arabia or anything, I always feel uncomfortable. What will people around me think? That I am related? That I agree with what's going on?"

Being a teenager in North Carolina after 9/11 had been rough. She wasn't going to force her own daughter to live through the kind of taunting and hazing she'd experienced. Piling on uncertainty about the hospital's future added to her doubts. "Listen," she told her husband, "we have to have a plan B. What if they go bankrupt? What if they close, or Parkview comes and takes them?" She trusted Ennen. Without him at her back, she wasn't sure what to expect. "If it gets too difficult, we will just leave."

9

They Don't Have to See

**The Limits of the
Band-Aid Station**

Tim Thuering and Mike Thomas settled into their recliners inside the Williams County EMS headquarters for the night shift ahead. Thuering had worked as a printer most of his adult life before taking up medic work, figuring it would be a more fulfilling retirement than messing around in the yard. Thomas was younger, nearing middle age. He'd begun riding ambulances as a Boy Scout and took to it. Tonight they'd be Life Squad 2, assigned to cover the southern half of the county. Life Squad 1 would take the northern half.

The previous night, a sixty-eight-year-old male DOA had taken up a lot of their shift. The other squad picked up a thirty-seven-year-old male DOA: a drug overdose case. They hoped this night would be a quiet one—Thuering wanted to catch *Jeopardy*. He was a fan of the show and the current champion was on a streak. Sometimes the big flat-screen hanging from the wall could be finicky, so he turned it on to make sure it would tune to the right station.

Life Squad 1 took a call from Rassini Chassis, up in Montpelier. A fire had broken out in one part of a building, as it sometimes did at Rassini, where they bent hot metal. Nobody knew if there'd been any injuries, but the squad would drive up just in case, prepared to help the firefighters. It wouldn't be an up-and-back trip. Life Squad 1 would have to wait, which meant it might be unavailable to accept any other calls for a while.

A short time later, Thuering and Thomas decided to visit "Station 4," the Circle K store in central Bryan. Most stops at Station 4 unfolded in the same way: the crews would come in and fill a soda cup, maybe pick out a candy bar or chips, and then make a show of attempting to pay. The cashier would do a little head nod or say "Nah," and the crew would say, "Thanks a lot," and walk out with Mountain Dew, or with coffee and a Kit-Kat. A man about thirty, in a hoodie and camo ball cap, got to the cashier first, though, to buy a couple of Bud Light tallboys and some beef jerky, so it took a minute for Thuering to catch the cashier's eye. He checked his watch. They could just make it back to headquarters in time for *Jeopardy*.

Thuering's butt hit the recliner at just about the same moment that the beeps and buzzes sounded from the radio loudspeaker, followed by a dispatcher's voice: code 4—auto with entrapment on the Ohio Turnpike. That would have been Life Squad 1's call, but they were at Rassini, so Thuering and Thomas scrambled out of their chairs and into the ambulance. It was 7:15 PM on a dark, cold, wet night. Once they left the garage, Williams County's residents would have no full-time, professional EMS available to take another call.

Thuering drove. Eighteen minutes later, after the ambulance passed through the toll gates by Holiday City, it sat motionless on the turnpike, siren screaming. Interstate 80 had turned into a long, narrow parking lot. Thuering maneuvered to the inside shoulder, then accelerated as fast as he dared to squeeze the truck between the median guardrail and the stopped traffic. When he pulled up to the scene of the accident, both men thought they had another DOA.

An overturned red 2008 Ford F150 pickup lay on its side, the undercarriage facing a farmer's field. Engine fluids and blood pooled outside the driver's-side window, which was now hard against the pavement. The pickup truck had hit the guardrail—at full speed, from the look of things—peeling about ten yards of steel rail and wood posts out of the interstate. It had then slid for some distance.

Jim Hicks had already arrived. He wasn't on duty, but he lived out in the country nearby. Hicks kept the dispatch signal on in his house, and when he heard the call, he had run to his truck, driven it off-road, and then parked it on a rise above the berm off the turnpike so its headlights would shine onto the road. As Thuering and Thomas approached, they found Hicks smashing the windshield with a hatchet.

"Cover your eyes!" Hicks shouted to the driver, John Ryder,* a man who was, by some fluke of physics, alive.

"What are you doing to my windshield!" Ryder shouted after the first strike.

"Windshield's the least of your worries!" Hicks shouted back. "Cover your eyes!"

A Montpelier fire truck pulled up, and Hicks asked the firefighters to affix an adjustable brace to the undercarriage. The truck was wobbling with each of his strikes, and Hicks didn't want it tipping over. Other firefighters used cutting tools to open the roof like a can of peas. "My truck!" Ryder shouted. "My whole life is in this truck!"

And it was. The cab was packed with a walker, a three-legged cane, a box of Winston cigarettes, Tagalong Girl Scout cookies, clothing, soft-drink cups, open snack packages, broken pretzels, white trash bags, a BiPAP breathing machine, and money: lots of money, bundled in plastic wrap. A toilet inside a big cardboard box had been in the bed, but it now lay shattered and scattered on the turnpike like a broken pot at an archeological dig.

Ryder was a big dude. Hicks had intended to pull him out of the windshield opening once the glass was removed. But, when it became clear the man wasn't going to die any second, Hicks stopped smashing the glass to assess the situation further. He realized there was no way Ryder was going to be pulled out through the windshield frame: extraction would have to wait until the saws did their work to peel the roof back so they could roll the man out. Then they had to hope he could stand long enough to lay himself down on the ambulance gurney, because, as Thuering and Thomas were about to discover, Ryder weighed 477 pounds. He was fifty years old.

"Thank God I had my seat belt on!" Ryder said to nobody in particular. The combination of the seat belt and his bulk—his body was its own airbag—may have saved his life.

A state trooper walked around the accident site, taking it all in and jotting down notes. With the benefit of a few minutes to wait, Ryder began to think. And, when he thought, it occurred to him that a state trooper might have questions about bills wrapped in plastic film and boxes of Girl

Scout cookies in a bag with more cash on an interstate that every drug cop coast-to-coast knew was a narcotics delivery route to Detroit and Chicago.

"I work for a troop of Girl Scouts," he said, again to nobody in particular. And then, to Hicks: "I brought my life savings with me. Fifteen thousand dollars."

Hicks, wanting to keep Ryder calm, said, "I carry cash a lot, 'cuz I don't trust the banking system." Hicks may or may not have trusted the banking system, but he for sure never carried thousands of dollars around in his truck.

Once the roof and windshield frame were opened wide enough, firefighters cut the seat-belt strap, and then a group of them helped maneuver the man out from the truck. With help, he was able to lie down on the ambulance gurney. Thuering and Thomas exchanged glances. They were grateful Hicks insisted on buying mechanized lifts for their trucks to raise the gurney into the ambulance. These days, the people they carried were just too heavy.

"Save my Girl Scout cookies!" Ryder shouted. "My bag. They're in my bag. Can you bring my bag?" Pumped with adrenaline and cortisol, he launched into a monologue while Thomas worked on his bloody arm and took vital signs and Thuering drove. Thomas asked his name, date of birth, and if he had any health conditions. "I got sarcoidosis, neuropathy, high blood pressure," he said. He lived in West Virginia and was driving to Michigan for a long weekend at his brother's place.

"I just took this real deep cough—took a drink of my Mountain Dew, then put it down, and took a real deep cough, and then it went in slow motion." The truck had swerved, hit the guardrail, and flipped. His arm scraped along the road, and his body was banged up and hurting, but his injuries didn't appear serious.

"I cannot frickin' believe I did this to myself. They're gonna think I'm a drug addict going across the country. I was bringin' my brother a toilet. I got tired of sittin' on his girlie toilet. I finally got my damn disability. I've watched enough TV to know what they're thinkin'," he said of the state police. "Finally got a chance to buy some family land." That was why he was carrying his $15,000 life savings. And the cash in the bag with the cookies was Girl Scout money. "I've made half the payments on that truck. Now I pissed it off real good. I just got my ACA insurance three months ago. It's real good."

Ryder asked Thomas for his phone, then dialed his brother. "Hey, bro! Guess where I'm at! In an ambulance, so I'm gonna be late." He laughed. Then he turned to Thomas: "Where you takin' me?" He put the phone back to his ear and told his brother, "They're takin' me to some town called Bryan, Ohio."

███

The town talked. It talked over the warm olives and wine at Kora's. It talked over the craft beers at Father John's, the pancakes at the Four Seasons diner, the soup at the Seasons café, the deep-fried cheesecake at Shaffer's. What was up with Phil Ennen? They talked about him at the Knights of Columbus fish fry—where, for just $9.50, you could eat all the fried fish, baked beans, coleslaw, mac 'n' cheese, and green beans your stomach could hold. "I heard Phil Ennen is on leave," a middle-aged woman at the fry said to an older companion. They speculated, as everyone did, about what was going on. Surely Ennen hadn't done anything wrong.

"He's such a nice man," the older woman said. "Well, you know, Rusty— Rusty was wonderful." They knew Brunicardi had trained Ennen, and felt that was a good thing for the hospital and for the town.

The Knights of Columbus hall sat hard by the railroad tracks. It was a blustery evening: chilly, spitting rain, a hard wind blowing. A train clacked by, hauling freight to cities far away from Bryan and drowning out conversation.

After a pause, the middle-aged woman said, "That hospital is so important to this community."

"We're so lucky to have it," her friend added.

Keith—and people like Keith—didn't talk about Ennen. He'd never heard of Ennen. He'd never set foot inside Kora's. Nobody he knew had been to Kora's.

Jim Watkins didn't know what to make of Ennen's suspension, but he figured "it was a great way to shoot yourself in the sack. It wouldn't be the first time." He pointed out all the good Ennen had done around Bryan and the county. When Watkins contacted Ennen, all he could get out of him was "It's for the lawyers to work out."

Only a handful of people knew the truth—that Phil Ennen had already been fired. Chris Cullis had called the Ennens while they were still out of town to deliver the verdict. The board decided Ennen had violated hospital policy, Cullis said.

Of course he had. Ennen had violated the hospital's human resources policy in the way he'd handled the alleged harassment of Kim Owen. He should have turned it over to Angelia Foster right away. Nobody needed the two-week investigation by CHWC's Columbus law firm to prove that, because nobody, including Ennen, ever disputed the basic events. But saying Ennen violated a policy and then firing him for it was like arresting a driver in the Indy 500 for breaking the speed limit. Ennen believed that CHWC existed because its leadership, starting with Brunicardi and continuing with Ennen, sometimes fudged policies and processes and procedures—not in the way CHWC took care of patients or of safety concerns, but in the politics of the medicine business. That's what you had to do if you wanted to survive.

It wasn't just the way CHWC had started the cath lab. The other moneymaker, the radiation oncology center itself, wouldn't have been in Bryan if Brunicardi and Ennen hadn't played the political game. At the time Brunicardi first tried to start the center, Ohio was governed by what was known as "certificate of need": too many hospitals and other facilities had been built with Hill-Burton money, legislators thought, and so to avoid wasting resources though duplication—like having two CT scanners across the street from each other—operators of proposed facilities had to apply for a certificate of need to gain approval. Big hospitals often tried to use certificate of need to block competition, and they often succeeded. Toledo hospitals argued that Bryan didn't need a radiation oncology center and lobbied hard against it. But Ennen and Brunicardi had figured a way around the denial.

Everybody—the nurses in Montpelier who massaged patient reports so people could receive the help they needed, administrators who "upcoded" diagnostic notes so Medicare or private insurance would fully reimburse for services, drug company CEOs who tacked a pointless molecule onto an old drug so they could patent it all over again—knew that American medicine was one big grift. The only question was whether you were grifting to benefit people or to cash in. Whatever your motivation, you had to game the system. The CHWC board had often congratulated Ennen on such maneuvers because they'd helped to keep the hospital alive and independent.

"He spent his entire life threading needles," Chris Kannel, the young board member and Montpelier council member, said of Ennen and the board's vote. "He thought if he could thread this one right, he could fix it."

Now the board thought that he'd tried to thread the wrong needle and had placed the hospital in legal jeopardy. The lawyers at Bricker, the law firm, Cullis said, "were certainly very influential." It wasn't only the harassment situation, though: the board considered Ennen's payout to the GI specialist, his reluctance over strategic planning, the way he walked out after being notified of the Bricker investigation, his impolitic emails in his moment of panic over the possible loss of his job, his apparent lack of contrition when interviewed by the investigator.

(My presence in the hospital also caused concern. Bricker, as was typical of a law firm, opposed allowing access to a journalist. At Ennen's insistence, Bricker acceded, but drafted a nondisclosure agreement so restrictive it would have been impossible to report this book. Ennen drafted a new version with an expiration that would predate publication. On the day Ennen was suspended, Tinkel, with support from some board members, revoked my access. Other board members prevailed, however, and my access resumed a month later.)

Ennen did not deny his mistakes. He admitted he'd let his satisfaction over landing a GI specialist—any GI specialist—for Bryan lull him into rationalizing the hiring of the doctor, in the hope he would adapt to CHWC culture. He wound up having to pay $1 million. He'd wanted to protect Kim Owen, and also ease out the radiation oncology group, without creating drama. He got drama. He screwed up. He deserved some sort of reprimand, he thought, for not using the HR executive he'd hired. But he felt the totality of his successes at CHWC far outweighed his errors.

Nobody on the board questioned Ennen's motivations or his integrity. "It was a culmination of that consistent, pervasive threading of needles that progressively eroded the board's confidence in Phil," Kannel said. The final vote wasn't close. Swanson regretted having to vote to remove Ennen, but he did so. So did Kannel and most of the rest of the board. Cullis voted against. The episode, Cullis said, "was the most difficult thing I have ever gone through in my life." (He would later apologize to his friend for failing to protect him.)

After getting Cullis's call, Ennen and Mary drove back to Bryan and sequestered themselves in their house. Dean Spangler, whose brother sat on the board and had voted with the majority, dropped by. He was furious—a member of "Team Pitchforks and Torches"—and told Ennen there'd be a local revolt. Nick Walz, the now-retired family doctor and local institution, was angry, too, Spangler said. There was talk of mounting some sort of countermove to rescind the termination—but, though nobody said so, it was clear they all recognized that the well had been poisoned, the decision made. The only question left centered on terminology: would Ennen be fired, or would he be "allowed" to resign?

After a few days, some consultations with an attorney, and a little negotiation, the Bricker lawyers drafted a separation agreement. Ennen hesitated to sign it. Several days later, though, he woke up to the realization that, as shattered and bitter as he was, at least he didn't have to worry about what to do when Kesireddy retired, or how to find another ob-gyn, or whether the cash would flow, or any of a dozen other things. He could move on. He was still only fifty-five. There was time for a second chapter. And if he resigned, he'd keep his severance package and health insurance.

He called a group of friends to come for lunch. Walz, Spangler, and others gathered around in the Ennen kitchen, ate sandwiches and potato chips, and listened as Ennen announced his decision and his reasoning.

His thirty-two years at the hospital—and his life in Bryan—were over. Before the year was out, he and Mary, the Bryan natives, would sell the house across the park from the hospital, store the family treasures, pack up the car, and drive out of town. Bryan would lose another bit of the glue that held it together. Chad Tinkel announced Ennen's resignation to the hospital staff with tears in his eyes.

■ ■ ■

Days after Ennen took Cullis's call, concerned local officials held another meeting. This time they gathered in the basement of the county health department in Montpelier. Tracy Plouck, an Ohio University addiction services expert, had gotten hold of some grant money. Now she was there to ask how she could help the county better confront the problem of drug abuse. Fred Lord, chief of the county's Jobs and Family Services (JFS) agency; Anna Meyers, a JFS supervisor; Brian Davis and Terry Rummel, county commissioners; the health department's Jim Watkins and its director of nursing, Rachel Aeschliman; Rob Giesige, the new chief of the Four County ADAMhs board; and several others sat around a long table.

Meth was still the drug of choice for abusers, but lately police and the ER had been seeing an increase in fentanyl, and sometimes meth with fentanyl. This, they told Plouck, was their first aggravation. After wishing away the opioid epidemic, Ohio state government had finally begun facing it and appropriating money for enforcement, interdiction, and treatment. But because most OD deaths—and news about OD deaths—involved opioids, the money had been designated for only that. It couldn't be used for meth-related projects. This was folly, they said.

Sociologists had tried for years to tell politicians that drug abuse was a symptom, not a cause. The kind of drug was irrelevant. Yes, heroin and fentanyl were deadlier than meth, and meth might be deadlier than alcohol. Alcohol might be more immediately dangerous than obesity, lousy dental care, poverty and low wages, crummy housing, depression, trauma, and anxiety. They were all part of the same pathology, though, and arguing about which was worse obscured the underlying causes of the abuse.

That message was a much tougher sell than going after a single drug. Few people wanted to question some of the most basic presumptions about how the country operated—and why. Most politicians preferred not to think too hard about why people might be depressed, anxious, and traumatized. Even when they did, they latched onto easy answers that resonated with their electorate.

There was no better example than the comments of politicians at the April 2019 "opioid summit," a weekend-long community event held at Northwest State Community College and hosted by the college and CHWC under the sponsorship of the Montpelier auto parts maker Rassini Chassis (more evidence that opioids attracted the money). During the wrap-up summation and Q-and-A session in the college's auditorium, Craig Riedel, a state representative, stood and took the microphone. The state spent $30 billion on Medicaid and education, he said. The opioid issue took up another $2 billion. Yet the drug problem grew. In case the implication wasn't clear enough, Riedel made it explicit: "Government isn't going to solve this," he declared. Watkins, who was sitting at a table in the back of the room with Bryan's mayor, Carrie Schlade, sighed.

"Our religious community has to be very involved in this," Riedel continued. "I believe that, as a society, we have to be more Christ-focused. I believe we will be relying heavily on our religious community and Christ to get this thing solved."

Watkins's forehead hit the table in front of him. He rolled it back and forth. Schlade, a woman who'd opened a Bryan Chamber of Commerce event "in Jesus's name," shook her head. The audience applauded, though; it was the first time it had applauded all afternoon.

"We've been working with faith-based for thirty years!" Watkins said over the applause. "So, how's that going?" It would be tough to find a more conservative Christian part of Ohio than the northwest corner, where separation of church and state was considered more advisory than mandatory. A giant marble slab carved with the Ten Commandments sat embedded in the front lawn of the Paulding County Courthouse. IN GOD WE TRUST. WITH GOD ALL THINGS ARE POSSIBLE, read a framed sign depicting the U.S. and Ohio flags mounted in the main hall of the Fayette public high school. The obituaries of the overdose dead often cited their religious affiliation and their love of Jesus.

Watkins dug his phone out of his pocket. He looked up the percentage of Americans who declared no religion—about a quarter. And what of the six million or so Jews? And the more than three million Muslims? Throw in Hindus, Buddhists, Zoroastrians, Sikhs, and Confucians, and Riedel was writing off an awful lot of Americans.

Riedel's Christian chauvinism wasn't what bugged Watkins most, though. "Why did he run for office?" he asked. "If government can't do anything, why run for a government office?"

Most of the people around the table in the basement in Montpelier were government employees of one kind or another. Most of them wanted to channel the energies of government to improve the health of the people they served. Doing so in Williams County, however, came with the extra burden of knowing that so many people there distrusted—and sometimes even hated—government. From the time Ronald Reagan declared that "government is not the solution to our problem; government is the problem" in his 1981 inaugural address, that slogan, too, had become part of the Williams County gospel, reinforced over and over through the decades by the politicians voters elected to government offices.

The resistance Ennen met when advocating for all employees to get flu shots wasn't only the result of false beliefs like "the flu shot will give you the flu," a common one in the county. The county commissioners didn't require EMS crews to get flu shots because they didn't think government should tell people they had to get vaccines. In the ER one day, Marv Stalter asked a young single mother who worked at Menards and who relied on

Medicaid if her small child was up to date on his vaccinations, and she made it clear she didn't trust pronouncements from the government. "Oh, we do not vaccinate," she said. Stalter made a short sound of concern with the intake of his breath, then launched into the same litany he preached to every such young parent—about polio and iron lungs and lives saved—but he knew not to bother being too insistent. When Jan David spoke to a neighbor about the importance of getting a flu shot, the neighbor replied, "That's from the government. You don't know what they'll put in it." A hospital employee filled out the required statement explaining why she refused to be vaccinated: "Religion is Pentecostal. Obamacare is putting a 'chip' in the flu shot to track people's whereabouts for the '666.' Not going to take the 'devil's shot.' Took it last year but felt forced into it. Husband was very upset. This is already happening in Wyoming and other countries." The employee was apparently referring to an anti-Obama conspiracy theory about radio-frequency identification tags being injected into human beings via vaccines.

For all the county's antipathy toward big government, it lived off big government—just as in the days of the Great Depression, when the feds made all those payments to farmers and built part of Bryan's infrastructure. Williams County residents received medical payments of $150,323,000 from government in 2018. Total government transfer payments to individuals came to $339,480,000. In 2019 and 2020, more federal money arrived via payments to county farmers from the Market Facilitation Program, the compensation to farmers hurt by Trump's trade war. Farmers who qualified could receive $67 an acre, up to $250,000 per person or farm corporation. Even if they didn't plant a crop, they could receive $15 an acre.

Of course, Bryan's biggest employer, the hospital, would shut its doors without federal payments, as Ennen had always liked to point out. "Very conservative community we live in," he told a group of employees at the Montpelier hospital during a meeting. "'Socialized medicine.' Well, if you are opposed to socialized medicine, wow, you are way too late. That horse left the barn a long time ago."

Some of those around the table, like the county commissioners, approved of government welfare for corporations—most recently granted to Love's Travel Stops, an Oklahoma-based chain of over five hundred truck stops owned by the billionaire Love family. The new truck stop would employ fifty people, Love's promised, half of whom would make $9 an hour.

They didn't approve of welfare payments to people, though, and the state legislature agreed.

The Republican Party enjoyed a supermajority in the legislature, thanks to gerrymandering, and it used that power to cut taxes over and over again. Meanwhile, state funding for Jobs and Family Services ranked fiftieth out of fifty states. "It would bankrupt the state just to get us to forty-ninth," JFS chief Lord said. Counties were expected to contribute money to the local JFS outlets, too.

The problems Lord faced—like the drug abuse being discussed around the table—only grew. In 1979, Williams County's poverty rate had been 7 percent. Now, in 2019, it was 13.5 percent, despite full employment. With poverty and near-poverty came drug abuse and a host of other ills, Jim Watkins said. The data showed it, and everybody knew where the hot spots were: on Bryan's east side and in depressed Montpelier.

When Tracey Plouck asked about mental health facilities for treatment and overdose care, Rob Giesige, the new ADAMhs board chief, pointed out that there were no crisis stabilization beds in the entire four-county region where they could put a person suffering from an overdose or mental health breakdown. Instead, they used the ERs at CHWC and other counties' hospitals, where they could at least put someone for twenty-four hours. Otherwise, everybody had to be sent to Toledo—and beds there were always in short supply.

To Lord and JFS administrator Anna Meyers, their biggest drug-related problem was children. Ten children had been taken into protective custody to shield them from drug-abusing caretakers in just the past couple of weeks, Meyers told the group. Williams County was swamped with such children. As it was, Brian Davis said, the county had spent $900,000 on child placement. "This is unsustainable," Davis told Plouck. He appealed to big government for help. "Hopefully, Medicaid will pick that up."

"Our ability to reunify with these people is almost zero," Lord said. He turned to Meyers. That was right, she confirmed; in the past three years, not one family had been reunited. "It's easy to say all those people need to be arrested and thrown in jail," Lord said, "but most of these people have kids. What happens to those kids once they go into foster care?"

Lord's small team of investigators was poorly paid, and abuse and threats were routine parts of their jobs. (In the spring of 2019, police would break up a murder-for-hire plot targeting one of them.) As a group, they managed about a hundred cases at a time. At a morning case intake meeting, eleven women—investigators, intake specialists, and a school social worker—received a briefing on the day's new business. A baby born at CHWC had tested positive for THC and amphetamine; the mother suffered from paranoia. Another mother living in a trailer had been monitored by JFS for a while. There'd been some steadying of the family after the child's father got a job, but now the little one had been found climbing out a window while the couple was having sex.

Another mother who showed up at Janis Sunderhaus's Bryan Community Health Center had revealed there was no refrigerator in her house and that she'd been storing food outdoors to keep it cold. She had no stove. She used a George Foreman grill to cook. The family had recently been homeless. Her husband was bipolar. Another woman with five children, all under age five, suffered from severe postpartum depression after the birth of her youngest.

Most people in Bryan had no idea of this reality. "They don't want to see," an investigator said. "Or they don't have to see."

With so many children in need of so much—and without places to put those children or the money to support them—JFS had no choice but to accept a low bar for parenting. "For us, if they have a roof over their heads, food in their stomachs, clothes on their backs, and [parents] are not doing drugs in front of the kids or beating them, we count that as a win," Meyers said.

The JFS investigators worked at the edge of what Montpelier's police chief, Dan Magee, saw as intergenerational dysfunction. Allison Rosenbrock, a JFS investigator, represented the front-line troops. She'd been out of college for a year and made about $16 an hour.

One day Rosenbrock drove out to West Unity to check on Shilo and Jimmy. Shilo had an interview later that afternoon for a job at a gas station in West Unity. That was good news, but there'd been a report of an altercation between them. A little rocking horse had tipped over. One of the children was injured. Shilo may have kicked Jimmy out of the house. Or maybe not. She might have just been waiting for him to cool off and learn his lesson. Rosenbrock wasn't sure.

She knocked on the door. Shilo welcomed her into the tiny living room. She was wearing a pair of floral cotton tights, which hid most of an elaborate tattoo, and an old hoodie. Both children slept soundly on a little couch, head to feet. A big candy-pink Barbie bag belonging to the mother sat on the living room floor. Barbie's blond hair fell in sharp bangs just above the frames of her heart-shaped sunglasses, and she flashed perfect, white, straight teeth. One of the boys "got a best new student award," Shilo told Rosenbrock. (Clients liked to headline any positive news to investigators.) The boy had been very proud. Shilo and Jimmy, amused by their little boy's bragging, had made fun of the award. She hadn't done it to be mean, she told Rosenbrock. She just wanted to let the boy know, "Look, kid, they give those things out all the time." She didn't want him to have any illusions. The boy still treasured it, though, so she framed it and put it on the kitchen counter for everyone to see.

Rosenbrock asked a few questions, took a few notes, and then informed Shilo about the Bryan Community Health Center. She drove out of the village and past a FOSTER PARENTS NEEDED sign on an empty storefront. Fifteen minutes later, she was cruising slowly through Montpelier, searching for a house. She pulled up to a shack with a long-dead lawn mower out front. "Last time I was here," she said, "there was a door there." There wasn't one now; instead, a thick, old blanket hung over the front doorway to the shack. The temperature was about 40 degrees.

The mother, Jessica,* bedraggled and holding a newborn baby on her hip, met Rosenbrock in the doorway. So did four other small children, in various states of nakedness. Two enormous dogs, a St. Bernard and a Rottweiler, sniffed the newcomers. A row of thirteen cereal boxes, all generic knockoffs of famous brands, sat on a one-by-six plank that had been nailed to a wall. The place smelled of dog piss and poop and mess. The power was on, though—for now. "Our shut-off date is usually the twenty-ninth," the mother explained.

Rosenbrock interviewed Jessica as the children clung to the visitors. She said that the father of some of the children—the man with whom she was living in the shack—had started a new job that very day, at an injection-molding company. They were behind on rent ($425 a month), but she hoped they could catch up in a month or so. She also hoped she could get in to see one of the Parkview doctors for her crippling depression. But she was worried: "They won't take my children because of depression, will they?"

That afternoon back in Bryan, Mindy Lemon, a veteran social worker at twenty-seven, knocked on the door of a single-wide trailer in a run-down trailer park. The mother inside had lost her children to Jobs and Family Services due to drug use. But the agency, desperate for a reunification, had since returned them. Lemon could show up at any time to check on them, and so she did.

A tall, skinny man with a military unit's ball cap on his head answered the door. He was the mother's fiancé. He, the mother, two boys, and the father of the boys all lived in the trailer together. The five-year-old boy was autistic. The eight-year-old often punched himself in the face.

The mother and the fiancé and the ex had bought the single-wide as a used, empty shell "because we been evicted so many times, nobody will rent to us," the mother explained. Ever since, they'd been trying to add walls to the interior. So far the walls consisted of two-by-four framing draped with towels and sheets.

The mother, the ex, and the autistic boy all sat on an uncovered mattress in the trailer's main room with a pizza box between them. A dog in a cage—some sort of Rottweiler mix—barked and lunged against its prison like a lunatic.

Things had been going pretty good, the mother told Lemon over the noise. She'd held on to her job at an auto-parts supplier across the border in Indiana and had received a raise to $16.50 an hour after she put in for and was granted an assignment to the swing shift, from two in the afternoon to ten at night. She brought home about $300 a week. So did the fiancé, who worked at the same plant.

She was worried, though, about medical care for her boys. Now that they were back in her custody and she was working, the boys would lose Medicaid coverage as of the first of the month. Obtaining coverage for the children would be an expensive proposition, especially when she was just finding her footing. Lots of people JFS served faced the same kind of problem. Often they made just enough money to disqualify themselves or their families from Medicaid, but not enough to afford coverage offered by an employer or via the Affordable Care Act.

Lemon invited the eight-year-old to show off his bedroom. She wanted to see how and where he was sleeping. The two of them walked to the back of the trailer and into a small bedroom furnished with stacked bunk beds. The eight-year-old slept in the top bunk.

"What happened to your sheets?" Lemon asked after seeing the bare mattresses.

"I took 'em off," the boy answered. "I don't like sheets."

"How are you doing?" she asked. "You know I worry about you."

"I know you do," he answered. "I'm okay. I just get mad sometimes."

In the early 1990s, medical researchers noticed that people who had survived childhood sexual abuse were more likely to suffer from a variety of physical maladies in adulthood. So in 1995, a group of physicians and public health experts from Kaiser Permanente in San Diego, Emory University, the University of Arizona, and the Centers for Disease Control and Prevention began a study of adverse childhood experiences, or ACEs. They screened thousands of people using Kaiser's medical services in San Diego, conducting physical exams and having people fill out long questionnaires designed to elicit information about household dysfunction when they were children, including such things as substance abuse in the home, physical and emotional abuse, and violence. The more categories of adverse experiences these people were exposed to as children, the greater their later risk of smoking, obesity, physical inactivity, depressed mood, and suicide attempts as adults. They were more likely to be alcoholics and drug abusers, and to engage in risky sex. And they were more likely to be sick with conditions like heart disease, cancer, emphysema, bone fractures, hepatitis, and general poor health.

Over the next twenty years, physicians, public health researchers, sociologists, and demographers explored the links between socioeconomics and health. Between 1959 and 1979, life expectancy in the United States increased from about seventy years to about seventy-five. There were multiple reasons for this: vaccines against childhood diseases, improved community infrastructure, better antibiotics, and improved treatments for diseases like cancer. It was no coincidence, though, that during this period economic inequality in America decreased. There are a number of ways to measure inequality, and a number of organizations, economists, and government agencies that do the measuring. But all of them show that inequality in America declined in the decades following World War II. Ronald Reagan was elected president in 1980, ushering in an era of union-busting, financial deregulation, leveraged buyouts, and the financialization of the American economy. What ensued was a precipitous increase in inequality, whether measured by income or by accumulated wealth, and except for short pauses, it kept rising. By 2019, the United States was one of the most unequal countries on earth.

Inequality itself was unequal. The gap between whites and blacks grew, and so did the gap between places and education. The well educated flocked to metropolitan areas and worked "knowledge economy" jobs. Rural counties, with few college graduates and a reliance on manufacturing, began to look more and more like poor neighborhoods in urban centers. In fact, many white people in Williams County had a lot more in common with poor black people in places like the Franklinton neighborhood of Columbus than they may have wished to admit.

The gap in mortality rates between whites and blacks began to converge. In 1999, the death rate for non-Hispanic white people ages fifty to fifty-four with a high school degree or less was roughly 30 percent lower than that of blacks. By 2015, it was 30 percent higher. The lines crossed for other age groups, too. Frederick Hoffman, the racist insurance data guru of the early twentieth century, had gotten it wrong: it wasn't race that made African Americans less healthy, but poverty, lack of education, lack of everything.

The effect held across generations. The life expectancy at age fifty for people born in 1930 was about five years higher in the top 20 percent of income than for those in the bottom 20 percent. But that chasm had grown much wider over the generations. By the time they were fifty years old, those who were born in 1960 and at the top 20 percent of income earners could expect to live until they were nearly eighty-nine. Those who were born in 1960 and at the bottom 20 percent of earnings could, at age fifty, expect to live to seventy-six, a difference of about thirteen years.

The same effect held by location, too. People in rich, better-educated counties lived longer, healthier lives than people living in poorer, less-educated counties.

The increase in socioeconomic inequality brought stress and frustration with it. The constant stress of barely making a living, of hustling for the next meal, of having to keep track of what date the power company would shut off the electricity, of worrying about every bill and every penny, of feeling hopeless about the future, and of knowing that you could work two or three jobs for the rest of your life and never really break out of the cycle in which Valerie Moreno, Keith Swihart, and so many others found themselves living could erode both mental and physical health—not least by creating actual physical changes in both the brain and the body. Family distress was one symptom of the disease, and it generated more adverse childhood experiences. And the wheel turned over to the next generation.

Lack of money wasn't the only ingredient in the American pathology, so escaping the cycle became tougher all the time. Family, community, and meaning had all broken down as disadvantage in one realm, like financial security, spread the malaise and surrender to other realms, like education. Social mobility in the United States had regressed. Fewer people were able to stand on the shoulders of their parents to make the all-American climb.

If a young person wanted to take a step up—say, by going to a university to earn a four-year degree—politicians made it harder to do so. Tuition plus room and board at Ohio University in Athens cost a state resident almost $26,000 a year. In 1980, it had been about $3,000 a year (roughly $10,000 in 2019 dollars). Ohio State cost about $28,000. Such hikes were typical across the country as states cut back on funding for higher education. Alaska cut state support for the University of Alaska by $100 million in 2019.

Schools around Williams County were starved for money. Bryan's would rack up a $2 million deficit in 2019, and more deficits were projected in succeeding years. Education suffered. Bryan city schools, Montpelier village schools, and the school in West Unity all received F grades for meeting achievement indicators when rated by the state of Ohio. Montpelier received an F for preparing students for later success. Overall, West Unity and Montpelier received D grades, while Bryan city schools earned a C.

Meanwhile, the Trump administration proposed big cuts to the programs that helped keep people like Keith alive. After Trump's tax cuts for corporations and the wealthy blew up the federal deficit, he proposed eliminating student loan subsidies, cutting Medicaid (which could be disastrous for hospitals like CHWC), and reducing housing assistance and funding for food stamps. The Trump Administration slogged through the courts in an effort to eliminate the Affordable Care Act.

Local policies didn't always make it easy for those who stumbled to get back up. Back in Montpelier in the basement of the health department's headquarters, Plouck, the Ohio University expert, asked the officials assembled around the table about a needle exchange program. A few of them chuckled. Several years before, a small town in neighboring Indiana had wound up with a localized HIV epidemic that resulted from sharing used needles. Williams County itself had a growing number of hepatitis C diagnoses, and the trend was beginning to shift to younger people.

"There's no way here," Watkins told Plouck. "We'd worry about the sheriff taking license plate numbers" of cars pulling into a needle exchange location. Many in the county regarded any accommodation to drug users, even in the

name of public health, to be encouraging drug abuse. Though medically assisted treatment, or MAT, had been proven effective in treating addicts by
providing them with a transitional prescription medication to ease the crav-
ing for opioids, many opposed that, too. Handing out Narcan, the drug that
could rescue people who overdosed, was "not so politically viable," either,
Watkins said. The belief in a prelapsarian utopia based on universal personal
responsibility was too strong in Williams County to tolerate easy access to
Narcan, MAT, or needle exchanges. You just had to teach kids to resist the lure
of drugs. You had to teach them to comply with the accepted norms of society.

So Sheriff Steven Towns insisted on money for the DARE program
(Drug Abuse Resistance Education) in schools, though DARE had been
shown to be worse than ineffective back in the early 1990s. (Towns would
resign his position in February 2020 in lieu of being charged with felony
crimes involving misuse of public money.)

This philosophy contributed to the pervasive belief in drug testing by
employers. Few business owners and managers questioned the wisdom of
testing applicants and employees—and of insisting, when some failed, that
nobody could pass a drug test.

Dave Swanson was a notable exception to this dogma. Why were employers testing in the first place? His company, Daavlin, didn't. As was the
case for most other employers, Swanson's workers weren't flying airplanes,
handling nuclear fuel, or slicing open a patient for heart surgery. He reckoned that a small minority of his employees might use drugs at least sometimes (he knew some had, in fact), but if anybody were to show up too high
to work, coworkers would notice. Keeping people from working because
they had THC or even a trace of meth in their system would only guarantee
that that person would keep on using—maybe more and more—as they
slipped further down the economic and social ladders.

Swanson did bring drug-sniffing dogs through his plant sometimes on
weekends, when it was shut down, because he didn't want anybody stashing
drugs on his property. But this idea that having used drugs should keep you
out of a job seemed counterproductive to him at a time when the country
was facing an epidemic of drug use, and when Williams County businesses
were crying out for workers. You'd just wind up making a lot more poor
people. Nothing was a guarantee, of course—and people with great jobs
could become addicts, too—but Swanson believed that a decent job was
more effective at fighting addiction than Jesus Christ was.

At the meeting, when Plouck and the others discussed a number of factors that contributed to the drug problem, they highlighted the same kinds of troubles many other places faced in post-recession America. They talked about housing and transiency, transportation and access to good food, wages and aging and education. They talked of enlisting the help of religious communities.

Jim Watkins was one of the few people in the county to recognize that Americans were faced with a new, deep, and abiding national sickness. He'd begun working with Bowling Green State University's Center for Regional Development in an effort to bring its expertise to bear on the housing problem and on the low-wage economy. "What's the reason people are going down this road in the first place?" he asked.

He already knew the answer: too many people in Williams County were being used the way mining companies used coal in West Virginia. Human beings were the object of an extractive industry. They were mined for their labor and for their money. Too often, they were a "workforce" and not people at all. The goal was to pay them as little as possible and to get as much work out of them as possible while taking the least amount of responsibility possible. The modern American version of capitalism encouraged—even demanded—that employers extract the value from their employees while returning scraps to them and their communities. And then others—like some medical professionals, business owners, politicians—questioned why poor and working-class people didn't take care of themselves. Why didn't they comply? This was the same argument employers had used in 1916 to oppose a state health plan, blaming the working class for "absences caused by intemperance, by ball games." If they were sick, they had only themselves to blame.

People were already sick. The medical industry and public health experts had a name for this mix of factors: "social determinants of health." But even the biggest systems couldn't do much about them. Those systems were packed with the fanciest gadgets and well-trained doctors and nurses. At CHWC, at least, there was a caring, sometimes even loving staff. Yet, simultaneous with the rise of the giant hospital corporation and the wealth-extracting medical industry, American life expectancy and well-being declined. Decades of research showed that social determinants had an enormous impact on health and longevity—more than medical care itself, which accounted for only about 15 percent of the inequity in mortality.

The medical economy itself, though, was also an exercise in inequality. In 1932, the Committee on the Costs of Medical Care concluded that "as one ascends the economic scale, medical care becomes more adequate. This results in a postponement of death in a certain number of instances." Since then, nothing had changed. Hospitals, drug companies, doctors, device makers, and insurers were consolidating furiously to protect their power to raise prices. Medical care cost too much because it *could* cost too much.

The health industry, like other industries, had also figured out how to siphon off what wealth people had and add that to its own bottom line. There was no better example than diabetes: between the insulin, the monitors, the test strips, and the pumps, diabetes was a rich vein of cash that would last as long as a diabetic lived.

Valerie and her family, Greg Coleman's flock in West Unity, the patients at the Bryan Community Health Center, and CHWC itself were all being crushed by the parallel economy of American medicine. Poor and working-class people, like Roger Metzger dying of cancer in the ER and Sheila Carpentar transported from the nursing home, even *died* differently than the rich did. Bryan, Ohio, wasn't much different from many other places. It was a microcosm of America's sickness.

Life Squad 2 wasn't back at headquarters long before another call came in at about 10:00 PM: law-enforcement assist on a county road not far from headquarters, just outside Bryan's city limits. A deputy was on the scene.

The ambulance pulled up to a trailer park of mostly single-wides, most of them giving way to corrosion. An old Chevy Malibu was parked in a little driveway amid the huddle of aluminum-and-tin homes. A deputy leaned into the passenger-side window. He spoke with soft words.

"I think you could use a little help," the deputy said to a pretty young woman. She was about twenty-five years old, with dark hair and a sad, worn look in her overdosed eyes. Want-ad sections of a newspaper lay crumpled on the car's passenger-side floor, along with wrinkled, official-looking pieces of white paper: Medicaid forms. "Let these fellas take you to the hospital and get ya checked out," he said.

She laid her face on the steering wheel and sighed. "I want help. I just don't wanna get checked out." Because she wasn't passed out, EMS couldn't take her to the hospital involuntarily. She'd overdosed, but not quite enough.

The deputy tried again. He reassured her. In her confused state, she insisted she wanted help but didn't want to be helped. She wanted *it*—addiction, hopelessness, depression, whatever it was—to go away, as if wishing it away would make it so.

The deputy and the EMS crew stepped over to a group of three people who'd been watching from the front of a crumbling single-wide, shivering in the nighttime cold. The young woman's mother took a cigarette out of her mouth and said, "She's been speedballin'." Her father, warmer in an Ohio State jacket and an Ohio State baseball cap, stood mute.

After a little discussion that amounted to nothing, the deputy declared that there was no point in sticking around because there would be no patient transported. The crew of Life Squad 2 drove away.

For all the talk in Bryan, Ennen's shove out the door of CHWC didn't matter much to most people. For them, nothing had changed.

The day after Ennen was fired, Valerie Moreno sat at a card table in the common room/kitchen of the church, counting out Girl Scout cookie money with her daughter and another Girl Scout mother. Betty Franks, the wife of the former pastor and a retired public schoolteacher, was there, too.

Valerie still worked three jobs. Her back still ached. And she was still coughing from something—maybe the flu, maybe a bad cold—that a coworker at Sauder had brought into the factory. Valerie wound up with bronchitis, an inner ear infection, and a sinus infection, but she didn't miss any work because she had no paid sick leave. "No! I went to work every day," she said, laughing, which called forth a brief coughing fit. She did visit the Sauder corporate clinic. The nurse practitioner there said, "You're sick," and Valerie said, "Yes, I am."

Her work at Sauder involved mostly standing for eight to ten hours as she wrapped foam and upholstery around sofa arms. "It was tough to go to work," she said. "I coughed and coughed and coughed." She was proud she was getting faster on the Sauder line. The day before, her line had completed twenty-one sofas. She'd received a raise—to $13.75 an hour—plus a $1 premium for working the third shift, from 11:00 PM to 7:00 AM. "Fridays, I don't sleep. I was up thirty-nine hours yesterday."

Valerie grossed $1,312 for two weeks of work, bringing home $793 after the $186 for healthcare was taken out, along with a little for her 401(k), a little into a health savings account (encouraged by the company with an HSA incentive payment), and some withholding. After the deductions, her take-home total amounted to about $19,200 a year. Her bus job added another $280 a month if she didn't miss any days, and Franks paid her $150 a month for looking after Franks's husband. Valerie and her husband were also trying to save for college tuition for their thirteen-year-old daughter—the Girl Scout—who wanted to become a nurse practitioner. And Valerie was determined to make that trip to Disney World.

Valerie did have a little more money in her checking account now, but she didn't feel any more secure. "I get paid every two weeks. So you eat well the first week, but the second week is a straggler." She counted out hundreds of dollars in cookie money, arranging them in neat stacks on the table.

With her teacher's pension and healthcare and her husband's retirement and Social Security, Franks didn't feel the same gravity of worry as Valerie, but facing the medical industry was still stressful. She and her husband had a $500 drug deductible. At the start of the year, she went to the drugstore to buy his Symbicort inhaler "and found out it was $300."

"Isn't that ridiculous?" Valerie chimed in. "For a medicine they have to have, it is $300 because they haven't met their deductible." "And the insurance wouldn't pay for the other drug he was prescribed," Franks added, "because that was $400." After the deductibles were met, they paid about $40 a month for the inhaler. "And I have a good policy!" Franks said, speaking of her state teacher's insurance. She wondered how other people coped.

"If you are on Medicaid, you are fine," Valerie said. "But if you're in between, you have got a real problem." Valerie knew a lot of people in between.

Valerie's daughter double-checked the cookie money count. She was excited by the sales. The troop had talked about a big project: some way to bring good food to the small villages around the county—or at least to the West Unity area. Maybe they could get a food truck, or build a greenhouse, growing fruits and vegetables year-round and selling them for just enough money to keep the project going.

Beth Pool understood the dilemmas faced by Valerie and Betty Franks better than anybody else in Williams County. Pool ran a small insurance agency, based in Bryan, that wrote a lot of healthcare policies for small and midsize employers, including CHWC. Over the previous decade, both her business—and the entire universe of American medicine—had begun to feel like they were built on sand during a rising tide.

When she looked over the insurance plan for her own twenty-nine employees, she had to laugh. The plan cost her agency $170,000 annually. "I looked at that big number and thought, 'How many insurance policies do I have to sell to pay that amount?' And it's more than I sold last year." She wasn't alone—employers all over the county faced the same problem.

Deductibles weren't always part of health insurance. They were introduced with arguments appealing to "personal responsibility" and "skin in the game." Without deductibles, some insisted, people would abuse insurance, and not take care of themselves. By 2008, deductibles had become a way for employers to lower rocketing premiums. After the recession, though, the deductibles kept rising, and so did the premiums. Employers passed the costs on to their employees, but the employers' costs still rose. One of her small business clients, for example, paid $335,173.56 in premiums. Employees insuring only themselves paid $509.33 a month as their share. An employee also insuring a spouse paid $1,013.53—close to half what Valerie made each month at Sauder, and Valerie's wages were typical.

To renew this plan for the following year, the insurance company would charge the employer 5 percent more, bringing the total to $352,001.52 annually. The employees' share would rise, too. Pool figured out a new plan that allowed the employer to reduce the annual outlay to $282,577.80. The employees would pay about $100 less each month. But they'd carry a $5,000 deductible for themselves and a $10,000 deductible for their family, and those amounts would double if they had to go out of network for any services.

"You have insurance, but it doesn't do you any good," Pool said. "I get that. That is a sad reality." For small employers like her, she said, this was not sustainable. Like the businesses she helped, you could scramble for a little while—push more costs on to somebody else—but eventually it would all fail. The farmers she insured could move to one-person and two-person group plans, which were a little less expensive than individual ones, but "they won't be able to do that forever and ever."

Dave Swanson knew that all too well. He liked to provide good coverage for his Daavlin employees. To do it, he had to drop a regular insurance company's plan and switch to a self-insured one by creating a pool of the company's own money. The plan included a stop-loss to prevent catastrophe. In 2019, when an employee submitted a claim for a drug that cost hundreds of thousands of dollars a year, Swanson's plan administrator had to figure a one-time way around the first-year cost of the drug. That maneuver worked, but it left Swanson uncertain about the future. "Fourteen months from now, we may be totally screwed," he said. "I don't know what we are going to do, because I like to have good coverage. But I am unlikely to be able to afford it. Everyone is going to get hurt. If the insurance pool was 340,000,000 strong," Swanson said, referring to Medicare for all, "it wouldn't be a problem."

Pool believed the entire system of employer-based health insurance was going to collapse sooner or later—maybe even sooner than many thought. She was skeptical of Medicare for all. On the other hand, the system had grown by accident, by ad hoc "solutions" over many years, decade upon decade. If it ever had made sense, it sure didn't now. "There is so much broken," she said, "I don't know what the answer is."

Jim Watkins was right: there was no system at all. "It isn't a system!" agreed Kim Bordenkircher, the CEO of Henry County Hospital. "We do not have a system here!"

What America *did* have was a jumble of ill-fitting building blocks: the doctoring industry, the hospital industry, the insurance industry, the drug industry, the device industry. They'd all been able to tweak and sand the corners of proposed "solutions" to benefit themselves. Lobbyists and political action committees spent millions to do so until the edifice of American medicine looked like a fragile Tower of Babel, rotten with holes and the crooked passageways where money was hidden. There was so much money. Trillions. And there was so much incentive to embrace the insanity because the insanity was so lucrative.

"It's crazy!" Nick Walz, the now-retired doctor, said in March 2018 as we sat over dinner in Father John's. "Really. The whole thing is insane." A year later, he hadn't changed his mind—and pretty much everybody agreed with him: other doctors, Ennen and other hospital administrators, patients, hospital social workers. Everybody.

There was no end of reform plans. America had been working on reform for a century. Shelves of books, stacks of government reports, entire staffs of think tanks were devoted to reforming American healthcare. Reform had become its own healthcare industry, complete with its own cadre of experts.

Around Bryan, though, just about everybody also agreed on solutions. The answers seemed so obvious. If Mike Liu, the Parkview surgeon, was correct that medical care was a human right, then what? Well, you could blow up the entire crazy structure and start over. The United States could create a national health plan, proposed over a hundred years ago. The government could go into the drug business to manufacture drugs that had gone off patent. It could regulate drug prices, especially for drugs that had been created with the help of taxpayer research money. It could shorten patent protection and ban copycat patents. Medical school costs could be slashed, especially for general practitioners and family practitioners. Hospitals could be funded with grants, and in return charge patients nothing: many hospitals, including CHWC, already received most of their income from the government.

Even in conservative Bryan a lot of people thought such ideas might be good ones. Yet, just as they all agreed that the current medical economy had become a perverse funhouse, they all also agreed that there was nothing to be done about it.

America had gone too far down a bad road and had no choice but to keep going. There was too much money at stake to blow it up. Doctors would make less. So would the drug companies and their shareholders. So would the big hospital systems and the private equity outfits that were beginning to dominate American medicine. The device makers would make less, too, and so would the consultants, the accountants, the medical records software companies, and the ambulance companies. Lots of people in the insurance industry would lose their jobs. Not in a million years, everybody agreed, because nobody wanted to give up their current piece of the pie.

So much depended now on the medical industry. In 1938, at a National Health Conference convened to explore the need for a government health plan, American Federation of Labor lawyer Joseph Padway argued that health was "not an article of commerce." Ninety years later it had replaced manufacturing as the nation's big driver of commerce. It had also become a substitute taxing agency for cities looking to replace local revenues with industry largesse, though the upstream source was the pockets of patients. Many medical jobs were in fact low-wage—assistants could expect to make about $33,000 a year, janitors and housekeepers about $26,000, home health aides $24,000, food service workers $22,000—but cities counted on the high prices people paid to the medical economy to help finance billions for new buildings and attract high-paying jobs. Officials at Toledo's Regional Growth Partnership, a multicounty economic development agency, were ecstatic when ProMedica took over an old steam plant in downtown Toledo and transformed it—with the help of massive subsidies from federal, state, and local government—into its new headquarters campus. ProMedica, they said, would turn Toledo's inner city around. They imagined chic loft apartments, new cafés, rising property values. The *Toledo Blade*, which called ProMedica's CEO, Randy Oostra, "a local hero," declared that "without Mr. Oostra, we are in trouble." Nobody wanted to wreck the chances of all that coming true by curing the insanity.

That's why private equity was taking over so much of healthcare. PE firms may not have known how to run companies, but they weren't stupid. Like Willie Sutton, the thief who when asked why he robbed banks supposedly replied, "Because that's where the money is" (words he later denied ever saying), PE investors knew healthcare was the biggest casino in the American economy.

Many patients didn't want to cure the insanity, either—their distrust of government was too deep. Jennifer Stantz, a young woman who incurred so much medical debt that she and her husband had to sell their house, didn't approve of the Affordable Care Act. Because her husband was the sole proprietor of his construction company, he didn't have insurance, and neither did Jennifer. An Obamacare plan would cost $1,400 a month, she said. "That's my whole income! How could I feed everybody?" Her own medical debt was about to pile up again because she'd been recommended to have surgery for a heart valve condition. "I'm screwed if I get that surgery," she said.

Yet she rejected the idea of a single-payer government plan. "No, no, no!" she said. "Because then your quality of care is going to be dictated by the government." Instead, she argued, she should be able to get Medicaid. The state had ruled that she made $200 too much. She was appealing that decision. All three children were already insured by Medicaid. Somehow, Medicaid didn't seem like a government plan.

Marc Tingle felt the same way. "I don't believe it should be put in the hands of the federal government that is so inept at handling anything," he said. "That is the last thing we need to do—I have no faith in them at all." Yet the Tingles relied on Ohio's Children with Medical Handicaps program to pay for the many bills resulting from their son's spina bifida. Funding for that program came from the federal government, along with state funds, county funds, and donations.

░░░

Even if the dream of a new system were to come true, what ailed the nation was so much deeper than whether or not people could afford health insurance. Donald Amos was fifty-five when he shot and killed himself at home in Stryker. He had a wife, children, grandchildren, and brothers. He liked camping, hot rods, car shows, motorcycles, and his dog. He was a truck driver for Menards.

Jonathan Fifer was a round-faced kid who liked to fish and play video games. He hung out at the Circle K in Montpelier, took classes at the Four County Career Center, and planned on joining the Marines. Then he and his friend Nicholas Rowland, of Swanton—over in Fulton County—drove a 2009 Ford Fusion about as fast as it would go into a tree up in Michigan's Lenawee County. The coroner there ruled it a suicide.

The next day, police searchers found thirty-five-year-old Anthony Wyse's body in the St. Joseph River, out by County Road J. He'd drowned. Kevin Park ruled his death unintentional, but nobody could explain why or how Wyse wound up drowning in a frigid river.

In May, Mick Frisbie, a fifty-year-old deputy sheriff, parked in an empty lot, put the barrel of his service handgun in his mouth, and pulled the trigger. He was taken to CHWC's ER, where the staff worked on him, but everybody knew it was pointless.

Keith thought about it: Why wouldn't he? He was sinking like a wounded ship. He was a very sick man. He was more than broke. And he still mourned Stephanie. "I get tired of staring at the same four walls all the time," he told Carolyn Sharrock-Dorsten as she checked on his amputation wound. She'd asked how he was doing, and he'd replied in his usual way—"I'm doin' good"—but it lacked even the little bit of enthusiasm he'd been able to muster in the past.

"You know, Keith," she said as she kept working, shaving off bits of skin, "it's okay to get help on all different levels. We have some resources at the hospital across the street. And at Parkview, too."

"I see what you're sayin'," Keith said, which was what he said when he had no intention of following advice but didn't want to be rude.

Keith's life revolved around doctors. A Parkview doctor scheduled a colonoscopy for him, though Keith didn't understand why, given every-thing else that was wrong with him. But Keith wanted to be cooperative, so he complied.

His eyes began to ache again. His left one, the worst of the two, throbbed. So he made an appointment with the same doctor in Toledo. Bobbi drove him there early one morning. Keith sat, slumped over, in the waiting area of St. V's, his red-checked flannel pajama pants baggy around his legs and a brown hooded jacket draped over his torso. Once they called him, the surgery didn't take long. The ophthalmologist installed a bolus of silicone oil in Keith's eye to replace the gas he'd tried last time. The staff told Keith to "take it easy," but he wasn't sure how much easier he could take it. He spent most of his days in the recliner, hopping to the front door to greet Caleb when he came home from school.

As the drama over Ennen's resignation played itself out at the hospital, Keith and Bobbi moved, one carload at a time, up to Hillsdale. Keith wasn't so sure he wanted to go. All of his doctors were in Bryan, and he liked the way the schools treated Caleb. He'd taken up with Bobbi because she was willing to help. She did help, too, but now she wanted to move back up to Hillsdale, into a Section 8 apartment because it had a decent washer and dryer and was closer to her family. Keith gave in. They left just ahead of a shut-off notice from Bryan Municipal Utilities.

A month later, Keith opened the door to his new apartment. He was wearing just a pair of long, sagging gym shorts—no shirt. Sallow skin hung from his waist. His face was drawn. He squinted at the April sun as if emerging from a long slumber in a cave. The amputated foot looked wor-rying: unbandaged, scabbed, with signs of pus in spots. A new wound had appeared above the ankle on his lower calf. He didn't know how he'd gotten it. Maybe the move. The vision in his good eye had grown fuzzy. Toys lay scattered everywhere, and potato chips had been ground into the carpet. Bills—some opened, some not—sat in a pile.

The job Bobbi had hoped to get by moving up to Hillsdale didn't pan out, so she took one at Clemens, a hog-processing plant near Coldwater. She started at $12.50 an hour. She didn't last long. Every day her body ached; every morning she woke with back pain, the result of the physical intensity of meatpacking. She eventually got a job at a McDonald's.

Keith was just so stressed. That was easy enough to believe. A few days before, he'd thought he was dying. His heart seemed to be knocking itself out of his chest, and his chest hurt, too, and the room swirled a little. Bobbi took him to the Hillsdale hospital's ER, but they didn't find anything. When it happened again the next day, the symptoms worsened, so he called an ambulance. Hillsdale ran more tests but again drew blanks. Frustrated, Bobbi drove him to a hospital in Jackson, Michigan. They ran tests, too, keeping him for four hours and concluding that Keith was probably experiencing severe anxiety. "I think I might need a counselor," he said. "I might be depressed."

Soon after, the day Pete Buttigieg announced he'd be running for president and Tiger Woods won the Masters, Keith spent most of the day in bed. He asked if I'd drive up to Hillsdale to take him to a hospital. When I arrived, Keith was up, and sitting so close to a computer screen that his nose almost touched it. He was trying to watch a movie. A cartoon played on the big TV, the boys screamed, and Bobbi heated frozen pizza in the oven. She handed a styrofoam plate with two pieces on it to Keith. "I know it's not salad," he said.

Keith was now almost entirely blind in his left eye. He could no longer see shapes—only a small amount of light. Despite the uselessness of his left eye, it still caused him pain. It kept him awake. He wanted to visit the doctor in Toledo, "but that's twenty bucks," he said, referring to the gas money. They were broke until Caleb's Social Security check arrived in four days.

Keith looked at me. As if to answer an unasked question, he said, "I admit it, Brian. I do cry at night more. I know you're worried about me. But I ain't gonna do anything to myself. I have too much to live for. I have Caleb and Bobbi and Gabe."

On April 23, 2019, Keith called to ask if I'd give him a ride to see the ophthalmologist in Bryan. The pain in his eye had gotten worse, and he couldn't stand it anymore. I picked him up in Hillsdale and we drove south into Bryan, to the chain ophthalmology outlet, where an assistant measured the intraocular pressure in Keith's eyes. His right eye tested at 18 millimeters of mercury. Between 10 and 20 is considered normal. His left eye measured 53.

"You need to go to the Kellogg Eye Center up in Ann Arbor," Dr. Mandar Joshi told Keith.

"Okay," Keith said. "I'll make an appointment."

"No," Joshi said. "You need to go right now. Get in your car and go."

We drove the ninety minutes to Ann Arbor and checked into the ER at the University of Michigan Medical Center. Since I'd met Keith, he'd had two amputations, three eye surgeries, and one colonoscopy. He'd been in six hospitals. The question arose as to how all of that might have been prevented if—way back, when he was first diagnosed—his insulin and his care had been free to him: just a benefit of being a taxpaying American citizen. There would have been costs for every taxpayer, of course. But those costs would have been a fraction of the Medicaid tab Keith had racked up—and would continue to rack up. And Keith would still be working and paying taxes himself.

Sana Qureshi, a petite New Yorker in her first year of an ophthalmology residency at Michigan, walked into the exam room and greeted Keith with an open smile and a gentle manner. She took his intraocular pressure and explained the situation to Keith in a way he hadn't heard quite the same way before, telling him that he had a very small chance—15 percent, tops—of regaining any sight in his left eye. His goal should be to protect his right one.

We were in for a long night. He sat, worried and despondent, on the edge of an exam table, waiting for Qureshi to return.

"I wish I woulda made a lot of different choices in my life," he said. "Before, in my life, I was in control. I had money, marriage, a lotta things." In the months since I'd first met him, Keith often talked about "control," as if he were controlling his own life the way he controlled an RC car. Most of that control had slipped away. He sighed. He was compliant. Really, he'd always been compliant—at least in terms of the big picture. "You have to accept how things are, because you can't change it all," he said. "Ya gotta work with the hand you're dealt. My dad always said that. That wise old trucker."

Keith wound up being admitted to the hospital. The next day I called to check on him, and he said, "Doin' good, buddy. Doin' good."

Part III

Winter/Spring/Summer, 2019–2020

Epilogue

Then Everything Changed

Covid-19

The board announced Chad Tinkel's appointment as permanent CEO on April 18, 2019. Tinkel was thrilled. He'd wanted the job—he was miffed that some board members had argued for a candidate search—and now he had it. He started right away to enlist support from the staff. "He was out politicking!" one employee said of Tinkel's appearance in the cafeteria. "He was working the room. I was surprised he wasn't kissing babies."

Nobody had much doubt about the outcome. Tinkel was the Bryan guy. His wife was Bryan. After all the tumult, he represented continuity. Some employees were pleased and others were wary, but everyone knew what they were getting, so the announcement calmed nerves.

The future looked brighter, too. CHWC had achieved a margin again, easing the financial worry a little, and so thoughts of strategic plans seemed a little less like hope and a little more like possibility.

The executives started setting goals the day after Tinkel's appointment. Patrick, David, Foster, and Tinkel (the original six had been whittled down to four) attached numbers to all the new business they wanted CHWC to generate. They projected that by October 1, 2020, the start of a new fiscal year, MRI revenue would grow by 5 percent, gastrointestinal by 5 percent, orthopedics by 7 percent, and wound care by 3 percent. CHWC should have a new phone system by then, too. They talked of a new PET/

CT scanner—which cost in the range of $1.5 to $2 million—to boost CHWC's imaging offerings. They planned a geriatric/psychiatric center in Montpelier.

All the clinics would stay open, they said. Though Michael Nosanov would retire by 2021, they'd keep the ENT clinic going by hiring a new doctor. If Parkview didn't go after an interventional cardiologist to replace Kesireddy, they'd recruit one of their own. They wanted the joint-venture cancer clinic with Parkview to be up and running by July 2020. Maybe there'd be a new marketing campaign to sell CHWC, and maybe they'd boost CHWC's Hospital Consumer Assessment of Healthcare Providers and Systems (HCAHPS) scores by giving "a patient experience that leverages a concierge approach." They laid out a big menu that would cost a lot of money.

Off they went into their bright future. CHWC made a margin every month. The specialty clinics began paying off, as more Williams County people stayed local for such services. Surgeries were up, and so was imaging. Expenses declined. Ennen's "glide path" had worked so well that in February 2020, CHWC was named a top twenty rural and community hospital by the National Rural Health Association.

Tinkel used the hospital's stabilizing finances to solve some of his most immediate concerns. Since there'd been no agreement with Jim Hicks and the Williams County EMS on how to handle the transfers to Toledo and Fort Wayne, and with the cutoff deadline approaching, Tinkel bought time by paying subsidy money from the hospital to EMS as a way to compensate Hicks's team. Meanwhile, he explored either creating a dedicated CHWC long-distance ambulance service or contracting for one.

When a general surgeon from the Bryan Parkview group announced his retirement, Parkview—over the objections of the group in Bryan—refused to hire a replacement. That convinced Tinkel that he couldn't cross his fingers and hope Parkview would hire an interventional cardiologist: The fear that Parkview would refuse to do so in a desire to force Williams County heart patients like Marc Tingle into the Fort Wayne system was too real. So after Kesireddy finally announced that he'd retire by the summer of 2021, Tinkel began searching for two candidates to take on Kesireddy's mammoth work hours.

Kim Owen, figuring that Parkview might wind up owning CHWC

someday, and feeling that life at the hospital couldn't go back to normal for her, quit and took a job with Parkview. Hanan Bazzi extended her contract for another three years, relieving Tinkel of his concern about having to recruit a new ob-gyn to head the Women's Clinic. And when Samar Hassouneh had a baby in early 2020, he dared to hope she'd become even more integrated into the Bryan community and decide to stay as well.

But Angelia Foster was never going to be satisfied with a supporting role on Tinkel's executive team. She'd wanted to be CEO, but she knew that, barring any unlikely stumble on his part, Tinkel might be ensconced at the top for as long as Ennen had been. So Foster and Tinkel conferred. She assured him that she'd remain on "Team Chad" for at least two years before trying to move on. Tinkel understood her ambition. As a consolation prize, he named her executive vice president and chief administrative officer, with a special emphasis on strategic leadership. The title didn't make much practical difference. It was a résumé-fluffer—a gift from Tinkel so Foster could better position herself with potential employers.

The gift worked too well. Just a few months later, Foster informed Tinkel she was leaving by early 2020 to accept a job as chief administrative officer of a chain hospital in Wisconsin. Tinkel was surprised. "We made it not quite a year," he said. "But the opportunity she got, I, as a friend, didn't resent it. I was ecstatic for her and proud of her. The only thing was the timing. I thought it would be another year."

Foster had a second motive to leave. She had come to think that some Bryanites "would like to see me burned at the stake," because they held her responsible for Ennen's forced resignation. She welcomed the chance to watch Bryan recede in her rearview mirror.

The CHWC-Parkview Cancer Center didn't open after all. Parkview insisted CHWC adopt its electronic medical records system, but CHWC hadn't yet made a decision on EMRs, so rather than wait, Tinkel decided to go it alone for now. He hired a radiation oncologist (eliminating the need for a contracted group), saying he might also employ a medical oncologist who could run chemotherapy. "We are trying to become more independent from a provider standpoint," Tinkel said. "We're becoming less dependent on [the Parkview Physicians Group]."

Swanson and Ennen were both right about Tinkel. He was an excellent CFO, but being a CFO was different from being a CEO. As CFO, "the job was to do this, get it done in a good way, provide this, and when you finish, people thank you, and you continue on. It was somewhat repetitious." Now he discovered that though he'd worked just down the hall from Ennen and had shared countless meetings, plans, and thoughts with Ennen, he still didn't fully grasp the CEO experience. "In this job, you're making decisions on a regular basis. One day you get praised, and they say how well you're doing and see the positive impact of it—and the next day somebody is tearing you apart."

Like Ennen, he embraced the family ethos. But he underestimated the emotional payload. The highs were higher than he'd imagined, but so were the lows—"and the going between the two is so much more frequent than I thought it could ever be."

The experience "enlightened" Tinkel about Ennen and the ways he'd managed to cope. Even after years of working with him, Tinkel had still been mystified at times by Ennen's behavior. Now he believed Ennen must have felt the same kinds of pressures—the same highs and lows—that Tinkel was presently feeling, but that Ennen's way of coping was to take those ups and downs home with him, to sit in the back of the room during meetings, and to skip the party at Jackie Blu's after the Joint Commission inspection.

Though CHWC had stepped back from its financial brink, the crisis of independent community hospitals remained. Three years after being freed from ProMedica, St. Luke's in Maumee succumbed. Citing an inability to build a solid financial footing in an outpatient world, it sold itself to Mc-Laren, a big nonprofit system based in Michigan. Efforts like joining the Vantage Ohio group that CHWC and the other small hospitals had formed in order to bulk up their purchasing heft weren't enough. Urban "safety net" hospitals fared no better. The University of Toledo Medical Center—the hospital ProMedica had cited to the FTC as proof that ProMedica didn't dominate the Toledo market—found itself on the verge of collapse and being taken over by ProMedica, which offered to operate it. Toledo residents protested and Toledo congresswoman Marcy Kaptur appealed to Ohio's governor, Mike DeWine, to intervene.

Still, Tinkel believed his hospital would cope better. The plans he and the others made would keep the momentum going—he could see that. His optimism seemed justified when two interventional cardiologists stepped in to signal their willingness to come to Bryan to replace Kesireddy. Tinkel was talking contracts. "Then," he said, "everything changed."

∎∎∎

At first, life outside CHWC seemed normal. Marc Tingle and his daughter, Summer, returned to swinging hammers.

Valerie Moreno made it to Disney World with her younger daughter and her husband, and they had "a blast on vacation: four parks in five days!" She found out her older daughter was pregnant. Her daughter didn't have health insurance because she made too much money in tips to qualify for Medicaid, and her employer didn't provide a plan. Valerie's back still hurt. Even so, she reduced the amount of the OxyContin she'd been taking for the pain because it scared her. She stopped working the bus route and caretaking for Betty's husband. When she did all those things, she found out what it was like to get seven hours of sleep: "Amazing!"

Chris Cullis put the *Bryan Times* building up for sale, quit the paper his family had run for three generations in order to save the paper the cost of his salary, and went to work for Dave Swanson at Daavlin, the dermatological light company. The paper itself continued to publish, though on a diminished schedule. Bryanites speculated about how long it could survive.

Greg Coleman had a hernia operation at CHWC. Mike Liu did the cutting. Coleman was back to preaching in no time, but Liu left Bryan for the Cleveland Clinic.

Keith kept visiting doctors. The long night I spent with him in the University of Michigan ER was the first of many long nights for him. He and Bobbi made regular trips to the Kellogg Eye Center at the University of Michigan–Ann Arbor in an effort to save the vision in his good eye. The interventions worked, for the most part: his sight in that eye stabilized. He also routinely visited doctors in Hillsdale to check on his foot wound.

But the rest of 2019 was a painful one for him, involving admissions to different Michigan hospitals, anxiety so severe he thought he was dying, another infection in his foot, a bone debridement in the foot to remove the infection, severe nausea, the removal of his gallbladder—another piece of Keith gone missing—courses of antibiotics, and a stint in a rehab nursing home where he was taught a series of exercises to strengthen his arms and legs. Doctors worried his kidneys might be failing. He returned to Kellogg for more eye procedures. The ophthalmologists removed scar tissue and blood from his left eye. They also wanted to administer a steroid into Keith's good eye, but a national shortage of the generic drug forced a delay. Nobody wanted to make the drug. There wasn't enough profit in it.

Keith and Bobbi and the boys lived off Bobbi's McDonald's pay, Caleb's Social Security payments, and Gabe's government money. Keith didn't receive any disability, though he didn't understand why. As far as he could tell, the bureaucrats wanted proof he was disabled to an extent that prevented him from working. Keith wouldn't receive any disability payments until May 2020. Until then, the other income was just enough for food and the Section 8 rent. Gas money was scarce, though, and buying the fresh fruit and vegetables Keith was supposed to be eating wasn't always possible. Frozen meals and pizza were far cheaper. The good thing, he said, was "those nurses up at U of M." They gave Keith gas cards so he could put fuel in the tank of the Saturn and make it to his appointments. "The ladies there are just wonderful. It's nice they have nurses like that."

Keith stopped talking. He thought about how everything had changed in three years. Three years ago, "I'd be working twelve hours, six days a week. My life has been turned upside down." He paused again. "You gotta make do with what you have in life."

One day, Keith had Bobbi drive him in the Saturn down to the cemetery in Bryan, out on the edge of town by the Arby's and the Walmart. The headstone was finally in place and Keith wanted to see it. He was proud of it: the deep carved letters spelling out SWIHART, the panel engraved with Stephanie's name and the dates of her birth and death, an etched image of Stephanie and Keith in the center—she in sunglasses, her head resting on his shoulder, and he with his arm around her, both of them smiling. There was another panel that read KEITH A., JUNE 1, 1979. That one had no second date.

He tried not to think too much about the future. Caleb remained his focus. He wanted to stick around on this earth for him. But he knew that his life was fragile, so he arranged to make Bobbi Caleb's legal guardian in the event of his death. He sounded stronger, though, when he said, "I'm doin' good, buddy. Doin' good."

▌▌▌

In late January 2020, at just about the same time that Keith was admitted to a hospital in Michigan for his bone debridement, Williams County health

director Jim Watkins received notices from Ohio's public health surveillance system. Chinese scientists in Wuhan, Hubei Province, had linked a
virus—a variant of the coronavirus family—to a rash of pneumonia cases in
the city. Days later, Japan, South Korea, and Thailand reported that people
in those countries had been sickened, too. On January 21, 2020, Washington State reported a case in the United States. Soon people were dying from
what became known as Covid-19. (Though it wasn't yet known, the first
U.S. cases and deaths occurred in California in January.)

The crisis seemed to smother the United States and the world with
sudden fury, but it wasn't sudden at all except in its particulars. Over the
previous forty years, fissures radiating from the deepening fault lines of
inequality, racism, suspicion, paranoia, and the propaganda of financial
self-interest carved their way through America's landscape until the country
and its people had become fragile. Covid-19 just exploited the weaknesses until the crust collapsed, revealing to Americans what had become
of their nation. If it hadn't been Covid-19, it would have been some other
catastrophe.

Though the triggering event didn't have to be a pandemic, a natural
attack on the nation's health seemed metaphorically apt, given Americans'
declining vigor and life expectancy and the rottenness of the country's
medical care. Just such a pandemic had been predicted for decades. The
public health community warned over and over that a novel disease would
eventually strike and spread around the world. In 2009, the U.S. Department of Health and Human Services advised that "any large-scale incident
such as a natural disaster or an infectious disease pandemic that affects the
health of critical workers and compromises a society's ability to provide
food, water, healthcare and, more broadly, economic productivity endan-
gers the security and stability of that society. Conversely, a society that can
accommodate and function effectively during such an incident is inherently
more secure."

There'd been close calls: Ebola, severe acute respiratory syndrome
(SARS), Middle East respiratory syndrome (MERS), deadly flu strains. All
these diseases killed people. Only quick action by world public health investigators and doctors had prevented millions of deaths across the globe.

For public health experts like Watkins, the Spanish flu pandemic of
1918, which had led to the creation of so many hospitals in the United
States and which had spurred Bryan to consider building one of its own,

served as a talismanic reminder. They'd studied it in school. Nobody knew
how many people had died of the flu in the years surrounding 1918—
maybe fifty million, maybe a hundred million—but nobody holding a job
like Watkins's could doubt how disastrous such a thing could be, or that its
arrival, someday, was certain.

When it finally came to America, the virus seeped into the fault lines
created by America's pathologies. The country had changed from being an
ongoing project to improve democratic society and live humanistic ideals
to being a framework for fostering corporate profit. Politicians declared
their intentions all the time: America should be run like a business and
led by a businessman. And so a program of starving the nation of public
goods while showering private interests with dollars entrenched itself until
it seemed as if America had always been that way and the new version of
capitalism came to be equated with patriotism. But that new capitalism was
killing people.

Even as public health officials like Watkins worried, their budgets were
cut. Across the United States, local health departments withered. While
medical industry costs rose far above the rate of inflation, and while Americans spent 52 percent more of their dollars on healthcare than during the
previous decade, the country reduced its spending on public health by
24 percent. About fifty thousand people who worked for health departments like the one Watkins ran for Williams County lost their jobs. The
federal government slashed the money it allocated to prepare for an emergency like Covid-19 from $940 million in 2002 to $667 million in 2017. By
2018, Ohio was spending just $13 per person on public health. Only three
states spent less.

After M. V. Replogle—the first person to hold Watkins's job—judged
Williams County to be an unhealthy place in the early 1920s, he pushed
for change. Grudgingly, the county did change. It took a local smallpox epidemic to get people vaccinated, but when they finally were, smallpox disappeared. America was once rife with yellow fever and malaria. The public
war on disease-carrying mosquitos, as well as improved public sanitation,
erased those diseases from the collective mind (though at the cost of pollution from the insecticide DDT).

Diseases of poverty and malnutrition, such as pellagra and rickets,
almost disappeared after the people of the United States, through their
government, funded campaigns to enrich food, and formed the Tennessee

Valley Authority to produce energy, reclaim land, and improve public health and welfare. Polio crippled Franklin Roosevelt in 1921 and terrified children and their parents into the 1950s. After Jonas Salk and his team produced a vaccine, the federal government licensed six manufacturers to make it, supported vaccination drives in conjunction with the March of Dimes and other charities, and provided money so that no child would be denied a vaccine because of inability to pay for it. Polio was wiped out in the United States. Thanks to vaccines, whooping cough, measles, mumps, and other diseases no longer plagued childhoods.

America had a long history of investing in the health of its people, but the public health infrastructure eroded from inattention and financial starvation in the same way other public goods like bridges, water systems, and education eroded, and so the health of Americans eroded, too. For decades, rising levels of obesity, high blood pressure, drug and alcohol abuse, suicide, heart disease, and lack of access to medical care rooted themselves in many millions of Americans. All these were quieter, more insidious epidemics, but they were epidemics just the same. And, as it happened, these conditions—all of them prevalent in Bryan and in Williams County, just as they were across the country—made the people who suffered from them more likely to suffer and die from Covid-19.

The decline in American health was abetted by deliberate policy. When a team of demographers, sociologists, a physician, and a political scientist led by Jennifer Karas Montez of Syracuse University studied the impact of state laws on longevity, they found a powerful correlation. In 1959, life expectancy in Oklahoma was 71.1 years. So was life expectancy in Connecticut. At the time, both states' policies in a number of realms studied by the team—labor, wages, environment, and so on—were pretty similar. But after 1980, those policies began to diverge. Lobbying and pressure inside state legislatures from organized groups such as the American Legislative Exchange Council (ALEC)—funded by big energy, drug, telecommunications, and tobacco companies and by the Koch-created Americans for Prosperity, and which favors minimal government expense and low minimum wages—began changing state laws. Oklahoma's minimum wage was $7.25 an hour in 2020, for example, while Connecticut's was $11.

In 2017, life expectancy in Connecticut was 80.7 years. But it was now 75.8 in Oklahoma, about 5 percent lower. Such correlations held up for states across America. People in states that passed labor, wage, environmental, and health laws that were often opposed by ALEC and business interests lived longer than people in states who adopted ALEC-like policies. The correlation did not prove a direct cause and effect, but the team's findings were robust.

Covid-19 was a crisis, all right—a bad one—but it was far from the first epidemic to hit the United States, or even the deadliest. The United States had been living with epidemics for decades but had pretended otherwise, soothing itself by saying that the epidemics existed only among the undisciplined, the noncompliant. Covid-19 stripped away the fiction.

There'd been an epidemic of financial manipulation, of dismantling the rights of workers, of eroding the social contract and therefore eroding community. There'd been an epidemic of sending work outside the country or to "right-to-work" states, of using the poor and working class—as well as, increasingly, the middle class—as "human capital" suitable for sacrifice in the service of the market. (The lieutenant governor of Texas, Dan Patrick, made the attitude explicit by saying Texas had to reopen its economy in the face of Covid-19 because "there are more important things than living.") There'd been an epidemic of consolidation in industry, and an epidemic of deregulation that allowed those industries to acquire more power than ever. There'd been an epidemic of ignorance, disinformation, and rank propaganda in the service of vote-getting and profit-making. All these epidemics killed many more people than Covid-19 would, even as the Hundred Years' War waged against the manufactured evil of "socialized medicine" left behind casualties of its own.

America had become an unforgiving nation, a fearful place, hiding behind a pyroclastic flow of guns, flag-waving, and ever-emptier jingoistic bragging. Then Covid-19 arrived. It just showed up, like lightning. There was no way to wrap it up in the comforting notion that the victims were to blame. It killed 170,000 by August 2020 and would probably kill many more, experts said.

▌▌▌

Watkins and his staff did what they could to protect Williams County, but it wasn't easy. Nurse Rachel Aeschliman and other staff members formulated detailed plans. They worked seven days a week, often late into the night. They drew up a set of actions, made long lists, and tried to prepare local officials, including the county prosecutor, the county commissioners, the

police, the sheriff, and mayors. Aeschliman organized extra nurses to help
with contact tracing investigations. She, Watkins, and the rest of the department coordinated with rehab facilities and nursing homes to limit visitors.

By early March, while New York City was being ravaged by Covid-19,
forecasting models from Ohio State University suggested that Williams
County could expect about a hundred hospitalized patients. That projec-
tion scared both Watkins and Tinkel. On an average day, about twenty-five
people occupied inpatient beds at CHWC in Bryan. Montpelier held about
ten. Few of those patients would normally suffer from infectious diseases
that could require intensive care, ventilators, respiratory therapists, and
nurses, all while in isolation.

Then when Kevin Park (the Parkview doctor who also served as both
coroner and medical director for the county's nursing homes) fell ill with
symptoms that looked a lot like those associated with Covid-19, they became alarmed. If Park had visited facilities when he was already infected,
CHWC could be flooded with cases. "There was a little panic," Tinkel said.
"Like, 'Oh my gosh, this is terrible! All the nursing homes are going to be
affected.'" After tests showed that Park was ill with something else, Watkins
and Tinkel felt that Williams County had escaped a serious threat.

At CHWC, some physicians urged Tinkel to shut down all discretion-
ary surgeries and clinic appointments. Tinkel could see his grand plans for
using the 2020 operating surplus he'd anticipated crumble a little more by
the hour. He was relieved when, on March 22, Governor DeWine ordered a
stop to all elective surgeries across the state. At least CHWC wouldn't be at
a competitive disadvantage by unilaterally ceasing the operations: patients
wouldn't be able to go to Napoleon, Hicksville, or Toledo, either.

Crews quickly reconfigured the hospital, even turning second-floor office space into a negative-air-pressure unit by rigging flexible ducting to
air movers and sealing the rooms with plastic sheeting. They augmented
CHWC's four ventilators by modifying anesthesia carts, which held machines that administered gases much like a vent did. By the time they were
through, they'd turned CHWC from a 50-bed hospital into a 107-bed hospital. The hitch, though, was that it didn't have the staff to be a 107-bed
hospital. At most, Tinkel could staff 64 beds. If more were filled, "we'd have
to stretch resources," he said.

While he awaited Covid-19 patients, Tinkel shifted personnel. Nurses
became door screeners, taking temperatures and interrogating anybody

trying to enter the hospital. Other staff became daycare workers, to mind the children of employees once all the daycares in the county closed. Nobody was laid off, though some employees worked reduced hours. Bazzi still delivered babies, of course, and the ER remained open, but with most normal functions of the hospital suspended, an uncanny, nervous silence settled over the Bryan building.

Without surgeries, lab tests, imaging, and the bills CHWC could send for them, money bled out as if from a gushing wound: $800,000 in March, and about $3 million by mid-April. After Congress passed the Coronavirus Aid, Relief, and Economic Security (CARES) Act, CHWC was given $1.5 million in emergency funding, but its days of cash dwindled down to 250. By August, Tinkel figured CHWC had lost $10 million, though eventually government payments roughly equaled the losses. After DeWine lifted restrictions on surgeries and outpatient procedures, CHWC's business returned as people who'd been forced to wait rushed in for service. July set a record for outpatient business: $10,298,475.

Other hospitals weren't as lucky. Some had thirty days of cash; a few had less than that. Thirteen small hospitals around the country closed between January 2020 and August 1—not all necessarily because of Covid-19, but the closures reflected the precarious state in which many community hospitals existed going into the crisis. What Tinkel gleaned from his conversations with other Ohio CEOs made him think there'd "be some small hospitals, before this is over, that will end up having to close their doors." By one estimate, a quarter of all rural hospitals in the United States were in danger.

While Tinkel juggled money and managed the logistics for the expected Covid-19 cases, Phil Ennen helped coordinate equipment needs between some Ohio hospitals and the state. The Ohio Hospital Association had hired him to consult from his temporary quarters in Florida for the duration of the crisis. He spoke with Tinkel for the first time in months and offered to help however he could.

At first, Watkins felt encouraged by the reaction to the crisis within the county. A few, like the woman who owned a beauty salon and dropped off an opened box of protective gloves to the health department headquarters, displayed the communitarian spirit for which the Midwest is known. "I have been truly impressed with the public," Watkins said early on. Some local officials mimicked Trump, claiming the whole thing was a hoax, but

Watkins held his tongue—he knew his county—and got most of the cooperation he needed. But as the shutdown dragged on, and as the expected wave of cases failed to materialize in Williams County, the Trumpist agitation grew louder and angrier, unleashing the same American disinformation-driven paranoia that plagued many other places.

By mid-April, six cases had been discovered. One person died. The day after that death, "some people were saying, 'This is made up; that person didn't really die from it,'" Watkins said.

As Trump sent insurrectionist messages to his Twitter followers, encouraging them to "liberate" states, the mood in the county darkened. The danger really was a hoax, some said. Trump was right. The threat was overblown.

"The stuff coming out of Washington was horrible," Watkins said, referring to the Trump administration. "It was doing nothing but causing problems for us. At times we had to battle against that."

Trump was a lying sociopath. But many in Bryan, and in the state and the nation, believed he was *their* lying sociopath, and anybody who contradicted his increasingly lunatic pronouncements became an enemy of freedom and right. Dr. Amy Acton, the state health chief, faced abuse from Republican members of the state legislature. Representative Nino Vitale accused her of destroying liberty and called her "an unelected Globalist Health Director," using a slur known to refer to Jews; Acton was Jewish. State senator Andrew Brenner likened Acton's health mandates to actions taken by Nazi Germany. Gun-toting protesters appeared on Acton's lawn. She received death threats.

Craig Riedel, the legislator who'd insisted that Jesus Christ could solve the drug problem, said DeWine should allow counties to determine whether it was safe to release themselves from shutdowns and distancing. "You can't do that!" Watkins retorted. Saying such things put the onus on county health departments like his at a time when their staffers were already receiving death threats. "A colleague of ours in [another county], who used to work for us, had a Facebook post saying they were gonna slit her throat," Watkins said. "Another one of my colleagues has police stationed outside her house because she's received so many threats." Anthony Fauci, the director of the National Institute of Allergy and Infectious Diseases, required full-time protection after receiving threats against himself and his children.

Acton finally had enough and resigned. By the end of July, forty-nine health officials in twenty-three states had either resigned or been fired, often after threats, harassment, or having property vandalized.

Watkins and his staff tried to ignore the fires Trump and his followers were stoking and simply do their jobs. As if to validate his argument that Williams County would not escape Covid-19 so easily, the number of cases doubled in one day when a hot spot of infection broke out inside a local prison. And as the weeks rolled by, the number of cases continued to rise.

By June, Watkins was receiving emails like "YOU ARE A FUCKING ASSHOLE, YOU SON OF A JACKASS!!!!!!!!!!" The mayor of Pioneer, Ed Kidston, seemed to think Covid-19 was an enemy coming over the hill to attack a fort. "Americans are not do-nothings!" he wrote to the *Bryan Times*. "We never sat silent and let the enemy creep in, regardless of the casualties." It was the "regardless of the casualties" part that worried Watkins. When attending a meeting to discuss the cancellation of much of the county fair, the president of the Williams County fair board wore a "Don't Tread on Me" baseball cap (the slogan used on the so-called Gadsden flag, featuring a coiled snake, which had been adopted by the Tea Party and white nationalist groups) and a white mask on which he inked a sarcastic, and grammatically incorrect, whine: "IT'S FOR THE KID'S!!"

As protests sparked by the killing of an African American man named George Floyd in Minneapolis roiled the nation, some resorted to racism. The agitation in the streets, they said, proved that warnings over Covid-19 were a false flag, meant to intimidate white people and keep Trump from winning reelection—a theory floated by Trump himself, who said Covid-19 numbers were inflated and that masks shouldn't be mandatory. "My favorite comment I've heard so far," Tinkel said in late summer, "is the belief that Covid will go away after the election and this is all a liberal media hoax."

But just as Watkins had warned, when Ohio loosened restrictions and people defied what orders and cautions remained, the numbers spiked again. People who often preached "personal responsibility" and "compliance" refused to take personal responsibility or comply. A winery in Napoleon held a "Name That Tune" contest with more than seventy attendees, none of whom were masked, said guests. Tracers attributed upward of eighty cases to the one event, at least thirteen of which were Williams County residents. Somebody held a bridal shower; cases spread from it. By August, now with 132 cases and three deaths, Watkins was frustrated and exhausted. "I'm getting very discouraged," he said. One of his nurses quit, saying she'd had enough. Watkins felt sure that the autumn would be worse. He suggested that 300,000 Americans, the number of people who lived in Cincinnati, might die.

Watkins's discouragement was fueled by social-media-spread disinformation, hatred of government, ignorance, and selfishness. Some favored the myth that wearing a mask could lead to low oxygen levels and brain damage. Others echoed legislators that mask mandates were an infringement on civil liberties and the first step toward state control of Americans' lives. For some years, as fears of diseases like polio and smallpox faded, Americans who distrusted government stoked an anti-vaccine creed that, like disease itself, infected people such as the young mother Stalter tried to convince in the CHWC ER. As a result, dangerous maladies like measles and whooping cough reappeared. Now, as the world hoped for a Covid-19 vaccine, the anti-vax, anti-government conspiracy theorists turned their attention to Microsoft founder Bill Gates, since the Gates Foundation was helping to finance vaccine research. Gates was part of a worldwide, "deep state" plot, they said, and nobody should trust any Covid-19 vaccine.

But other Americans discovered just what life without effective national government was like. Cases and deaths rose until the United States had the worst record of Covid-19 response in the industrialized world.

America's long racism sickness also aided the virus. In Michigan, for example, by late summer, the rate of Covid-19 infections in African Americans was 14,703 per million; in white people it was 4,160 per million. As of midsummer, African Americans, who comprised roughly 13 percent of the population, accounted for nearly 25 percent of the Covid-19 deaths. Native Americans and Americans of Hispanic origin were more likely to suffer from the virus, too. In response, Ohio state senator Stephen Huffman (an emergency room doctor employed by TeamHealth, the Blackstone-controlled ER staffing agency) asked, "Could it just be that African Americans, or the colored population, do not wash their hands as well as other groups or wear a mask or do not socially distance themselves? Could that be the explanation of why the higher incidence?"

The answer to that racist question was no, just as it had been way back when Frederick Hoffman suggested that African Americans were less healthy because of personal moral failings, and just as it was in Bryan when people suggested the poor and the sick had only themselves to blame.

African Americans were more likely to be poor, to live in crowded house-holds, to be "essential workers" (grocery store clerks, truck drivers, delivery people, nursing assistants), to suffer from obesity or diabetes or high blood pressure, to have lousy health insurance or no insurance at all, to have crummy access to medical care—all like their poor white counterparts in Williams County.

They were all the victims of economic warfare, America's deepest fault. Across the United States, while those who had "knowledge" jobs worked from home, binge-watched TV series, and joked about gaining weight, cauldrons of infection erupted in meatpacking plants, in prisons, and in nursing homes among people who had to go to work.

Valerie worked. Sauder, the furniture-making factory where she made sofas, closed early on. The company paid a supplement to the furloughed workers that amounted to about half their lost wages, which Valerie appreciated. She was able to keep her health insurance, too—but with the proviso that once she returned to work, she had to pay the company back out of her first paycheck for her share of the premiums. Soon, long before Ohio lifted statewide restrictions, Sauder declared itself an essential business. That seemed like a dubious claim, but Sauder did make furniture that was sold to hospitals, so it stuck. Like it or not, Valerie went back on the line. She had mixed feelings: her family needed the money, and she took comfort in Sauder's extra sanitation procedures and new policy of spacing workers six feet apart. "They're doing amazing at keeping us safe," she said. But she was nervous. "Safe" was a relative term during a pandemic of a deadly contagious disease. The extra $1.50 per hour of "hazard pay" that Sauder gave her seemed to confirm as much.

Her first paycheck, for $580, was gutted by all the carve-outs. She ended up taking home $199.45. She felt lucky to have once again landed a second job, this time working as a home aide for a company called Visiting Angels. She made $10 an hour going to the homes of elderly people and attending to their needs. Visiting Angels also tacked on an extra $1.50 per hour as hazard pay to compensate. (Valerie would eventually, finally, have her back surgery, and it would be successful. After rehab, she'd go back on the line at Sauder.)

Valerie was grateful to have work at a time when many others had lost their jobs. Williams County's unemployment rate shot up to 21.2 percent by April, though it would drop back to about 9 percent by the end of the summer. Some jobs would never come back. Rassini Chassis announced in August 2020 that it would close its Montpelier plant for good.

Millions of people around the country lost jobs. And when they lost those jobs, many of them, an estimated 5.4 million, lost health insurance because their insurance was tied to their employment. The Consolidated Omnibus Budget Reconciliation Act (COBRA), passed in 1985, allowed people faced with job loss to keep the employment-based insurance they'd had, but now they were responsible for paying both their and their employer's share. For a family, that could amount to over $20,000 per year at a time when they had no income. They could get insurance through the Affordable Care Act marketplace now that they'd experienced a "life-changing event," but ACA insurance would be expensive, too, and would carry high deductibles. It was now obvious to everyone that what Americans called the "healthcare system" was no system at all.

While small community hospitals tried to stay afloat, big hospital systems had truckloads of money to ride out the crisis. The richest figured out how to take government money anyway. By the end of June, ProMedica had taken $240 million, though it sat atop a hoard of $2.2 billion in cash and investments. For the quarter ending June 30, the "nonprofit" made a 10.8 percent operating margin. UPMC, the University of Pittsburgh Medical Center organization—the "nonprofit" that built hospitals in Italy and started its own venture capital outfit—swept up about $1 billion in government payments and loans by the beginning of summer, though it had an investment portfolio of about $6.6 billion. The for-profit Hospital Corporation of America (HCA), which once paid its CEO $109 million, received about $1 billion. Private-equity-owned businesses like EmCare borrowed about $1.5 billion from the taxpayers. Such generosity, though, did not stop the operators from slashing jobs. Beaumont, the Michigan system that went into the real estate development business with a shopping mall and hotel project, laid off 2,475 people and permanently eliminated 450 jobs. HCA threatened layoffs if staff did not agree to wage freezes.

The shoddy edifice of American medicine trembled. It had turned itself into just another industry, and like other industries it had grown addicted to the dogma of return on investment, high dollar revenues, and just-in-time supply chains. It had put money into shiny machines, new buildings, and mergers that would boost return on investment—but not into stores of masks, gowns, ventilators, and beds. The refusal to prepare for a crisis they'd been warned about forced hospitals to make mafia-like deals in parking lots to buy masks and to negotiate with shady foreign characters charging extortionate prices for equipment.

The private-equity wheeler-dealers, though they had billions under management, pleaded poverty so that they, too, could take government money. Despite their own assets and the government loans, they still forced employees to take pay cuts. And in a move that recalled the old New York League for Americanism, which had helped defeat New York's proposed health insurance law in 1919, KKR and Blackstone spent millions to form a front group called Doctor Patient Unity. They then used this group to continue their advertising and lobbying effort toward defeating surprise-billing reform in the U.S. Congress.

The big nonprofit hospitals continued to act like corporate for-profits, but now, with Covid-19, the screen that hid their true nature collapsed. When nurses and other employees went public over a lack of safety precautions and gear, hospitals fired them or clamped gag orders on them.

Parkview and Anthem decided, in the middle of a pandemic, to stage a fight over reimbursement rates. The old contract between the big health system and the big insurer expired on July 28 after months of negotiations failed. A quarter of a million Anthem enrollees across the region, including many in Williams County, faced the loss of their doctors. Anthem argued that Parkview's rates were too high (they were), while Parkview argued that it provided value and the insurer could afford to pay for it. Two days later, as would-be patients panicked, the two businesses signed a deal, though both sides claimed the details of the contract, such as how much medical care would really cost, had to be kept secret.

Consolidation within the medical equipment industry now seemed to have been a bad idea, too. For example, in 2012, Covidien—the Tyco spinoff that was purchased by Medtronic several years later—bought a maker of ventilators called Newport Medical Instruments. Regulators suspected Covidien bought Newport because Newport had designed a cheaper vent that threatened to compete with Covidien's expensive one. Covidien, they thought, wanted to squash the cheaper design. Two years before the buyout, Newport had signed a deal with the federal government in which Newport would make thousands of vents at a cost to the government of $3,000 per unit, as a way to bulk up the national stockpile in case of an epidemic. Covidien backed out of the government deal after it bought Newport, and the ventilators were never made. As a result, states found themselves competing against each other to obtain ventilators to treat Covid-19 victims, and paying ransom-level prices to companies when they found some. New York paid about $59,000 per unit.

The drug industry tried to wield the same power it had been throwing around for generations. A draft emergency spending bill designed to address the crisis contained language that prevented drug companies from setting high prices for vaccines or therapies by allowing the federal government to usurp patent rights, especially for products whose development had been funded by taxpayer dollars. The industry argued that it wouldn't have the incentive to conduct research and development if it couldn't earn its profits. The bill's language was weakened. Meanwhile, after a drug called remdesivir was found to help some Covid-19 patients with severe disease, Gilead Sciences, the drug's maker, said it would charge up to $3,120 for a course of treatment, though the government had helped fund the drug's development in the first place. Attorneys general for several states urged the feds to "march in" on Gilead's patent rights, but that didn't seem likely to happen.

Covid-19 tests, critical for mitigating the spread of the virus, fell into the disjointed whirl of American medical care. Some people were charged about $100, while others were charged nearly $2,000; some tests were free. Many tests were inaccurate. Some public officials believed the testing process should have been nationalized and free to all. The wisdom of that approach was proved when Ohio tried to use corporate pharmacies as testing stations but the state's Medicaid department had no idea how to pay the pharmacies. Thirty days into the program, not a single test had been run through the system. Meanwhile, people around the country waited up to two weeks for test results from the two oligopoly labs, Quest and LabCorp, rendering the testing pointless.

There was much renewed talk of change, but most of the talk didn't penetrate the surface. American cruelty had germinated the dysfunction, and it didn't stop even as a virus killed more than a thousand people every day. The Trump administration still fought in court to dismantle the Affordable Care Act. By July 29, American renters owed $21.5 billion in back rent. An estimated one-third of all renters and homeowners with mortgages were behind on payments. Early in the pandemic, cities, states, and the federal government slapped eviction bans on landlords to avoid a blitz of homelessness, but by July 31, the federal government, which had power over rental properties financed with federally backed loans, allowed its ban to expire. Republicans in Congress refused to extend it. They refused to extend an extra $600 per week in unemployment booster payments by not renewing Federal Pandemic Unemployment Compensation, so that expired, too. Senate Republicans held up the renewal of the law by relying on the same gospel heard all over Bryan: people didn't want to work. Between the unemployment and the $600 boost, some made more money by not working, the senators said, and while that may have been true in some instances, studies showed that it didn't slow down hiring. It did, however, highlight just how little many people earned.

The kinds of policies explored by the Syracuse demographers would continue to kill people even if some system, like Medicare for all or something like a Canadian or British program, were to appear in a magic instant. There would still be many Keiths, many Valeries, many Marcs—millions of them. Until the cruelty was neutered, the best government plan in the world wouldn't fix American health, and hospitals like CHWC would continue to be Band-Aid stations in a war.

When pathologist Shannon Keil had held Keith's toes in her hand, she looked down at them, then back up at me, and sighed: "What a fucking failure." She didn't mean the operation, and she didn't mean Keith. She meant the forces that had swept Keith's toes into that small plastic tub.

Acknowledgments

Hospitals are notorious among journalists for being unforthcoming. When Phil Ennen and I held our first conversations about *The Hospital*, I asked for complete access: meetings, papers, finances, treatment areas, staff—everything. Ennen agreed, in the face of some initial resistance from a couple of board members and the hospital's law firm, because he believed the story of healthcare in America, especially from the perspective of rural healthcare, was important and not adequately told. He exacted no promises from me in return that would limit the substantive content or point of view of this book. He could not have known the twists that awaited him back in March 2018 when I made my first trip to Bryan. Yet even during the most vulnerable and unpleasant moments of his life, Ennen kept his word. He didn't hide, obfuscate, or resist my intrusions when it would have been easier for him to do so. This book exists because Ennen honored his promise.

The staff of CHWC, including those who feature prominently in the book, and many others who do not, weren't always sure of the wisdom of allowing me to become part of the fabric of the hospital, but they were all gracious, welcoming, and kind. Dave Swanson and Chris Cullis, in the belief that the hospital had nothing to fear from truth, championed my access. Civic, political, religious, and business leaders of Bryan and Williams County were open and willing, especially Jim Watkins and the employees of the Williams County Health Department, who went far out of their way to be helpful, and Fred Lord and Anna Meyers of Jobs and Family Services. When I asked Jim Hicks about riding along with his EMS crews, he said, "You bet!" and that was that. The staff of the Williams County library helped me locate sources of historical import.

Keith Swihart, Valerie Moreno, Marc Tingle, and all the other people who allowed me into their lives have done a service for which I am grateful. Their stories are the stories of millions.

Chip Wood, owner of Bryan Ford Lincoln, gave me a sweet deal on a 2013 Hyundai Accent with 140,000 miles on it. George and Mary Jo Magill allowed a stranger to shack up in their lake house in return for very little rent, mouse extermination services, snow shoveling and plowing, and assistance installing a new bathtub. I got the best of the bargain.

I imposed upon other writers, academics, and experts to read all, or portions of, the text, and was met with generosity. Historian Nancy Tomes, of Stony Brook University, and Carnegie Mellon economist Martin Gaynor read select chapters, offered helpful insights, and saved me from errors. Beatrix Hoffman (no relation to Frederick), historian at Northern Illinois University, read the text—sometimes in rough form—and offered important advice and encouragement; I'm grateful for her patience. Cynthia Pearsall, a nurse and former executive of a small-town hospital, also read the text and provided context and corrections. Author Suzy Spencer took time away from her own work to critique and make suggestions. Anne Carney acted as my trial average reader. She proofread the text, challenged my presumptions, and made incisive queries. I am also grateful to the many journalists upon whose work I have relied for information, background, facts, numbers. Many of them are cited in the Notes section. Support your local newspaper. All errors are mine alone, of course.

Susan Heard copyedited my drafts, improved my grammar and sentences, and provided the occasional pep talk, despite my annoying habit of starting, stopping, restarting, and do-overs. As he has for decades, Alex Heard continues to encourage, as does Shelley Metcalf, who has given me attaboys for over twenty years. I'm grateful for her continued friendship and affection.

Many thanks to Howard Yoon, who helped refine the idea of *The Hospital*. Henry R. Kaufman provided the kind of comfort that only a diligent and expert veteran attorney can provide. No writer could ask for a more nurturing and tolerant editor than Elisabeth Dyssegaard. She and the crew at St. Martin's are the best there is.

NOTES

The reporting for this book was conducted between March 2018 and August 2020 and included reference to over 3,100 documents and my own observations and interviews. The following books provided important background, insights, and facts: *In Sickness and in Wealth: American Hospitals in the Twentieth Century*, by Rosemary Stevens (Baltimore: Johns Hopkins University Press, 1999); *Health Care for Some: Rights and Rationing in the United States Since 1930*, by Beatrix Hoffman (Chicago: University of Chicago Press, 2012); *Remaking the American Patient: How Madison Avenue and Modern Medicine Turned Patients into Consumers*, by Nancy Tomes (Chapel Hill: University of North Carolina Press, 2016); *Selling Our Souls: The Commodification of Hospital Care in the United States*, by Adam D. Reich (Princeton, NJ: Princeton University Press, 2014); *An American Sickness: How Healthcare Became Big Business and How You Can Take It Back*, by Elisabeth Rosenthal (New York: Penguin Books, 2017).

I attempted to interview Michael Packnett, CEO of Parkview, and Randy Oostra, CEO of ProMedica. Both declined through their press officers.

The following selected notes are not a complete list of sources or attributions.

Prologue

2 *Hundreds more such hospitals, over six hundred by some estimates*: Sharita R. Thomas et al., "Geographic Variation in the 2019 Risk of Financial Distress Among Rural Hospitals," North Carolina Rural Health Research Program, April 2019; "NRHA Endorses Reintroduction of Save Rural Hospitals Act to New Congress," press release, June 20, 2017.

3 *18 percent of the entire economy, health was the nation's largest industry by far*: "US Health Spending Recovers After Two Slow Years: CMS," Reuters, December 5, 2019.

3 *four hundred nursing-care facilities in thirty states and $1.16 billion in revenue*: Genesis earnings release, Q1, 2019.

8 *while Hillsdale County, Michigan, where Hi-Lex was located, hit 20 percent*: Unemployment rate in Hillsdale County, Michigan, St. Louis Federal Reserve.

Chapter 1: A Ready Haven of Refuge

15   *He used this sole white outpost as a base from which to annihilate Native American villages*: https://ohiohistorycentral.org/w/Fort_Defiance?rec=703.

15   *Twenty years later, just 265 people lived in the new city of Bryan, the county seat*: Presentation by Kevin Maynard, Wiliams County Public Library, March 25, 2019.

16   *"People are negligent as to health conditions"*: Logs and notebooks of the Williams County Health Department, 1922.

18   *The chief's enthusiasm failed to sway tightfisted taxpayers*: "Chief Bowersox Suggests Use of Cherry School for Hospital," *Bryan Democrat*, April 12, 1918.

18   *By 1926, there were 6,946*: Vital Statistics, Health, and Nutrition (Series C 1-155), 1789–1945, National Office of Vital Statistics.

19   *All he asked was that the city come up with a matching $25,000*: "Committee of 29 Given Charge of Hospital Project," *Bryan Press*, September 16, 1926.

20   *The winning children in each age group received $5*: "Healthiest Kids at Fair to Get Prizes," *Bryan Press*, September 9, 1926.

21   *"Logically, the next step would seem to be to institute sickness insurance"*: "Sickness Insurance and Its Possibilities in Mining and Railroading," *The National: A Journal Devoted to the Interests of the National Window Glass Workers of America*, August 1915.

22   *"We are not yet ready therefore to assent to the advantage of a system so startling to our American theories and ideals"*: *Proceedings of the Conference on Social Insurance, December 5–9, 1916*, Workmen's Insurance and Compensation Series, Department of Labor, Bulletin of the United States, number 212.

22   *by the work of a statistician named Frederick Ludwig Hoffman* (and subsequent information and quotes from Hoffman): Beatrix Hoffman, "Scientific Racism, Insurance, and Opposition to the Welfare State: Frederick L. Hoffman's Transatlantic Journey," *Journal of the Gilded Age and Progressive Era* 2 (April 2003): 150–190.

24   *by branding such legislation as "Bolshevistic"*: "Women Assail Welfare Foes," *New York Times*, March 23, 1920.

25   *The measure passed both houses of Congress by wide margins in 1921*: Sheppard-Towner Maternity and Infancy Protection Act (1921), Embryo Project Encyclopedia, https://embryo .asu.edu.

25   *"The legislation is economically unsound. It did not accomplish what its proponents claimed for it"*: "Deplores Passing of Personal Doctor," *New York Times*, September 22, 1927.

25   *from 76 per 1,000 live births when the law was passed to 65 in 1927*: "CB and the Sheppard-Towner Act of 1921," Department of Health and Human Services.

26   *The median net income of a Shelbyville County doctor in 1930 was $3,066*: Committee on the Costs of Medical Care, Publication Number 6, *A Survey of the Medical Facilities of Shelby County, Indiana*, 1929.

26   *"The difficulty now is that its cost is beyond the reach of a great majority of people"*: "$6,000,000 Sought for New Hospital," *New York Times*, October 3, 1929.

26   *A simple hospital tonsillectomy would cost a week's pay*: *History of Wages in the United States from Colonial Times to 1928*, Bulletin of the United States Bureau of Labor Statistics, number 604, United States Bureau of Labor Statistics, October 1929.

27   *in Chester County, Tennessee, the average net annual income of a physician was $991*: "Reports Ten States Lack Medical Care," *New York Times*, November 18, 1932.

27   *But those rich households accounted for 9.8 percent of hospital cases*: Data derived from Rosemary Stevens, *In Sickness and in Wealth: American Hospitals in the Twentieth Century* (Baltimore: Johns Hopkins University Press, 1999), 136; National Bureau of Economic Research, bulletin number 46, May 1, 1933.

28 *The Los Angeles Medical Association expelled them*: "Dr. Donald Ross, Pioneer in Prepaid Health," *Washington Post*, June 18, 1981.

28 *Other physicians who deviated from AMA orthodoxy regarding payments were denied hospital privileges or were harassed*: "Moderate Medical Costs," *New York Times*, July 11, 1929.

29 *He called the proposed group practice idea "medical soviets" and warned of the "destruction of private practice"*: Morris Fishbein, "The Committee on the Costs of Medical Care," *Journal of the American Medical Association*, December 3, 1932.

29 *Fishbein argued that the public should trust doctors and the AMA*: "Abstract of Dr. Morris Fishbein's Lecture at Battle Creek, December 6, 1932," *Journal of the Michigan State Medical Society*, January 1933.

29 *"It is absurd for the editor of a leading American medical journal"*: Isidore Falk, "The Present and Future Organization of Medicine," *Milbank Memorial Fund Quarterly* 12, no. 2 (1934).

31 *By the end of 1933, there were 930 fewer cars and trucks in the county than there'd been in 1929*: "Fewer Autos; More Taxes in 5 Years," *Bryan Press*, May 3, 1934.

31 *two people committed suicide in 1929*: Records of the Williams County Health Department, various years.

31 *federal money had flooded into the pockets of more than 1,100 of the county's farmers*: "AAA Knocked Out, Many Farmers in County Affected," *Bryan Democrat*, January 6, 1936.

32 *an inventor and entrepreneur named John C. Markey sold more than two thousand shares of ARO Equipment Corporation*: "Wesley Life Learns About Aro, Ancestry," *Bryan Times*, March 30, 2012.

32 *ARO was listed on the New York Curb Exchange*: "Listings Increased by Curb Exchange," *New York Times*, June 13, 1940.

32 *Cameron, who practiced in Fort Wayne, married the daughter of the U.S. congressman who represented Angola*: "Memoirs of Two Hospitals: As Recalled by Don F. Cameron M.D.," Cameron Memorial Hospitals, Inc.

Chapter 2: Everybody Is Coming After This Hospital

34 *for a −2 percent operating margin*: CHWC IRS Form 990, Year Ending September 30, 2018; Phil Ennen memo to CHWC Employees, November 15, 2018.

35 *His chief financial officer, Chad Tinkel, figured it could happen within three years*: Interview with Dave Swanson, January 23, 2019.

36 *loan covenants with Fifth Third Bank that required it to maintain a cash-to-debt ratio of 1.25*: Reimbursement Agreement by and between Community Hospitals and Wellness Centers, an Ohio nonprofit corporation, and Fifth Third Bank, dated July 1, 2008.

38 *The board, he thought, gave him the autonomy to "find a glide path that gets the job done"*: Interview with Phil Ennen, June 21, 2018.

39 *the hospital received a pitch from a firm called Quest Health Enterprises*: 1994 letter from James R. Swope, CEO, Quest Health Enterprises, to Rusty Brunicardi.

39 *By 2007, Quest was charging hospitals $1 million a year to license the software*: June 20, 2007, letter from James R. Swope, CEO, Quest Health Enterprises, to Rusty Brunicardi.

42 *"Are you hiring Isis?" it read*: Interview with Phil Ennen, November 11, 2018.

43 *"They wanna shut me out?"*: Interview with Hanan Bazzi, February 18, 2019.

43 *his family had to force him to go on vacation*: Interview with Demoder Kesireddy, April 24, 2019.

44 *Kim Owen, the radiation oncology center director, was beginning to rethink her own career with CHWC*: Interview with Kim Owen, April 23, 2019.

44 *"An apple a day won't keep this doctor away"*: Interview with Angelia Foster, February 9, 2019.

44 *"That uncorks a variety of bad things, like a more public airing, perhaps questioning"*: Interview with Phil Ennen, February 23, 2019.

46   *In 1985, Todd Shipyards, in deep financial trouble, raided ARO to add its solvent pension fund to Todd's assets*: "Todd Shipyards to Acquire Aro," *New York Times*, October 22, 1985; interview with Dean Spangler, March 7, 2018.

46   *Mohawk, caught up in a wave of consolidation of auto suppliers*: "Acquisition of Montpelier Mohawk Tools Is Completed," *Crescent-News*, November 4, 1986.

46   *shut down about the same time as ARO*: *Federal Register*, February 4, 1992, "Notices," Department of Labor.

46   *When the recession hit, unemployment in the United States rose to 10 percent, but in Williams County it was 17.2 percent*: Federal Reserve of St. Louis, using U.S. Bureau of Labor statistics.

46   *so only a few hundred people still farmed full-time*: 1978 Census of Agriculture, Williams County, Ohio; 1997 Census of Agriculture, Williams County, Ohio; Ohio County Profiles, Williams, State of Ohio.

47   *because she'd just started, she had no health insurance and no paycheck yet*: Interview with Valerie Moreno, December 3, 2018.

47   *They offered sketchy loans to buyers with poor credit scores, who then snapped up the homes*: Mike Baker and Daniel Wagner, "The Mobile-Home Trap: How a Warren Buffett Empire Preys on the Poor," *Seattle Times*/Center for Public Integrity, April 2, 2015.

47   *their homes were repossessed, and manufacturing slowed until, finally, as the recession hit, it stopped altogether*: Interview with Marc Tingle, March 9, 2019.

50   *one of the 920 people in Ohio who would kill themselves with guns that year*: "Years of Lost Life: Firearm Fatalities 2009–2018," Ohio Alliance for Innovation in Population Health.

50   *Besides, the last time she'd had the test, the results were okay*: Stephanie Swihart's medical information derived from medical records and billings viewed by the author, with permission from Keith Swihart.

52   *Hassouneh knew the diagnosis had come far too late*: Interview with Samar Hassouneh, April 22, 2019.

52   *Cameron united his Angola and Bryan operations into a single tax-exempt charitable corporation*: Letter from Dallas A. Riddle, Ohio Hospital Association, to Donald F. Cameron, March 15, 1961.

53   *in the mold of beneficent medical pioneers like the Mayo brothers*: Draft letter from law firm Baker Hostetler & Patterson to the Internal Revenue Service, May 1962.

53   *"among indigents, a medical triumph often adds to the taxpayer's burden"*: Donald Cameron speech to the Quest Club of Fort Wayne, Indiana, April 8, 1960.

54   *By 1962, Cameron was receiving $500 a month*: Letter with attached history and finances of Cameron Hospitals, Inc., from Baker Hostetler & Patterson to the Internal Revenue Service, May 1960; Financial Report, Cameron Memorial Hospitals, Inc., February 29, 1964; affidavit of Lloyd Leo McCormack to Internal Revenue Service agent Robert Cantwell, July 29, 1960; affidavit of Ramesh Carpentar to Internal Revenue Service agent Robert Cantwell, August 5, 1960; draft letter from law firm Baker Hostetler & Patterson to the Internal Revenue Service, May 1962.

54   *By 1973, the hospital found itself in deep trouble*: Letter from Ralph Hause to Miss Ada Mitchell and Robert Dilworth, M.D., September 11, 1972.

55   *Brown called Brunicardi*: Interview with Rusty Brunicardi, February 19, 2019.

57   *"Effective immediately, I am placing the hospital on a fiscal watch"*: Phil Ennen memo to CHWC employees, October 8, 2008.

58   *"The economic recovery that Washington keeps talking about has not arrived in Northwest Ohio"*: Phil Ennen memo to CHWC employees, December 10, 2009.

58   *The two teenagers earned a little extra spending money by helping Brunicardi compile a database of rural hospitals*: Interview with Kim Jerger, April 16, 2019.

Chapter 3: Chasing the Symptoms

62 *charging between $10,000 and $20,000 a talk*: www.allamericanspeakers.com/speakers /3157/Chris-Spielman.

63 *Main Street turned out to be a stark dividing line*: PowerPoint presentation by Jim Watkins and Meagan Riley, Williams County Health Department.

63 *"the stage at the time of diagnosis was advanced in the east side of Bryan"*: Bryan Cancer Cases Study 2017 Data, February 15, 2019.

64 *In Franklinton, a neighborhood in Columbus, the average life expectancy was sixty*: Joann Viviano, "Report: Two Columbus Neighborhoods Among Lowest in Ohio for Life Expectancy Rates," *Columbus Dispatch*, October 17, 2018.

64 *a seven-year chasm had opened between states*: Andy Miller, "Life Expectancy Rates Vary Across Census Tracts," *Georgia Health News*, September 17, 2018; Laura Dwyer-Lindgren et al., "Inequalities in Life Expectancy Among US Counties," *Health Care Policy and Law*, July 2017; Vital and Health Statistics, Series 2, Number 181, September 2018, National Center for Health Statistics; Steven H. Woolf and Heidi Schoomaker, "Life Expectancy and Mortality Rates in the United States, 1959–2017," *Journal of the American Medical Association*, November 26, 2019.

64 *When the Robert Wood Johnson Foundation issued rankings for counties*: Lynn Thompson, "Latest County Health Rankings Released," *Bryan Times*, March 18, 2019.

64 *Ohio ranked forty-sixth out of the fifty states*: 2019 Health Value Dashboard, Health Policy Institute of Ohio.

64 *"negative trends in premature death, life expectancy and overall health status"*: State Health Assessment Ohio 2019 (Preliminary Draft), Health Policy Institute of Ohio and Ohio Department of Health.

64 *815.7 people out of 100,000 (age-adjusted) died of all causes*: Deaths: Final Data for 2010, National Vital Statistics Reports, volume 61, number 4.

64 *By 2017, 849.7 died*: Deaths: Final Data for 2017, National Vital Statistics Reports, volume 68, number 9.

65 *Sixteen percent of young people said they seriously considered suicide*: 2019 Williams County Health Needs Assessment, Williams County Health Department, Community Hospitals and Wellness Centers.

65 *"We saw four thousand more patients in 2017 than we did in 2016"*: Interview with Les McCaslin, December 3, 2018.

66 *It was called to twenty-eight attempted suicides in 2018*: Montpelier Police Department 2017 Annual Report; Montpelier Police Department 2018 Annual Report.

66 *Six days after Keith's buddy Chad killed himself*: Williams County Year-to-Date Filed Deaths 2017, Williams County Health Department; Holly Hedegaard et al., "Suicide Mortality in the United States, 1999–2017," NCHS Data Brief, no. 330, November 2018.

66 *Nearly half of all people ages thirty to sixty-four were obese*: 2019 Williams County Health Needs Assessment, Williams County Health Department, Community Hospitals and Wellness Centers.

67 *Williams had a higher rate of infections of the sexually transmitted disease*: Ohio 2018 Chlamydia Rates, Ohio Department of Health, STD Surveillance.

71 *The Joint Commission was a private body with roots stretching back to 1913*: www.facs.org /about-acs/archives/acshistory.

71 *By 1952, several organizations agreed to carve out a stand-alone hospital standards group*: Rosemary Stevens, *In Sickness and in Wealth: American Hospitals in the Twentieth Century* (Baltimore: Johns Hopkins University Press, 1999).

72 *The 2018 edition of* Hospital Accreditation Standards: 2018 Hospital Accreditation Standards, The Joint Commission, January 2018.

78 *he emptied his 401(k) account of the little that was left*: Interview with Keith Swihart, February 15, 2019.

79 *"Final request for payment," the invoice for $852.84 from Mercy Health announced*: Invoices from consulting pathologists, Mercy Health.

80 *Twelve percent of adults—including 16 percent of all men and 27 percent of all people over age sixty-five—in Williams County had been diagnosed with diabetes*: 2019 Williams County Community Health Needs Assessment, Williams County Health Department, Community Hospitals and Wellness Centers.

80 *The ER bill alone, just for the doctor's time, was $1,250*: Invoice from Schumacher Clinical Partners dated November 21, 2018.

81 *Barb Purvis, the nurse practitioner at the community health center, saw Keith*: Medical records for Keith Swihart, Bryan Community Health Center.

82 *"There's no point in kicking the can down the road"*: Phil Ennen memo to CHWC departments, November 15, 2018.

Chapter 4: Powers Beyond Us

88 *"Or they can't pass a drug test"*: Interview with Brian Davis, March 8, 2018.

88 *"We have good, hardworking people, and they are the reason for our continued growth"*: 2017 WEDCO Annual Report (presented at the 2018 annual meeting).

89 *"The sense I get is that people look at Bryan as 'our best days are behind us'"*: Interview with Kevin Maynard, December 5, 2018.

89 *Only three permits to build new houses would be issued in the city of Bryan in 2018*: Max Reinhart, "Planning and Zoning Director Issues Annual Report," *Bryan Times*, February 12, 2019.

89 *while there'd be 567 permits issued to carry a concealed gun in Williams County*: Ron Osborn, "Williams County Issues 567 Concealed Carry Licenses in 2018," *Bryan Times*, March 3, 2019.

90 *Snyder was sentenced to two years in prison and ordered to pay back $781,000*: "Former Ruralogic Chairman Sentenced to Two Years in Prison," *Bryan Times*, November 30, 2018.

91 *"The only thing that can save our community is Jesus"*: Interview with Chris Kannel, April 16, 2019.

92 *Valerie tried to stay as involved as she could in the life of her younger one*: Interview with Valerie Moreno, December 3, 2018.

93 *Fayette Tubular was sold to a French conglomerate that shut the plant and moved the jobs to Tennessee*: "Fayette Tubular," *New York Times*, December 6, 1995; "Hutchinson Seeks a Place in U.S. Hose Market," *Automotive News*, July 7, 1997.

93 *In 2010, Global Automotive Systems closed the Bryan factory as part of its "global optimization strategy"*: "Auto Parts Supplier in Bryan to Close," *Bryan Times*, December 2, 2010.

94 *Contrary to the gospel, five families in the entire county received government cash assistance*: Interview with Fred Lord, March 22, 2019.

95 *The median household income . . . in Williams County was $47,593*: Ohio County Profiles, Williams County, Ohio Office of Research.

95 *About 13.5 percent of Williams County residents lived in poverty*: The Ohio Poverty Report, February 2019, Ohio Development Services Agency.

95 *Williams County, with a population of about 37,000 people, had about 4,600 ALICE households*: Williams County Health Department via U.S. Census Bureau.

96 *"People talk about that all the time"*: Interview with Chastity Yoder, March 26, 2019.

99 *Some flouted the law for decades*: Beatrix Hoffman, *Health Care for Some: Rights and Rationing in the United States Since 1930* (Chicago: University of Chicago Press, 2012).

99 *there was an incentive for hospitals to plead poverty to the government and report lots of uncompensated care*: "Hospital Uncompensated Care," United States Government Accountability Office, June 2016.

99 CHWC reported nearly $3 million in bad debt: Community Hospitals and Wellness Centers, IRS Form 990, FY Ending September 30, 2018.

100 Henry County Hospital, over in Napoleon, was losing money every month, too: Interview with Kim Bordenkircher, March 14, 2019.

102 "Transformational changes dictate that leaders within the physician enterprise focus on enterprise sustainability": www.dhg.com/services/advisory/healthcare-consulting/achieve; DHG Healthcare Executive Brief.

103 a few board members hankered for a more formal process: Interview with Chris Kannel, April 16, 2019.

104 Ennen, without consulting the board, paid for his mistake with a million-dollar buyout of the physician's contract: Interview with Phil Ennen, April 24, 2019.

107 "But they'd leave Bryan alone, because of its isolation, and we weren't competitive": Interview with Phil Ennen, February 8, 2019.

111 Younger doctors, he thought, were preoccupied with money: Interview with Nick Walz, January 19, 2019.

Chapter 5: Pray

114 Coleman had run his own little contracting company up in Michigan: Interview with Greg Coleman, December 4, 2018.

114 DHL got another $122 million in state-paid road construction and tax breaks: "Wilmington Closes Deal to Finance DHL Expansion," *Dayton Daily News*, March 7, 2007; Jack Lyne, "Blockbuster Deal," *Site Selection Magazine*, week of July 5, 2004.

114 The mayor of Wilmington called the closure "catastrophic": Bob Driehaus, "DHL Cuts 9,500 Jobs in U.S., and an Ohio Town Takes the Brunt," *New York Times*, November 10, 2008.

116 He founded what became Menards in 1958 in Wisconsin: www.menards.com/main/footer/company-information/about-us/our-history/c-3588.htm.

116 State regulators did, however, and levied a $1.7 million fine: Michael Isikoff, "Secret $1.5 Million Donation from Wisconsin Billionaire Uncovered in Scott Walker Dark-Money Probe," Yahoo Politics, March 23, 2015; Mary Van de Kamp Nohl, "Big Money," *Milwaukee Magazine*, April 30, 2007.

116 The company paid $2 million: "Menards Inc. Fined $2 Million in Pollution Case," *Milwaukee Business Journal*, August 9, 2005; Bruce Murphy, "Murphy's Law: The Strange Life of John Menard," *Urban Milwaukee*, June 20, 2013.

116 The billionaire had given $1.5 million in "dark" money to a group supporting Walker's campaign: Isikoff, "Secret $1.5 Million Donation"; "Influence Peddler of the Month—John Menard, Jr.," Wisconsin Democracy Campaign, June 1, 2016.

116 "your income will automatically be reduced by sixty percent (60%)": Bill Lueders, "Managers at Menards Stand to Lose Big Money if Unions Form," *The Progressive*, December 8, 2015.

116 In 2015, the company paid a $1 million settlement in a race discrimination case: "Menards Ends Discrimination Claim for $1 Million," *Pioneer Press*, February 7, 2012.

116 they had to pay for their own lawyers as well as half the cost of the arbitration process, even if Menards was found to be at fault: Faber v. Menard, No. C 03-3034-MWB, United States District Court, N.D. Iowa, Central Division, June 17, 2003.

117 In 2015, it wrote to the commissioners of Kansas's Douglas County: December 7, 2015, letter to Douglas County Commission from Scott R. Nuttelman.

117 Menards lapped up $23,321,779 in subsidies: Subsidy Tracker, GoodJobsFirst.org.

117 Hundreds of thousands of dollars' worth of infrastructure—including a road, water and sewer systems, and power systems—were used to build what Menards wanted built: Williams County Engineer Todd Roth, May 12, 2020.

117 Menards was by far the biggest beneficiary: Williams County Single Audit for the Year Ended December 31, 2016, Dave Yost, Auditor, State of Ohio.

117 Roughly nine hundred people worked at Menards: Housing Opportunities Assessment, Williams County, Ohio, July 17, 2018.

118 If they tried to lower those premiums by enrolling in a "B" plan, their deductibles could rise into the thousands: Menards Benefits at a Glance, last updated January 1, 2019.

118 The 2019–2020 "B" plan deductible for a single Menards employee was $5,750: "Health and Dental Information 2020," Menards. (Author's note: Repeated calls, over a period of months, to Menards human resources in Holiday City and to the Menards general number in Holiday City went unanswered.)

118 CHWC cut their bill in half and wrote off $8,500 as charity: CHWC Charitable Care Program intake form.

119 A private equity firm, Taglich Private Equity LLC, had created Unique Fabricating: U.S. Securities and Exchange Commission, form 10-Q, Unique Fabricating, Inc., for the quarterly period ended September 29, 2019.

119 Unique Fabricating decided to close the Bryan plant: Josh Ewers, "Unique-Chardan Plant to Close," *Bryan Times*, January 3, 2020.

119 Hassouneh continued to see the woman—who, now pain free, was able to get a job and begin pulling herself out of debt: Interview with Samar Hassouneh, April 22, 2019.

120 ER nurse Heather Gaylord found herself fighting the urge to judge: Interview with Heather Gaylord, April 13, 2019.

121 "they're not keepin' it controlled because they can't afford the meds and the services": Interview with Jim Hicks, December, 6, 2018.

124 A lot of people in such places had bad credit and low incomes: Heather Long, "A Record 7 Million Americans Are 3 Months Behind on Their Car Payments, a Red Flag for the Economy," *Washington Post*, February 12, 2019.

124 they were "selling money, not cars": Rex Collins, "Buy Here/Pay Here Dealerships Can Generate Substantial Profit," July 1, 2016, https://www.hbkcpa.com/buy-herepay-here-dealerships-can-generate-substantial-profit.

124 "In BHPH one fact of life is vehicle breakdowns": "BHPH News & Articles," NABD, bhphinfo.com/bhph-library#2.

125 NIADA made generous campaign contributions: Schedule B, Itemized Disbursements, National Independent Automobile Dealers Association PAC Fund, 2016 and 2019.

125 Trump signed it into law on May 21: "Statement of Administration Policy," SJ Res. 57, April 17, 2018; Neil Haggerty, "Trump Makes Repeal of CFPB Auto Lending Rule Official," *American Banker*, May 21, 2018.

125 Zach shot himself almost two years to the day: Williams County Health Department, 2018–2019 Deaths.

127 When he wasn't working, Zach liked to go fishing for catfish at night, hang out with his bros, drive his car with the stereo blasting, and go target shooting: "Lance Corporal Zachary Allan Rhinard (1998–2019)," *Bryan Times*, January 17, 2019.

129 The call would be one of four hundred runs Jim Hicks's EMS crews would make in January: Interview with Jim Hicks, January 21, 2019.

132 If you were a police and fire dispatcher in Bryan, you started at $11.76 an hour, about what Taco Bell offered: Max Reinhart, "Council Approves Pay Increase for Police Dispatchers," *Bryan Times*, May 21, 2019.

132 Working-class wages in the United States just about flatlined from 1979 to 2017: Cumulative Percent Change in Real Annual Wages, by Wage Group, 1979–2017, "State of Working America: Wages 2018," Economic Policy Institute; Cumulative Percent Change in Real

Annual Wages, by Wage Group, 1979–2017, "State of Working America: Wages 2019," Economic Policy Institute.

132 *Only 14.6 percent had a bachelor's degree*: "Ohio County Profiles: Williams County," Ohio Office of Research.

133 *"We put this stuff on the outside, but inside—who we are? Who are we?"*: Interview with Tonie Long, January 23, 2019.

135 *And so you learned from disappointment and defeat*: A rich academic literature has explored these effects of inequality. Among the many consulted for this book: Michael J. Solomon Weiss et al., "What Explains the Negative Consequences of Adverse Childhood Experiences on Adult Health?," *American Journal of Preventive Medicine* 14, no. 4 (1998); J. T. Maguire et al., "Decision Makers Calibrate Behavioral Persistence on the Basis of Time-Interval Experience," *Cognition*, August 2012; Shannon Monnat, "Place-Based Economic Conditions and the Geography of the Opioid Overdose Crisis" and "The Contributions of Socioeconomic and Opioid Supply Factors to Geographic Variation in U.S. Drug Mortality Rates," Institute for New Economic Thinking, January 2019; Shannon Monnat, "Our Problem Is Bigger Than Opioids," *U.S. News and World Report*, February 26, 2019; Hawre Jalal et al., "Changing Dynamics of the Drug Overdose Epidemic in the United States from 1979 Through 2016," *Science*, September 21, 2018; Aaron Antonovsky, "Social Class, Life Expectancy and Overall Mortality," *Milbank Memorial Fund Quarterly*, April 1967; Anne Case and Angus Deaton, "Mortality and Morbidity in the 21st Century," Brookings Papers on Economic Activity, BPEA Conference Drafts, March 23–24, 2017; Nancy E. Adler and Katherine Newman, "Socioeconomic Disparities in Health: Pathways and Policies," *Health Affairs* 21, no. 2, 2002; Atheendar S. Venkataramani et al., "Association Between Automotive Assembly Plant Closures and Opioid Overdose Mortality in the United States: A Difference-in-Differences Analysis," *JAMA Internal Medicine*, December 30, 2019; Priya Fielding-Singh, "A Taste of Inequality: Food's Symbolic Value Across the Socioeconomic Spectrum," *Sociological Science*, August 2017; Norman J. Waitzman and Ken R. Smith, "Separate but Lethal: The Effects of Economic Segregation on Mortality in Metropolitan America," *Milbank Quarterly* 76, no. 3 (1998); Ichiro Kawachi and Bruce P. Kennedy, "Income Inequality and Health: Pathways and Mechanisms," *Health Services Research*, April 1999.

135 *Montpelier police chief Dan Magee arrested generations of the same families*: Interview with Dan Magee, March 20, 2019.

136 *"And some other people make less, and they have kids. That's stressful"*: Interview with Sarah Vashaw, March 8, 2018.

138 *"Because there's so many factors in their life that they can't control if that paycheck doesn't come through"*: Interview with Carrie Schlade, February 14, 2019.

139 *38.6 percent of the children qualified for free or reduced-price school lunch*: Data for Free and Reduced Meals, Ohio Department of Education.

139 *equipped that school with forty-eight security cameras*: Presentation of school resource officers, November 13, 2018, Bryan, Ohio.

139 *Meadow Creek, built by an out-of-town development company*: *United States of America v. Miller-Valentine Operations Inc. et al.*, United States District Court for the Southern District of Ohio Western Division, filed May 9, 2019.

141 *In 2015, Wisconsin governor Scott Walker tried to change the state university's mission statement*: Valerie Strauss, "A University of Wisconsin Campus Pushes Plan to Drop 13 Majors—Including English, History and Philosophy," *Washington Post*, March 21, 2018.

141 *DeMaria set the standard in consultation with industry as a way to tailor the "workforce" to its needs*: Patrick O'Donnell, "Ohio Graduates Won't Have to Be 'Proficient' in Math or English, Under State Superintendent's Plan," *Cleveland Plain Dealer*, February 22, 2020.

Chapter 6: What Free Market?

147 *The highest price listed for a CT scan at Parkview's flagship hospital in Fort Wayne was over $4,000*: Parkview Chargemaster.

147 *but even the lower prices were higher than the prices in almost any other peer country in the world*: Irene Papanicolas et al., "Health Care Spending in the United States and Other High-Income Countries," *Journal of the American Medical Association*, March 13, 2018.

147 *Even within the same market region, the price in one hospital could be double the price in another*: Zack Cooper et al., "The Price Ain't Right? Hospital Prices and Health Spending on the Privately Insured," NBER Working Paper no. 21815, December 2015.

148 *"And maybe that's how it feels for them"*: Interview with Angelia Foster, February 15, 2019.

150 *It had already closed its wound care clinic, home healthcare service, pain clinic, and an urgent care center*: "Sturgis Hospital Restructuring Plan: Frequently Asked Questions."

151 *Emilia Pearl Miller became the last baby born in Sturgis Hospital*: Michelle Patrick, "Emilia Miller Is Final Birth at Sturgis Hospital," *Sturgis Journal*, January 3, 2019.

151 *The CEO would be fired, but Sturgis's financial crisis would continue*: Anuja Vaidya and Kelly Gooch, "Michigan Hospital CEO Ousted," *Becker's Hospital Review*, January 29, 2019.

153 *A few paid $1,600*: Interview with John Rymer, March 6, 2018.

153 *"We pay anywhere from three times as much as they might"*: Interview with Chad Tinkel, March 6, 2018.

153 *"But I don't have the volume"*: Interview with Kim Bordenkircher, March 14, 2019.

154 *including a $14 billion deal between Zimmer and Biomet in 2015*: "Zimmer Completes Combination with Biomet," press release, June 24, 2015.

154 *35 percent of the knee market and 31 percent of the hip market*: Zimmer Biomet Holdings, Inc., 2018 Annual Report.

154 *In 2018, Zimmer Biomet CEO Bryan C. Hanson made about $9.7 million*: www.execpay.org/news/zimmer-biomet-holdings-inc-2018-compensation-1112; Zimmer Biomet Holdings, Inc., proxy statement, 2018 annual meeting.

154 *the firm spent nearly $1 billion buying back its own shares*: Fortuna Advisors, 2019 Fortuna Buyback ROI Report, April 19, 2019.

154 *for repeatedly violating the Foreign Corrupt Practices Act*: "Biomet Charged with Repeating FCPA Violations," U.S. Securities and Exchange Commission, January 12, 2017.

154 *Zimmer had to pay $169.5 million for violating anti-kickback laws*: "Five Companies in Hip and Knee Replacement Industry Avoid Prosecution by Agreeing to Compliance Rules and Monitoring," United States Department of Justice, U.S. Attorney, District of New Jersey, September 27, 2007.

154 *subpoena from the Office of Inspector General for the U.S Department of Health and Human Services demanding the company produce additional records*: Zimmer Biomet Holdings, Inc., 2018 Annual Report.

155 *B. Braun Medical . . . would raise its price for them by 100 percent*: Jared S. Hopkins, "Drugmakers Push Their Prices Higher," *Wall Street Journal*, July 1, 2019.

155 *Insulin medications like the ones Keith needed ballooned in cost by 700 percent*: Drew Pendergrass, "How Insulin Became Unaffordable," *Harvard Political Review*, January 22, 2018; Max Filby, "Insulin Prices Double, Forcing Diabetics to Carefully Budget," *Columbus Dispatch*, December 9, 2019; Megan Henry, "Insulin Prices Double, Pinching Diabetics' Budgets," *Columbus Dispatch*, December 9, 2019.

155 *was forced to pay $7 million to buy its way out of price-fixing accusations*: Ed Silverman, "Heritage Pharma Admits to Price Fixing as Part of Far-Reaching Generic Drug Probe," Pharmalot, May 31, 2019.

155 *the drug would now cost them nearly $200,000 per year*: Rebecca Spalding, "Celgene Boosted the Price of Its Top Cancer Drug on the Same Day of Mega-Deal," Bloomberg News, January 4, 2019.

156 *New York City hospitals pioneered the strategy in 1910*: Rosemary Stevens, *In Sickness and in Wealth: American Hospitals in the Twentieth Century* (Baltimore: Johns Hopkins University Press, 2012).

158 *Established in 1906*: www.stlukeshospital.com/about.

158 *good care at lower prices than some of the other regional hospitals*: *United States District Court, Northern District of Ohio Western Division Federal Trade Commission, Plaintiffs v. Promedica Health System, Inc., Defendants*, Docket No. 3:11CV47 (various documents).

159 *so Anthem capitulated*: *In the Matter of ProMedica Health System, Inc.*, Docket No. 9346, Opinion of the Commission.

159 *St. Luke's was so troubled by ProMedica's tactics, it considered mounting an antitrust lawsuit*: Transcript of TRO Hearing Before the Honorable David A. Katz, United States District Judge, January 13, 2011.

160 *pay us a little more now, or you'll have to pay us a lot more later when we become a ProMedica hospital*: *In the Matter of Promedica Health System, Inc., Respondent*, Initial Decision.

160 *"stick it to employers, that is, to continue forcing high rates on employers and insurance companies"*: United States of America Before the Federal Trade Commission Office of Administrative Law Judges, in the matter of Promedica Health System, Inc., a corporation; Docket number 9346.

161 *In 2008, he'd accused ProMedica of taking "the greatest resources from the community" and performing "poorly in terms of costs of outcomes"*: Complaint Counsel's post-trial reply brief.

161 *"sure would make life much easier right now, though"*: United States of America Before the Federal Trade Commission Office of Administrative Law Judges, in the matter of Promedica Health System, Inc., a corporation; Docket number 9346.

162 *In 2018, Atrium Health, a North Carolina "nonprofit" system, was forced by the FTC*: Ames Alexander and Cassie Cope, "Atrium Health to Settle Federal Antitrust Suit over Health Care Costs," *Charlotte Observer*, November 15, 2018.

163 *Stung, the FTC retreated*: Email from Martin Gaynor, January 14, 2020.

164 *"One, pass it on to the public; two, increase the bottom line?"*: Transcript of Preliminary Injunction Proceedings Before the Honorable David A. Katz, Senior United States District Judge, February 11, 2011.

164 *Michigan's Spectrum Health, for example*: "Spectrum Health System and Affiliates Consolidated Financial Statements," June 30, 2019.

165 *Parkview Health System reported gross receipts of $2,130,554,741*: Parkview Health System, IRS Form 990, year ending December 31, 2017; 2018 Parkview Health System, Inc., and Subsidiaries Consolidated Financial Report.

165 *ProMedica reported net assets of $2,467,501,418*: ProMedica 2017 IRS Form 990.

165 *paid to R. Milton Johnson, CEO of for-profit hospital operator Hospital Corporation of America: $109,050,692*: Axios Healthcare Executive Compensation, 2018.

165 *Employers Forum of Indiana asked the Rand Corporation to study Indiana hospitals*: "Hospital Prices in Indiana: Findings from an Employer-Led Transparency Initiative," Chapin White, 2017.

166 *a Ball State University study*: Michael J. Hicks, "Indiana Has a Monopoly Problem in Healthcare: Preliminary Evidence and Recommendations," Center for Business and Economic Research, Ball State University.

167 *Hospital services rose over 200 percent*: Mark J. Perry, "Chart of the Day . . . or Century?," *Carpe Diem* (blog), American Enterprise Institute, July 12, 2019, www.aei.org/carpe-diem /chart-of-the-day-or-century-2.

167 *In Colorado, hospital profits increased 280 percent from 2009 through 2018, from $538 per patient to $1,518*: Colorado Hospital Cost Shift Analysis, Colorado Department of Health Care Policy and Financing, January 2020.

167 *ProMedica parked money in "Central America and the Caribbean"*: ProMedica IRS Form 990, 2016.

168 *Indiana University's center closed in 2014*: Jay Hancock, "As Proton Centers Struggle, a Sign of a Health Care Bubble?," *Kaiser Health News*, May 2, 2018.

168 *in 2020 it would announce that its UPMC Enterprises arm, a venture capital outfit, would invest $1 billion in a drugs, devices, and diagnostics business*: Tina Reed, "JPM20: UPMC Venture Arm Announces $1B Life Sciences Commitment," Fierce Healthcare, January 14, 2020.

168 *then asking for a city schools tax abatement of nearly $20 million on the for-profit drug company*: Alissa Widman Neese, "Nationwide Children's Asks Columbus School Board for Tax Abatement on For-Profit Company," *Columbus Dispatch*, January 21, 2020.

168 *While it was possible that a takeover* could *improve the health of Williams County residents, such acquisitions often raised prices and reduced the quality of care*: Many studies over years have shown such effects. Among those consulted for this book: Patrick S. Romano and David J. Balan, "A Retrospective Analysis of the Clinical Quality Effects of the Acquisition of Highland Park Hospital by Evanston Northwestern Healthcare," Federal Trade Commission Working Paper 307, November 2010; "Diagnosing the Problem: Exploring the Effects of Consolidation and Anticompetitive Conduct in Health Care Markets," Martin Gaynor, statement before the Committee on the Judiciary Subcommittee on Antitrust, Commercial, and Administrative Law, U.S. House of Representatives, March 7, 2019; Martin Gaynor, "What to Do About Health-Care Markets? Policies to Make Health-Care Markets Work," Brookings Institution, Policy Proposal 2020-10; Nancy D. Beaulieu et al., "Changes in Quality of Care After Hospital Mergers and Acquisitions," *New England Journal of Medicine*, January 2, 2020; Martin Gaynor, "2013 MacEachern Symposium: On a Collision Course? Health Care Integration and Antitrust," June 5, 2013.

169 *they'd charged the Medicaid program $224 million more for dispensed drugs than they had actually paid out to pharmacies*: Marty Schladen et al., "Local Pharmacies and Their Personal Care in Danger of Disappearing," *Columbus Dispatch*, July 15, 2018.

169 *The AMA issued regular reports on competition in metropolitan statistical areas*: "Competition in Health Insurance: A Comprehensive Study of U.S. Markets," American Medical Association, 2018 update.

170 *becoming part of National Pain and Spine Centers with offices in seven states*: Jonathan LaMantia, "Physician Practices Increasingly Turn to Private Equity for Capital," *Modern Healthcare*, April 26, 2019.

170 *Advanced Dermatology and Cosmetic Surgery became the country's largest provider in its specialty*: Katie Hafner, "Why Private Equity Is Furious Over a Paper in a Dermatology Journal," *New York Times*, October 26, 2018.

170 *Kohlberg Kravis Roberts (KKR) bought a controlling stake in Heartland Dental*: "Global Healthcare Private Equity and Corporate M&A Report 2019," Bain and Company.

170 *at an average of 637 percent of what Medicare would charge*: Zack Cooper et al., "Surprise! Out-of-Network Billing for Emergency Care in the United States," Institution for Social and Policy Studies Working Paper, July 2017.

170 *TeamHealth agreed to settle Justice Department charges that the company used fake billings to defraud the government. It paid $60 million*: "Healthcare Service Provider to Pay $60 Million to Settle Medicare and Medicaid False Claims Act Allegations," United States Department of Justice, February 6, 2017.

170 *Brown Brothers Harriman gained control of American Physician Partners, doubling its size in a year*: "BBH Capital Partners Completes Recapitalization of American Physician Partners," BBH press release, January 11, 2017.

170 *In 2018 alone, private equity made 855 deals into which it invested $100 billion*: Eileen Appelbaum, "Private Equity's Engagement with Health Care: Cause for Concern?," Report to the Institute for New Economic Thinking, December 27, 2019.

171 *paid $1,000 per night for hotel rooms that normally cost $200*: Rebecca Spalding, "Ex-Banker Walks into a Conference, Walks out with $480 Million," Bloomberg News, January 10, 2019.

171 *The journal removed it from its website*: Hafner, "Why Private Equity Is Furious."

172 *Seven children died over three states*: Sabrina Willmer, "When Wall Street Took Over This Nursing Company, Profits Grew and Patients Suffered," Bloomberg News, October 22, 2019.

172 *Under Carlyle's ownership*: Peter Whoriskey and Dan Keating, "Overdoses, Bedsores, Broken Bones: What Happened When a Private-Equity Firm Sought to Care for Society's Most Vulnerable," *Washington Post*, November 25, 2018.

172 *In 2016, Schumacher rolled up another ER staffing company, ECI, for $140 million*: "Management's Discussion and Analysis and Financial Statements," Onex, December 31, 2016.

173 *ER company revenues rose 21.9 percent over just five years*: Cooper et al., "Surprise! Out-of-Network Billing."

173 *The bill stalled*: Elizabeth Dexheimer, "Blackstone-KKR Hidden Hand in Ad Blitz Unleashes Washington Fury," Bloomberg News, January 8, 2020.

Chapter 7: The Crap End of the Stick

176 *Brooks swerved, but there wasn't much he could do about it. George hit him head-on*: "A Two Vehicle Accident Wednesday Afternoon Claimed the Life of a Frontier Man," *Hillsdale Daily News*, January 24, 2019.

180 *Brian George would be arrested*: "Trial Scheduled in Fatal Drunk Driving Case," *Hillsdale Daily News*, December 13, 2019.

181 *Brooks's wife and some of the children were there. It was an emotional scene for everybody*: Interview with Wade Patrick, February 13, 2019.

182 *"I told Chad, 'Show me you've got some heart'"*: Interview with Dave Swanson, January 23, 2019.

186 *Around the country, fourteen rural hospitals closed in 2018, and there were already reports of more closings in 2019*: Rural Health Research Program, University of North Carolina.

186 *Ellwood stiffed its employees by missing payroll*: Patrick O'Shea, "Another Payroll Delay Reported at Ellwood City Medical Center," *Ellwood City Ledger*, November 15, 2018.

186 *That deal blew up in 1998, and the hospital limped into the twenty-first century*: Patrick O'Shea, "Ellwood City Hospital Workers Might Benefit from Revamped Grove City Medical Center," *Ellwood City Ledger*, January 11, 2020.

186 *"We desperately need this hospital to prosper"*: "'We Desperately Need This Hospital': Ellwood City Medical Center Closes to Inpatient, ER Services," KDKA, November 29, 2019.

187 *"If we try to live our values, then we'll make the best of a difficult situation"*: Phil Ennen memo to CHWC Leadership Council, January 28, 2019.

196 *She would think about Marc's case for weeks afterward, rehashing it in her mind*: Interview with Heather Gaylord, April 24, 2019.

197 *all were either in short supply or not available at any price*: CHWC Drug Shortage List.

197 *the U.S. Food and Drug Administration suggested the harms from the shortages were "drastically underestimated"*: "Drug Shortages: Root Causes and Potential Solutions, 2019," U.S. Food and Drug Administration.

198 *"because of the costs they tell you, 'I am going to choose to die'"*: Interview with Mike Liu, February 14, 2019.

199 *It also had the lowest rate of meeting colorectal screening guidelines in the state*: Ohio Cancer Atlas, 2019.

199 *Studies linked hundreds of thousands of cancer deaths around the world to the effects of the Great Recession*: Mahiben Maruthappu et al., "Economic Downturns, Universal Health Coverage, and Cancer Mortality in High-Income and Middle-Income Countries, 1990–2010: A Longitudinal Analysis," *The Lancet*, May 25, 2016.

199 *An estimated ten thousand American and European suicides were attributed to it*: Karen Weintraub, "Great Recession Tied to More Than 10,000 Suicides," *USA Today*, June 11, 2014.

199 *Blood pressure and blood sugar measures worsened in American adults*: Teresa Seeman et al., "The Great Recession Worsened Blood Pressure and Blood Glucose Levels in American Adults," *Proceedings of the National Academy of Sciences*, March 27, 2018.

Chapter 8: Puppies Are Drowning

200 *she couldn't help but be outraged and then try to do something about it*: Interview with Janis Sunderhaus, March 15, 2019.

204 *"Dispensaries" were as old as the United States . . . and they could be affiliated with a nearby hospital or with a charity or social service organization*: Beatrix Hoffman, *Health Care for Some: Rights and Rationing in the United States Since 1930* (Chicago: University of Chicago Press, 2012).

204 *George W. Bush reinvigorated federally qualified health centers by pouring money into an effort to open twelve hundred of them during his first five years in office*: Kevin Sack, "Community Health Clinics Increased During Bush Years," *New York Times*, December 26, 2008.

205 *Barb Purvis, the nurse practitioner who cared for Keith, made $120,000 a year, plus a bonus that was dependent upon her patient volume*: Interview with Barb Purvis, April 18, 2019.

206 *During the rise of the Great Society clinics, AMA president Milton Rouse called them "unnecessary" and "wasteful"*: Hoffman, *Health Care for Some.*

207 *not a single private-practice dentist in Williams County accepted Medicaid patients*: Interview with Carl Cheney, August 13, 2019.

208 *The Ohio Turnpike Commission paid ADW $342,000 a year to keep that plaza clean*: Ohio Turnpike Commission, Resolution Awarding Agreements for Janitorial Services at the Commission's Middle Ridge and Vermilion Valley Service Plazas (Agreement TRM-10D), the Blue Heron and Wyandot Service Plazas (Agreement TRM-10E), and the Indian Meadow and Tiffin River Service Plazas (Agreement TRM-10F).

212 *"That is almost $1 million more than our budgeted margin for this year"*: Phil Ennen memo, November 22, 2011.

213 *"I wish I could always give everyone more clarity"*: Email from Phil Ennen to CHWC leadership, February 13, 2019.

214 *He loaned a personal car to Vasi's wife*: Interview with Zoher Vasi, January 21, 2019.

214 *Ennen wrote to the area's federal legislators in the wake of Donald Trump's 2017 anti-Muslim travel ban*: "Ennen: Ban Has Negative Effect on CHWC," reprinted in *Bryan Times*, February 8, 2017.

215 *CHWC sometimes had no choice but to offer top salaries*: CHWC IRS Form 990; "2018 Review of Physician and Advanced Practitioner Recruiting Incentives," Merrit Hawkins.

216 *physician compensation rose over 16 percent in the four years between 2013 and 2017*: Stephen Zuckerman et al., "Analysis of Disparities in Physician Compensation," Report by the Urban Institute and SullivanCotter for the Medicare Payment Advisory Commission, January 2019.

218 *"I have no desire to lose my job"*: Email from Phil Ennen to CHWC vice presidents, February 14, 2019.

220 *When KKR sold all of its stake in 2013, the company was worth three times what KKR paid for it, and the financial press hailed the play's success*: Phil Wahba, "Making Billions at the Dollar Store," *Fortune*, May 22, 2019; Matt Jarzemsky, "KKR, Goldman Exit from Dollar

General Stake with $252 Million Stock Sale," *Wall Street Journal*, December 12, 2013; Daniel Gross, "How KKR Scored with Dollar General," *Newsweek*, June 10, 2009.

220 *often wiping out small-town grocers and preventing any new independent stores from ever opening*: Marie Donahue and Stacy Mitchell, "Dollar Stores Are Targeting Struggling Urban Neighborhoods and Small Towns. One Community Is Showing How to Fight Back," Institute for Local Self-Reliance, December 6, 2018.

221 *"published by the Department of Agriculture in the Federal Register on December 15, 2016"*: www.congress.gov/bill/115th-congress/house-bill/244/text?overview=closed.

221 *Lobbyists for the convenience-store industry convinced legislators that requiring more fresh fruits and vegetables . . . was too burdensome*: Memorandum to NACS from Doug Kantor, Eva V. Rigamonti, RE: SNAP "Variety" Proposed Rule, Providing Regulatory Flexibility for Retailers in the Supplemental Nutrition Assistance Program (RIN 0584-AE61), Steptoe and Johnson LLP, April 11, 2019.

221 *So a can of ravioli in tomato sauce counted as a vegetable*: "What Are Staple Foods?," U.S. Department of Agriculture, updated March 5, 2018.

221 *The SNAP program paid billions of dollars a year—about $4 billion, by one estimate*: Nicole E. Negowetti, "The SNAP Sugar-Sweetened Beverage Debate: Restricting Purchases to Improve Health Outcomes of Low-Income Americans," *Journal of Food Law and Policy* 14, no. 1 (2018).

222 *"one doctor bill or one car repair bill away from not being in such good shape"*: Nathaniel Meyersohn, "Dollar General Is Opening 1,000 New Stores Next Year," CNN Business, December 5, 2019.

224 *Cullis now found himself in the most uncomfortable spot of his life*: Interview with Chris Cullis, April 22, 2019.

225 *Cullis finally sent a confidential memo on CHWC letterhead to the entire staff*: Memo from Chris Cullis to CHWC staff, March 5, 2019.

227 *"If it gets too difficult, we will just leave"*: Interview with Hanan Bazzi, March 7, 2019.

Chapter 9: They Don't Have to See

238 *Williams County residents received medical payments of $150,323,000 from government in 2018*: Williams County Profile, Ohio Office of Research, 2018.

238 *Total government transfer payments to individuals came to $339,480,000*: Williams County Profile, Ohio Office of Research, 2018.

238 *Even if they didn't plant a crop, they could receive $15 an acre*: Lucas Bechtol, "Third Round of MFP Payments Released to Farmers," *Bryan Times*, February 9, 2020.

238 *the county commissioners, approved of government welfare for corporations—most recently granted to Love's Travel Stops*: Williams County Resolution 19-0123, April 8, 2019; Lisa Lockwood, "Kylie Jenner Makes Forbes List of America's Richest Self-Made Women," *Women's Wear Daily*, July 11, 2018.

238 *half of whom would make $9 an hour*: Don Koralewski, "Schools and Government Agree on Tax Financing District for Love's," *Bryan Times*, April 8, 2019.

243 *And they were more likely to be sick with conditions like heart disease, cancer, emphysema, bone fractures, hepatitis, and general poor health*: Vincent J. Felitti et al., "Relationship of Childhood Abuse and Household Dysfunction to Many of the Leading Causes of Death in Adults: The Adverse Childhood Experiences (ACE) Study," *American Journal of Preventive Medicine* 14, no. 4 (1998).

243 *Between 1959 and 1979, life expectancy in the United States increased from about seventy years to about seventy-five*: Steven H. Woolf and Heidi Schoomaker, "Life Expectancy and Mortality Rates in the United States, 1959–2017," *Journal of the American Medical Association*, November 26, 2019; U.S. Census, "Life Expectancy at Birth, at 65 Years of Age, and at

75 Years of Age, by Race and Sex: United States, Selected Years 1900–2007," Health, United States, 2010, Trend Tables.

243 *By 2019, the United States was one of the most unequal countries on Earth*: Drew DeSilver, www.pewresearch.org/fact-tank/2013/12/19/global-inequality-how-the-u-s-compares/; https://www.stlouisfed.org/on-the-economy/2017/october/how-us-income-inequality -compare-worldwide; www.cia.gov/library/publications/the-world-factbook/rankorder /2172rank.html; Catherine Rampell, "Why Income Inequality Is So Much Worse in the U.S. Than in Other Rich Countries," *Washington Post*, April 11, 2017.

244 *The lines crossed for other age groups, too*: Anne Case and Angus Deaton, "Mortality and Morbidity in the 21st Century," Brookings Papers on Economic Activity, March 17, 2017.

244 *Those who were born in 1960 and at the bottom 20 percent of earnings could, at age fifty, expect to live to seventy-six, a difference of about thirteen years*: Katelin P. Isaacs and Sharmila Choudhury, "The Growing Gap in Life Expectancy by Income: Recent Evidence and Implications for the Social Security Retirement Age," Congressional Research Service, May 12, 2017.

244 *People in rich, better-educated counties lived longer, healthier lives than people living in poorer, less-educated counties*: Laura Dwyer-Lindgren et al., "Inequalities in Life Expectancy Among US Counties: 1980 to 2014," *JAMA Internal Medicine*, July 2017.

244 *Family distress was one symptom of the disease, and it generated more adverse childhood experiences*: Among the research supporting this statement: Melissa T. Merrick et al., "Estimated Proportion of Adult Health Problems Attributable to Adverse Childhood Experiences and Implications for Prevention—25 States, 2015–2017," *Morbidity and Mortality Weekly Report*, November 8, 2019; Ichiro Kawachi and Bruce P. Kennedy, "Income Inequality and Health: Pathways and Mechanisms," *Health Services Research*, April 1999; Woolf and Schoomaker, "Life Expectancy and Mortality Rates in the United States, 1959–2017"; Jacob Bor et al., "Population Health in an Era of Rising Income Inequality: USA, 1980–2015," *The Lancet*, April 8, 2017; Raj Chetty et al., "The Association Between Income and Life Expectancy in the United States, 2001–2014," *Journal of the American Medical Association*, April 26, 2016; Peter A. Muennig et al., "America's Declining Well-Being, Health, and Life Expectancy: Not Just a White Problem," *American Journal of Public Health*, December 2018; Nancy E. Adler and Katherine Newman, "Socioeconomic Disparities in Health: Pathways and Policies," *Health Affairs*, March/April 2002.

245 *Overall, West Unity and Montpelier received D grades, while Bryan city schools earned a C*: Ohio Schools Report Cards, Ohio Department of Education, https://reportcard.education .ohio.gov/district/overview/043679.

246 *though DARE had been shown to be worse than ineffective back in the early 1990s*: Steven L. West and Keri K. O'Neal, "Project D.A.R.E. Outcome Effectiveness Revisited," *American Journal of Public Health*, June 2004.

246 *Towns would resign his position in February 2020 under threat of being charged with felony crimes involving misuse of public money*: State of Ohio v. Steven M. Towns, June 20, 2019.

247 *more than medical care itself, which accounted for only about 15 percent of the inequity in mortality*: Steven H. Woolf, "Necessary but Not Sufficient: Why Health Care Alone Cannot Improve Population Health and Reduce Health Inequities," *Annals of Family Medicine*, May/ June 2019.

249 *The nurse practitioner there said, "You're sick"*: Interview with Valerie Moreno and Betty Franks, March 9, 2019.

250 *Beth Pool understood the dilemmas*: Interview with Beth Pool, February 15, 2019.

253 *Joseph Padway argued that health was "not an article of commerce"*: Beatrix Hoffman, *Health Care for Some: Rights and Rationing in the United States Since 1930* (Chicago: University of Chicago Press, 2012).

254 *They imagined chic loft apartments, new cafés, rising property values*: "ProMedica Breathes New Life into Toledo's Downtown Riverfront," press release, JobsOhio.

255 *In May, Mick Frisbie*: Williams County Health Department death records; Shannon Keil.

Epilogue

262 *he explored either creating a dedicated CHWC long-distance ambulance service or contracting for one*: Interview with Chad Tinkel, April 16, 2020.

267 *In 2009, the U.S. Department of Health and Human Services advised*: William Lazonick and Matt Hopkins, "How 'Maximizing Shareholder Value' Minimized the Strategic National Stockpile," The Academic-Industry Research Network, July 2020.

268 *About fifty thousand people who worked for health departments like the one Watkins ran for Williams County lost their jobs*: Jeneen Interlandi, "The U.S. Approach to Public Health: Neglect, Panic, Repeat," *New York Times*, April 9, 2020.

268 *The federal government slashed the money it allocated to prepare for an emergency like Covid-19*: "New Report: Funding for Public Health Has Declined Significantly Since the Great Recession," Trust for America's Health, March 1, 2018.

268 *Only three states spent less*: State Health Compare, State Health Access Data Assistance Center, University of Minnesota.

269 *After Jonas Salk and his team produced a vaccine*: Dwight Eisenhower, "Statement by the President," May 31, 1955.

269 *The decline in American health was abetted by deliberate policy*: Jennifer Karas Montez et al., "US State Policies, Politics, and Life Expectancy," *The Millbank Quarterly*, August 2020.

271 *She, Watkins, and the rest of the department coordinated with rehab facilities*: Interview with Jim Watkins, April 16, 2020.

272 *Tinkel figured CHWC had lost $10 million*: Interview with Chad Tinkel August 5, 2020.

272 *July set a record for outpatient business*: Memo from Chad Tinkel to CHWC employees, August 6, 2020.

272 *Thirteen small hospitals around the country closed between January 2020 and August 1*: Closures Database, North Carolina Rural Health Research Program, University of North Carolina.

272 *By one estimate, a quarter of all rural hospitals in the United States were in danger*: Alex Kacik, "A Quarter of Rural Hospitals Are at Risk of Closing," *Modern Healthcare*, April 8, 2020.

272 *Representative Nino Vitale . . . called her "an unelected Globalist Health Director*: Brett Zelman, "Ohio State Rep. Nino Vitale Calls Dr. Amy Acton, Who Is Jewish, a Globalist," *Cleveland Scene*, May 1, 2020.

273 *State senator Andrew Brenner likened Acton's health mandates to actions taken by Nazi Germany*: Darrel Rowland, "Wife of Ohio State Senator Compares Dr. Amy Acton Statement with Nazi Mandates," *Columbus Dispatch*, April 22, 2020.

274 *By the end of July, forty-nine health officials in twenty-three states had either resigned or been fired*: Michelle R. Smith and Lauren Weber, "Health Officials Are Quitting or Getting Fired amid Outbreak," AP and Kaiser Health News, August 10, 2020.

274 *"regardless of the casualties"*: Lucas Bechtol, "Local Reaction to State Plan Mixed," *Bryan Times*, May 3, 2020.

274 *A winery in Napoleon held a "Name That Tune" contest*: Emily Tian, "Henry County Winery Event Linked to 83 Coronavirus Cases," *Toledo Blade*, July 28, 2020.

275 *the rate of Covid-19 infections in African Americans was 14,703 per million*: Governor Gretchen Whitmer, EXECUTIVE DIRECTIVE No. 2020-9, August 5, 2020.

275 *African Americans, who comprised roughly 13 percent of the population, accounted for nearly 25 percent of the Covid deaths*: Samrachana Adhikari, et al., "Assessment of Community-Level Disparities in Coronavirus Disease 2019 (COVID-19) Infections and Deaths

in Large US Metropolitan Areas," *JAMA Network*, July 28, 2020; "Minorities Are Disproportionately Affected by COVID-19. This Is How It Varies by State," *USA Today*, July 21, 2020; CDC, https://www.cdc.gov/nchs/nvss/vsrr/covid19/health_disparities.htm.

275 **Ohio state senator Stephen Huffman**: Adriana Velez Kalsekar, "It's Not Unhealthy Behavior. It's Systemic Racism," EndocrineWeb, July 10, 2020.

277 **an estimated 5.4 million lost health insurance because their insurance was tied to their employment**: Sheryl Gay Stolberg, "Millions Have Lost Health Insurance in Pandemic-Driven Recession," *New York Times*, July 13, 2020.

277 **The richest figured out how to take government money anyway**: Natasha Lindstrom, "UPMC to Get $1 Billion in Federal Aid After Hard Hit from Coronavirus Pandemic," *Tribune Review*, May 29, 2020; Jessica Silver-Greenberg, Jesse Drucker, and David Enrich, "Hospitals Got Bailouts and Furloughed Thousands While Paying C.E.O.s Millions," *New York Times*, June 8, 2020; David Kocieniewski and Caleb Melby, "Private Equity Lands Billion-Dollar Backdoor Hospital Bailout," Bloomberg News, June 2, 2020.

277 **ProMedica had taken $240 million**: Jon Chavez, "Federal Aid Protects ProMedica During Pandemic," *Toledo Blade*, August 17, 2020.

277 **Private equity-owned businesses like EmCare borrowed about $1.5 billion from the taxpayers**: Rosemary Batt and Eileen Appelbaum, "Hospital Bailouts Begin—for Those Owned by Private Equity Firms," *American Prospect*, April 2, 2020; Kocieniewski and Melby, "Private Equity Lands Billion-Dollar Backdoor Hospital Bailout."

278 **they still forced employees to take pay cuts**: Katherine Doherty, "KKR-Backed Envision Withholds Doctor Pay as Routine Care Slows," Bloomberg News, April 3, 2020.

278 **They then used this group to continue their advertising and lobbying efforts**: Isaac Arnsdorf, "Medical Staffing Companies Cut Doctors' Pay While Spending Millions on Political Ads," ProPublica, April 20, 2020.

278 **the two businesses signed a deal, though both sides claimed the details of the contract**: Rosa Salter Rodriguez, "Parkview, Anthem Sign Contract," *Journal-Gazette*, July 31, 2020.

278 **Covidien backed out of the government deal after it bought Newport, and the ventilators were never made**: Ben Remaly, "Ventilator Merger Scrutinised as Potential 'Killer Acquisition,'" *Global Competition Review*, March 31, 2020; Nicholas Kulish, Sarah Kliff, and Jessica Silver-Greenberg, "The U.S. Tried to Build a New Fleet of Ventilators. The Mission Failed," *New York Times*, March 29, 2020; William Lazonick and Matt Hopkins, "How 'Maximizing Shareholder Value' Minimized the Strategic National Stockpile," The Academic-Industry Research Network, July 2020.

279 **The bill's language was weakened**: Sarah Karlin-Smith, "How the Drug Industry Got Its Way on the Coronavirus," *Politico*, March 5, 2020.

279 **Attorneys general for several states urged the feds to "march in" on Gilead's patent rights**: Ron Leuty, "Feds Should 'March In' on Covid Drug Remdesivir, State AGs Say. Gilead Says They're Wrong," *San Francisco Business Times*, August 5, 2020.

279 **Thirty days into the program, not a single test had been run through the system**: Catherine Candisky, "Efforts to Expand Ohio COVID Testing to Community Pharmacies Stalls," *Columbus Dispatch*, July 30, 2020.

279 **By July 29, American renters owed $21.5 billion in back rent**: Michelle Conlin, "U.S. Renters Owe $21.5 Billion in Back Rent; Republicans Offer No Eviction Relief," Reuters, July 29, 2020.

Index